American Popular Music

Country

American Popular Music

Blues
Classical
Country
Folk
Jazz
Rhythm and Blues, Rap, and Hip-Hop
Rock and Roll

General Editor: Richard Carlin

Editorial Board:

Barbara Ching, Ph.D., University of Memphis

Ronald D. Cohen, Ph.D., Indiana University-Northwest

William Duckworth, Bucknell University

Kevin J. Holm-Hudson, Ph.D., University of Kentucky

Nadine Hubbs, Ph.D., University of Michigan

Craig Morrison, Ph.D., Concordia University and McGill University

Albin J. Zak III, Ph.D., University at Albany (SUNY)

American Popular Music

Country

Richard Carlin

Foreword by Barbara Ching, Ph.D.
University of Memphis

☑️ Facts On File
An imprint of Infobase Publishing

American Popular Music: Country

Facts On File, Inc.
An imprint of Infobase Publishing
132 West 31st Street
New York NY 10001

Library of Congress Cataloging-in-Publication Data
Carlin, Richard, 1956–
   American popular music : country / Richard Carlin ; foreword by Barbara Ching.
     p. cm.
   Includes bibliographical references and index.
   ISBN 0-8160-5312-X (hc : alk. paper)
1. Country music—Encyclopedias. 2. Popular music—United States—Encyclopedias. I. Ching, Barbara, 1958– II. Title.
   ML102.C7C37 2005
   781.642'0973'03—dc22   2004028882

Text design by James Scotto-Lavino
Cover design by Nora Wertz

Printed in the United States of America

VB FOF 10 9 8 7 6 5 4 3 2 1

This book is printed on acid-free paper.

Contents

Foreword

This encyclopedia can teach readers many things about the most important songs, styles, and artists in country music, although no book can begin to describe all the country music played since the early days of radio and sound recording. In this foreword, I hope readers will think about how country music is defined and why people listen to it, even love it.

Musicians make country music with pedal steel guitars, twin fiddles, and nasal, regionally accented vocals, although not all of these prominent stylistic features appear in all songs or in all stages of the music. This book's chronology includes country music's earliest recordings and other landmarks, and its introduction describes well the music's historical development; this foreword stresses how the music, from the early days of recording and radio broadcasting through the 21st century, directs its listeners to a specific place in the nation as it amplifies the dual locations implied by the word *country*. We all live in a country, and some of us live in the country, still more of us used to live in the country. The music's early entrepreneurs and advocates thus found a market for the music by contrasting it with more refined and urban entertainment. The story of the *Grand Ole Opry*'s christening illustrates the contrast well. In the 1920s many radio stations featured "barn dance" programs showcasing fiddlers and other rural acts. In late 1925 Nashville's WSM began broadcasting a Saturday night program of old-time music with George Hay as host. Two years later, when the program began to follow Dr. Walter Damrosch's *Musical Appreciation Hour,* Hay opened a broadcast with a quip that turned into the show's title: "For the past hour we have been listening to music taken largely from grand opera, but from now on, we will present the grand ole opry." Scholars have shown how Hays deliberately created rural imagery by giving regular performers folksy names such as Dr. Humphrey Bate and His Possum Hunters and encouraging them to forgo their Sunday best in favor of gingham and denim country costumes.

Early recorded music similarly constructed a specific country style. Ralph Peer, originally an agent of the Victor Talking Machine Company's "Old-time Melodies of the Sunny South" division, became one of country music's first record producers when he scouted out stars such as Fiddlin' John Carson, the Carter Family, and Jimmie Rodgers. In tune with the Victor Company's nostalgic marketing of the old South, Peer choose songs that directed listeners to a lost rural idyll; examples are Carson's "Little Old Log Cabin in the Lane," the Carter Family's "Lonesome Homesick Blues," and Rodgers's "Dear Old Sunny South by the Sea." Peer also pioneered the recording of African-American artists, inventing the term "race records" to describe this music. By contrast, implicit in Peer's work with musicians like Rodgers and the Carter Family is some notion of whiteness, and by the mid-1920s, the genre term most often used to signify this association was *hillbilly.*

Billboard magazine began charting country music in 1944 as "Folk Records." The word *country* was officially attached to the music in 1949 when

Billboard changed the title of its "Hillbilly" charts to "Country and Western." In 1962, the magazine dropped "Western," leaving "Country" to stand alone. Later attempts to capture a broader market for the music, such as the countrypolitan movement of the 1970s and the "Hot New Country" that followed, promise some form of sophistication (the play on "cosmopolitan") or progress (the promise of something excitingly "new") at the same time that they restate their attachment to the ever-present country. Interestingly, attempts to refine and modernize country music usually coexist with movements that emphasize a return to the music's past, such as the "new traditionalist" singers of the mid-1980's (Dwight Yoakam, George Strait, and others).

Another expression used to describe this music is "white man's blues." While the mutual influence of blues and country has been documented many times, the few exceptional black country musicians that have risen to prominence throughout the music's history only demonstrate the lasting influence of the business decision to separate rural music into white and black markets. African-American harmonica player Deford Bailey appeared regularly on the *Grand Ole Opry* from 1926 to 1941. After Ray Charles established himself as a blues star, he released his 1962 album *Modern Sounds in Country and Western Music* featuring his utterly convincing renditions of many country standards. Charley Pride achieved country superstardom between the mid-1960s and the 1980s with his covers of Hank Williams's standards and newer happy-go-lucky love songs such as the chart-topping "Kiss an Angel Good Morning" (1971).

In the United States, a young country, rural roots lie beneath many family trees, and thus, for many Americans, country music evokes "home"— whether in a nostalgic look back or in a patriotic look at the flag. So while many songs express pride in being American (hear Lee Greenwood's 1984 "God Bless the USA" for a perfect specimen), others depict a tension among Americans about where the country has been and where it is headed. Merle Haggard's 1969 hit "Okie from Muskogee," for example, pitted hippie anti-war protesters against supposedly more upright prowar middle Americans. More recently, Chely Wright's "Bumper of My SUV" supports the military despite the scorn of a minivan-driving middle-class mom for peace.

Country music also gives voice to the situation of rustic outsiders unable or unwilling to keep up with the pressures and pleasures of modern city life. In fact, the honky-tonk, the bar, dance hall, and soundstage, subjects of so many country songs, seem to be a sort of home away from home for these refugees. In Hank Williams's "Honky Tonk Blues" (1952), he sings about how country music and the city bars where it is played soothe his homesickness. Other classics, such as Bobby Bare's "The Streets of Baltimore" (1963) and "Detroit City" (1966), continued to develop the themes of displacement and alienation. Dwight Yoakam mastered it in songs set amid the false allure of Los Angeles such as "Guitars, Cadillacs," "He Sang Dixie," and his duet with Buck Owens, "The Streets of Bakersfield" (first recorded in 1973 by Owens and his band, the Buckaroos).

People also use *country* as a term to describe themselves; self-professed "country" boys and girls abound in Nashville's galaxy. Little Jimmy Dickens described himself as a "Country Boy" (1949). In "You're Lookin' at Country" (1971), Loretta Lynn asserted that anyone who looked at her would see "country," described in this song as a set of traditional beliefs and virtues such as delaying sex until marriage and appreciating nature. Similarly, Barbara Mandrell bragged about being "Country (When Country Wasn't Cool)" (1981). Even the most pop-oriented artists such as John Denver sang this sort of song (1975's "Thank God I'm a Country Boy"). Other songs dramatize the difference between affluent urbanites and struggling rural residents. In a 1982 song that begins with the story of a friend's fatal mugging on a Manhattan street, Hank Williams Jr. promised that "A Country Boy (Will Survive)." Gretchen Wilson defends herself from urban scorn with a chorus of like-minded sisters in "Redneck Woman" (2004). In fact, nearly all country artists profess to relate to their fans as members of their community rather than as admirers of their glamour.

Country music makes much of its own tradition by often singing about itself. Songs like Eddie Dean's 1950 "I Dreamed of a Hillbilly Heaven" can be endlessly adapted to memorialize country's dead stars. George Jones's "Who's Gonna Fill Their Shoes?" similarly mourns and praises country's dead. Waylon Jennings paid tribute to Hank Williams in his "Are You Sure Hank Done It This Way?" (1975), a song that other singers often perform or cite. Other songs pay tribute to country music's living stars by referring to them: countless lyrics make reference to Haggard and Jones. Many songs refer to country classics; Emmylou Harris and Buck Owens, for example, sang together on "Play 'Together Again' Again" (1976) a song that requests Owens's earlier classic "Together Again" (1964). Country music also self-consciously works with its favorite themes; in "You Never Even Called Me by My Name" (1975), David Allan Coe proclaims he created the perfect country song by reworking Steve Goodman's original to include references to drinking, motherhood, trucks, and prison.

Country's most popular songs, like the most popular songs in many commercial music genres, provide the soundtrack for life's good times and bleak moments. Sung at weddings and funerals, they tell stories about the joy and heartbreak in love affairs and family matters. But even in these perennial themes, country songs maintain their identity. George Jones's "He Stopped Loving Her Today" (1980), voted the top country song of all time by readers of the fan magazine *Country America,* not only describes a funeral but also tells the life story of a man who devoted his life to mourning a failed romance, staying behind while a woman moved on. While a sobbing steel guitar sets the mood, it is the dogged devotion to loss, losing, and the things money can't buy that mark the song as country.

Barbara Ching, Ph.D.
University of Memphis

Preface

American popular music reflects the rich cultural diversity of the American people. From classical to folk to jazz, America has contributed a rich legacy of musical styles to the world over its two-plus centuries of existence. The rich cross-fertilization of cultures—African-American, Hispanic, Asian, and European—has resulted in one of the unique musical mixtures in the world.

American Popular Music celebrates this great diversity by presenting to the student, researcher, and individual enthusiast a wealth of information on each musical style in an easily accessible format. The subjects covered are:

Blues
Classical music
Country
Folk music
Jazz
Rock and Roll
Rhythm and Blues, Rap, and Hip-Hop

Each volume presents key information on performers, musical genres, famous compositions, musical instruments, media, and centers of musical activity. The volumes conclude with a chronology, recommended listening, and a complete bibliography or list of sources for further study.

How do we define *popular music?* Literally, any music that attracts a reasonably large audience is "popular" (as opposed to "unpopular"). Over the past few decades, however, as the study of popular music has grown, the term has come to have specific

meanings. While some might exclude certain genres covered in this series—American classical music leaps to mind—we felt that it was important to represent the range of musical styles that have been popular in the United States over its entire history. New scholarship has brought to light the interplay among genres that previously were felt to be unrelated—such as the influence of folk forms on classical music, opera's influence on jazz, or the blues' influence on country—so that to truly understand each musical style, it is important to be conversant with at least some aspects of all.

These volumes are intended to be introductory, not comprehensive. Any "A to Z" work is by its very nature selective; it's impossible to include *every* figure, *every* song, or *every* key event. For most users, we hope the selections made here will be more than adequate, giving information on the key composers and performers who shaped each style, while also introducing some lesser-known figures who are worthy of study. The Editorial Board and other outside advisers played a key role in reviewing the entry lists for completeness.

All encyclopedia authors also face the rather daunting task of separating fact from fiction when writing short biographies of performers and composers. Even birth and death dates can be "up for grabs," as artists have been known to subtract years from their lives in their official biographies. "Official" records are often unavailable, particularly for earlier artists who may have been born at home, or for those whose family histories themselves are shrouded in mystery. We have attempted to draw on the latest research and most reliable sources whenever possible, and have also pointed out when key facts are in dispute. And, for many popular performers, the myth can be as important as the reality when it comes to their lives, so we have tried to honor both in writing about their achievements.

Popular music reflects the concerns of the artists who create it and their audience. Each era of our country's history has spawned a variety of popular music styles, and these styles in turn have grown over the decades as new performers and new times have arisen. These volumes try to place the music into its context, acknowledging that the way music is performed and its effect on the greater society is as important as the music itself. We've also tried to highlight the many interchanges between styles and performers, because one of the unique—and important—aspects of American cultural life is the way that various people have come together to create a new culture out of the interplay of their original practices and beliefs.

Race, class, culture, and sex have played roles in the development of American popular music. Regrettably, the playing field has not always been level for performers from different backgrounds, particularly when it comes to the business aspects of the industry: paying royalties, honoring copyrights, and the general treatment of artists. Some figures have been forgotten or ignored who deserved greater attention; the marketplace can be ruthless, and its agents—music publishers, record producers, concert promoters—have and undoubtedly will continue to take advantage of the musicians trying to bring their unique voices to market. These volumes attempt to address many of these issues as they have affected the development of individual musicians' careers as well as from the larger perspective of the growth of popular music. The reader is encouraged to delve further into these topics by referring to the bibliographies in each volume.

Popular music can be a slave itself to crass commercialism, as well as a bevy of hangers-on, fellow travelers, and others who seek only to make a quick buck by following easy-to-identify trends. While we bemoan the lack of new visionary artists today like Bessie Smith, Miles Davis, Pauline Oliveros, or Bob Dylan, it's important to remember that when they first came on the scene the vast majority of popular performers were journeymen musicians at best. Popular music will always include many second-, third-, and fourth-tier performers; some will offer one or two recordings or performances that will have a lasting impact, while many will be celebrated during their 15 minutes of fame, but most will be forgotten. In separating the wheat from the chaff, it is understandably easier for our writers working on earlier styles where the passing of time has helped sort out the important from the just popular. However, all the contributors have tried to supply some distance, giving greatest weight to the true artists, while acknowledging that popular figures who are less talented can nonetheless have a great impact on the genre during their performing career—no matter how brief it might be.

All in all, the range, depth, and quality of popular musical styles that have developed in the United States over its lifetime is truly amazing. These styles could not have arisen anywhere else, but are the unique products of the mixing of cultures, geography, technology, and sheer luck that helped disseminate each style. Who could have forecast the music of Bill Monroe before he assembled his first great bluegrass band? Or predicted the melding of gospel, rhythm and blues, and popular music achieved by Aretha Franklin during her reign as "Queen of Soul"? The tinkering of classical composer John Cage—who admitted to having no talent for creating melodies—was a truly American response to new technologies, a new environment, and a new role for music in our lives. And Patti Smith's particular take on poetry, the punk-rock movement, and the difficulties faced by a woman who leads a rock band make her music particularly compelling and original—and unpredictable to those who dismissed the original rock records as mere "teenage fluff."

We hope that the volumes in this series will open your eyes, minds, and, most important, your ears to a world of musical styles. Some may be familiar, others more obscure, but all are worthy. With today's proliferation of sound on the Web, finding even the most obscure recording is becoming increasingly simple. We urge you to read deeply but also to put these books down to listen. Come to your own conclusions. American popular music is a rich world, one open to many different interpretations. We hope these volumes serve as your windows to these many compelling worlds.

Richard Carlin,
General Editor

Acknowledgments

Thanks to Gene Brissie for inviting me to edit this series and to write two volumes for it, and to James Chambers and Vanessa Nittoli at Facts On File for shepherding the manuscript through production. Thanks also to John Wright, my long-suffering agent; David Stanford at Penguin Books; Bob Nirkind at Billboard Books; and Sylvia Miller at Routledge, all of whom in their own way have supported my habit for writing about country and other musical styles.

All encyclopedia writers owe considerable debt to the "real heroes," the scholars who have dug through archives and spent their lives chasing down the facts so that the details of these life stories can be told. I am particularly indebted to the tireless Charles Wolfe, Tony Russell, Colin Escott, and Rich Kienzle, whose writing and determination to uncover the facts have inspired me for many years. I am, of course, responsible for any errors and omissions that this work may contain; I know that critics like nothing less than to find the small faults and omissions in a work that pretends to be "encyclopedic" and look forward to using this information to update and correct future editions of this—and other—works.

My brother, Bob Carlin, is another dogged researcher and hero to me as a musician and long-time adviser. He played me the first country records that I heard, and without him I undoubtedly would never have been able to write this book. Long may his banjo ring!

Finally, to Jessica Myers, this—indeed all—of my work is humbly dedicated. It is a meager token for so great a love.

Introduction

This book offers an introduction to the key people, songs, musical instruments, and styles that have made country music a unique part of the American popular music tradition. Until very recently, country music was viewed as the poor half-sibling of such styles as blues, jazz, or rock; today, thankfully, with the growth of interest in American "roots music," country is coming into its own. Always popular in terms of record sales and radio play, country is now recognized as one of America's unique styles.

Very broadly defined, country music encompasses a series of musical traditions that have developed since about 1850. Drawing on both Anglo-American and African-American folk traditions, the musical style has passed through several developments:

1. Old-time country (c. 1880–1920s). The fiddle tunes, and songs of Appalachia encompass the old-time tradition. String bands playing for local dances, banjo players singing dance songs, and even unaccompanied ballad singers all made up part of this tradition. Some old-time performers highlighted in this work include Uncle Dave Macon and Doctor Humphrey Bate.

2. Songsters (c. 1920s). Performers such as Jimmie Rodgers and the Carter Family were the first to focus primarily on the vocal music tradition. Like pop singers Bing Crosby and the Andrews Sisters, they gained devoted followings and helped turn country music away from primarily an instrumental tradition to one focusing on musical personalities.

3. Cowboy singers (c. 1930s). The craze for cowboys and the "Old West" began in the 1930s and helped spawn a large group of popular singers who emphasized the cowboy image both in their dress and in their repertoires. Singers such as Gene Autry, Patsy Montana, and Roy Rogers represent this tradition.

4. Western swing (c. 1935–50). Taking the cowboy tradition and melding it with jazz, bandleaders in the Southwest—notably Texas and Oklahoma—made a new style of music in the 1930s known as western swing. A key creator behind this movement was Texas fiddler Bob Wills.

5. Bluegrass (c. 1945–1960). In the early 1940s a new style of music arose that melded the older string band tradition with the more modern cowboy/western swing traditions. Beginning with mandolin player Bill Monroe and his group the Blue Grass Boys, bluegrass music became a popular style just after World War II on record and radio.

6. Honky-tonk music (c. 1945–55). Also after World War II small combos playing in local bars known as honky-tonks became popular. Often fronted by a singer/guitar player, honky-tonk bands created repertoires that reflected the barroom life: songs of drinkin', lovin', losin', and fightin'. The greatest honky-tonk songwriter and performer was Hank Williams, who influenced an entire generation of country singers.

7. Nashville sound (c. 1955–70). In the 1950s, trying to escape the "hillbilly" image that clung to

country music, a group of performers and instrumentalists in Nashville began incorporating new styles, primarily drawn from jazz and popular music, into their recordings. A key figure in this movement was guitarist Chet Atkins, who served as producer for RCA Records, and his counterpart at the Decca label, Owen Bradley. Together they helped move country into a more mainstream pop direction. Artists such as Patsy Cline and Jim Reeves represented this new style.

8. Outlaw country (c. 1970–85). A group of Nashville-based songwriters and performers including Willie Nelson, Kris Kristofferson, and Waylon Jennings rebelled against the smooth Nashville sound. They wanted to return country to its honky-tonk roots, and also wanted to address a wider range of subjects—often controversial ones in the conservative Nashville world. Known informally as "the outlaws," this generation of artists helped usher in a new era in country music.

9. Countrypolitan (c. 1970–80). At the same time that the outlaws were rebelling against the Nashville sound, many in the country industry were moving even further toward soft rock and other pop styles in their recordings. Artists such as Kenny Rogers, Eddie Rabbitt, and Barbara Mandrell were all drawing on adult contemporary and soft rock in their performances. This music represented the least traditional of all country styles, and yet was very successful during the 1970s.

10. New country (c. 1985–2000). A return to the roots sound of country music, without the hard edge of outlaw country, occurred in the early-to-mid 1980s with such new artists as Ricky Skaggs, Randy Travis, and Patty Loveless, among many, many others. The so-called new country artists drew on a variety of traditional styles, from old-time and bluegrass to honky-tonk and western swing.

Of course, any "time line" approach to charting the history of a musical genre papers over the important fact that history does not develop in a straight line. Styles have a way of lasting beyond their original period of popularity, returning in new forms, or merging with other styles in various ways. Bluegrass, for example, has returned to popularity since the mid-1970s after a period of being in relative eclipse; western swing has also made several comebacks, both in its pure original form and in various combinations with more contemporary influences from rock, jazz, and country.

This book is not meant to be all-encompassing; rather, I've selected people, songs, musical styles, and musical instruments that I feel are central to the history of country music. Many could argue with this selection, and undoubtedly I have passed over some figures or styles that deserve fuller discussion. I hope it serves as a brief introduction to the riches that can be found within the country genre. If it encourages you to read and listen more, I will have achieved my goal.

A-to-Z Entries

"Achy Breaky Heart" (1991) *Billy Ray Cyrus hit*

This was the first—and only—major hit for singer BILLY RAY CYRUS. The song and performer were heavily hyped by the record company as the "next big thing" in country music. The song was test-marketed in country dance clubs, and a new dance was developed to be performed to it. Cyrus's hunky good looks were also a major asset to the song and accompanying video. Despite the money invested in this song, Cyrus was unable to equal its success with later recordings.

"Act Naturally" (1963) *hit song for the Beatles and Buck Owens*

A number-one hit recording for Buck Owens, spending four weeks at the top of the charts on its original release and remaining on the top 100 charts for an impressive 28 weeks. This country song was covered by the Beatles, sung by Ringo Starr, who was a big fan of American country. It was released on the British version of the sound-track to the Beatles film *Help!* (although it was not included in the film) in 1965, and a year later turned up on the U.S.-only Beatles album *Yesterday . . . and Today.* Their affectionate recreation of Owens's song made it the perfect vehicle for Ringo's sad-sack vocal. This record influenced other rock stars to experiment with country songs, helping to inspire a new genre, COUNTRY ROCK. Starr and Owens recorded a new duet version of the song decades later in 1989.

Acuff, Roy (1903–1992) *singer and businessman*

Born to a middle-class family in Maynardville, Tennessee, on September 15, 1903, Acuff originally hoped to be a professional ballplayer. However, a case of severe sunstroke left him bedridden for two years, during which time he took up the fiddle. He formed his first band in the early 1930s, performing on Knoxville radio. Acuff enjoyed his first hits, "The Great Speckled Bird" and "The Wabash Cannonball," in 1936, and made his first appearance on the *Grand Ole Opry* two years later, where he became a major new star. He scored his last big hit, "Wreck on the Highway," in 1942. That same year, Acuff formed a music-publishing partnership with songwriter Fred Rose, which would become the major publisher of country songs.

The late 1940s were difficult years for Acuff because musical styles were changing. In 1948 he tried his hand at politics, running as the Republican candidate for governor of Tennessee. (He lost.) Although he continued to record during the 1950s, Acuff focused more of his attention on the music business. In 1953 Acuff and Rose founded the Hickory record label, which became Acuff's home as a recording artist four years later. In 1962 he became the first living inductee into the Country Music Hall of Fame. Three years later, a bad car accident sidelined Acuff's performing career, although he made some personal appearances outside of Nashville through the early 1970s. In 1974, with the opening of the theme park Opryland USA, Acuff retired from active touring. Despite increasingly poor health, Acuff continued to perform on the *Grand Ole Opry* through the late 1980s and early 1990s, making his last appearance just a month before his death on November 23, 1992.

Roy Acuff with fiddle in appropriate countrified dress, c. 1938 (University of North Carolina, Southern Historical Collection, Southern Folklife Collection, University Archives)

Adkins, Trace (b. 1962) *singer*

Tracy Darrell Adkins was born in Springhill, Louisiana, on January 13, 1962. Adkins's father was a paper mill worker in rural Louisiana, where Adkins was raised in the town of Sarepta. He performed in a local gospel group, the New Commitment, while still in high school, singing bass and appearing on two locally issued albums. After graduation Adkins attended Louisiana Tech to study petroleum engineering, and also played on the college's football team. A knee injury ended his sports ambitions, but he continued to study and eventually worked on oil derricks for about 10 years in the Gulf region. He continued to perform semiprofessionally, including a stint with a local band called Bayou, which played in the Gulf region and enjoyed some success.

In 1992 Adkins resettled in Nashville, determined to pursue a musical career. Working local bars, he was "discovered" by producer Scott Hendricks, then president of Capitol Nashville, and signed to the label. His debut album appeared in mid-1996 and quickly produced hits; his own upbeat love song "There's a Girl in Texas" reached the top 20, then the ballad "There's a Light in the House" climbed to the top five. In 1997 he reached number one on the country charts for the first time with "(This Ain't No) Thinkin' Thing."

Adkins continued to enjoy great success with his second album, *Big Time,* released in autumn 1997. It yielded more hits, primarily ballads, including the classic honky-tonk weeper, "Lonely Won't Leave Me Alone." His success led to a shower of awards, including the Academy of Country Music's best "New Male Vocalist" title of 1997, and a nomination for the Country Music Association's "Horizon Award" in 1998. Adkins next released his 1999 album, *More . . .* including a clever, western-swing-flavored anthem, "All Hat, No Cattle," as well as "Working Man's Wage."

Chrome followed in 2001, producing a top-five country hit with "I'm Tryin." An arrest for drunken driving that year, however, slowed his career, although he returned to the charts in 2003 with "Chrome," his 2001 album title track, released as a single. *Coming on Strong* followed later that year, with the lead track, "Hot Mama," an ode to marital love, performing well.

Alabama *vocal group*

Alabama, formed in 1975, is a pop-rock-influenced vocal group that was most popular in the early and mid-1980s. They were one of the first vocal bands to introduce a hard-rocking style to country music, while they continued to project a good-time nostalgic message through their music.

Originally formed around a quartet of cousins (Randy Yuell Owen [vocals, guitar]; Jeffrey Alan Cook [vocals, guitar]; Teddy Wayne Gentry [vocals, bass]; Jackie Owen [1975–79: drums]; Mark Joel Herndon, [1979–ongoing: drums]), the group worked as a bar band from the mid-1970s to about 1979. In 1980 their single "My Home's in Alabama," cowritten by first cousins Randy Owen and Teddy Gentry, became their signature song and first top 20 hit. That same year they signed with RCA. For the next decade the group enjoyed a string of number-one country hits, including 1982's "(Play Me Some) Mountain Music," 1984's "Roll On (Eighteen Wheeler)," and 1988's "Song of the South." Their last number one to date came in 1993, but the group continues to enjoy success on the road and to release new albums.

Allen, Rex (1920–1999) *cowboy singer and actor*

Allen was a cowboy actor and singing star who was most active from the mid-1940s through the late 1960s. Born in rural Willcox, Arizona, Allen was already working the amateur rodeo circuit in his early teens; at the same time, he took up guitar and fiddle playing. He worked on radio as a cowboy performer, most notably on Chicago's popular *National Barn Dance* radio show from 1945 to 1949. Then he traveled to California to host his own radio show and appear in the first of a series of westerns for Republic Studios, home to GENE AUTRY and ROY ROGERS. He also helped to pioneer the western genre on television in his *Frontier Doctor* program, broadcast in 1949–50 on CBS TV. In the early 1950s Allen signed with Decca Records, producing a string of western hits. He continued to record throughout the 1960s, drawing heavily on cowboy

standards along with his own self-penned western songs. Allen retired from music in the early 1970s and died on December 17, 1999, in Tucson, Arizona. His son, Rex Allen Jr. (b. Chicago, August 23, 1947), has continued the family tradition of performing cowboy-style music.

"All My Ex's Live in Texas" (1987) *honky tonk number-one hit*

Texas honky-tonk revivalist GEORGE STRAIT put this song on the country charts for 13 weeks. Strait's popularity was so great in the late 1980s that he scored 11 number-one country hits in a row between May 1986 and August 1989; this song was fourth in that series. Combining a typical honky-tonk rhythm and accompaniment with contemporary lyrics, the song was a defining one for Strait, establishing his retro-hip persona.

"All My Rowdy Friends (Have Settled Down)" (1981) *Hank Williams Jr. number-one hit*

HANK WILLIAMS JR. cemented his hell-raising image with this humorous song. While breaking free of being just the son of HANK WILLIAMS, nonetheless Hank Junior, as he is known, still references his dad (along with friends like WAYLON JENNINGS) in this song about settling down in old age. Hank Junior also recorded an answer song, "All My Rowdy Friends Are Coming over Tonight," in 1984, in which the urge to party overcomes the creaking muscles of maturity.

"Always Late (With Your Kisses)" (1951) *number-one hit for Lefty Frizzell*

Lefty Frizzell's second number-one hit, this song topped the country charts for 12 weeks in 1951 and remained on the charts for 16 weeks more; it also topped disc jockey, jukebox, and best-seller lists. Co-credited to Frizzell and Blackie Crawford, the song is a classic lovelorn ballad, with a sad "Why do you want to do me this way" refrain. Neo-honky-tonker DWIGHT YOAKAM revived the song in 1989 for a number-nine country hit.

Anderson, John (b. 1954) *performer and songwriter*

Anderson was born in Apopka, Florida, on December 13, 1954. He performed in a high school rock band and, after his graduation, moved to Nashville to pursue a music career, performing with his sister Donna. Anderson worked for a couple of years as a songwriter, and then signed with Warner Brothers in 1977. He began recording in the late 1970s featuring a hardcore Texas honky-tonk sound. He enjoyed three top country hits in the early 1980s, most notably 1983's "Swingin'." In 1988 Anderson returned to his roots with the excellent *10* album, emphasizing his world-weary vocals against simple, tasteful traditional accompaniments, and his original compositions. Major hits came in 1992 with the number-one "Straight Tequila Night" and "Seminole Wind," perhaps his best-known song, although it only reached number two on the country charts. Of late he has not been a major presence on the country charts, but Anderson has continued to record and perform.

Anderson, Lynn (b. 1947) *singer*

Lynn Anderson is a smooth-voiced vocalist who is best remembered for her 1970 hit "I Never Promised You a Rose Garden." She is the daughter of honky-tonk songwriter Liz Anderson (b. Elizabeth Jane Haaby, Roseau, Minnesota, March 13, 1930, best known for the hits she wrote for Merle Haggard, including "Lonesome Fugitive" and "My Friends Are Gonna Be Strangers"). Lynn was born in Grand Forks, North Dakota, and raised in California. She first found success on the local horse-show circuit while also working as a singer on *The Lawrence Welk Show*. In 1968 she moved to Nashville. A year later she had a number-three country hit with "That's a No No." She wed producer/songwriter R. Glenn Sutton, who produced her biggest hit in 1970, "I Never Promised You a Rose Garden," the title song of a successful film. A string of pop-country hits followed. Anderson split from her husband in the mid-1970s. By the early 1980s she had returned to a career as a horsewoman.

Anderson, "Whispering" Bill (b. 1937) *singer and songwriter*

Known as "Whispering Bill" because of his famous vocals on the 1963 hit "Still," Anderson was born in Columbia, South Carolina, but raised in suburban Atlanta. He was already leading his own country band and writing songs while in high school. After graduating from college, he pursued a part-time career as a songwriter and performer; RAY PRICE heard his 1958 recording of "City Lights" and covered it, achieving a gold record. Thanks to this success, Anderson began writing for many of the big Nashville recording stars of the day, including Jim Reeves, Hank Locklin, and Porter Wagoner.

Anderson achieved his greatest success as a solo performer in the early 1960s, joining the *Grand Ole Opry* in 1961. He first topped the country charts with 1962's "Mama Sang a Sad Song," and then crossed over into the lucrative pop market with "Still" in 1963. In the late 1960s he recorded some popular duets with Jan Howard and in the early 1970s with Mary Lou Turner, whom he discovered. After that, Anderson's recording career slowed, although he continued to tour. In 2001 he was inducted into the Country Music Hall of Fame, and he remains a member of the *Grand Ole Opry*.

Arnold, Eddy (b. 1918) *guitarist and singer*

The son of an old-time fiddler father and guitar-playing mother, Richard Evert ("Eddy") Arnold took up the guitar at age 10, abandoning his schooling soon after to help during the depression years on his family's farm. After performing at local dances, Arnold was hired to perform on local radio, which in turn led to further jobs in Memphis and St. Louis. Arnold enjoyed his first success as a performer when he was hired in the early 1940s to sing with Pee Wee King's Golden West Cowboys, a popular group on the *Grand Ole Opry.* From his early experiences on the farm, Arnold took the nickname "The Tennessee Ploughboy."

In 1944 Arnold signed as a solo act with RCA. He had his first string of hits with honky-tonk and cowboy numbers in the late 1940s and early 1950s, including 1948's sentimental "Bouquet of Roses," 1951's "I Wanna Play House with You," and 1955's western epic, "Cattle Call." In the mid-1950s, Arnold hosted his own syndicated TV program and also made guest appearances on many of the popular variety programs catering to a general audience. Arnold's greatest success came during the 1960s. On records like "Make the World Go Away," "Lonely Again," and "Turn the World Around," Arnold successfully wed blue-and-lonesome subject matter with mainstream appeal. Arnold continued to record and perform through the mid-1980s, when he retired.

Asleep at the Wheel *western swing band*

Asleep at the Wheel, formed in 1970, is a rockin' western swing revival band that was most popular in the mid-1970s. It is said to have employed more than 75 musicians in its 30-plus years of existence. Lead guitarist/vocalist Ray Benson is the motivating force behind the band, and the only original member left. He is one of those rare true believers who has been able to keep his band going against the odds.

Benson's love of western swing music began when he was a teenager in suburban Philadelphia, playing music with steel guitarist Reuben Gosfield (aka Lucky Oceans). The duo moved to a farm in West Virginia in 1970, forming the nucleus of the original band. By 1973 the band was headquartered on the West Coast, where they were signed by United Artists Records. In 1975 they scored a top-10 country hit with "The Letter That Johnny Walker Read," their greatest chart success. In the early 1980s Benson cut back on the size of the outfit, for financial and artistic reasons. Through the 1980s and 1990s, and into the 21st century, the band soldiered on.

Atkins, Chet (1924–2001) *guitarist and record producer*

Chester Burton Atkins (b. June 20, 1924) came from a musical family; his grandfather was a well-known fiddler, and his father, a preacher, taught music and tuned pianos. His parents separated when he was young, and Chet got his first guitar from his stepfather when he was about nine years old. He already was playing a homemade banjo, and had learned the basics of ukulele and fiddle. Suffering from childhood asthma, Atkins moved to Columbus, Georgia, from the Appalachian hamlet of Luttrell, Tennessee, when he was 11 years old, where his father lived with his new wife.

At age 17 Atkins got his first radio work, playing fiddle with the *Bill Carlisle–Archie Campbell Show,* out of Knoxville, Tennessee. After the band's show was canceled, the station manager hired Atkins as staff guitarist. Beginning in the mid-1940s, Atkins worked as an accompanist for various country acts (including the CARTER FAMILY and country comedians HOMER AND JETHRO) on radio and the road. He began recording as a soloist in the late 1940s. He also appeared on the *Carter Family and Chet Atkins Show* on radio, which was picked up for national syndication, and joined the Carters when they appeared on the *Grand Ole Opry.*

Atkins's best work was done from the late 1940s through the early 1950s, when his electric guitar instrumentals set new standards for performance, including 1947's "Canned Heat," 1949's "Galloping on the Guitar," and his best-known composition, "Country Gentlemen" in 1953. His appointment as manager of A&R (artists and repertoire) at RCA's new Nashville studios in the mid-1950s ended Atkins's career as an instrumentalist. In his new

Chet Atkins served as the guitarist for "Mother" Maybelle Carter and her daughters ("The Carter Sisters") in the late 1940s and early 1950s, as shown in this photograph. (University of North Carolina, Southern Historical Collection, Southern Folklife Collection, University Archives)

position, Atkins gave a new professionalism to Nashville's recordings, helped mold the careers of Elvis Presley, the BROWNS, and Skeeter Davis, among many others.

Atkins's later recordings often paired him with another musician, among them Les Paul, Doc Watson, or Scottish rock guitarist Mark Knopfler. He retired from working for RCA as a producer in the late 1970s to return to his first love, performing. His last work was with singer SUZY BOGGUSS. Among his many achievements, Atkins was elected into the Country Music Hall of Fame in 1973. Beginning in the mid-1990s, he suffered from cancer. He underwent a brain-tumor operation in

1997, and finally succumbed to complications from the disease on June 20, 2001.

autoharp

The autoharp, a type of mechanical zither, was invented in the late 19th century by an eccentric American music theorist named Charles Zimmerman, who designed the instrument to show the advantages of his new system of music writing. Although Zimmerman's theories didn't catch on, the instrument did become popular, thanks to aggressive sales through mail order catalogs and traveling musicians.

The autoharp features a unique mechanism for automatically playing standard chords. In order to dampen unwanted notes and prevent them from sounding, the instrument features "chord bars"; when depressed, the G chord bar, for example, prevents all the notes from sounding that are not part of a standard G chord. The other chord bars work in a similar fashion.

The autoharp was first popularized in country music by the famous CARTER FAMILY. Sara Carter played the instrument on almost all of their popular recordings. Another early country star who featured the instrument was Ernest Stoneman, whose records sold well through the late 1920s. But it was really thanks to merchandisers like Sears, Roebuck and Montgomery Ward that the instrument became widely known; their mail order catalogs were sent throughout the country, even to the most rural areas, and featured inexpensive instruments that could be delivered through the mail.

A revival of interest in the instrument came in the late 1950s thanks to the folk music revival. Mike Seeger was one of the first enthusiasts to champion the instrument, recording earlier performers including Stoneman and Mother Maybelle Carter, as well as performing with it himself. In folk-rock circles, John Sebastian of the Lovin' Spoonful featured the instrument on several of that group's hits. In the 1970s a new breed of younger virtuosos came on the scene, notably Bryan Bowers.

Autry, Gene (1907–1998) *singing cowboy*

The most famous singing cowboy, Autry transformed the image of the country singer with his introduction of western costumes and cowboy lore into his performances. Born September 29, 1907, Orvon Gene Autry was the son of a Texas farmer who lived and worked in the small town of Tioga Springs. He began his musical career as a member of the church choir, where his grandfather was the preacher. He purchased his first guitar by mail order in his early teens and began playing at local

Early publicity shot of Gene Autry, before he got his cowboy gear (University of North Carolina, Southern Historical Collection, Southern Folklife Collection, University Archives)

events. The family moved to Oklahoma when he was a teenager, and Gene found a job with a local railroad line as a telegraph operator. Autry began his career imitating the popular style of JIMMIE RODGERS, one of country's most beloved performers. Autry's first radio job was singing on Tulsa radio, where he was billed as "Oklahoma's Yodeling Cowboy." In October 1929 Autry went to New York and broke into the recording world. He had his first hit in 1931 with "That Silver Haired Daddy of Mine." This led to a radio contract with the influential and powerful WLS station out of Chicago, where he would remain through mid-1934.

In 1934 Autry gained his first movie role in support of cowboy star Ken Maynard in *In Old Santa Fe;* in the next year, he starred in his first serial. Autry would appear in almost 100 cowboy films, usually accompanied by his favorite horse, Champion. From 1939 to 1956, he starred on radio in *Gene Autry's Melody Ranch,* further underscoring his cowboy image. Autry recorded dozens of western-flavored songs during this period that became major hits. These include "Tumblin' Tumbleweeds," "Back in the Saddle Again," and "The Last Roundup."

After serving in the Army Air Corps in World War II, Autry returned to civilian life. However, while Autry was away, a new star, ROY ROGERS, had gained fame as a singing cowboy, and Autry's last recording successes came with children's records, including "Rudolph, the Red-Nosed Reindeer," "Frosty the Snow Man," "Here Comes Santa Claus," and "(Here Comes) Peter Cottontail." Besides continuing to make films, Autry became an early TV star, appearing in *The Gene Autry Show* for six years beginning in 1950. Autry retired from making music in the mid-1950s to focus on his lucrative business ventures. In 1969 he was inducted into the Country Music Hall of Fame. He died on October 2, 1998.

"Back in the Saddle Again" (1939) *Gene Autry classic*

Typical western-flavored song coauthored by Autry and fellow cowboy singer Ray Whitley and popularized by GENE AUTRY in 1939. He subsequently rerecorded it in 1946 and 1952. It was featured in the 1939 Autry film *Rovin' Tumbleweeds,* and has remained a cowboy standard. Autry's recording was used to humorous effect on the soundtrack of the 1993 romantic comedy *Sleepless in Seattle.*

Bailes Brothers, The *performing brothers*

The Bailes Brothers—guitarists Walter Butler Bailes (1920–November 2000) and John Jacob "Johnny" (1918–1989), fiddler Homer Abraham Jr. (b. 1922) and bass player Kyle (b. 1915)—hailed from a small farm community near Charleston, West Virginia. The boys performed together at home and church, where they learned the classic shape-note style of harmony singing that would be echoed in their recordings. Their father was a Baptist preacher, and two of the four sons would eventually follow him into this profession.

Johnny was the first successful musician, working with Red Sovine in 1937 and then hooking up with Skeets and Laverne Williamson (Laverne later gained fame as Molly O'Day) and "LITTLE" JIMMY DICKENS, working out of Beckley, West Virginia, on radio. He also began performing with brother Kyle as a vocal duet; soon after, Walter replaced Kyle, and the Bailes Brothers was born.

In 1942 ROY ACUFF brought the two brothers to the *Grand Ole Opry,* and they remained popular performers for six years. They were signed to Columbia, where they recorded many of their classic compositions, including "I Want to Be Loved (But Only by You)," "Oh, So Many Years," "Dust on the Bible," and "Give Mother My Crown." All of these recalled the vocal sound and accompaniment of recordings of a decade earlier; in fact, the Bailes vocals resonated with the age-old mountain ballad singing style as it was filtered through rural churches.

In 1948 the duo switched to the rival *Louisiana Hayride* radio program, performing for one more year before the act dissolved. Although Johnny and Walter continued to work sporadically as a gospel duo through the early 1950s, Walter curtailed his performing to focus on the ministry. Johnny ended up in the late 1970s managing one of WEBB PIERCE's country radio stations, and Walter, while still a minister, was also performing. Homer followed Walter into the ministry, but Kyle went into the air-conditioning business.

Bailey, DeFord (1899–1982) *harmonica player*

Born in rural Bellwood, Tennessee, on December 14, 1899, Bailey suffered from infantile paralysis, which stunted his growth. Bailey was discovered by DR. HUMPHREY BATE, also a harmonica player, who led his own string band and performed on the Nashville radio station WSM, home of the *Grand Ole Opry.* Bate brought Bailey to the producer GEORGE HAY for an audition, and he was quickly given a prominent spot on the broadcast. For decades, Bailey was the lone African-American performer on the program. Bailey's talents on the harmonica were awesome, and besides being hired to perform on the *Grand Ole Opry,* he was among the first artists to be recorded in Nashville in 1928. His famous "Pan American Blues," with its imitations of train whistles and the sound of a speeding freight train, influenced generations of musicians.

Although Bailey continued to perform on the *Grand Ole Opry,* the novelty of his few numbers began to wear thin in the 1930s, and he was phased off the program by 1941. Bailey blamed racism for his career's failure; Hay blamed Bailey for his failure to learn new material. Bailey spent the final decades of his life an embittered man, turning down recording offers and most other opportunities to play. He operated a shoeshine stand in Nashville until his retirement in the 1970s and died on July 2, 1982.

Bakersfield sound

About 100 miles north of Los Angeles lies the oil-boom town of Bakersfield. In the late 1940s many displaced southwesterners, particularly from Oklahoma, came to the town in search of work. The oil industry provided good jobs that paid well, and soon a local club scene was thriving to cater to the tastes of the displaced Okies.

One of the first stars from the area was Okie TOMMY COLLINS, who featured a stripped-down honky-tonk sound in his band and recordings, thanks to lead guitarist BUCK OWENS, another Okie. Owens was soon a star on his own, leading a hot country combo from the late 1950s through the 1960s, featuring lead guitar parts and vocal harmonies by Don Rich, who played the newly introduced Fender Telecaster, as well as steel guitarist Tom Brumley. A Bakersfield native named MERLE HAGGARD furthered the roots-oriented style, performing songs about his life experiences.

The Bakersfield sound was first captured on record by tiny labels that sprang up in the area, but was really given a boost when Los Angeles–based

Capitol Records signed Collins, and then his protégé Owens, and finally Merle Haggard. The Bakersfield sound has recently been revived by such new country stars as DWIGHT YOAKAM, who have taken the blend of rock, honky-tonk, and traditional country to a new audience.

Bandy, Moe (b. 1944) *guitarist and singer*

Marion "Moe" Bandy was born in Meridian, Mississippi, on February 12, 1944, the same town where famed singer JIMMIE RODGERS was born. However, Bandy's family relocated to San Antonio, Texas, when he was just six years old, and his musical legacy is pure Texas honky-tonk. Both of Bandy's parents were musical, particularly Moe's father, who had his own country band for a while. He encouraged his son to learn fiddle and guitar, but Moe was more interested in pursuing a career as a rodeo rider. After several years of hard knocks and little pay, he abandoned the rodeo life to take up a job as a sheet-metal worker during the day and a honky-tonk singer at night. He formed his first band, Moe and the Mavericks, in 1962, and recorded sporadically for the next decade for many small Texas labels.

In 1972 Moe met record producer Ray Baker, who took an interest in his career. Baker gave him the song "I Just Started Hatin' Cheatin' Songs Today" to record, and it was released a year later on GRC Records, out of Atlanta. The song shot to number five on the country charts, and was followed by similar honky-tonk anthems, including "Honky Tonk Amnesia" and "Don't Anyone Make Love at Home Anymore." In 1975 Bandy cowrote with LEFTY FRIZZELL a song recalling his rodeo days, "Bandy the Rodeo Clown," his last hit for GRC.

In that same year Bandy signed with Columbia, still under Baker's guiding hand. They continued their string of beer-soaked laments through the early 1980s, including "Here I Am Drunk Again," "She Just Loved the Cheatin' out of Me," "Barstool Mountain," and 1979's duet with JANIE FRICKE, "It's a Cheatin' Situation." In the same year, Moe made his first recording with Joe Stampley, "Just Good Ol' Boys," the beginning of a string of successful duets with a good-natured, humorous tone, culminating in 1981's top-10 "Hey Joe, Hey Moe."

Although Moe continued to tour (accompanied by his backup band, the Rodeo Clowns) and record, he faded from the charts during the onslaught of "new Nashville" artists in the mid-1980s. He has made his home in Branson, Missouri, since the early 1990s, appearing at his own theater.

banjo, five-string

The five-string banjo was developed in the mid-19th century, probably derived from earlier African instruments. White minstrel star Joel Walker Sweeney is generally credited with adding the short fifth or drone string to the banjo, which previously had been made in four-, six-, eight-, and 10-string models. Early banjos were generally made with wooden bodies and rims, a fretless neck, and a skin head. The original banjo playing style has been variously called clawhammer, frailing, rapping, or knocking. It involves brushing the back of the hand across the strings while catching the thumb on the fifth string. There are many different varieties of clawhammer styles, from highly melodic to highly percussive.

Around the turn of the 20th century, ragtime players like Fred Van Epps and Vess L. Ossmann popularized a picked style using three fingers; this style is known as "classical" or "ragtime" banjo today. Improved instrument designs helped increase the banjo's popularity. Makers such as the Vega company of Boston introduced new metal tone rings that helped project the instrument's sound, enabling it to be heard in a band setting. The famous instruments of the teens and twenties, such as Vega's Whyte Laydie and Tubaphone models, were favored by banjoists working both as soloists or in a band.

In the mid-1940s, a new style of banjo playing helped transform it from a background (or accompaniment) role to new prominence as a melody

A Vega Tubaphone Banjo number two from the mid-1920s (George Gruhn)

instrument. Two-finger and three-finger picking styles had existed among folk banjoists at least from the turn of the 20th century, particularly in North Carolina and the upper South. These evolved into bluegrass-style picking, originally introduced by Earl Scruggs (see FLATT AND SCRUGGS) as a member of BILL MONROE's Blue Grass Boys. Here, three fingers are used, with metal picks, to play rapid chord rolls and melody parts. Bluegrass musicians began playing a newly styled banjo marketed by the Gibson company called the Mastertone; it featured further improvements in the design of the tone ring, including a raised head, as well as a full resonator to further increase the instrument's sound.

Although old-time styles continue to be performed today, particularly among urban revivalists, bluegrass-style banjo playing dominates commercial Nashville music. The mid-1970s progressive bluegrass movement helped introduce jazz and rock techniques into the banjoist's repertoire; some of the leading practitioners of this latest banjo style include Tony Trischka and Bela Fleck, who leads the jazz-pop band the Flecktones.

Bare, Bobby (b. 1935) *singer*

Robert Joseph Bare was born in Ironton, Ohio, on April 7, 1935. He was raised in relative poverty on a farm by his father (his mother had died when he was five years old). He began working as a farm laborer when he was 15 and eventually landed a job in a clothing factory. He sang in a local country band and, in 1958, recorded his first solo song, "All American Boy." The song was a hit when it was released by the Fraternity label a year later under the name "Bill Parsons," but Bare did not profit much from it because he had sold his rights to the number for $50. The record was so successful that Fraternity sent a stand-in "Bill Parsons" out on the road who lip-synched to Bare's recording.

Soon after, Bare signed with RCA records, having minor hits with his own "Shame On Me" and "Detroit City" in 1962–63. He recorded an arrangement of the traditional folk song "500 Miles away from Home" that Bare, folksinger Hedy West, and Charles Williams took credit for as "arrangers." He continued to score minor hits on the country and pop charts through the 1960s. He moved to Mercury in the early 1970s but returned to RCA in 1972, having rock-influenced country hits with "Daddy What If" and "Marie Laveau," both penned by Shel Silverstein. (Bare would collaborate again with Silverstein in 1980 and 1982.) He was an early fan of then-progressive country songwriters like Billy Joe Shaver, KRIS KRISTOFFERSON, and Mickey Newbury.

Bare was heavily promoted by rock entrepreneur Bill Graham in the late 1970s, who got him a contract with Columbia Records, hailing him as the "Bruce Springsteen of country music." However, Bare's career faded. He ended up back in country music in the mid-1980s, hosting his own show on the then fledgling Nashville Network. After some years off the country radar, Bare returned as part of the (aging) supergroup, The Old Dogs, including JERRY REED, MEL TILLIS, and WAYLON JENNINGS for a 1998 album of new songs by Shel Silverstein; it was Silverstein's last major work, because he died soon after it was released. Bare has been less active over the last decade.

Bate, Dr. Humphrey, and the Possum Hunters

The Possum Hunters were one of the first old-time string bands featured on the *Grand Ole Opry*. They were led by the harmonica-playing physician Humphrey Bate, who was born in Castallian Springs, Tennessee, on May 25, 1875, and died on June 12, 1936.

Bate led several old-time bands in the Nashville area. He was already performing on Nashville radio in 1925, before the *Grand Ole Opry* was first broadcast, and he was immediately invited to perform when the show was launched. Soon after their *Grand Ole Opry* debut, the band recorded for Brunswick records. Bate's two children—Alcyone, who began performing with her father when she was 13 and continued to play with various versions of the band through the early 1960s, and Buster—were prominent members of the group, with other members floating in and out as recording sessions or radio work came their way. After Bate's death the band continued until the late 1940s under the lead of fiddler Oscar Stone, and then into the early 1960s led by Alcyone and guitarist Staley Walton. In the early 1960s the band merged with the Crook Brothers, another old-time string band and long-time performer on the *Opry*.

"Battle of New Orleans, The" (1959)
folk-styled hit

Arkansas-born JIMMIE DRIFTWOOD composed a number of songs in the late 1950s in a folk ballad style. RCA released an album of these songs performed by Driftwood in 1958, but it saw little success until "The Battle of New Orleans" topped the country charts in a cover version by singer JOHNNY HORTON in early 1959. The ballad told the story of the last battle of the War of 1812 between the British and the Americans, which took place outside New Orleans in 1814. It was set to a traditional fiddle tune, "The 8th of January." Horton's version topped the charts for 10 weeks, and reached gold (million-selling) status. This led RCA to release Driftwood's version that June, for a top-25 country hit.

"Behind Closed Doors" (1973) *hit song for*
Charlie Rich

Although singer/pianist CHARLIE RICH first recorded for Sun Records in the late 1950s, he did not achieve significant success as a performer until he signed with Epic Records in the early 1970s and began working with producer Billy Sherrill. The result was Rich's massive hit, "Behind Closed Doors," which reached number one on March 10, 1973, was certified gold, and named as the Country Music Association's Single of the Year. In the song (which Rich wrote), Rich praises his "baby" because "she never makes a scene/By hangin' all over me in a crowd"—yet in Rich's smoky-voiced rendition, there is a hint of stormy sexuality lurking below the surface. It remained the song most closely associated with the singer through the rest of his career.

Bellamy Brothers, The *pop-country duo*

Born in Derby, Florida, keyboard player David (b. September 16, 1950) and guitarist Howard (b. February 2, 1946) have had long careers in country-pop music. Their father was a farmer who played dobro and fiddle in an amateur bluegrass band.

David was the first to make it into the musical big time as a member of an R&B band called the Accidents in the mid-1960s, backing stars such as Percy Sledge and Little Anthony and The Imperials. The brothers began performing together in a country-rock band called Jericho in the late 1960s, playing the southern club circuit through 1971, when they disbanded. The Bellamys then went to work as jingle writers and songwriters.

Their big break came in 1975 when JIM STAFFORD scored a hit with David's composition "Spiders and Snakes." They were signed to Warner Brothers, and had a minor hit with 1975's "Nothin' Heavy." In 1976 they covered the Neil Diamond–Larry Williams pop anthem "Let Your Love Flow," replete with their sweet harmonies and jangling acoustic guitars. The record was an enormous hit on country and pop charts. The Bellamys continued to record in this acoustic rock style through the 1970s, scoring minor hits with songs like "If I Said You Had a Beautiful Body Would You Hold It against Me" in 1979.

In the 1980s they turned to more mainstream country sounds, recording a number of minor hits mostly written by David, including 1982's "Redneck Girl," 1983's "Dancing Cowboys," and 1986's "Too Much Is Not Enough." In 1987 they recorded "Kids of the Baby Boom" with the Forester Sisters, a nostalgic look at growing up in the 1950s that had broad appeal. They continued to perform through the 1990s, releasing their work after 1991 on their own Bellamy Brothers label and on other small labels.

"Big Bad John" (1961) *number-one hit for*
Jimmy Dean

JIMMY DEAN's first number-one hit, this song topped the country, adult contemporary, and pop charts in 1961. Like many country hits of the late 1950s and early 1960s, this song imitates a folk ballad in its language and song structure. Written by Dean, the song tells the story of a mysterious man known only as "Big Bad John," who comes to the aid of his fellow miners after a disaster leaves them trapped in the mines. The biggest and strongest of the lot, John held up the sagging timbers while the others escaped; however, his life was lost performing this heroic act.

Black, Clint (b. 1962) *performer and songwriter*
Although born in Long Branch, New Jersey, on February 4, 1962, Black was raised in Houston, Texas, from the age of six months. He played bass as a teenager in his brother's band and soon began working as a soloist in local clubs, where he hooked up with guitarist Hayden Nicholas. The two began writing songs together, and they produced a demo tape, which landed Black a contract with RCA. Black's first single, "A Better Man," cowritten with Nicholas, hit number one in 1989, a rare feat for a first recording. It was followed by another chart buster, "Killin' Time." Black had several more number-one hits through the mid-1990s in a similar style, but then began to fade from the charts. He continues to record and perform.

Blackwood Brothers, The *gospel vocal group*
The Blackwood family were sharecroppers in the Mississippi Delta. Like many others, they were caught up in the gospel fervor that swept the South, propelled by traveling revivalists. At one such revival the brothers' mother was "saved," inspiring her sons to also follow the Lord. Sometime during the mid-1920s, Roy (b. Fentress, Mississippi, December 24, 1900–March 21, 1971) became a traveling preacher while brothers Doyle (b. Ackerman, Mississippi, August 22, 1911–October 3, 1974) and James (b. Ackerman, Mississippi, August 4, 1919–February 3, 2002) began performing religious material at local revival meetings and schoolhouses. In about 1933 they joined with a local singing school teacher to form the Choctaw County Jubilee Singers. Doyle briefly traveled to Birmingham to work with another professional gospel group, but by early 1935 Doyle, James, Roy, and Roy's son R. W. (Ronald Winston, b. Ackerman, Mississippi, October 23, 1921–June 24, 1954), were all back in Mississippi. The first quartet began at around this time.

After broadcasting on several small stations, the group got its big break when it began a daily program on the powerful KWKH station, out of Shreveport, Louisiana. With its strong signal, the station could be heard through much of the South and Midwest. The group expanded its repertory to include country and pop songs as well as gospel numbers around this time. The Stamps-Baxter Publishing Company, which specialized in gospel music, was impressed by their radio broadcasts and hired the Blackwoods to travel to promote their songbooks. Stamps arranged for them to broadcast out of Shenandoah, Iowa, where the group spent the early 1940s. The group briefly disbanded during the height of World War II.

In 1946 the group broke from Stamps-Baxter and formed their own recording company. Between 1946 and 1948, Doyle left the group and was replaced by the first nonfamily member, Don Smith. The group moved increasingly toward pop material, gaining such popularity that by 1948 they formed a separate unit, the Blackwood Gospel Quartet, to focus on religious material. Doyle returned to lead this group.

In 1950 both Doyle and the eldest brother, Roy, decided to retire. James and R. W. took the group to Memphis, where they had their own radio show broadcast twice a day. They also signed with RCA records and scored several hits, beginning in 1952 with "Rock My Soul," reflecting the influence of black gospel groups. During this period, Roy's son Cecil (October 28, 1934–November 13, 2000) formed a "junior" quartet for the younger family members and friends, called the Songfellows. It was this group that a young Elvis Presley hoped to join, but he was turned down after an audition. In 1954 the senior group seemed poised for greater success after appearing on the Arthur Godfrey TV show, but then R. W. and group member Bill Lyles were killed in a plane crash following a performance.

After a period of mourning, the group reformed and became even more popular in Memphis. Cecil and James's son James Jr. (b. July 31, 1943) came on board, along with bass singer J. D. Sumner. During this period, the group also became a prime force in the gospel music industry, founding and buying several gospel publishing houses, including the Stamps-Baxter company, which had originally sponsored them. In 1956 the group organized the National Quartet Convention, which has become an important annual event in Memphis, and also the Gospel Music Association, which brought greater organization to the field.

The Blackwoods continued to record and perform through the end of the 20th century, with varying personnel. James Blackwood, the last remaining of the original brothers, continued to be the group's guiding force through 1970. He subsequently "retired," although as late as 1999 he was still making many appearances, both with the group and sometimes as a guest of others. He was inducted into the Gospel Music Hall of Fame in 1974, and won numerous Dove Awards as best male gospel singer from the late 1960s through the late 1970s. In 1998 the group was inducted into the Gospel Music Hall of Fame. Cecil became the de facto leader for the last quarter-century, until his death in 2000; his son Mark continues to sing with the group.

bluegrass music

Sometimes called "country music in overdrive," bluegrass music is often caricatured as high-speed, high-pitched, high-energy music. Taking its name from the legendary band led by mandolinist BILL MONROE in the late 1940s, bluegrass actually is more than just fancy pickin' and breathless singing. It is a music of great emotional power and musical sophistication that borrows from country, gospel, honky-tonk, and, more recently, jazz and rock music to form a unique musical union.

All bluegrass bands owe a debt to Bill Monroe, who brought together a group of five musicians to form the first classic lineup of his Blue Grass Boys in 1946. These included FLATT AND SCRUGGS on lead guitar and banjo, respectively, fiddler Chubby Wise on fiddle, Monroe on mandolin and high tenor vocals, and Cedric Rainwater on bass. Earl Scruggs had evolved a unique method of playing the five-string banjo, a three-finger picking style that changed the instrument from primarily an accompaniment to a melodic lead instrument. Lester Flatt developed a new way of playing guitar accompaniments, using bass runs rather than chords as "fills" to bridge the gaps between chord progressions. Monroe was a master mandolin player, and Wise was a fiddler influenced as much by western swing as he was by old-time styles. Vocally, the group offered a strong contrast between the relaxed, almost crooning lead vocals of Flatt and the intense, high-pitched harmonies and leads of Monroe. It is not an exaggeration to say that Monroe's band not only invented bluegrass vocally and instrumentally but also became the model for every other band.

When this band performed on the *Grand Ole Opry,* their effect was immediate and revolutionary. Bands such as the STANLEY BROTHERS, who had been playing in a more traditional style, immediately switched to bluegrass; in 1948, Flatt and Scruggs left Monroe to form a less mandolin-oriented ensemble. Monroe continued to work through the 1990s, composing many classic bluegrass tunes and songs while refining the overall sound.

In 1959 Mike Seeger recorded a number of groups for an anthology for Folkways Records called *Mountain Music: Bluegrass Style.* While a few urban players had been aware of bluegrass before this album was issued, this opened the floodgates, with many groups forming in urban centers, including New York, Boston, Baltimore, Washington, San Francisco, and Los Angeles. So-called progressive bluegrass was born, a wedding of traditional bluegrass instrumentation with a broader palette of material. Banjoist Bill Keith, who briefly performed with Monroe, introduced "melodic" bluegrass banjo, almost eliminating accompaniment chords from his playing. Bands such as Washington's Country Gentlemen, Boston's Charles River Valley Boys, Los Angeles's Kentucky Colonels (featuring legendary guitarist Clarence White), and New York City's Greenbriar Boys all represented a new approach to the bluegrass style.

The older acts, like Monroe, the Stanleys, and Flatt and Scruggs, had eked out a living through the 1950s existing on the edge of country music. The folk music revival, along with the growth of progressive bluegrass, helped them gain a larger audience, although they still remained on the fringes. Flatt and Scruggs came the closest to widespread popularity, thanks to their appearance on TV's *Beverly Hillbillies* and the soundtrack to the film *Bonnie and Clyde.* By the end of the 1960s, Scruggs was pursuing a country-rock audience performing with his sons, while Flatt formed a more traditional bluegrass band.

The 1970s brought a second wave of bluegrass innovators. These bands and solo acts tended to emphasize flashy instrumental work over vocals. Country Cooking, out of Ithaca, New York, featured the twin banjos of Tony Trischka and Pete Wernick on original bluegrass-flavored instrumentals (the band never recorded vocals). New York–area mandolinist David Grisman began recording what he called "dawg" music, a synthesis of swing and bluegrass. Newgrass Revival, under the leadership of mandolinist Sam Bush, combined the energy of rock (and heavy metal's power) with bluegrass instrumentation.

In the 1980s Bill Monroe began to gain the wide acceptance that his stature as the "father of bluegrass music" deserved. Meanwhile, progressive bluegrassers began returning to more traditional material, while traditionalists showed the influence of the progressive crowd. The new country explosion featured many ex-bluegrassers, most prominently Ricky Skaggs, Kathy Mattea, and Vince Gill. They brought many traditional bluegrass songs and instrumentation into mainstream country music. Bands such as the Johnson Mountain Boys arose as virtual clones of traditional bluegrass

outfits, recreating the look, style, and sound of a generic 1950s bluegrass ensemble. Meanwhile, the Nashville Bluegrass Band and others continued to broaden the bluegrass repertory while remaining true to the roots of the music.

The later 1990s saw yet another bluegrass revival. Singer/fiddler Alison Krauss has achieved remarkable success, both as a solo performer and with her band Union Station. Krauss in turn discovered the band Nickel Creek, a group of young bluegrass players who recorded a less aggressive form of the music. They have become a popular act on the country charts and the CMT cable network. Ricky Skaggs, who had previously crossed over to mainstream country, returned to the bluegrass fold in the later 1990s with his group Kentucky Thunder. Earlier bluegrass stars such as Del McCoury also began to enjoy wider followings. Bluegrass achieved such high visibility that in early 2002 CMT featured a "Bluegrass Rules" weekend featuring concerts and videos.

"Blue Moon of Kentucky" (1947) *classic bluegrass song*

Bill Monroe's "Blue Moon of Kentucky" has the distinction of being both a classic bluegrass song and appearing on the B side of Elvis Presley's first record. State-themed waltzes enjoyed a brief run of popularity in the late 1940s, so Bill Monroe wrote and performed this song originally in waltz (3/4) time. When Elvis went into Sun studios to cut his first single, he chose the R&B song "That's Alright, Mama" as the A side. Asked for another song by producer/engineer Sam Phillips, Elvis supposedly began "goofing around," singing "Blue Moon of Kentucky" converted to a 4/4, rockabilly tune. Phillips liked what he heard, and the new version was placed on the back of Elvis's first single. Monroe later acknowledged Elvis's innovation by performing the song first in waltz time, and then switching to an upbeat 4/4 version. In 1989 the Kentucky legislature named the song the state's "Official Bluegrass Song."

Blue Sky Boys, The   *vocal duo*

Bill (b. Hickory, North Carolina, October 28, 1917) and Earl Bolick (November 16, 1919–Suwanee, Georgia, April 19, 1998) were among the first "brother" acts in country music, and one of the most popular. The boys were raised in the mountainous western section of North Carolina on a small family farm. They learned their repertoire of traditional songs from family members, gospel hymns from the local church and mail-order hymnals, and sentimental songs from the recordings of 1920s country artists.

After performing on radio in Asheboro, North Carolina, in the early 1930s, the boys were signed by RCA Victor to a recording contract in 1936, enjoying immediate popularity. Among their hits were the sentimental favorite "The Sweetest Gift (A Mother's Smile)" and "Short Life of Trouble," along with the more upbeat "Sunny Side of Life," and "Are You from Dixie?," their radio theme song.

The brothers were inactive in the 1950s, returning to recording in the early 1960s for the Starday label and then retiring again until the old-time music revival of the mid-1970s brought them back

Bill (left) and Earl Bolick, c. 1950, the Blue Sky Boys (University of North Carolina, Southern Historical Collection, Southern Folklife Collection, University Archives)

to the studio. Even though Starday added a fuller country band to the accompaniment, the sound and style of their music never really changed.

Bogguss, Suzy (b. 1956) *performer and singer* Bogguss was a popular singer/performer in the 1990s country revival. She was born on December 30, 1956, in Aledo, Illinois, and took up guitar and singing as a hobby when she was a teenager. Bogguss arrived in Nashville in 1984, and two years later, she was the lead attraction at Dollywood, the theme park run by DOLLY PARTON. Bogguss sold a self-produced cassette during her stage shows that attracted the attention of Capitol Records. Capitol signed her in 1987. She enjoyed her first hits with covers of older country songs, and had her greatest success in 1991 with her recording of Nancy Griffith's "Outbound Plane." Legendary guitarist/producer CHET ATKINS admired her style, and the two made an album together in 1994. Since then, Bogguss has recorded less frequently, and has had few hits.

Suzy Bogguss, 1996 (Raeanne Rubenstein)

Bond, Johnny (1915–1978) *guitarist and performer*

Cyrus Whitfield Bond was born in the farm community of Enville, Oklahoma, on June 1, 1915, and raised on a number of small Oklahoma farms. Bond said he could remember listening to his parents' Victrola, and was particularly fond of "The Prisoner's Song" and "The Death of Floyd Collins," both tremendously popular recordings by early country star VERNON DALHART. Bond was a member of the brass band in high school, where he learned the rudiments of music. At about this time he invested 98 cents in a Montgomery Ward ukulele. He quickly graduated to the guitar, and was playing locally during his high school years.

At age 19 Bond made his radio debut on a station out of Oklahoma City, and three years later, he was hired by Jimmy Wakely, who led a western trio called the Bell Boys. In that same year, 1937, Bond made his first solo recordings for Columbia Records, including his classic cowboy ballad "Cimarron" and the country weeper "Divorce Me C.O.D." In 1940 Wakeley's group was hired to back popular cowboy star GENE AUTRY on film and his popular *Melody Ranch* radio show, a relationship that lasted 16 years. In 1943 Bond hooked up with TEX RITTER, with whom he would star in numerous cowboy films, tour, and form a music publishing company called Vidor Publications.

In 1953 Bond and Ritter were hired to host the syndicated *Town Hall Party* TV show, taped in southern California, giving them national exposure for the next seven years, while Bond continued to work TV and radio with Autry, SPADE COOLEY, and Wakeley. He also began writing prolifically, adding to his catalog such songs as "I Wonder Where You Are Tonight," "Gone and Left Me Blues," and "Tomorrow Never Comes." (Bond is said to have written more than 500 songs, many of which became classics.) In 1960 his song "Hot Rod Lincoln" was a major rock and roll hit for him on Autry's Republic record label, and he had one further hit, 1965's tongue-in-cheek classic "Ten Little Bottles," issued by Starday.

In the 1970s he retired from active performing to focus on music publishing. He also wrote two books, a biography of Ritter and his own memoirs. Bond died on June 22, 1978. In 2000 he was elected to the Country Music Hall of Fame.

Boone, Debby (b. 1956) *singer*

Daughter of pop singer Pat Boone, Debby was born in Hackensack, New Jersey, during the height of her dad's teen-idol success, on September 22, 1956. She came to her musical talents naturally; her grandfather was the legendary country showman RED FOLEY, and her father was a major hitmaker of the late 1950s. Young Debby followed in their footsteps, first shooting up the charts in 1977 with "You Light Up My Life." She had a couple more country hits, including the number-one 1980 ode "Are You on the Road to Lovin' Me Again." After 1982 Boone primarily recorded gospel material.

"Bouquet of Roses" (1948) *Gold record and major hit for Eddy Arnold*

EDDY ARNOLD's second major hit, and his first gold record, "Bouquet of Roses" is a sentimental tearjerker on the common theme of the jilted lover. It managed to sell more than 1 million copies without placing on the pop charts, an unusual feat for a country song during that era. *Billboard* ranks it as the sixth best-selling country single since country charts were first compiled in 1944.

Bowen, Jimmy (b. 1937) *performer and producer*

James Albert Bowen was born in Santa Rita, New Mexico, on November 30, 1937. He began his career working as a musician, partnering with guitarist Buddy Knox in a group known as the Rhythm Orchids that they formed while still in college in 1955 at West Texas State. They made some recordings for Norman Petty (the same person who recorded and produced BUDDY HOLLY), which were leased to Roulette in 1957. The pair had a two-sided hit: "Party Doll," credited to Knox, and "I'm Stickin' with You," credited to Bowen. Bass-playing Bowen was only a marginal singer, however, and, after he recorded one album for Roulette, his career as a performer ended.

By the mid-1960s Bowen had relocated to Los Angeles, where he became a producer for Reprise Records, then owned by Frank Sinatra. In 1977 he moved to Nashville, where he shaped the careers of EDDIE RABBITT and the resurgence of HANK WILLIAMS JR. In 1984 he was hired to run the country division of MCA. He played a central role in molding REBA MCENTIRE into the glitzy, mainstream act that she became. In the early 1990s he moved to Capitol Records, which had little if any country roster. He immediately discovered and nurtured GARTH BROOKS, whom he built into a megastar. Bowen wrote an autobiography detailing the behind-the-scenes world of a record producer in the later 1990s, and he continues to work in Nashville.

Boxcar Willie (1931–1999) *performer*
Lecil Travis Martin was born in Sterrett, Texas, on September 1, 1931. Although his father was a railroad worker (and a part-time fiddler), Willie never worked on the rails, despite his colorful stage name. He had a number of professions while pursuing his avocation, a love of music, ranging from disc jockey to mechanic to refrigeration and flight engineer. In the mid-1970s he decided to scrap it all for the life of an entertainer, relocating from his native Texas to Nashville, and taking on his hobo persona. Scottish agent Drew Taylor caught him performing at a local club, and arranged for several English tours, where he became a major success.

In 1979 he returned triumphantly to the United States, making his *Grand Ole Opry* debut. He had a minor hit in 1980 with his "Train Medley." He followed this with a number of half-sung, half-spoken novelty numbers, including 1982's European hit "Bad News," which also charted on the lower ends

of the U.S. country charts. He also was a regular performer on the syndicated version of *Hee Haw* in the early 1980s.

Willie established himself as a prime draw at the new country-music capital, Branson, Missouri, in the 1980s. He often performed six shows a day at his own theater, which was one of the first and most successful in town. When he died of leukemia at his Branson home on April 12, 1999, flags were flown at half-mast throughout the town.

Boyd, Bill (1910–1977) *western swing performer*
William Lemuel Boyd (b. near Ladonia, Texas, September 29, 1910) was one of 13 children born to Lemuel and Molly Jared Boyd, both originally of Tennessee. The family migrated to Texas in about 1902, settling on a large ranch. There the young Boyds were exposed to hard work and music; both parents were singers and many of the ranch hands played music in the evening. Bill got his first guitar through a mail order catalog and was soon performing with his younger brother Jim (b. 1914).

When the depression hit Texas, the family relocated to Dallas, where Bill began working a series of odd jobs from laborer to salesman, while pursuing music on the side. Brother Jim enrolled in the Technical High School, where he met Art (b. Audrey) Davis, a talented musician who played clarinet, fiddle, and mandolin.

While Jim and Art were getting their act together, Bill got his first radio job as a member of a trio known as the Alexanders Daybreakers for a local early-morning show. By 1932 the Daybreakers had become the Cowboy Ramblers, moved to station WRR, and Jim and Art were brought on board. The group was signed to the Victor budget label, Bluebird, in 1934, and would continue to perform together for nearly 20 years.

Through the 1930s, the Boyds made classic western swing recordings for Bluebird, including blues like "Fan It" and "I've Got Those Oklahoma Blues," instrumentals like "Beaumont Rag" and "New Steel Guitar Rag" (picking up on the popularity of BOB

WILLS's recording of "Steel Guitar Rag"), and novelties like the silly "Wah Hoo," complete with animal sound effects. Their recording of "Under the Double Eagle" remained in print for more than 25 years, making it one of the best-loved of all western swing recordings. They also recorded the obligatory cowboy numbers, including "The Strawberry Roan" and "The Windswept Desert." Younger brother John played steel guitar on several of their later recordings, as well as forming his own band, the Southerners, in the late 1930s. He continued to perform until his death in 1942.

During the 1940s the two brothers relocated to Hollywood, following in the footsteps of other swing bands that found lucrative work in southern California. They also appeared in a number of the low-budget westerns that small Hollywood studios produced during this period. In the late 1940s and early 1950s Jim formed his own band, the Men of the West, to cash in on the cowboy craze.

In the 1950s live music on the radio was gradually edged out by records, and the two brothers switched to working as disc jockeys. Bill retired in the early 1970s, but his brother Jim was still working part time as late as 1975. Bill died on December 7, 1977.

"Boy Named Sue, A" (1969) *Johnny Cash hit*

Only ultra-macho JOHNNY CASH could have made a country hit out of Shel Silverstein's sly parody of a classic country ballad. Abandoned as an infant by his no-good father, the song's hero is cursed by the only legacy his father left him—the name Sue. He vows to hunt down his pa and kill him for this shame. Discovering him in a bar, he nearly kills him when his father tells him that he named him Sue to toughen him up in this "mean old world." Moved by this admission, the two have a tearful reunion, although the son still hates his name! Cash bravely performed this song for the first time in front of an audience of prisoners at San Quentin; recorded live, the song became an unexpected hit, spending 12 weeks on the country charts.

Bradley, Owen (1915–1998) *performer and producer*

Along with CHET ATKINS, Bradley was the man most responsible for the growth of the Nashville Sound. Bradley was born in Westmoreland, Tennessee, northeast of Nashville, on October 21, 1915. He began his career as a pianist and guitar player in various pickup pop bands in and around Nashville after World War II. In 1947 he was selected to be the orchestra leader for radio station WSM, home of the *Grand Ole Opry*. In that same year he was hired to produce recordings for Decca Records, which wanted to establish a presence in country music. Although Bradley recorded everything from BILL MONROE's traditional bluegrass to ERNEST TUBB's original honky-tonk sessions, he is most famous for his late 1950s and early 1960s recordings of crossover artists such as BRENDA LEE and PATSY CLINE. In 1962 Bradley was promoted to chief staff producer for MCA (then the parent company of Decca). Through the 1960s he was country's premier producer, working with such major country singers as CONWAY TWITTY and LORETTA LYNN. After retiring in the early 1970s, Bradley occasionally returned to the studio to work with acts ranging from Elvis Costello to K. D. LANG. He died in Nashville on January 7, 1998.

Although best known as a producer, Bradley also had a recording career with Decca, from 1949 through the 1950s. Bradley's younger brother Harold (b. Nashville, January 2, 1926) worked as a guitarist on many of his brother's sessions, and is credited as the most recorded guitarist in history.

Branson, Missouri

A formerly sleepy town of some 3,700 inhabitants that was best known for its natural springs, Branson has become a center for (mostly older) country and pop performers who have built lavish theaters there to present their music.

The Branson story has been oft told. Nestled in the foothills of the Ozarks, the town was first put on the map by Harold Bell Wright in his 1907 best-selling romance, *The Shepherd of the Hills*. Decades later, a small theme park, Silver Dollar City, opened in 1960, followed by a couple of music clubs. Presley's Mountain Music Jubilee, which opened its doors in 1967, is said to be the first country-music attraction in town.

After their major hit-making days were over, many older country acts spent a large part of each year on the road, performing a grueling round of one-nighters, and wished they could stay put in one place and let their core audience come to them. ROY CLARK had often vacationed in the Branson area and thought it would be as good a place as any to open a year-round music theater. He set up shop in 1983. Soon Clark brought other older country stars to the area, including MEL TILLIS. Both had long been off the country charts, but they proved to be major draws in Branson. They opened their own palatial theaters, with architecture and floor shows reminiscent of those in Las Vegas. A second wave of musical immigrants, such as Andy Williams and Wayne Newton, came from other mainstream musical genres and discovered that Branson was hospitable to their talents as well. The number of theaters multiplied, and the town's main drag became a glittering strip of marquees and neon.

A featured segment on *60 Minutes* in 1989 cemented the town's growing reputation as middle America's country entertainment mecca. A highlight of this report was an interview with Japanese violin virtuoso Shoji Tabuchi, who became one of the town's major attractions. Tabuchi played everything from Mozart to Broadway tunes to high-speed bluegrass standards, and put on a spectacular show, including lasers, smoke bombs, "genies" emerging from bottles, and "magic carpets." Another Branson standout is the Baldknobbers, a country comedy act who had been performing in Branson long before the town ascended to its legendary status. And to this day Roy Clark continues to offer one of the better music shows in the area.

Britt, Elton (1913–1972) *singing cowboy and yodeler*

An amazing yodeler, Britt was a singing cowboy who appeared in movies and early TV as well as on radio and recordings. Born James Elton Baker in Zack, Arkansas, on June 27, 1913, Elton was the son of a champion fiddler/small-time farmer, and learned to play guitar as a youngster. At age 14, he was discovered playing locally in an amateur show, and was hired to perform on radio station KMPC, out of Los Angeles, where he was given his stage name. He began recording almost immediately, and in 1937 signed a contract with RCA, which would last for over 20 years.

Britt's 1942 patriotic ballad, "There's A Star Spangled Banner Waving Somewhere," was the first country recording to be awarded a gold record, although it took two years to achieve this feat. This led to an invitation from President Roosevelt to perform at the White House. Other popular recordings include 1948's "Chime Bells," famous for Britt's show-stopping falsetto yodeling. He also recorded many duets with Rosalie Allen, including 1949's "Quicksilver." Britt's recording career continued through the 1950s, but was upstaged somewhat by his film and TV work. He retired from active performing between 1954 to 1968, although he returned to perform occasionally during the last four years of his life. He died on June 23, 1972.

Brooks, Garth (b. 1963) *singer and songwriter*

Brooks was a phenomenon in the 1990s; his albums and singles crossed over to the pop charts, and before his popularity faded he had nearly eclipsed the Beatles as a best-selling pop artist. Brooks's mother, Coleen, was an amateur country singer who worked sporadically in their native Luba, Oklahoma, on recordings and radio. Brooks grew up interested in sports, entering Oklahoma State University on a track-and-field scholarship, with a specialty in javelin throwing. His guitar playing career began in high school and continued in college. On a trip to

Garth Brooks, 1997 (Raeanne Rubenstein)

Nashville in 1987, Brooks attracted the attention of Capitol Records and producer Allen Reynolds. His first album was successful, producing the number-one country hit "If Tomorrow Never Comes." However, the follow-up, *No Fences,* was a phenomenon: It sold 700,000 copies in its first 10 days on sale and stayed on the pop charts for over a year. It had major hits, including the pop ballad "The Dance" and the joyous honky-tonk number "Friends in Low Places." Brooks's third album, 1991's *Ropin' the Wind,* entered the pop charts in the number-one position, the first country album ever to do so. His next four albums would repeat this achievement.

Brooks's 1992 album, *The Chase,* reflected a further move toward mainstream pop, particularly in the anthemic single "We Shall Be Free." It was less successful than his previous releases but still sold several million copies. Brooks followed it with 1993's *In Pieces,* featuring a selection of high-energy honky-tonk numbers. After a gap due to a disagreement with his record label, Brooks released *Sevens* in 1997 and then a two-CD live set, his last major successes as of 2004.

In 1999 Brooks portrayed a fictional pop singer named Chris Gaines in both an album and a film; the album was released first and was so poorly received that the film was never shown. Brooks withdrew from the public eye in 2000, amid announcements that his longtime "storybook" marriage was coming to an end. Never one to give up easily, Brooks came roaring back with his album *Scarecrow* in autumn 2001. Announced as his "last" album, it returned him to the sound and style of his earlier country outings, and the fans responded by making it a major hit. In May 2005 Brooks became engaged to be married to longtime girlfriend TRISHA YEARWOOD.

Brooks and Dunn

Leon Eric "Kix" Brooks (b. Shreveport, Louisiana, May 12, 1955; lead guitar, vocals) was a singer/songwriter who had spent some time working in Alaska on the pipeline before settling in Nashville in the early 1980s where he established a successful career as a songwriter. Ronnie Dunn (b. Tulsa, Oklahoma, June 1, 1953; guitar, vocals) came out of Oklahoma. Originally pursuing a career as a Baptist minister, he began performing in local venues as a singer/guitarist. Dunn won a Marlboro Talent Contest in 1988, where one of the judges was Scott Hendricks, who was a major country producer for Arista Records. Hendricks brought Dunn together with Brooks to write some songs for a solo album. The pair clicked, and they debuted with a dance hit, "Boot Scootin' Boogie," in 1990.

Through the early 1990s the duo was rarely off the charts, racking up hits with their nouveau honky-tonk anthems such as "Brand New Man" and 1992's "Hard Working Man." They also dominated the award shows, winning numerous "Best Country Duo" nods. However, the hits dried up somewhat in the later 1990s as tastes changed, and it looked like Brooks and Dunn would never return to their top-of-the-charts glory. But in 2001, they came back strongly with "Ain't Nothin' 'Bout You." They followed with "Only in America," a patriotic song that gained a significant sales boost after the terrorist attacks on September 11, 2001. They remain one of the most popular touring acts in country music.

Brown, "Junior" (b. 1952) *guitarist and singer*
Jamieson Brown was born in Cottonwood, Arizona, on June 12, 1952. The son of a pianist, he took up guitar early in life, and counts among his influences everything from country to Jimi Hendrix. Although born in Arizona, he was primarily raised in rural Indiana. After a stint playing local clubs in the Albuquerque, New Mexico, area in the mid-1970s, he settled in Austin, Texas, in 1979, just as alt-country was beginning to develop. He worked as a guitarist in several local bands, and then taught guitar and pedal steel at nearby Rodgers State College in Oklahoma in the mid-1980s. At that time he designed a new musical instrument, the "Guit-Steel," a twin-necked guitar that combines the tonal qualities of both conventional electric and steel guitars. Guitar maker Michael Stevens made the first Guit-Steel to Brown's specifications in 1985.

While teaching at Rodgers State, Brown met guitarist/vocalist Tanya Rae, whom he wed in 1988, and she joined his band. Brown self-released his first album, *12 Shades of Brown,* which was licensed by a British label, Demon Records, in 1990. Two years later he made a stunning and well-received debut at Austin's South by Southwest music conference, and was signed to Curb Records.

In 1993 Curb reissued Brown's debut album and also issued *Guit with It.* It featured a remake of Red Simpson's 1950s-era road epic, "Highway Patrol," which—in a remixed version and promoted with a humorous video—became a chart hit in 1995. Another minor hit was the humorous "My Wife Thinks You're Dead," also promoted with a clever video (it won an Academy of Country Music award for best country video of 1995). The loping beat of the tune perfectly suits the somewhat tongue-in-cheek lyrics. He followed with his third album, *Semi Crazy,* in 1996, but it did not produce any further hits.

Besides his traditional-sounding baritone vocals, Brown is a very talented guitarist. He mixes into his lead guitar work traditional country licks along with references to Jimi Hendrix and acid rock. His steel work is more traditional, and his Guit-Steel hybrid guitar allows him to move effortlessly between twangy lead work and sliding steel licks.

Brown issued *Long Walk Back* and *Mixed Bag* in 1998 and 2001, respectively, both featuring a more eclectic mix of music. *Long Walk Back* even included two tracks with Hendrix drummer Mitch Mitchell. However, it failed to win any new fans for Brown. Nonetheless, Brown continued to write and perform, releasing the album *Mixed Bag* in 2001.

Brown, Milton (1903–1936) *vocalist and bandleader*
Milton Brown was born in Stephensville, Texas, on September 8, 1903. Brown began his career as a partner of BOB WILLS, forming a band in 1931 known originally as the Aladdin Laddies (named for its radio sponsor, the Aladdin Lamp Company). When new sponsor Light Crust Flour hired the group in 1932, they became the Light Crust Doughboys. Brown soon struck out on his own, as did Wills.

From 1934 until his death two years later, Brown led one of the first and hottest bands in western swing, the Musical Brownies, who were far more hard-edged than Wills's band at the time. The band featured a swinging fiddler (originally Cecil Brower, who was replaced in 1936 by Cliff Bruner), a jazz-style pianist, Fred Calhoun, and legendary steel guitarist, Bob Dunn, whose staccato bursts of sound were unequaled at the time. Dunn is said to have been the first player to use an electric instrument on a country recording, and certainly his unique playing style made the instrument stand out. The group further capitalized on this novelty by doubling the fiddle lead with the steel guitar, an effect that was often imitated on other western swing and later country recordings. The band's repertoire was heavy on blues, jazz, and pop standards, with the occasional country number thrown in. They avoided ballads, perhaps because they worked primarily as a dance band, and probably also because Brown's vocal style, a combination of Cab Calloway–style jive and Bing Crosby–style smooch, was ill-suited to slower numbers.

When Brown died in a car accident on April 18, 1936, his brother, guitarist Durwood, managed to keep the band going for a few years, but most of the key members soon defected to other outfits or to lead their own ensembles.

Browns, The *vocal trio*

The Browns—Ella Maxine (b. Samti, Louisiana, April 27, 1932); James Edward (Jim Ed, b. Sparkman, Arkansas, April 1, 1934); and Bonnie (b. Sparkman, Arkansas, July 31, 1937)—were not dirt-poor country folks; their father operated a sawmill, and for a while Jim Ed studied forestry with the idea that he would take over the family business. However, his sister Maxine was ambitious and longed for a career as an entertainer. The two had been singing together since junior high school, and began performing together in the early 1950s on Little Rock radio station KLRA after winning a talent contest sponsored by the station. They eventually worked their way up to being featured on the larger KWKH's *Hayride* program, also originating out of Little Rock. They made some early recordings for the local Abbott label in 1954 to 1955 that feature some nice country harmony singing, including their own composition "Looking Back to See," along with lots of country

novelty songs. Their backup on these sessions included on guitar JIM REEVES (who would later encourage RCA to sign the group) and pianist FLOYD CRAMER.

In 1955 younger sister Bonnie joined the act, and the group toured as headliners with the Ozark Jubilee. Thanks to Reeves, they got a contract with RCA, and the group had a hit with a cover of the LOUVIN BROTHERS' "I Take a Chance" in 1956. The Browns were inactive on the recording scene for a few years while Jim Ed served in the army (although another sibling, Norma, temporarily joined to help out with touring), but scored a big pop and country hit in 1959 on Jim Ed's return with "The Three Bells," a cover of Edith Piaf's "Les Trois Cloches."

Some more pop-country hits followed, as well as covers of traditional folk songs, such as 1961's "Groundhog," performed in the manner of the popular folk revival groups of the day (such as the Kingston Trio or Peter, Paul, and Mary). In 1963 the Browns were invited to join the *Grand Ole Opry*, but internal disagreements in the group, sparked by the marriages of the two women, ended their career in 1967.

Jim Ed had already recorded successfully as a soloist in 1965, and continued his solo career on RCA through the early 1980s, appearing regularly in the late 1960s at Lake Tahoe as a lounge singer. He also scored as a partner with Helen Cornelius from 1976 to 1981. His first hit with Cornelius was the slightly racy, "I Don't Want to Have to Marry You," followed by other country-pop heartache numbers (even a cover of Neil Diamond's three-hanky weeper "You Don't Bring Me Flowers"). Maxine made a successful solo single in 1968 ("Sugar Cane Country," issued by Chart), but soon retired from performing.

Brumley, Albert E(dward) (1905–1977)
gospel songwriter and music publisher
Albert Brumley was born in Spiro, Oklahoma, on October 29, 1905. He was trained by the best of the gospel songwriters from an early age. He attended many local singing schools and conventions on the

Oklahoma/Arkansas border. But most important, as a teenager he enrolled at Hartford (Arkansas) Music Institute, where he encountered Virgil O. Stamps, the founder of the Stamps quartet and publishing company. The institute served as a training ground for songwriters, and had its own affiliated publishing arm to take advantage of the school's output.

After his marriage in 1931, Brumley settled in the rural Ozarks in the small town of Powell, Missouri; that same year he wrote his first (and perhaps most famous) gospel classic, "I'll Fly Away." Brumley eventually penned more than 800 songs, many of them now standards in the country and bluegrass repertoire. Among his classics are "Rank Stranger to Me" (1942), which became one of the favorites in the Stanley Brothers repertoire, and "Turn Your Radio On" (1938). Other favorites include 1933's "Jesus Hold My Hand," 1937's "There's a Little Pine Log Cabin," and 1939's "I've Found a Hiding Place." Brumley's songs were recorded by a wide range of gospel and country artists, including RED FOLEY, the CHUCK WAGON GANG, and BILL MONROE, among many others.

Brumley also became a gospel publishing mogul, with his own Albert E. Brumley Music company, publishing gospel songbooks beginning in the 1930s. These songbooks helped spread his songs throughout the South and West, and many artists used them as resources for their radio or record work. In the late 1940s Brumley purchased the Hartford Music company, which owned the rights to his earliest songs. He continued to live in Powell, Missouri, through his death on November 15, 1977.

Brumley's children have all been active in the music business. His son Al began his performing career in honky tonk music, primarily working in California. However, for the last two decades, he has made a career out of performing his father's songs on the gospel circuit. Tom Brumley is perhaps the most famous of Albert's children; he played steel guitar with Buck Owens's Buckaroos in the mid-1960s and then cofounded one of the first country rock bands, the Stone Canyon band, with singer

Rick Nelson, later that decade. Both Tom and Al (and their children) are involved with the Brumley Music Show, which is staged in the family theater in Branson, Missouri. Brumley's other children are also involved in the music publishing business that he founded.

Bryant, Boudleaux and Felice *songwriters*
Boudleaux Bryant's (b. Shellman, Georgia, February 13, 1920–June 25, 1987) first love was classical music; as a classical violinist, he worked for a year with the Atlanta Symphony, before turning to jazz and leading a series of small combos. While touring the Midwest he met and befriended an elevator attendant at Milwaukee's Shrader Hotel; she was Felice Scaduto (b. Matilda Genevieve Scaduto, Milwaukee, Wisconsin, August 7, 1925–April 22, 2003), and the couple were married soon after World War II. At about the same time, Boudleaux joined Hank Penny's band as a country-style fiddler, and he began writing country songs with his young wife.

The Bryants began writing country songs together. Their first hit was "Country Boy" recorded by "LITTLE" JIMMY DICKENS in 1949, leading to a contract with FRED ROSE of the powerful Acuff-Rose publishing company. They produced hits for both pop singers (Tony Bennett's "Have a Good Time") and mainstream country acts (CARL SMITH's "Hey Joe," later covered by Frankie Laine, and a number of hits for EDDY ARNOLD, including "I've Been Thinking" and "The Richest Man," both released in 1955).

Fred Rose's son Wesley introduced the Bryants to an up-and-coming country duo called the EVERLY BROTHERS in 1957, asking them to come up with some teen-style hits for the pair. They quickly produced "Bye Bye Love," the Everlys' first hit, followed by "Wake Up, Little Susie" in the same year, 1958's "All I Have to Do Is Dream," "Bird Dog," and "Problems," and 1959's "Take a Message to Mary" and "Poor Jenny." Their success with the Everlys led to other teen popsters covering their material, including Buddy Holly ("It's Raining in My Heart") and Bob Luman ("Let's Think About Living"). In these songs, the Bryants combined classic country sentiments of love gone wrong with teen angst; even the nonhits, like the Everly Brothers' "Love Hurts" (later covered by Roy Orbison and Gram Parsons) have had a long shelf life.

In the 1960s, with the growing influence of the New York–based Brill Building songwriters, the Bryants returned to writing primarily for country performers, including Sonny James's 1964 hit, "Baltimore," and ROY CLARK's 1973 hit, "Come Live with Me." The Bryants were inducted into the Country Music Hall of Fame in 1991.

Butler, Carl and Pearl *vocal duo*

Carl Roberts Butler (b. Knoxville, Tennessee, June 2, 1927–September 4, 1992) first worked as a solo recording artist, charting in the early 1960s with the honky-tonk throwbacks "Honky Tonkitis" (1961) and 1962's "Don't Let Me Cross Over." The second recording featured his wife, Pearl (b. Pearl Dee Jones, Nashville, Tennessee, September 30, 1927–March 3, 1989) on harmony vocals, although she was uncredited on the label. It became a major country hit, so the duo followed up with a number of similar-sounding weepers, from 1963's "Loving Arms" to 1969's "I Never Got Over You." In 1967 the duo appeared in the B-grade film *Second Fiddle to a Steel Guitar*. In the 1970s they retired from performing.

"Bye Bye Love" (1957) *pop and country hit for the Everly Brothers*

Although remembered as the first pop hit for the EVERLY BROTHERS, this song also topped the country charts, thanks to its Nashville production, the Everlys' sunny harmonies, and the songwriting skill of FELICE AND BOUDLEAUX BRYANT. Throughout their early pop success, the Everlys enjoyed equal exposure on the country charts, reflecting their rural roots and the roots of their sound in acts like the BLUE SKY BOYS.

Byrd, Tracy (b. 1966) *singer*

Byrd was born in the small Texas town of Vidor on December 18, 1966. The nearest big city was Beaumont, 15 miles away, where Byrd made his "recording" debut at a local shopping mall, cutting his own version of "Your Cheatin' Heart" to a prerecorded accompaniment. Surprisingly, the clerk operating the pay-to-record machine was impressed by Byrd's baritone, and immediately signed him to appear at a local amateur show he sponsored on a monthly basis. Byrd was soon playing in Beaumont clubs, where he met future country star MARK CHESNUTT; he even took Chesnutt's place at the popular Cutter's Nightclub when Chesnutt left town for Nashville in 1990. Chesnutt recommended Byrd to his producer at MCA, hitmaker Tony Brown, who signed Byrd in 1992.

Byrd's 1993 debut album was fairly successful, producing a number-one hit with the tears-in-my-beer ballad "Holdin' Heaven." But it was 1994's *No Ordinary Man* that launched him into the big time as a platinum-selling country hitmaker. It featured two novelty hits, "Watermelon Crawl" and "Lifestyles of the Not So Rich and Famous," that remain two of the songs most closely associated with Byrd. Byrd would repeat the formula of pseudo-western swing up-tempo numbers mixed with pop-country balladry on his followup albums through the 1990s, but his hitmaking days slowed toward the decade's end.

In 2000 Byrd left MCA and signed with RCA Nashville. Boldly declaring his independence, he vowed to return to his earlier western swing style. But like many other successful 1990s acts, Byrd appeared to be having trouble establishing himself long-term, at least as a chart-topping artist.

Unlike many other country stars, Byrd has resisted the siren call of living in Nashville. He remains in Beaumont, where he has become something of a local booster. He sponsors an annual homecoming weekend, which features an all-star concert, and trout-fishing and golf tournaments. An avid outdoorsman, Byrd hosted a long-running TNN program on the joys of fishing and hunting.

Cajun music

A revival of interest in the traditional music of southern Louisiana in the 1970s and 1980s led to a "rediscovery" of Cajun music, the songs and dance tunes performed by the descendants of the original French Acadians who arrived in the area in the 18th century.

The Acadians originally hail from the island of Acadia, a French colony off of Canada (now known as Nova Scotia); when the French ceded the island to the British in 1713, the settlers moved south to what was then still French territory in Louisiana. There, they intermixed with English, Spanish, and African Americans, while developing their own unique language (known as Louisiana French or Creole) and musical style. Through the 19th century, the musical styles of Europe—waltzes, quadrilles, cotillions, mazurkas—came to the area and entered the musical repertoire. In the 18th century the fiddle and triangle had been the primary musical instruments, but the 19th century brought first the newly introduced accordion and its many relatives and, later, the guitar.

Cajun music was first recorded in the 1920s when the record industry was quickly discovering the commercial potential for musics directed at specific regional groups. Fiddlers Dennis McGee and Sady Courville made the first twin-fiddle recordings. In the 1930s, 1940s, and 1950s western swing and pop styles swept the area, and several Cajun musicians—notably fiddler/bandleader Harry Choates, who wrote the big country and Cajun hit "Jole Blon"—modernized the music to reflect these outside influences.

After World War II, Cajun sounds occasionally crossed over into the country charts. HANK WILLIAMS had a hit with the Cajun-style song "Jambalaya," and DOUG KERSHAW (with his brother Rusty) began recording for both country and Cajun markets. Meanwhile, the folk revival of the late 1950s and early 1960s led to a renewed interest in more traditional Cajun music. Groups such as the New Lost City Ramblers added Cajun music to their acts, and traditional family bands like the Balfa Brothers from Mamou, Louisiana, were successful on the festival and folk-revival trail. Accordionist Nathan Abshire, who had originally recorded in the 1930s without much success, was rediscovered and became a big concert attraction.

Along with Cajun music, its sister sound, known as zodico or zydeco, gained new popularity also in the 1970s and 1980s. Zydeco is the wedding of African-American blues and jazz styles with Cajun dance and song; its proponents are mostly African-American Creoles. One of the greatest zydeco musicians was Clifton Chenier, an accordionist who recorded extensively through the 1960s and 1970s.

Revival bands began springing up in the 1970s and appealed to a more educated, upscale market. Fiddler Michael Doucet was one of the most active of the younger Cajun musicians; eventually he formed the group Beausoleil, which wedded Cajun sounds with folk-rock instrumentation. Their music was celebrated in MARY CHAPIN CARPENTER's first big country hit, "Down at the Twist and Shout" (the band also performed on the track). Other popular Cajun and zydeco revivalists include Rockin' Dopsie and the Twisters (who appear on Paul Simon's *Graceland* album), Rockin' Sydney (popularizer of the much-recorded "My Toot Toot"), and Jo-el Sonnier.

Callahan Brothers, The *vocal duo*

Born in the mountains of western North Carolina, in the small town of Laurel, guitarist Walter T. ("Joe"; January 27, 1910–September 10, 1971) and his mandolinist brother, Homer C. ("Bill"; b. March 27, 1912–September 12, 2002) absorbed the traditional dance music, balladry, and religious songs that were performed throughout the region. They made their professional debut at the 1933 Asheville, North Carolina, folk festival, and were immediately signed by a Knoxville radio station.

A year later the Callahans made their first recordings for the budget American Record Company (ARC) label. In 1935 they made one of the first recordings of the traditional folk blues "The House of the Rising Sun," released under the name "Rounder's Luck." They scored big hits with "Curly Headed Baby" and "St. Louis Blues," also cut at this session. They also published a series of songbooks that they promoted through their radio shows and personal appearances, greatly influencing the repertoire of many other traditional musicians.

The Callahans moved throughout the South and West to play on various country-music radio programs, including a stint with RED FOLEY on Cincinnati's WLW and another with the country musical comedy act, the Weaver Brothers and Elviry, out of Springfield, Missouri. They finally settled in Texas in the early 1940s, broadcasting simultaneously out of Dallas and Wichita Falls, where they worked with LEFTY FRIZZELL. After recording a good deal of traditional material in the 1930s, they moved into more blues and jazz-oriented sounds in the 1940s, expanding their band (now called the Blue Ridge Mountain Folk) into a cross between the sound and style of old-time bands and more modern western swing orchestras. Their recordings included country blues numbers like "Step It Up and Go" and a cover of Bill Carlisle's (of the CARLISLE BROTHERS) "Rattlesnakin' Daddy."

The Callahans were a link between old-time country style and newer cowboy and western acts that emphasized bluesier styles. Although they continued to perform through the early 1960s (primarily on radio and in personal appearances), their greatest impact was in the 1930s and 1940s when this period of transition was occurring.

Campbell, Glen (b. 1936) *guitarist and singer*

Born on April 22, 1936, in Delight, Arkansas, Campbell began playing the guitar at age four; by his teens, he was touring with his own country

Glen Campbell at Lake Tahoe, 1975 (Raeanne Rubenstein)

band, the Western Wranglers. At age 24 Campbell relocated to Los Angeles, where he quickly found employment as a session guitarist. In the mid-1960s he was signed to Capitol as a solo artist. The company first tried to promote him as an instrumentalist, releasing an album of 12-string guitar instrumentals aimed at a pop market. However, it was Campbell's clear tenor, with only a hint of a country twang, that gained him his hits. His first hit, a cover of John Hartford's "Gentle on My Mind," came in 1967, followed by a string of Jimmy Webb–penned soft-country hits ("By the Time I Get to Phoenix," "Wichita Lineman," and "Galveston"). Campbell's career was furthered by his exposure on his own TV variety show in 1969, plus some film roles, most notably with John Wayne in *True Grit.* Campbell had his last chart hits in the mid-1970s with "Rhinestone Cowboy" and "Southern Nights." During this period he was married to TANYA TUCKER, and their stormy relationship often landed them in the tabloids. Although he continues to perform both as a vocalist and instrumentalist, Campbell has failed to capitalize on his earlier success.

Carlisle Brothers, The *vocal duo*

Clifford Raymond Carlisle (b. Mount Eden, Kentucky, March 6, 1904–April 2, 1983) and his brother Bill (b. Wakefield, Kentucky, December 19, 1908–March 17, 2003) were raised in the hills of Kentucky, although the family originally hailed from Tennessee. Their father led singing schools in rural churches, teaching gospel songs in the traditional shape-note style, but his kids were more interested in the sounds coming over the radio from Nashville.

Cliff learned to play the Dobro, and apparently toured the South as a youngster playing on the Keith vaudeville circuit, specializing in railroad songs and Hawaiian numbers. The novelty of playing the guitar with a steel bar to perform pseudo-Hawaiian songs made him an instant success. He signed with the Indiana-based Gennett label when

he was 26, initially recording with guitarist Wilbur Ball; inspired by JIMMIE RODGERS, the pair specialized in blues numbers featuring closely harmonized yodeling. In fact, Carlisle played on some of Rodgers's recordings, providing Dobro accompaniment for the famous musician.

The brothers formed their duet in 1931, and they performed together on many recordings for various labels, as well as on radio stations out of Lexington, Kentucky, and Charlotte, North Carolina. They specialized in train songs (such as "Pan American Man" and the hobo numbers "Just a Lonely Hobo" and "Ramblin' Jack") along with the "blue yodeling" that Cliff had originally performed with his first partner; both of these styles showed their debt to Jimmie Rogers. They also performed comic novelty numbers, including risqué, suggestive songs such as "Tom Cat Blues," and Hawaiian instrumentals, both vestiges of Cliff's vaudeville days. Bill has said that as part of the act he appeared as a barefoot comedian, a country hayseed character called "Hotshot Elmer." He also developed a stunt where, in mock anger, he would place a chair between himself and his brother, jumping over it to confront him and then jumping back to hide; this earned him the nickname "Jumpin' Bill Carlisle," which he would use for years after the brother act ended. Meanwhile, Cliff continued to perform and record with other musicians, including his original partner, Wilbur Ball, and Fred Kirby.

Cliff retired in 1947, and Bill formed a new family group called the Carlisles. Bill made his *Grand Ole Opry* debut in 1952, following his hit with the comic novelty number "Too Old to Cut the Mustard," a Carlisle original. He also wrote a follow-up hit "No Help Wanted," followed by further novelties with "Is That You, Myrtle?" (cowritten with the LOUVIN BROTHERS) and "Rough Stuff." Bill continued to record through the late 1960s, having one more hit with another country comedy number, "What Kinda Deal Is This," in 1966. He appeared on the *Grand Ole Opry* through the 1990s, when he himself was in his nineties, and was elected to the Country Music Hall of Fame in fall 2002 as the oldest member of the Opry. He died in early 2003.

Carlson, Paulette (b. 1983) *singer*

Highway 101 is a hard-rockin' country outfit formed originally to accompany smoky-voiced singer Paulette Carlson (b. Northfield, Minnesota, October 11, 1953) that has managed to survive her leaving the band to pursue a solo career. Carlson first came to Nashville in 1978 when she was 24, working on the staff of the Oak Ridge Boys's publishing company and singing backup vocals for Gail Davies. Carlson's solo recordings for RCA in 1983 and 1984 failed to chart, and she moved back to her native Minnesota in 1985, disappointed with her career progress.

Although Carlson was in semiretirement, her manager, Chuck Morris, felt that she could be successful if packaged correctly. Noting the increased interest in cowboy bands, he enlisted the help of a trio of California session musicians—guitarist, mandolin and bass player Curtis Stone (b. North Hollywood, California, April 3, 1950) drummer Cactus Moser (b. Scott Moser, Montrose, California, May 3, 1957), and guitarist/vocalist Jack Daniels (b. Choctaw, Oklahoma, October 27, 1949)—to form Highway 101 as a showcase for Carlson. The group's hits capitalized on her raspy singing by portraying her as a tough broad who is not to be slighted, from their first charting record, 1987's "The Bed You Made for Me" (a song Carlson wrote addressed to an ex-boyfriend who had cheated on her), "Whiskey If You Were a Woman," portraying the havoc brought on a marriage by a husband's dependency on alcohol, and 1988's "All the Reasons Why" (cowritten by Carlson) telling of a woman who is unafraid to end an unhappy relationship, and "Just Say Yes," in which the woman frankly and unabashedly pursues her man.

Carlson left the band in 1989 to pursue a solo career. Her first solo recording produced the minor hit "Not with My Heart You Don't." Nikki Nelson (b. San Diego, California, January 3, 1969) replaced Carlson as the band's focal point, visually and vocally, singing lead on their uptempo 1991 hit, "Big Bang Boom." However, the band could not follow this success, and after a failed 1993 album, Nelson was gone.

Neither Carlson nor the reconstituted Highway 101 enjoyed as great success on their own as they did when they were together. By 1995 Carlson rejoined for a reunion tour and new album. Since then, the group has appeared on the road and on two more albums issued on small labels. However, they have never been able to recapture their original commercial success.

Carpenter, Mary Chapin (b. 1958) *singer*

The daughter of a *Life* magazine executive, Carpenter was born in suburban Princeton, New Jersey, and spent most of her childhood there. Her mother played the guitar during the early 1960s, and gave her instrument to Carpenter when she expressed interest in learning to play. The family moved to Washington, D.C., in 1974 and, after college, Carpenter began performing in the Washington area. She hooked up with guitarist John Jennings, and the duo produced a demo tape which led to an audition for Columbia Records, which signed Carpenter and released her first album in 1987.

From 1987 to 1992 Carpenter developed a cult following. She scored a minor hit with 1989's "How Do," a flirtation song. But her breakthrough came in 1992 with the Cajun-flavored hit single, "Down at the Twist and Shout." She quickly followed up with her 1993 releases, "I Feel Lucky," another up-tempo number, and her cover of Lucinda Williams's "Passionate Kisses." However, Carpenter has struggled to duplicate her commercial success of 1993–94. Her follow-up albums to 1992's *Come On, Come On* have had a quieter, more introspective quality that continues to appeal to her fans, but has not resulted in country-radio hits.

Carson, Fiddlin' John (1868–1949) *singer and fiddle player*

Carson was born on a farm in rural Fannin County, Georgia. From an early age, he was a professional entertainer, although he held odd jobs as a painter or carpenter and probably also worked as a subsistence farmer. Carson was first recorded thanks to Polk Brockman, the Atlanta, Georgia, representative for OKeh Records. Brockman recognized Carson's local popularity and urged OKeh to record him; when his first recording, "Little Old Log Cabin in the Lane," released in 1923, became a major success, Carson was quickly brought to New York to record more songs and fiddle tunes. Carson often performed and recorded as a duo with his daughter Rosa Lee Carson (1909–92; known as "Moonshine Kate"), who sang harmony vocals and played the banjo and guitar.

Carson enjoyed his greatest popularity through the late 1920s, recording dozens of popular songs, many commenting on topical issues and local events. Perhaps his best-remembered song is "The Farmer Is the Man Who Feeds Them All," reflecting the difficulties that small farmers experienced trying to make a living. He recorded prolifically through the early 1930s, often with younger musicians in a string band. The depression ended his recording career, but Carson remained popular locally. He died in Atlanta on December 11, 1949.

Carson, Martha (b. 1921) *singer*

Irene Amburgey was born in the small town of Neon, Kentucky, on March 19, 1921. She got her first radio exposure when she was 18 years old in Bluefield, West Virginia. Her father was an old-time banjoist and her mother played organ; along with their daughters Bertha and Irene, they formed a sacred quartet that sang at religious revival meetings through the South. In about 1938 fiddler Bertha and guitarist Irene, along with younger sister Opal, who played banjo and mandolin, formed the Amburgey Sisters and began performing on Lexington, Kentucky, radio, followed by a stint in Bluefield, West Virginia, and finally joining the famous Renfro Valley Barn Dance, where they performed with legendary fiddler/banjoist Lilly Mae Ledford. In 1940 they went to Atlanta's WSB, where their act was renamed Mattie, Marthie, and Minnie (for Opal, Irene, and Bertha, respectively); they performed such patriotic wartime ditties as "I'll Be Back in a Year, Little Darling."

In the early 1940s the trio dissolved as the various sisters married and moved on to other careers. Opal wed Salty Holmes from the Prairie Ramblers, and the two became popular on the *Grand Ole Opry* performing as Salty Holmes and Mattie O'Neill; in the 1950s she took the new name of Jean Chapel and recorded for Sun Records as a rockabilly artist. Sam Phillips of Sun sold her contract to RCA, which billed her as "The Female Elvis Presley." She had a minor hit on RCA in 1956 with "Oo-ba-la Baby!" Bertha married a defense plant worker and retired, although she later returned to performing with her sisters in the early 1950s.

Martha married country songster and mandolin player James Carson (Roberts) in the early 1940s. He was the son of fiddler Doc Roberts, one of the finer old-time recording artists of the late 1920s. The two became known as the Barn Dance Sweethearts when they signed up with Atlanta's WSB in the mid-1940s, and had hits with sentimental numbers such as their cover of the BLUE SKY BOYS song "The Sweetest Gift," as well as the gospelesque "Man of Galilee."

The Carsons split in 1951, and Martha briefly reunited with her sisters. She joined the cast of the *Grand Ole Opry* a year later, bringing her gospel style to the stage of Nashville's premier radio show. Oddly enough, her fervent singing, a wedding of old-time religious sentiment, black gospel and R&B, and country styles, found a home in the rarefied supper clubs of northeastern cities in the mid-1950s, so that she became equally in demand for her appearances at such tony venues as New York's Waldorf-Astoria Hotel. Her solo recordings increasingly took on the trappings of 1950s pop, complete with wall-to-wall orchestrations accompanying Martha's big voice. She even took a stab at rock and roll, covering such numbers as Otis Blackwell's "Just Whistle and Call" and "Music Drives Me Crazy (Especially Rock 'n' Roll)," although she sounds less comfortable outside of the country milieu. Carson wrote more than 100 songs, all in a religious vein, including "Let's Talk about that Old Time Religion" and "Satisfied."

Although she continued to perform in the 1960s, 1970s, and even 1980s, Carson's career flourished at the outset, her initial successful days in the 1950s.

Carter, Wilf (1904–1996) *yodeling cowboy*

Better known in the United States as "Montana Slim," Wilf Carter (b. Guysboro, Nova Scotia, December 18, 1904–December 5, 1996) was one of the pioneering "yodeling cowboys," Canada's answer to the western craze.

Carter was one of the few cowboy-style performers who was not directly influenced by JIMMIE RODGERS, although he was certainly aware of Rodgers's remarkably successful recordings. He took up yodeling after hearing a Swiss yodeler who was performing on the Canadian vaudeville circuit. Carter was a real cowboy, too, having worked as a trail rider in the Canadian Rockies and performed at local rodeos.

Carter's big break came on Calgary radio in the mid-1930s, leading to a contract with Canadian RCA. He began performing in New York later in the decade, taking the stage name of Montana Slim. He recorded more than 500 numbers for RCA and its budget Camden label, as well as countless smaller labels. He's best known for his 1949 recording of "There's a Bluebird on Your Windowsill," the kind of cowboy pop that is treasured as a kitsch classic. In 1952 he left RCA, and then recorded for Decca through 1957. Beginning in 1953 he toured with his two daughters, billing themselves as "The Family Show with the Folks You Know." He recorded for Starday briefly in the early 1960s and then recorded for RCA in Canada, continuing to play mostly up north through the late 1980s. He retired during the last years of his life, and died in 1996 after being diagnosed with stomach cancer.

Carter Family *influential vocal trio*

The Carter Family was one of the first and most popular country vocal groups, whose unornamented, nasal harmonies, born and bred in rural church music, is probably the purest Appalachian sound ever recorded. The group coalesced around Alvin Pleasant Carter (known as A. P.; b. Maces Springs, Virginia, December 15, 1891–November 7, 1960; vocals), his wife Sara (b. Sara Dougherty, Flat Woods, Virginia, July 21, 1898–January 8, 1979; autoharp, vocals), and his sister-in-law Maybelle (b. Maybelle Addington, Nickelsville, Virginia, May 10, 1909–October 23, 1978; guitar, vocals). Sara usually sang lead and played the autoharp, with Alvin on bass vocals, and Maybelle on tenor and guitar. A. P. was a master collector of traditional songs. He reworked them into pleasant and memorable melodies that became the first country music hits, including "Keep on the Sunny Side," "The Storms Are on the Ocean," "Wildwood Flower," "Bury Me beneath the Willow," and their best-known song, "Will the Circle Be Unbroken," an adaptation of a shape-note hymn.

Their first and greatest success came recording under the supervision of Ralph Peer for RCA Victor from 1927 to 1933. The group continued to record through the later 1930s and early 1940s, even though A. P. and Sara's marriage dissolved in 1932. They gained great exposure in the late 1930s while working on XERA, an unregulated Mexican "border radio" station that had a much more powerful and far-reaching signal than did U.S. commercial stations. At this time various Carter daughters were also getting into the act. The last "original" Carter family performance came in 1943.

In the late 1940s Maybelle performed with her daughters (Anita [vocals, bass, guitar; b. Ina A. Carter, Maces Springs, Virginia, March 31,

1933–July 30, 1999], June [vocals, autoharp, guitar; b. Valerie J. Carter, Maces Springs, Virginia, June 23, 1929–May 15, 2003], and Helen [vocals, guitar, autoharp, accordion; b. H. Myrl Carter, Maces Springs, Virginia, September 12, 1927–June 2, 1998) as the Carter Family; the girls also performed in a more modern-sounding country act as the Carter Sisters. Mother and daughters became members of the *Grand Ole Opry* in 1950. Meanwhile, A. P. recorded in the early 1950s with his two children, Janette (b. Maces Springs, Virginia, July 2, 1932) and Joe (b. Maces Springs, Virginia, February 27, 1927–March 2, 2005).

Maybelle was rediscovered during the 1960s folk revival, and she became a popular performer on the autoharp, picking melodies on it rather than just strumming chords. She was also prominently featured on the NITTY GRITTY DIRT BAND's homage to country music, *Will the Circle Be Unbroken?*, in 1971. Although Sara performed with her at the 1967 Newport Folk Festival, she was mostly inactive after A. P.'s death in 1960. Janette Carter continues to run the Carter Family Homestead in Virginia, which includes a museum with memorabilia of the family's music career plus a dance/concert hall that features bluegrass and country acts. She recorded a duet album with her brother Joe in the 1970s.

June's daughter Carlene Carter (b. Rebecca Carlene Smith, Madison, Tennessee, September 26, 1955; her father was country singer CARL SMITH) returned the Carter name to the country charts in the 1980s and 1990s. Her music mixed rockabilly and classic country influences for a number of lighthearted hits, most notably 1990's "I Fell in Love" and 1993's "Every Little Thing." However, later in the 1990s a troubled personal life hampered her career.

Cash, Johnny (1932–2003) *singer and songwriter*

John Ray Cash was born in Kingsland, Arkansas, to a family of poor cotton farmers who lost everything in the depression. Cash joined the air force in the early 1950s and took up the guitar while stationed in Germany. On his return home, he formed a band called the Tennessee Two (Cash played guitar, backed by a second guitarist, Luther Perkins, and bass; later a drummer was added to make the group the Tennessee Three). Signed to the legendary rockabilly label Sun Records, Cash scored with his country classic, "I Walk the Line" (1956). Disappointed with Sun's commercial orientation, Cash signed to Columbia Records in 1959. Cash initially recorded topical songs about America's working class, American Indians, legendary figures such as John Henry, and outlaws, with the simple backup of his own band, unlike other country recordings of the day, which often featured strings and vocal choruses.

Cash's big break came with his legendary live concert at California's Folsom Prison (held in 1968), including the classic bad-man song "Folsom Prison Blues." Bob Dylan enlisted Cash's aid for his country album, *Nashville Skyline* in 1969, exposing Cash to a younger, rock and folk-oriented audience. In the same year, Cash had his first solid hit with "A BOY NAMED SUE," a comic song written by Shel Silverstein. Through the 1970s Cash recorded more mainstream pop-country material, while also developing an acting career. He often performed with a large revue, including his wife June Carter Cash, members of the CARTER FAMILY, and old friends such as CARL PERKINS.

In the 1980s Cash had a varied career. He recorded a successful series of albums with country "outlaws" WILLIE NELSON, KRIS KRISTOFFERSON, and WAYLON JENNINGS; the group took the name the Highwaymen. Cash's own solo recordings did not fare very well, and he was dropped by Columbia and then Mercury Records. Then, in the 1990s Cash began to receive renewed attention from both the rock and country worlds for his many contributions to music. In 1992 he was inducted into the Rock and Roll Hall of Fame for his early recordings. In the mid-1990s Cash signed with former rap music producer Rick Rubin to Rubin's American Records label. He eventually recorded four albums under

Rubin's guidance, all of which were critically and financially successful. Cash's health began to fail in the later 1990s, but he continued to perform and record until nearly the end. His final album release, in 2002, produced a hit with the eerie cover of the industrial-pop group Nine Inch Nails' song "Hurt." Cash succumbed to complications from diabetes on September 12, 2003.

His daughter ROSANNE CASH has been one of the most innovative and unusual country singer/songwriters of the last decade. His stepdaughter Carlene Carter combines rockabilly and 1970s rock styles with a country sound.

Cash, Rosanne (b. 1956) *singer and songwriter*

The daughter of singer/songwriter Johnny Cash, Rosanne was born in Memphis, Tennessee, but was raised by her mother in Southern California, and did not come directly in contact with her father's music until after high school graduation, when she joined his road show. In the late 1970s Rosanne Cash hooked up with Texas singer/songwriter/bandleader RODNEY CROWELL, and the two were wed in the early 1980s. Crowell served as her producer, recording her debut album, *Right or Wrong*. This was followed by *Seven Year Ache,* which netted her two number-one country singles and established her as a sophisticated singer/songwriter. Other notable albums include *King's Record Shop,* which reflects country music traditions, and *The Wheel,* which documents the breakup of her marriage. Cash has continued to record and perform through the 1990s, and has a strong cult following.

"Cattle Call" *major hit for Eddy Arnold*

A number-one country hit for EDDY ARNOLD that remained on the country charts for six months, and also placed in the top five of the juke box, best seller, and disc jockey charts. The song had been composed 20 years earlier by Tex Owens, and features a yodeling refrain in the manner of JIMMIE RODGERS.

In 1996 Arnold recorded the number again in a duet with new country star LEANN RIMES.

Charles, Ray (1930–2004) *singer and songwriter*

Although he's best known to the general listening public as an R&B singer, Charles recorded country music for more than a quarter-century and was one of the first black artists to cross over into the country market. Born Ray Charles Robinson in Albany, Georgia, Charles attended a local school for the blind, where he learned music. Playing in the South in small clubs for many different audiences, he mastered various musical styles, including country music, although he scored his initial success with his unique blend of gospel-tinged R&B.

In 1959 Charles scored a minor hit with HANK SNOW's "I'm Movin' On," revealing for the first time his unique take on country sounds. Joining the ABC label in the same year, Charles took control of his recordings and issued a series of country albums, notably 1963's hugely successful *Modern Sounds in Country and Western Music.* Charles's country hits include a cover of the DON GIBSON classic, "I Can't Stop Lovin' You," from that album; "Hit the Road Jack"; "Busted"; and HANK WILLIAMS's "Your Cheatin' Heart." Charles transformed the pop classic "Georgia on My Mind" into a slow country blues; his performance was so brilliant that he was invited to sing it for the Georgia legislature when it was made the official state song. Charles's long career as a performer continued over five decades, encompassing an eclectic mix of material, including country songs, all of which he transformed into the classic Ray Charles style. He died on June 10, 2004.

Chesnutt, Mark (b. 1963) *singer*

Born on September 16, 1963, and raised in Beaumont, Texas, Chesnutt came from a musical home; his dad had been a local country singer before giving up his dreams of making it big to open up a used-car lot. At age 16, Chesnutt began performing locally, filling in with day jobs as necessary, but mostly pursuing a performing career. He worked locally for 12 years, releasing his first single on a small Houston label. After his record was released, he managed to get it to GEORGE STRAIT (whose drummer had previously played in Chesnutt's band), who passed it along to producer TONY BROWN at MCA Records. Brown liked what he heard and signed Chesnutt, rerecording the song and releasing it in summer 1990. Buoyed by Chesnutt's pleasant voice, the song hit big, and soon Chesnutt was being compared to GARTH BROOKS as "the next big thing."

Actually, his second album was far superior, featuring far more of an individual personality, in such Texas-styled, light-hearted numbers as "Bubba Shot the Jukebox" and traditional weepers like "I'll Think of Something." He followed with another collection of honkers and weepers, including the 1993 hit "Almost Goodbye." Chesnutt proved successful through 1995, with several albums quickly going gold, but then the recordings came less frequently, as did the hits. Nonetheless, he continues to be a popular concert draw. In 2002 Chesnutt left MCA to join Columbia Records in an attempt to revive his career, and undertook a tour with JOE DIFFIE and Tracy Lawrence called the Rockin' Roadhouse Tour.

Chuck Wagon Gang, The *gospel group*

The Chuck Wagon Gang is one of the most enduring and popular country-gospel harmonizing groups, originally a small-town family group that has blossomed into a big country business.

D. P. "Dad" Carter (David Parker Carter, b. Milltown, Kentucky, September 25, 1889–April 28, 1963) was raised on a farm in West Texas. His family was very religious, and he met his future wife Carrie Brooks at a singing school sponsored by the local Baptist church. They raised nine children, including two particularly talented daughters, Rose

(Rose Lola, b. Noel, Missouri, December 31, 1915) and Anna (Effie, b. Shannon, TX, February 15, 1917–March 5, 2004), who became the center of the family's informal singing group. Along with brother Jim (Ernest, b. Tioga, Texas, August 10, 1910), the group appeared on radio out of Lubbock in 1935, and a year later won the sponsorship of Fort Worth's Bewley Mills, who named the group the Chuck Wagon Gang; at this time the group was signed to Columbia.

Although they always featured at least one gospel number in their radio act and in personal appearances, the group started out performing a mix of folk songs, pop, and sentimental numbers, led by the sweet harmonies of the two young daughters. However, listener response was so overwhelmingly strong for their gospel numbers that by 1938 they switched to an all-gospel format. From the traditional backwoods church, they took the call-and-response pattern that was typically used by preacher and chorus, and from pop music they borrowed sweet harmonies and slick instrumentation to achieve a more modern sound. They recorded many gospel standards, including "I'll Fly Away" and "We Are Climbing Jacob's Ladder," as well as publishing countless songbooks. A young songster named HANK WILLIAMS borrowed the melody of their 1941 recording of "He Set Me Free" for his own classic gospel song, "I Saw the Light."

After World War II country gospel gained new popularity, in part thanks to groups such as the Chuck Wagon Gang. They toured extensively, with some personnel changes over the years. The biggest blow to the group came with the retirement of the two lead singers in swift succession in 1965 and 1967 (Rose retired first, and then Anna wed songster/politician JIMMIE DAVIS, leading to her withdrawal from the family act). Although family members continue to work in the band today, it has become more of a business than a group, with new members brought in to carry forward the "Chuck Wagon" sound; since 1989, the two lead singers have been professionals recruited specifically to fit the bill.

Clark, Roy (b. 1933) *singer and performer*

Clark was born in Meherrin, Virginia, where his father worked a small tobacco farm, on April 15, 1933. The family relocated to Washington, D.C., when Roy was 11. Roy soon was performing locally, winning several local bluegrass contests. Clark spent most of the 1950s as a backup guitarist, first working with Jimmy Dean and eventually hooking up with singer Wanda Jackson, for whom he played guitar and wrote arrangements. Clark recorded as a solo artist beginning in the late 1950s for a variety of small labels, but success eluded him until he signed to Capitol in 1963. His first hit came the same year with the classic Nashville-sound instrumental "Tips of My Fingers." Clark gained his greatest recognition when he was hired to cohost the country comedy show *Hee Haw* in the late 1960s along with Buck Owens. Exposure on this show led to other charting songs, including 1969's "Yesterday When I Was Young" and the clever novelty number "Thank God and Greyhound (You're Gone)." He continued to score hits through the mid-1970s. Clark has continued to tour during the following decades. Since the 1980s he has been a popular attraction in Branson, Missouri, where he has his own theater.

Clark, Terri (b. 1968) *singer and songwriter*

Terri Sauson was born in Montreal, Quebec, on August 5, 1968, the daughter of a truck driver and secretary. After graduating from high school, she moved to Nashville in search of the proverbial fame and fortune. She soon befriended other up-and-coming performers and singers, and began pitching songs to established acts. Through her songwriting, she was heard by producer Keith Stegall, who had a production deal with Mercury Nashville. He signed her to the label in 1994, and her self-titled debut album was an immediate success. It contained a number of hits, including "When Boy Meets Girl" and "If I Were You," which went gold and garnered her a Best New Female Artist award from the Academy of Country Music.

Her 1996 follow-up album, *Just the Same,* was less successful than the first. It featured a hit cover of "Poor, Poor Pitiful Me" by Warren Zevon, first popularized in 1978 by Linda Ronstadt. After a slight slump in the later 1990s and a two-year hiatus from recording, Clark returned to the charts with the singles "A Little Gasoline" and "No Fear" from her *Fearless* album, released in 2000.

Clement, "Cowboy" Jack (b. 1932) *performer and producer*

John Henderson Clement was born in Memphis, Tennessee, on April 5, 1932. He took up music while stationed in Washington in the Marine Corps, performing locally with another country legend in the making, ROY CLARK. He worked briefly in the early 1950s with Buzz Busby as a duo called "Buzz and Jack, The Bayou Boys," then played Hawaiian-style music in the Washington area, but finally returned to Memphis to pursue an English degree at the local university.

Clement was hired by legendary recording studio owner Sam Phillips, who operated Sun Records (the original home of Elvis Presley, JOHNNY CASH, CARL PERKINS, and others) in the late 1950s and continued to work for him as a producer, engineer, and session player until he was fired in 1959. Phillips was out of town when a young piano player named JERRY LEE LEWIS came through the door; Clement was the one who auditioned him and encouraged the singer to return, launching his career. He was Sun's house arranger, working with the other musicians to perfect accompaniments for many classic recordings, as well as recording a few singles under his own name that flopped. He also wrote a couple of hits for Sun artists, including the country weeper "Guess Things Happen that Way" and "Ballad of a Teenage Queen," both recorded by Johnny Cash.

After leaving Sun, Clement briefly ran his own Summer label, and then relocated to Nashville, where he was hired as an assistant to CHET ATKINS at RCA. He spent a few years running a studio and label in Beaumont, Texas, before returning to Nashville in 1965, where he opened a successful music-publishing business and recording studio. He discovered some of the top Nashville stars of the era, including CHARLEY PRIDE and DON WILLIAMS. In the early 1970s he co-owned a record label, JMI, which lasted until about 1974. In 1973 he was inducted into the Nashville Songwriter's Hall of Fame. Later in the decade, he was a successful producer, working with country outlaws Johnny Cash and WAYLON JENNINGS, and he also made a solo album for Elektra Records in 1978.

Clement continued to run his studio, working with John Hartford in the late 1970s and early 1980s, and continuing to work with Johnny Cash. He was enlisted by Irish rockers U2 to man the boards at some of their sessions for their 1988 album, *Rattle and Hum.* In the 1990s he worked with a variety of artists, including newcomer Iris DeMent. He is a longtime friend of Georgia senator Zell Miller, and the two coauthored several humorous songs, including "Talking Pickup Truck Blues" in 2001 to support Miller's attempt to extend fuel regulations to these vehicles.

Cline, Patsy (1932–1963) *singer*

Born Virginia Patterson Hensley in Winchester, Virginia, Cline won an amateur talent contest as a tap dancer when she was four and began singing soon after. Winning an audition with Wally Fowler of the *Grand Ole Opry* when she was 16, young Cline so impressed him that he invited her to Nashville; however, she was unable to obtain a recording contract, and eventually returned to her hometown. She performed throughout her high school years, eventually signing with the local Four Star label in 1956. Her first hit came in 1957 with "Walkin' after Midnight," leading to a contract with Decca Records.

Cline worked with producer OWEN BRADLEY from 1957 to 1960, gaining moderate success on the country charts. It wasn't until 1961's "Crazy" (written by WILLIE NELSON), followed by "I Fall to Pieces"

(cowritten by HARLAN HOWARD and Hank Cochran) that her characteristic sad-and-lonesome vocal sound fell into place. A brief two-year hit-making career followed, including "When I Get Through with You," "Leavin' on Your Mind," and the posthumously released "Sweet Dreams."

Cline's death in an airplane accident on March 5, 1963, along with stars HAWKSHAW HAWKINS and COWBOY COPAS, helped solidify her place in the country-music pantheon. Many country stars cite her as an influence, including LORETTA LYNN, who was befriended by the older performer when she first came to Nashville, and new country star K. D. LANG. Cline's lasting impact was reinforced in 1986 by the release of the Hollywood film *Sweet Dreams* starring Jessica Lange.

"Coal Miner's Daughter" (1970)
autobiographical number-one hit song for singer/songwriter Loretta Lynn

This song became the title for LORETTA LYNN's best-selling autobiography and the 1980 film biography, starring Sissy Spacek, that was based on the book. Typical of Lynn's songs, it tells the story of her hardscrabble childhood in a simple narrative with a memorable chorus. Lynn asserted her pride in her backwoods upbringing, a brave position to take when many looked down upon the "hillbillies" who inhabited the Appalachians.

"Coat of Many Colors" (1971) *country hit for Dolly Parton*

Like LORETTA LYNN's "Coal Miner's Daughter," DOLLY PARTON's "Coat of Many Colors" tells the story of her upbringing in a poor Appalachian family. A number-four country hit, it tells how her mother stitched together clothing for her, making a quilt-like "coat of many colors" to keep her warm in the winter. The obvious allusion to the biblical story of Joseph and his many-colored coat gives the song added resonance.

Coe, David Allan (b. 1939) *singer and song-writer*

Born in Akron, Ohio, on September 6, 1939, Coe spent most of his youth in trouble with the law, ending up in the state penitentiary, where he allegedly killed another prisoner; only the end of the death penalty saved him from the electric chair. On his release in 1967, he hooked up with legendary country-pop producer Shelby Singleton, who signed him to his SSS label, impressed by the bluesy, soulful original material that Coe had composed while in prison. Two albums were produced showing a strong soul influence.

In 1974 Coe was signed to Columbia, where he remained for more than a decade. During this period he achieved his greatest success, although he continued to attract controversy. Many of his songs were confessional, including the outlaw ballad "Willie, Waylon and Me" and 1983's "The Ride," telling of an imaginary meeting with the ghost of HANK WILLIAMS. In 1984 "Mona Lisa's Lost Her Smile" was his biggest hit. Coe has a darker side as well; in the early 1980s, he issued on his own label two albums of songs that featured racist, homophobic, and obscene lyrics. (Although later disavowing this work, Coe rereleased the material on CD in the late 1990s.) In 1986, in another bizarre move, he issued an entire album of meditations on the death of his father, even featuring a photo of his dad decked out in his coffin on the inner sleeve.

Through the 1990s Coe ran the Willie Nelson and Family general store in Branson, Missouri. His career got a boost in 2000 when young rap star Kid Rock invited him to be his opening act; after the summer tour, the two also recorded some songs together.

As a songwriter Coe has placed a number of hits with mainstream country acts, including 1975's "Would You Lay with Me (in a Field of Stone)" recorded by a young TANYA TUCKER that created quite a stir (because of its mature theme), and the 1977 megahit "Take This Job and Shove It," immortalized by JOHNNY PAYCHECK.

"Cold, Cold Heart" (1953) *classic honky-tonk ballad*

Lovelorn HANK WILLIAMS wonders how he'll win over the distant—and icy cold—woman of his desires in this tune. The song was a number-one country hit, spending a total of 46 weeks on the country charts; additionally, it placed on several of the day's pop listings, reaching number one on the disc jockey charts (showing substantial radio play); number two on the best seller charts; and number four on the jukebox charts (indicating strong play in barrooms).

Williams's publisher, Fred Rose, pitched the song to pop singer Tony Bennett, who loathed the song, but nonetheless it was a major pop hit, showing that country songs could appeal to the mainstream market. It has been covered numerous times by pop, jazz, and country artists over the decades. Showing its continuing appeal, new jazz-pop vocalist Norah Jones covered the evergreen classic for an adult contemporary hit in 2002.

Collie, Mark (b. 1956) *performer*

George Mark Collie was born in Waynesboro, Tennessee, on January 18, 1956. Collie describes his hometown as "half-way between Memphis and Nashville" (musically as well as geographically). He originally hoped to join the army, but found out that he was ineligible because of his diabetes. He ended up in Memphis, looking for a vibrant music scene that had existed 20 or more years earlier; instead, he ended up bumming around with the few local players he could find.

After he married, his wife encouraged him to move to Nashville in 1986 and try to become a professional performer. Collie landed a bar job at Nashville's Douglas Corner club, playing for a year before he was discovered by MCA producer TONY BROWN. His first few singles didn't move very high up the country charts, but he finally scored with the top-five single "Even the Man in the Moon Is Crying," released at the end of 1992. Building on that momentum, his third album was released in 1993, and its first single, "Born to Love You," made the top 10. However, the follow-up recordings were not as successful. Collie moved to the Warner/Giant label in 1994, releasing *Tennessee Plates* a year later, his last album of new material to date. Collie has continued to tour and compose songs, and a live album is said to be in the works.

Collins, Tommy (1930–2000) *performer*

Leonard Raymond Sipes was born in Bethany, Oklahoma, on September 28, 1930. He had his first exposure on local radio before relocating to the Bakersfield, California, area, where many displaced Okies came in search of employment after World War II. He roomed with FERLIN HUSKY and soon became an important member of the local country scene, appearing on the influential *Town Hall Party* radio program that featured TEX RITTER, Rose and JOE MAPHIS, the Collins Kids (no relation), and many other local country acts. He signed with Los Angeles–based Capitol Records and had his biggest hits in 1954–55 with "You Better Not Do That," "Whatcha Gonna Do Now," "You Gotta Have a License," and "High on a Hilltop," all featuring BUCK OWENS in the backup band. Then, in 1956, Collins claimed he found Jesus, and for a while he abandoned his musical career to become a minister. He recorded some gospel material with his wife, Wanda Lucille Shahan, around this period.

Collins managed to return to the charts in the mid-1960s with a couple of singles for Columbia, including 1966's "If You Can't Bite, Don't Growl" and "Birmingham," and "I Made the Prison Band" in 1968. He remained popular in Europe during this time although his U.S. career was fading. In the later 1980s new country star GEORGE STRAIT covered some of his earlier honky-tonk numbers, including the number-one hit "If You Ain't Lovin' (You Ain't Livin')." In 1993 Collins signed with Ricky Skaggs Music as a songwriter, and he continued to write material until his death in Ashland City, Tennessee, on May 14, 2000.

Colter, Jessi (b. 1947) *singer and songwriter*

Miriam Johnson was born in Phoenix, Arizona, on May 25, 1947. She was raised in a strict household by her evangelist mother, who had her playing church piano by the time she reached adolescence. By her teen years she was singing professionally. Through her sister, who had married producer/songwriter "COWBOY" JACK CLEMENT, she was introduced to surf guitarist Duane Eddy, who was looking to record with a vocalist. The two married when she was just 16, and she became part of his road show, performing mostly in Europe (Eddy's hits had come a few years earlier in the United States, and by the mid-1960s he was something of a has-been).

In 1966 the couple resettled in Los Angeles, where Miriam Eddy (as she was now known) placed some of her original songs with DON GIBSON and DOTTIE WEST, before taking the stage name of Jessi Colter (after her great-great-uncle, Jess Colter, a small-time western outlaw and counterfeiter), and was signed to Lee Hazlewood's Jamie label. However, her first records failed to sell, and she returned to being a housewife briefly before divorcing Eddy in 1968.

While performing in Phoenix, Colter met the next man in her life, WAYLON JENNINGS, and the two were married in 1969. Jennings took her to his label, RCA, and the two issued a couple of duets, although Colter's solo career was slow to get started. She moved to Capitol in 1974, and the following year produced her sole number-one country hit, "I'm Not Lisa." Despite the fact that this song was an enormous hit, Colter's album tracks from the time were far superior to it, showing her to be an expressive vocalist not limited to sentimental singing. She followed this with a couple of other hits in the next two years, charting on both rock and pop charts.

In 1976 RCA issued an anthology featuring recordings by Jennings, Colter, WILLIE NELSON, and Tompall Glaser called *Wanted: The Outlaws*. This clever marketing move gave a name to the 1970s artists who refused to participate in the COUNTRY-POLITAN sounds of the decade, instead producing a rougher, rowdier, more rock-and-roll-oriented sound. The decision to include Colter gave her career a further boost, and she spent much of the rest of the 1970s touring with her husband and Nelson as part of the Outlaws.

In the late 1970s and early 1980s, Colter's career slowed down, and she returned to recording primarily for the country charts. Many of her albums of this period had cowboy themes. In 1980 she recorded a second album of duets with Jennings called *Leather and Lace*. She returned to Capitol Records in 1982, but her recording career slowed down; in 1985 she issued a gospel album under her real name, Miriam Johnson. A decade later, she issued a children's album.

Conley, Earl Thomas (b. 1941) *singer and songwriter*

Born to an impoverished rural family in the town of West Portsmouth, Ohio, on October 17, 1941, Conley originally studied to be an art student and didn't take up songwriting professionally until he was 26. In 1970 he relocated to Huntsville, Alabama, where he cut a demo tape with his brother Fred. The two brought it to a local insurance salesman and part-time record producer, Nelson Larkin, who signed Conley to his own Prize label. Conley had a few minor hits from the mid-1970s through the end of the decade.

In 1980 Conley recorded an album of original songs called *Blue Pearl*; Randy Scruggs, a musician and producer (as well as the son of legendary banjoist Earl Scruggs), worked on the sessions, beginning a long association with Conley. The album yielded a hit with "Fire and Smoke," and Larkin quickly licensed it to RCA. Larkin, Scruggs, and Conley moved to the new label together, producing a follow-up hit in 1982 with "Somewhere between Right and Wrong," a song that featured a rocking beat and horns. In 1983 Conley scored a string of hits from his next album, *Don't Make It Easy for Me*, all cowritten with Scruggs. The album yielded four number-one country hits for the duo.

Into the mid-1980s Conley and producer Larkin continued to move his recordings toward a more rock-oriented sound. Always a sporadic songwriter, Conley increasingly relied on material provided by Nashville's professional hit-making factory. In 1986 RCA convinced him to cut a duet with Anita Pointer, of the R&B group the Pointer Sisters (who had had a freak country hit 11 years earlier with "Fairytale"); the result of this collaboration was "Too Many Times," which made it to number two.

In 1988 Conley finally broke with Larkin, although he didn't go far in selecting a new guiding hand; Randy Scruggs handled the production duties on his next record, along with Nashville pro and session bass player Emory Gordy Jr. From these sessions came a pairing of Conley with sweet-voiced singer EMMYLOU HARRIS on "Happy Endings." Conley continued rocking Nashville's boat when he chose to release "What'd I Say" as his first 1989 single, a song that featured the phrase "Go to hell" repeated three times. Despite this controversial lyric, the song became another number-one hit. Conley scored his 16th consecutive number one later that year with "Love Out Loud," the last in his long, unbroken string of good luck. He was less active in the 1990s. Conley's last album of new material (to date) appeared on the small Intersound label in 1998.

Cooley, Spade (1910–1969) *fiddle player and bandleader*

Donnell Clyde Cooley was born in Pack Saddle Creek, Oklahoma, on December 17, 1910. He was descended from two generations of fiddle players, so it's not surprising that he played for his first dance at age eight. His family relocated from Oklahoma to Southern California, where the young Cooley performed with western-flavored groups, including Jimmy Wakeley's band. In the early 1940s Cooley formed his first band, and by the end of World War II they were permanently installed in the Santa Monica Ballroom, which Cooley leased as his home base, drawing several thousand western swing fans each night. Cooley's first band featured vocalist Tex Williams, as well as Joaquin Murphey's hot steel guitar and Johnny Weiss's guitar leads that were reminiscent of jazz great Charlie Christian. In 1943, they recorded Cooley's composition "Shame, Shame on You," with Williams on lead vocals, which would be his biggest hit and become his theme song. The entire band along with singer Williams quit in 1946 to go out on their own as The Western Caravan.

In 1948, Cooley was given his own variety show on a local Los Angeles TV station, which introduced country comic HANK PENNY. In the 1950s, Cooley's bands grew in size, sometimes numbering over a dozen members, including full string sections, harp, and accordian, and he slowly gravitated toward a more pop-sounding style. Increasing problems with alcohol led to a decline in his popularity later in the decade, and his personal problems came to a head in 1961 when he killed his wife in front of their teenage daughter. Cooley spent the 1960s in prison for his crime. He was released to perform at a benefit concert on November 23, 1969; following his performance, he died backstage of a heart attack.

Copas, Cowboy (1913–1963) *singer*

Lloyd Copas was born in Blue Creek, Ohio, on July 15, 1913. (He later claimed to have been raised on a ranch in Muskogee, Oklahoma, but this was untrue). By his late teens he was already touring as a musician in a novelty duo with a "pureblood Indian" called Natchee (actually Lesley Vernon Stover, and no more an Indian that Copas was a cowboy) who played the fiddle. In 1940 the duo broke up when Copas was hired as a single act for the Cincinnati-based radio show *Boone Country Jamboree.*

In Cincinnati, Copas met record producer Syd Nathan, who founded King and related labels in the 1940s to produce country and R&B acts. Copas recorded a number of hits for King, including "Filipino Baby," "Tragic Romance," "Gone and Left Me Blues," and "Signed, Sealed and Delivered" (not the same as the later R&B hit) in the mid-1940s that

were early songs in the honky-tonk style that would become increasingly popular after the war. In his performances Copas wed jazz, blues, and pop influences, making for a hot, high-energy style that predicted not only honky-tonk but the coming rockabilly craze.

In 1946 PEE WEE KING invited Copas to replace the smooth-voiced EDDY ARNOLD in his Golden West Cowboys, getting him his first exposure on the *Grand Ole Opry.* Copas stayed for two years, singing lead on the legendary 1948 recording of "Tennessee Waltz," securing his position in country music history. He then went solo again, with a few more hits including 1949's "Hangman's Boogie" and 1951's "Strange Little Girl."

Copas's career sagged in the 1950s but was revived toward the decade's end when he signed with Starday, returning to his original stripped-down sound on several hits, including the number-one 1960 hit "Alabam"; "Flat Top" and "Sunny Tennessee" from 1961; and his last hit, "Goodbye Kisses," in 1963. In that year Copas had the misfortune to play a benefit concert with HAWKSHAW HAWKINS and PATSY CLINE; the trio were killed when their chartered plane crashed on the way back to Nashville on March 5.

Cornelius, Helen (b. 1941) *singer and songwriter*

Born in Monroe City, Missouri, on December 6, 1941, Helen Lorene Johnson was raised in a musical family; her father was a big *Grand Ole Opry* fan, and her brothers were all amateur country musicians. Cornelius began her career as a child performing in a vocal trio with her sisters on the local country fair circuit. After a number of years working on an amateur level, she got her big break as a soloist appearing on the *Ted Mack Amateur Hour* in the mid-1960s.

However, it took a while for her career to get in gear. After failing to get very far as a solo artist, she took up songwriting, placing minor hits with other female country stars, including LYNN ANDERSON, JEANNIE C. RILEY, and SKEETER DAVIS. She recorded demos for MCA and Columbia and finally was signed to RCA in the mid-1970s, enjoying a minor hit with "We Still Sing Love Songs in Missouri."

RCA producer Bob Ferguson suggested that the young singer might make a good duet partner for Jim Ed Brown (previously lead singer of the BROWNS). The pair recorded "I Don't Want to Have to Marry You" in 1977; it was a number-one hit on the country charts. Inspired by this success, they recorded together for the next three years, even doing a country cover of "You Don't Bring Me Flowers," originally cut by Neil Diamond and Barbra Streisand.

In 1980 Cornelius and Brown split to pursue solo careers, and neither had much success. Eight years later, they reunited, but by then their style was outdated.

countrypolitan

Countrypolitan, a play on words combining *country* and *cosmopolitan,* is a name that has been applied to the music that came out of Nashville from the 1970s through the "new country" revolution of the mid-1980s. Producers and performers alike wanted to compete with middle-of-the-road pop music, in order to cross over to the more lucrative "adult contemporary" market. In countrypolitan music, Nashville's professional music establishment turned to pop styles and "countrified" them.

The movement began with soft-pop singers who tried to move a little more toward a rock sound. LYNN ANDERSON's upbeat 1970 hit "(I Never Promised You a) Rose Garden" is one of the first examples of a pop song that came out of the country charts. Perhaps the best-remembered song in this style was CRYSTAL GAYLE's 1978 hit "Don't It Make My Brown Eyes Blue," with its tinkling piano and oh-so-pleasant vocals. Other country stars soon jumped on the bandwagon. DOLLY PARTON made an attempt to cross over, releasing the perky dance number "Here You Come Again," as well as performing in more "contemporary" clothing. Late 1970s star EDDIE RABBITT represented the perfect blend of pop-rock and country styles, although it's hard to figure out what makes a song like "I Love a Rainy Night" country.

KENNY ROGERS was the ultimate countrypolitan star. Coming from a folk-pop background, Rogers had a husky voice, sexy good looks, and a repertoire of soft-pop ballads that appealed to a mainstream audience. Again, his dress style indicated a basic change in the country audience; no Nudie suits (western-style clothing from famous tailor Jamie Nudie) or 10-gallon hats for this cowboy, but rather ready-to-wear disco clothes, complete with unbuttoned shirts, chains, and bell-bottoms. Rogers reached out to the pop audience by recording duets with pop-rocker Kim Carnes on "Don't Fall in Love with a Dreamer" in 1980, and with R&B balladeer Lionel Richie on the ballad "Lady."

While the countrypolitan movement was in full flower, stirrings of revolt could be felt in two areas. The so-called outlaws turned their backs on Nashville, heading to places like Austin, Texas, to create a new music by focusing on older country styles. Meanwhile, the bluegrass revival was sweeping through the folk community, and many of its younger pickers would become the new country stars of the 1980s and 1990s.

country rock

Several performers have claimed the mantle of being the first to meld country and rock into a new style. Rick (Ricky) Nelson, a forgotten teen idol by the mid-1960s, was among the first to cut all-country albums, and he formed his Stone Canyon Band to further his country sound in 1969. The EVERLY BROTHERS—who had true country roots—also dabbled in country rock on two late 1960s albums. However, probably the first and most important country rock album was the Byrds' 1968 release, *Sweetheart of the Rodeo. Sweetheart* featured country standards, along with compositions by BOB DYLAN and new band member Gram Parsons in a country style, performed by the band along with some of the better, younger Nashville session men.

While this version of the Byrds was short-lived, the album they recorded became a model for later country-rock ensembles.

A year later, Bob Dylan gave the movement added legitimacy by releasing his *Nashville Skyline* album, in which he sang like a mellow country crooner and dueted with JOHNNY CASH. Young Nashvillians such as multi-instrumentalist Norman Blake and steel guitarist Pete Drake played on these sessions; these musicians knew country roots, but were influenced by more progressive sounds. Another influential album, oddly enough, was Ringo Starr's *Beaucoups of Blues,* recorded in Nashville in 1971; Ringo had sung BUCK OWENS's "Act Naturally" with the Beatles, and somehow his sad-sack vocals perfectly fit mainstream country songs. Steel guitarist Pete Drake approached Starr with the project, and he produced all of the tracks using Nashville's young talent.

Southern California was an important center for country rock. One of the first groups from this region was Poco, formed in 1969, and featuring Rusty Young on pedal steel guitar. Their theme song, "Pickin' Up the Pieces," on their first album, stated their mission quite clearly: to "pick up the pieces" of country tradition and modernize them for a new, young, hip audience. The NITTY GRITTY DIRT BAND was another West Coast band that began its life in rock and converted to country rock in the late 1960s. But again the Byrds provided the basis for the best remembered of these bands, the FLYING BURRITO BROTHERS. After *Sweetheart of the Rodeo* was completed, Byrds Gram Parsons and Chris Hillman wanted to take the country-rock experiment further, so they formed the Flying Burrito Brothers. Their first two albums, made while Parsons was still with the group, are considered classics today, combining traditional country subject matter and sounds with a decidedly new outlook. Parsons left the band and he had a short solo career before his untimely death; he helped launch the career of country-rock vocalist EMMYLOU HARRIS, who would later cross over in the mid-1980s to become

a pure country act. Chris Hillman later formed a progressive country band, The Desert Rose Band.

Even the Grateful Dead got in on the act on their early 1970s releases *Workingman's Dead* and *American Beauty.* Both albums featured songs with distinct country flavorings, along with some of the purest harmonies ever laid down by the Dead. Jerry Garcia, who began his career as a bluegrass banjoist and would from time to time return to this format through the 1970s and 1980s with his informal group Old and in the Way, took up the pedal steel guitar at this time to get that true country sound.

Country rock not only opened country music to a new audience—the young, literate audience for contemporary rock—but it also helped remind country of its roots in western swing, honky-tonk, and bluegrass, while pointing the way to a new music that could be created based on these roots. The country-rock revival would lead, in turn, to interest in other types of country music, such as the mid-to-late 1970s revival of rockabilly.

"Courtesy of the Red, White and Blue"
(2003) *song inspired by the invasion of Iraq*
TOBY KEITH, who has inherited MERLE HAGGARD's role as conservative spokesperson for country music, wrote the song to express his feelings of pride in the 2003 military operation. He often performed it, including on a tour of Iraq to entertain the soldiers.

cowboy songs
Although western and frontier literature has been popular in America since the days of James Fenimore Cooper and Zane Grey (and continues today with Louis L'Amour), cowboy songs were discovered by urban America with the publication of John A. Lomax's *Cowboy Ballads* in 1910, followed by several other collections. Lomax introduced such classics as "Home on the Range" and "Git Along, Little Doggies," providing the backbone for cowboy singer

repertoires for decades to come, and also solidifying the image of the cowboy as a lonesome songster.

Although not in the cowboy mold per se, JIMMIE RODGERS was also influential in developing the cowboy repertoire. His combination of a black, blues-influenced repertoire and vocal style with white sentimental songs and simple guitar accompaniments was influential on dozens of country performers, including a young GENE AUTRY, the first cowboy star. Rodgers's characteristic "blue yodel" also became an integral part of many cowboy acts.

The mid-to-late 1930s saw a blossoming of cowboy and cowgirl acts, influenced by successful movie serials starring Autry and other "singing cowboys." These horse operas, so called because they combined cowboy music with fanciful plots of the old West, were hugely popular in rural America because they provided images of a simpler, happier time when good guys wore white and bad guys were always successfully run out of town. Groups like the SONS OF THE PIONEERS and the GIRLS OF THE GOLDEN WEST were two of many who exploited the cowboy imagery and repertoire. These bands took 1930s and 1940s vocal harmonies and wed them to cowboy themes. Western swing stars like fiddler and bandleader BOB WILLS brought his group to Hollywood to join the cowboy movement and starred in a number of budget westerns in the 1940s.

With cowboys came cowgirls, particularly the popular PATSY MONTANA and ROSE MADDOX. Montana wore a fringed outfit while singing the popular "I Want to Be a Cowboy's Sweetheart," appealing to both male and female listeners.

ROY ROGERS and TEX RITTER would continue the image of the singing cowboy for a new generation on TV and films in the 1950s and 1960s. The popularity of the Disney film *Davy Crockett* in 1954 would also further the cowboy myth. Country performers began wearing increasingly flamboyant cowboy garb, culminating in the famous "Nudie suits" (named for their creator), of the 1960s with their garish rhinestones, embroidery, and exaggerated flared pants.

The good-guy cowboy of the 1930s through 1950s gave way to the outlaw cowboy of the 1970s, most notably WILLIE NELSON and WAYLON JENNINGS. Nelson even created a musical tale of the "old West," *Red-Headed Stranger,* a song cycle that changed the cowboy image to fit the idea that cowboys lived by their own rules, just as Nelson the singer/songwriter refused to obey the rules of mainstream Nashville. The early 1970s also saw country-rock bands in a cowboy mold, such as the New Riders of the Purple Sage. Another recent development in the cowboy myth has been spearheaded by country/cowboy MICHAEL MARTIN MURPHEY. He has been a champion of cowboy song and poetry, and a main mover behind the annual West Fest, a love-in for fans of cowboy lore. Poets specializing in reciting epic tales of the West have sprung up around the country.

The "singing cowboy" continues to be popular in folk and country circles, although he is more likely to be seen behind the wheel of a pickup truck than on horseback. Folklorist Doug Green has revived a 1940s-style cowboy combo in the retro band RIDERS IN THE SKY, who have become popular on the *Grand Ole Opry* stage. Nearly every male country star appears wearing a cowboy hat as at least a nod to the Western heritage.

Craddock, Billy "Crash" (b. 1939) *guitarist and singer*

William Wayne Craddock was born on a farm near Greensboro, North Carolina, on June 13, 1939, in relative poverty. His older brother began teaching him guitar when he was 11, and he debuted as part of a country duo during his high school years, playing with another brother, Ronald. Eventually the duo expanded into a foursome called the Four Rebels, who played rockabilly and upbeat country music. Billy earned his nickname, "Crash," in high school, thanks to his enthusiasm for tackling the opposing team's players on the football field.

In 1959 a field scout for Columbia caught the Four Rebels act and signed Billy to the label. Columbia brought him to Nashville, but instead of recording country or even straight rockabilly, they decided to mold him into a teen idol, in the style of crooners like Fabian. Oddly enough, Billy's greatest success in this phase of his career was in the Australian market, where he was hailed as the new Elvis Presley.

After his teen-pop career faded, Craddock returned to North Carolina to work in construction. Although he continued to perform locally, he spent most of the 1960s in semiretirement until a local pharmaceutical manufacturer named Dale Morris caught his act in 1969. Morris enlisted record producer Ron Chancey to engineer Craddock's comeback sessions, founding with him the tiny Cartwheel label. Billy's first hit was a countrified version of the old rocker "Knock Three Times" released in 1971, followed by remakes of "Ain't Nothin' Shakin' (But the Leaves on the Trees)" and the teen-pop ode "Dream Lover."

Craddock's early 1970s success interested ABC records, which bought out his contract, and released his first number-one country hit, the cute "Rub It In" in 1974 (a few years later, Craddock made an answer song "You Rubbed It In All Wrong," and then remade his original hit as an ad jingle for the muscle-soothing compound Absorbine Junior in 1986). ABC also had him record more rock remakes, including his next number one, a cover of the Leiber/Stoller classic "Ruby, Baby."

By the mid-1970s the novelty of doing old pop hits in a country style was wearing thin. Craddock began moving toward a mainstream country style, crafting one final hit with the country weeper "Broken Down in Tiny Pieces," featuring background vocals by JANIE FRICKIE, who was then working as a session singer. In 1977 he left ABC records for Capitol, and broke off his relationship with longtime producer Chancey. He managed to score a few more late 1970s hits, beginning with 1978's "I Cheated on a Good Woman's Love" and the saccharine "If I Could Write a Song as Beautiful as You" from a year later. In 1980 he returned to his old pattern of recording rock songs with a remake of "Sea Cruise." He left Capitol in 1982, recording an album three years later for Dot. Today, he continues to record and perform, although primarily focusing

on the Australian market, where he remains a living legend.

Cramer, Floyd (1933–1997) *pianist*

Cramer was born in Sampti, Louisiana, on October 27, 1933, but raised in tiny Huttig, Arkansas. He began piano lessons at age five, and first played professionally for local dances while still in high school. He joined the *Louisiana Hayride* radio program as a staff accompanist after his graduation from high school in 1951. He worked briefly for the Abbott label, and then teamed up with CHET ATKINS as house pianist at RCA, recording behind a young Elvis Presley, JIM REEVES, and countless others. Influenced by the picking of Mother Maybelle Carter and the piano playing of Don Robertson, he developed his characteristic "slip-note" style of playing, in which he imitates the sliding from note to note that is possible on guitar or fiddle by hitting one note and almost immediately sliding his finger onto the next key. Like Atkins, Cramer was influenced by the light jazz of such 1950s performers as Nat King Cole.

Cramer recorded a number of bluesy rockabilly songs in the late 1950s, including his first hit, "Flip, Flop and Bop," issued in 1957. He scored his biggest hits in the early 1960s, including 1960's "Last Date," 1961's "San Antonio Rose" (a cover of the BOB WILLS classic) and "On the Rebound," and finally 1967's "Stood Up." He reemerged from obscurity in the late 1970s with an album on which he played eight different keyboards through the miracle of overtracking, including synthesizer.

Less active in the 1980s and 1990s, Cramer died after a six-month battle with cancer at age 64 on December 31, 1997. He was inducted into the Country Music Hall of Fame in 2003.

"Crazy" (1961) *landmark hit for both its writer, Willie Nelson, and the performer Patsy Cline*

PATSY CLINE was seeking to cross over from the country charts to mainstream success and this tune helped her do it. Cline's mournful vocals—a legacy of her country career—were highlighted against a muted ensemble featuring a tinkling piano. For Nelson, who had been struggling to establish himself as a songwriter, the song validated him in the eyes of the Nashville establishment, although it would take another decade before he could achieve success as a performer.

"Crazy Arms" (1956) *Ray Price's biggest hit*
It remained in the number-one position on the country charts for an astonishing 20 weeks beginning in late May 1956, racking up an impressive 45 weeks total on the charts. It also was a DJ number-one hit for 20 weeks and a top-ranked best-seller for 11 weeks. These sales led *Billboard* to rank the song as the fourth biggest hit of all country releases since the country charts were begun in 1944. The song is a typical boy-loses-girl number. Price's country version was covered by JERRY LEE LEWIS in 1957, before his initial rock hits, and has been covered innumerable times by others including PATSY CLINE, Linda Ronstadt, Gram Parsons, and WAYLON JENNINGS.

Crowell, Rodney (b. 1950) *performer and songwriter*
Crowell performed with his father in a local country bar band when he was growing up. He moved to Nashville in the mid-1970s in search of a recording career. He was hired by EMMYLOU HARRIS to play in her Hot Band in 1975, where he worked for two years not only as a musician but also as an arranger; Harris also recorded several of his songs, including "Leaving Louisiana in Broad Daylight" and "Bluebird Wine." His songs began to be covered by country and pop acts; rocker Bob Seger scored a hit with his "Shame on the Moon," which led to Crowell's solo recording contract in 1977. Two years later he wed Rosanne Cash, with whom he recorded several duets (and for whom he produced several albums), until their marriage ended in the late 1980s.

Crowell's career slowed after 1995, when he was dropped by Columbia Records. After six years of trying to find a label interested in his songs, Crowell returned in 2001 with the album *The Houston Kid*. Crowell continues to go persistently in his own, sometimes eccentric direction, but his material is never less than interesting.

Cyrus, Billy Ray (b. 1961) *singer and actor*
Cyrus is the grandson of a preacher and began singing in his family's gospel group before attending school. An early enthusiasm for sports led to a

Billy Ray Cyrus, left, with his hero, Tom T. Hall (Raeanne Rubenstein)

baseball scholarship at Georgetown College. When he was 20, he formed a country band that played locally in the Kentucky/Ohio region in bars and small-time clubs. Cyrus spent the 1980s trying to establish himself as either an actor or musician but was unsuccessful until he finally signed a contract with Mercury Records in 1990. The good-looking star was heavily promoted, and his initial single, "Achy Breaky Heart," released in 1991, was a major phenomenon. Many in country music were dismayed by the song's pop-style production and dismissed Cyrus as merely the product of clever marketing. Their criticisms seemed to be justified as Cyrus didn't have much luck with his follow-up records, and he turned to acting in 2000, appearing as the lead on the cable TV show *Doc*.

d

Daffan, Ted (1912–1996) *performer and songwriter*

Theron Eugene Daffan was born in Beauregard, Louisiana, on September 21, 1912. He was raised in Houston, where he developed an interest in electronics, leading him to open one of the first electric-musical-instrument repair shops. The newly introduced electric steel guitar was particularly fascinating to the young musician/engineer; he even formed an amateur Hawaiian-style band called the Blue Islanders to play local gigs so he could practice. Western swing star MILTON BROWN patronized Daffan's shop, and also convinced him to become a full-time musician. Daffan first worked with the Blue Ridge Playboys led by guitarist Floyd Tillman in 1934.

Daffan's songwriting career got a good start with "Truck Driver's Blues," a big hit for western swing bandleader Cliff Bruner, who featured Texas honky-tonk singer MOON MULLICAN as his lead vocalist. This led to a contract for Daffan and his band, The Texans, with Columbia, and the 1940 hit "Worried Mind." This was followed through the 1940s by similar bluesy numbers, mostly on the classic honky-tonk themes of lovin', losin', and leavin'. These include 1943's weeper "Born to Lose," 1945's "Headin' Down the Wrong Highway," and the fine jump number "I've Got Five Dollars and It's Saturday Night" from 1950. Right after World War II Daffan had a steady job at the Venice Pier Ballroom near Los Angeles, but in 1946 he returned to Houston.

In the 1950s Daffan's career as a performer slowed down, even though he continued to write hits in the beer-soaked style that made him famous. In 1958 he joined forces in Nashville with Canadian HANK SNOW to form a publishing company, and turned his attention to the business side of songwriting and promotion. He returned to Houston in 1961 to continue working on the business side of the industry; that same year, Joe Barry had a million-selling hit with a remake of his "I'm a Fool to Care," previously recorded about a decade earlier by Les Paul and Mary Ford. Daffan died on October 6, 1996.

Daily, Harold "Pappy" (1902–1987) *producer*

Harold Daily was born in the small town of Yoakum, Texas, on February 8, 1902. A successful Houston-based businessman who had served in the Marine Corps in World War I, Daily established a jukebox and pinball distribution and service business in the 1930s. On the side he distributed records, recorded local talent, and then sold the masters to various small labels, and also ran a country radio program. Eventually he came to the conclusion that he was in an excellent position to press his own records, with a ready market of jukebox owners already established in his state. So, in 1953, he formed Starday records with Beaumont-based promoter Jack Starnes and his wife, Neva. A few months later, producer Don Pierce was made a third partner because of his wide contacts in the country business. (Pierce had previously worked for the West Coast–based 4-Star label.)

While Daily viewed the deal as a sideline to his business, Starnes saw the label as a means of promoting artists appearing at his clubs. Pierce was the only professional among them, and he soon aggravated Starnes by refusing to release records to correspond with club dates. Starnes left the label in 1954, selling his stake to Daily, shortly after recording a local singer who had been hanging out at his club: GEORGE JONES. Jones, under Daily's guidance, would become Starday's greatest asset, scoring big with his first hit, 1955's "Why, Baby, Why."

Mercury Records, a label that Daily already distributed in Texas, was impressed by the performance of Jones's record, and offered Pierce and Daily the opportunity to run Mercury's country division, beginning in early 1957. The deal lasted for a year and a half, and led to a falling out between Pierce and Daily. Daily wanted to stay with Mercury, having befriended label executive Art Talmadge there; Pierce wanted to remain independent. The two divided up Starday's publishing and recording assets, and Pierce went back to being an independent.

While still at Mercury, Daily had formed another side business, D Records, perhaps to keep one hand in that side of the record world. D would be the home of various Texas artists, including a local deejay who performed a funny half-spoken, half-sung routine he called "Chantilly Lace"—the Big Bopper. The record became a massive rock-and-roll hit after it was leased to Mercury. Daily kept D going through 1979; both WILLIE NELSON and GEORGE STRAIT recorded for it early in their careers.

Daily joined United Artists (UA) Records as director of its country division in 1960, following in the footsteps of his buddy Art Talmadge and bringing George Jones with him. Jones recommended a young female singer named MELBA MONTGOMERY to Daily, and she soon was one of the label's big hit makers, both in duet with Jones and on her own.

Daily left UA in 1964 to join, again with Art Talmadge, the Musicor label, and again Jones followed. But in 1971 Jones wanted to join his then-wife TAMMY WYNETTE at Epic Records, which offered a far more lucrative deal than Musicor—and also greater exposure. Talmadge and Daily were upset and threatened to sue. Although eventually resolved, this incident ended the relationship between Daily and Jones.

After folding D Records in 1979, Daily retired from the music business. He died on December 5, 1987.

Dalhart, Vernon (1883–1948) *singer*

Vernon Dalhart was born Marion Try Slaughter, in Jefferson, Texas, on April 6, 1883, the son of a rancher who worked the rich land of northeastern Texas. Young Slaughter worked as a cowhand in the region, but his true love was for the light classical and operatic music of the day. He entered the Dallas Conservatory of Music and then moved to New York, landing a job with the Century Opera Company in 1913. He took his stage name from the names of two tiny Texas towns, Vernon and Dalhart.

Dalhart first recorded as a popular tenor, beginning with the Edison label in 1916 and then moving to Victor, using more than 100 pseudonyms. Then, in 1924, he recorded "The Wreck of the Old 97," a song he learned from a recording made a year earlier by blind fiddler Henry Whitter. The record would sell more than 25 million copies during the next two decades, becoming country's first certified big hit. It was backed by the sentimental "The Prisoner's Song," which Dalhart would rerecord several more times, earning, it is said, more than $1 million in composer's royalties.

Dalhart's heyday was between 1925 and 1931. He worked with several accompanists, the best-known being guitarist/songwriter Carson Robison. Dalhart's repertoire was made up of a smattering of traditional songs, popular songs of the late 19th and early 20th century, and topical numbers, such as the ever-popular "Death of Floyd Collins" (written by Robison).

The depression slowed Dalhart's career, although he continued to record through 1939, when he made his final records for the budget Bluebird label. In the 1940s Dalhart relocated to Bridgeport, Connecticut, where he eventually became a hotel clerk; he died of a heart attack on September 15, 1948.

Dalton, Lacy J. (b. 1946) *singer and songwriter*

Jill Lynne Byrem was born in Bloomsburg, Pennsylvania, on October 13, 1946. She came from a solid working-class background; her father was a mechanic and hunting guide, while her mother worked as both a beautician and waitress. Both were also active amateur country musicians. Interested in art during her high school years, Dalton enrolled at Brigham Young University as an art major; she lasted only a year and a half in school, and then began performing with a friend in local coffeehouses. She passed through Minnesota for a while, returned home to Pennsylvania, and then headed out to California, where she fronted a folk-rock band called the Office, managed by her future husband, John Croston. However, the band was not a success, and her husband was killed in a freak auto accident, leaving Dalton to fend for herself.

In 1978 Dalton recorded an album in a friend's garage; she was able to sell about 3,000 copies locally. A local deejay passed a copy along to Columbia Records, where her songwriting abilities impressed veteran country producer Billy Sherrill. Sherrill suggested a name change, and Jill Byrem became Lacy J. (for Jill) Dalton; the last name came from a singer she admired, Karen Dalton. Her first single, 1978's "Crazy Blue Eyes," which she cowrote, was moderately successful. Her 1980 remake of the country classic "Tennessee Waltz" was a bigger hit.

Through the 1980s Dalton produced a body of work centering on a number of concept albums, often dealing with the difficulty faced by the rural poor, particularly women, in making a living. This streak began with 1980's "Hard Times," continued with the 1986 album *Highway Diner* and its hit "Working Class Man," and 1989's *Survivor* with the title song, "I'm a Survivor." (Between 1986 and 1989 Dalton struggled to overcome a growing problem with alcoholism.) Dalton released her last major-label album to date in 1992. Nonetheless, she has continued touring and releasing albums independently through the 1990s, appealing to her core audience.

Daniels, Charlie (b. 1936) *guitarist, fiddle player, and songwriter*

Born Charles Edwards Daniels in Wilmington, North Carolina, on October 28, 1936, Daniels played fiddle and guitar in a number of amateur country and bluegrass bands before turning professional at age 21. His first group was a rock and roll instrumental ensemble called the Jaguars. The group stayed together in one form or another for eight years, when Daniels came to Nashville to work as a session musician and songwriter. Daniels played on a number of landmark recordings, including Bob Dylan's *Nashville Skyline,* as well as touring with singer/poet Leonard Cohen.

After recording a solo album for Capitol, Daniels formed the Charlie Daniels Band in 1972, inspired by the success of the Allman Brothers; Daniels played lead guitar (and occasional fiddle). Their first big hit was 1973's "Uneasy Rider," followed a year later by the rebel-rousing anthem, "The South's Gonna Do It." By the end of the 1970s it was clear that the rock audience was turning away from southern bands, so Daniels shifted into a more country-oriented direction. His biggest hit in this mold was 1979's "The Devil Went Down to Georgia," full of flashy fiddle effects (not played by Daniels on record). The song was an enormous hit, and remains the number most closely associated with him to today. Daniels has continued to record and perform with various versions of his band, mostly featuring his old hits.

Davis, Jimmie (1902–2000) *singing cowboy*

Born James Houston Davis, in Beech Springs, Louisiana, on September 11, 1902, Davis came from a rural background, but eventually earned a master's degree and taught college for a while during the mid-1920s. Because of his country roots and his pleasant voice, he was invited to sing "old-time" songs in the late 1920s by a radio station out of Shreveport, Louisiana, leading to a performing career and recording contract with Victor Records. Davis's first phase of recording, from 1929 to 1934, featured a mix of sentimental "heart" songs and bluesy numbers sung in the manner of JIMMIE RODGERS.

In 1934 Davis moved to the Decca label and adopted a singing-cowboy image. Davis is said to have cowritten many of his 1930s hits. Some of these claims may be exaggerations, but he certainly was the first artist to record many songs that have become country standards, from 1934's "Nobody's Darlin' but Mine" to 1938's "(I Don't Worry 'Cause) It Makes No Difference Now" to 1940's "You Are My Sunshine." "Sunshine" was successfully revived in the 2001 film *Oh Brother, Where Art Thou?*, which helped popularize traditional country music for a new audience.

During World War II Davis moved into politics, successfully running for governor of Louisiana in 1944 and serving for one term, and then returning to the governor's office in 1960. In between, he became increasingly involved in publishing and business concerns; when he did record, he turned to gospel material. In 1969 he married Anna Carter, from the CHUCK WAGON GANG, a well-known country-gospel group. In 1971 he was among the first inductees into the Country Music Hall of Fame. Despite failing health, he continued to perform into the 1980s until he suffered a heart attack in October 1987. He made a few appearances in the 1990s and one final recording of "You Are My Sunshine" in 1998. He died on November 5, 2000.

Davis, Mac (b. 1942) *singer and songwriter*
Born in Lubbock, Texas, on January 21, 1942, Scott Davis was raised by his uncle on a ranch, and he first sang as a member of the church choir. By his teen years he was performing with friends in local pop-rock groups. In his late teens he moved to Atlanta. He began working as a record-label representative, and then took a job with a Los Angeles based music publisher in 1967. Davis's big break came when he placed one of his own songs, "A Little Less Conversation," with Elvis Presley in 1968; the song enjoyed some success, so Presley requested a

follow-up. Davis delivered what would become his first smash pop hit, "In the Ghetto." This was the first of Davis's songs to reflect a gritty reality. He wrote two more songs in this vein for Elvis ("Memories" and "Don't Cry Daddy").

In 1970 Davis decided to promote his own performing career, and began to appear on TV talk shows and play in Vegas. He was signed to Columbia Records and released his first album in 1971. He had a string of hits in the early 1970s, from "Beginning to Feel the Pain" and "I Believe in Music" in 1971 through 1973's "Everybody Loves a Love Song." Davis dropped off the pop charts by the mid-1970s but continued to have country hits, including "I Still Love You (You Still Love Me)" and "Picking Up the Pieces of My Life" in 1977. At the same time, he appeared on a number of televised variety-show specials that drew large ratings. In 1979 he appeared in the movie *North Dallas Forty*, enjoying some critical success, and it looked like a movie career might be on the horizons.

However, both Davis's music and movie careers faded in the 1980s. He still had hits, including 1980's "It's Hard to Be Humble" and "Texas in My Rear View Mirror." In the early 1990s Davis enjoyed a short run on Broadway as Will Rogers in the popular revue *The Will Rogers Follies*.

Davis, Skeeter (1931–2004) *singer*
Mary Frances Penick was born in Dry Ridge, Kentucky, on December 30, 1931. She took her stage name in high school when she performed with a friend named Betty Jack Davis (1932–53) in a vocal duo known as the Davis Sisters. They were discovered after appearing on the *Kentucky Barn Dance* radio show out of Lexington, which led to further radio work in Detroit and Cincinnati and finally a contract with RCA in the early 1950s. They scored big with 1953's "I Forgot More Than You'll Ever Know," but, in the same year, they were involved in a severe car crash following a performance that took Betty Jack's life and severely injured Skeeter. After

her recovery, Skeeter worked for a while with Betty Jack's sister Georgia, but then went out on her own.

Skeeter had several early 1960s hits, mostly in the form of the then-popular women's answer song to hits by male stars. Her 1960 song "(I Can't Help You) I'm Fallin' Too" was an answer to Hank Locklin's big number "Please Help Me I'm Falling," and 1961's "My Last Date (With You)" was a vocal version of FLOYD CRAMER's hit, "Last Date"; both songs were written by Davis. Her biggest hit came in 1962 with "The End of the World" followed by a crossover pop hit, "I Can't Stay Mad at You," a year later. In these songs Skeeter expressed "men-will-ramble-and-women-must-suffer" sentiments that made her the first in a line of long-suffering country women who were not exactly role models of liberation.

In the mid-1960s, after a brief flirtation with the pop charts, Davis had a couple more country hits, including duets with BOBBY BARE on 1965's "A Dear John Letter" and 1971's "Your Husband, Your Wife," as well as recording with PORTER WAGONER and GEORGE HAMILTON IV. She established herself as a Nashville outlaw by touring with the Rolling Stones during the 1960s and denouncing the Nashville police for brutality from the stage of the *Grand Ole Opry* in 1973.

Davis returned to performing in the later 1980s after her marriage to Joey Spampinato, the bass player of the roots rock ensemble NRBQ, with a new emphasis on the harder-rockin' side of her personality. She died of breast cancer on September 28, 2004.

Dean, Jimmy (b. 1928) *performer*

Seth Ward was born near Plainview, Texas, on August 10, 1928, and lived in near poverty in his earliest years; his father had abandoned his mother, who managed a local barbershop to make ends meet. As a child, he worked as a field hand, and he showed an early interest in music, learning in rapid succession piano, guitar, accordion, and harmonica. As for many other rural southerners, the military

served as an escape from his impoverished family life. While in the service in the late 1940s, he formed his first group, the Tennessee Haymakers.

By 1953 Jimmy was located in Arlington, Virginia, performing with a new backup band, the Texas Wildcats. They recorded "Bummin' Around," Dean's first single to gain national attention. Two years later he was hosting a local television program that caught the eye of the CBS network. In 1957 CBS launched a morning show hosted by Dean, which failed to find a national sponsor. In 1961 Dean signed with Columbia Records, where he enjoyed his greatest success. His first hit was "Big Bad John," a mock-ballad written by Dean that told the story of a backcountry hellraisin' coal miner. One year later he scored again with "P.T. 109," a patriotic anthem describing the exploits of John F. Kennedy during World War II.

Dean's good-natured, backwoodsy appeal brought him a second television contract, this time with ABC, where he remained through the mid-1960s. Although he continued to record for various labels through the mid-1970s, he was becoming a TV personality rather than a country musician. Since the early 1980s he's been best known for his line of country sausage that he personally promoted through radio and TV ads.

Delmore Brothers, The *vocal duo*

Alton (December 25, 1908–June 8, 1964; guitar, vocal) and Rabon (December 3, 1916–December 4, 1952; tenor guitar, vocal) Delmore were born in Elkmont, Alabama, and raised on a farm where their mother taught them the rudiments of gospel singing. As a singing duo they won a prize at a fiddler's contest in 1930. The brothers accompanied themselves on guitars, with Rabon playing the tenor guitar (with four strings tuned like a tenor banjo, this instrument has a smaller body and a sweeter tone than a standard guitar). The brothers began recording for Columbia in 1931, and joined the *Grand Ole Opry* in 1932, remaining there until 1938. Their first recordings featured their close harmonies, great bluesy material (including "Brown's Ferry Blues," "Gonna Lay Down My Old Guitar," and "Nashville Blues"), and Rabon's lead guitar work, which forecast the style of later pickers such as Doc Watson.

In 1944 the brothers began recording in an even bluesier style for King Records out of Cincinnati, often accompanied by electric guitars and string bass. Their 1949 recording of "Blues Stay Away From Me" was a smash country hit, staying on the charts for 23 weeks. The Delmores also worked with MERLE TRAVIS and GRANDPA JONES during this period as the Brown's Ferry Four. In the early 1950s they based their act in Houston, but the act began to disintegrate after the death of Alton's daughter, Sharon. He never recovered, becoming a heavy drinker. Rabon, meanwhile, contracted lung cancer, and returned to Alabama to die in 1952. Alton later worked as a traveling salesman and part-time guitar teacher before his death due to alcoholism 12 years later.

Denver, John (1943–1997) singer and songwriter

Born Henry John Deutschendorf, in Roswell, New Mexico, on December 31, 1943, Denver was the son of a career air force pilot. John performed in the early 1960s with the Chad Mitchell Trio, a popular folk-revival group. In 1965 he replaced leader Chad Mitchell, continuing to record with them until 1969 when the trio dissolved. Denver was signed to RCA as a solo artist that year, after his song "(Leaving on a) Jet Plane" was a hit for Peter, Paul and Mary.

Denver's big break came in 1971 with his recording of "Take Me Home, Country Roads," followed by a string of country-flavored pop hits, including "Annie's Song" and "Thank God I'm a Country Boy." Denver began a film acting career in 1977, and proved himself to be an affable comedian. He continued to record his own material through the mid-1980s with limited success. In 1988 he formed his own label to promote a country album, *Higher Ground*. Denver died while piloting a small airplane on October 12, 1997.

"Detroit City" (1963) a number-three country hit for Bobby Bare

"Detroit City" helped launch BOBBY BARE's career as well as that of the song's writer, MEL TILLIS. The song tells the story of a country boy who moves north to Detroit in search of employment, only to miss the simpler way of life back home. It has been covered by a surprising array of artists, including country star DOLLY PARTON, mainstream pop singer Dean Martin, and rocker Alice Cooper.

"Devil Went Down to Georgia, The" (1979) Charlie Daniels's biggest hit and best-known song

This song is loosely based on the folk belief that the fiddle is the "devil's instrument." It reached number one on July 21, 1979, remained at the top of the country charts for three weeks, and sold more than a million copies. Ironically, CHARLIE DANIELS is a talented guitarist and did not play fiddle on the original recording (although he has since made it a concert specialty). Daniels rerecorded the song with Mark O'Connor in the late 1990s.

Diamond Rio

Diamond Rio was born in the Opryland, USA theme park. Assembled to play "bluegrass" music (or at least what would sound like bluegrass to the park's visitors), the group grew to include three talented vocalists, with a smooth countryish lead provided by Marty Roe. The group's hot pickers—lead guitarist Jimmy Olander (who worked previously as a session picker with RODNEY CROWELL and Foster and Lloyd), mandolin/fiddle player Gene Johnson (an alumnus of J. D. Crowe's New South as well as folk rocker David Bromberg's band), and bassist Dana Williams (who is the nephew of the famous bluegrass pickers the Osborne Brothers)—are indeed impressive, and the group's harmonies blend a bluegrass sensibility with pop leanings.

They were signed to Arista Records in 1990 and given their new name and a splashy new act and look. Right out of the gate, they scored big with the hummable "Meet in the Middle," followed by "Norma Jeanne Riley" and three other top-five songs. Although the group's instrumental work enlivened many of these numbers, the result was a bland, middle-of-the-road sound that is the opposite of cutting-edge music-making. Diamond Rio followed up with a second album in 1993, leaning heavily on love ballads (the upbeat "Calling All Hearts" and the weepy "I Was Meant to Be with You" and "In a Week or Two").

After the mid-1990s the band's productivity—and hits—slowed. They have released new albums about once every three years since, but have failed to equal their previous success. Nonetheless, they remain popular on the road; fans know exactly what they're going to get at a Diamond Rio show. In 2001 they issued a new album, *One More Day,* which continued the basic style and sound of their earlier recordings.

Dickens, "Little" Jimmy (b. 1920) *singer*
James Cecil Dickens was born on December 19, 1920, the 13th child of a small-time rancher in rural Bolt, West Virginia. After attending the small local school, Dickens was accepted into the University of West Virginia, where he also landed a job as a performer on the local radio station. After radio stints in Cincinnati and Michigan, the pint-sized crooner, then billed as "Jimmy the Kid," attracted the attention of ROY ACUFF, who invited him to perform on the *Grand Ole Opry.* By the late 1940s he was a permanent member of the show, a position he holds to this day.

Dickens signed to Columbia, recording a string of novelty hits in the late 1940s, including his first top-10 country song, "Take an Old Cold Tater and Wait," earning him a second nickname, "Tater." Other novelty hit numbers included "I'm Little but I'm Loud," "A-Sleeping at the Foot of the Bed," and "Hillbilly Fever." Through the 1950s Dickens led a hot band called the Country Boys, which featured two lead guitars, pedal steel, and drums. Many of his recordings from this era share the energy of the best of rockabilly. For this alone Dickens deserves the seat in the Country Music Hall of Fame that he earned in 1983.

After his big pop hit with the silly "Bluebird of Paradise" in 1965, Dickens faded from the charts, but he continued to tour and perform, as well as to appear on the *Grand Ole Opry.* Today his appearances have more nostalgia value than anything else, maintaining a link with country's past.

Diffie, Joe (b. 1958) *singer and songwriter*
Joseph Logan Diffie was born in Tulsa, Oklahoma, on December 28, 1958, and raised in rural Duncan, Oklahoma, although his family relocated several times during his early years, moving as far west as Washington State. After attending college briefly, he returned to Duncan to work in an iron foundry while writing songs at night. His mother sent one of his early compositions to singer Hank Thompson, who bought it.

After nine years of heavy labor, Diffie was laid off due to tough financial times; with nothing to lose, he headed for Nashville to seek work as a songwriter. For the balance of the 1980s Diffie worked as a demo singer and songwriter. His demos were well received by the Nashville community, and eventually producer Bob Montgomery at Epic Records signed him, although he waited a few years to release Diffie's first album. Diffie had an immediate hit with 1990's "Home" and has followed it up with some spunky honky-tonk numbers, including 1992's "Honky Tonk Attitude" and 1993's "Prop Me Up (Beside the Jukebox If I Die)." He also recorded a duet with popular folk-country star MARY CHAPIN CARPENTER. Diffie continued to score hits through the 1990s, including "Texas Sized Heartache" in 1998 and "In Another World" in 2001.

Dinning Sisters, The *vocal trio*
Ella Lucille "Lou" Dinning (b. Auburn, Kentucky, September 29, 1920) and twins Virginia "Ginger" and Eugenia "Jean" (b. Braman, Oklahoma, March

29, 1924) were country music's answer to the Andrews Sisters. The Dinnings were popular stars of Chicago's radio program *National Barn Dance* in the 1940s and later had a minor career in musical short films and low-budget pictures.

Originally from Kentucky, the three sisters and five more siblings were raised primarily on a farm near Enid, Oklahoma. All eight children were musically inclined. Identical twins Jean and Ginger and elder sister Lucille formed a harmony group, performing on the local radio station. In 1939 they moved to Chicago, where elder sister Marvis had already begun a career as a big band singer; two years later, they were hired to perform on *National Barn Dance,* dubbed "The Sweethearts of Sunbonnet Swing." Their mix of down-home sweetness with pleasing harmonies won them an immediate audience, and soon they had their own radio show, plus an invitation to come to Hollywood to appear in cameo roles in a number of films.

By 1945 they had signed with the fledgling West Coast Capitol label, and they had a couple of hits with remakes of sugary pop numbers like 1947's "My Adobe Hacienda" (written by cowgirl star LOUISE MASSEY) and "Buttons and Bows" (1948); they also recorded swinging novelty numbers reminiscent of the Boswell Sisters, including 1946's "Iggedy Song." Elder sister Lou married country songsmith Don Robertson in 1946 (best known for writing "Please Help Me I'm Falling") and left the act; she was replaced first by Jayne Bundesen and, in 1949, by younger sister Delores Dinning.

The group's career faded in the 1950s. Jean later became a songwriter, best known for writing "Teen Angel," a pop hit of the early 1960s; sister Delores later joined the Nashville Edition, backup singers who appeared regularly on TV's *Hee Haw* as well as doing session work.

"Divorce Me C.O.D." (1946) *honky-tonk classic*
"Divorce Me C.O.D." was MERLE TRAVIS's first number-one hit. Its success inspired country covers by the King Sisters (1946; later better known as the

King Family, this group had its own network variety show in the 1960s) and Johnny Bond (it was Bond's first chart record, 1947).

Dixie Chicks, The
Originally known as the Dixie Chickens, the Texas-based group's first lineup, formed in 1989, consisted of sisters Martie (b. Dallas, Texas, 1970; fiddle, vocals) and Emily Erwin (b. Dallas, Texas, 1973; banjo, Dobro, vocals), along with guitarist/vocalist Robin Macy and bassist/vocalist Laura Lynch. All had backgrounds in bluegrass music, but they initially promoted themselves as a retro-cowgirl band. By the mid-1990s, however, they had thrown away the gingham and boots and settled on a more contemporary look and style. Macy defected from the group in the early 1990s, due to her objection to this more contemporary sound and the addition of a drummer to the group's touring band. The group continued as a trio, but still were unable to get what they really wanted: a contract with a major Nashville label.

Finally, in 1996 the Dixie Chicks got a bite from Sony Records. However, the company questioned the sex appeal and talent of Laura Lynch, suggesting she was too old to appeal to a wide audience. Vocalist Natalie Maines (b. Lubbock, Texas, 1975), the daughter of noted steel guitarist Lloyd Maines, was brought in to replace Lynch. She was considerably younger—and a more dynamic stage personality and singer—so the addition proved to be smart artistically as well as commercially.

The second single from the group's debut major-label album, *Wide Open Spaces,* shot to number one, the first trio recording to achieve this distinction on the country charts in more than a decade. The album garnered many awards for the group, and sold more than 10 million copies. Their second release, *Fly,* spawned several hit singles and went quadruple platinum. The hits included the tongue-in-cheek "Goodbye Earl," a song about an abusive husband who is killed by his long-suffering wife; and "Sin Wagon," an unusual song for a

The Dixie Chicks enjoying their award-winning streak (Raeanne Rubenstein)

female country group because it celebrated (rather than lamented) a "sinful" life over the usual "stay-at-home" stereotypes. The album also resulted in hit ballads, including the romantic "Cowboy Take Me Away."

Following this success, the Dixie Chicks fought with Sony over the details of their original contract, with claims and counterclaims flying for about two years. Finally, in 2002 they settled, and released a new album, *Home*. Recorded in Texas and produced by the band along with Lloyd Maines, the record had a bluegrass flavor. It again produced several hits, including an interesting acoustic arrangement of Fleetwood Mac's "Landslide." A two-CD live set was released in late 2003.

Dobro

The Dobro is a unique American musical instrument that has become central to the sound of modern bluegrass and country music. It is one of the key forerunners of the pedal-steel guitar.

The Dobro has its roots in the craze for Hawaiian music that swept the country in the 1920s. The classical guitar was introduced by Portuguese settlers in the islands around the 1830s; eventually, by the 20th century's end, Hawaiian musicians had taken to playing the guitar on their laps, tuning the strings to a full open or partially open chord (known as "slack-key" tuning), and noting the strings with a solid metal bar (hence the name, "steel guitar," referring to the bar used to damp the notes, not to the material used in making the guitar itself). Joseph Kekuku is generally cited as the first great Hawaiian player; he toured the United States and Europe at the turn of the 20th century, influencing hundreds of lesser-known vaudeville and tent-show musicians. One of the most popular recording stars of the 1920s in this style was Sol Hoopii, whose playing was emulated by both country and blues musicians.

Conventional guitars were modified for Hawaiian playing by being fitted with raised nuts (to increase string height), flush frets (so that the bar could be easily slid across the strings), hollow, square necks (to enable the instrument to sit flat on a player's lap), and stronger and larger body construction (to take the extra tension created by the steel strings used on these instruments, and also to increase volume). However, it was still difficult to produce a conventional guitar that would have enough power to be heard over an entire band.

One solution was the Dobro, invented by a family of Czechoslovakian immigrant instrument makers, the Dopyera brothers (hence the trade name do-bro used on some of their instruments). John Dopyera is generally credited with designing the original resonator used on Dobros, a system that employed a primitive nonelectric pickup mounted on the bridge of the instrument (like the needle used on early acoustic phonographs) that transmitted the sound down into a chamber that held three megaphone-like cones, facing down (or toward the back of the instrument). Dopyera was awarded a patent for his design in 1927, and a year later began producing instruments with his brothers under the National name; one of their first customers was Hawaiian star Hoopii. These instruments had steel bodies, so are commonly called National steels by today's players. Square-neck models for Hawaiian players and round-neck models for conventional players (highly prized among blues musicians) were both made through the 1930s.

In a complex business history, John eventually broke with National in 1929, coming up with a new design for a resonator instrument, the first true Dobro. This featured a single cone facing forward, with an elaborate eight-legged "spider" pickup that projected sound down from the bridge to the edges of the cone. In order to make a cheaper instrument than the National steel, the brothers decided to use a plywood body for their new instrument that they called the Dobro.

By the early depression years the National and Dobro companies had reunited, and were making a wide variety of both steel-bodied and wood-bodied guitars with either the single or tricone resonator. Soon after, a new technology in the form of electric (or amplified) lap guitars cut seriously into the popularity of these earlier so-called resophonic instruments. The Dobro probably would have disappeared from the musical scene if it had not been for a couple of influential players. "Bashful Brother Oswald" (aka Pete Kirby) played the instrument in ROY ACUFF's influential band from 1939 through the 1950s, appearing weekly on the *Grand Ole Opry*. In bluegrass music the pioneering FLATT AND SCRUGGS band featured a talented Dobro player, Uncle Josh (b. Burkett) Graves, who took Earl Scruggs's signature banjo roll and adapted it to the Dobro.

The Dobro fell out of popularity in mainstream country music recording circles from the mid-1950s to the mid-1980s, when the whine of the pedal steel guitar dominated recording sessions. It was the bluegrass revival of the 1970s that helped bring the instrument back to the fore, with young players such as Jerry Douglas showing that the Dobro was not just a relic of the past. Douglas has become one of the most in-demand session musicians of the 1980s and 1990s, and many other players have emulated his versatility on the instrument.

"Don't It Make My Brown Eyes Blue"
(1977) *Crystal Gayle hit*

Songwriter Richard Leigh was inspired by LORETTA LYNN's self-penned hit "I've Cried the Blue Right out of My Eyes." "Don't It" was intended for BRENDA LEE; however, Lee rejected it because her eyes *were* blue! Lynn recorded it, but it was her half-sister CRYSTAL GAYLE's record that became a major country and adult contemporary hit. The song topped the country charts for four weeks, and was certified gold. Its tinkling cocktail-piano accompaniment made it a classic of the mid-1970s COUNTRYPOLITAN style, which was noted for its smooth, pop-style arrangements.

"Down at the Twist and Shout" (1992)
breakthrough hit for new country star Mary Chapin Carpenter

Based in Washington, D.C., MARY CHAPIN CARPENTER was inspired by a local folk club that sponsored regular dances featuring the popular Cajun band Beausoleil. The band was featured on this single, which used a traditional Cajun two-step beat and melody for Chapin Carpenter's lyric. Chapin Carpenter and Beausoleil also performed the song as part of the halftime show at the Super Bowl (1993).

Downing, Big Al (b. 1940) *piano player and singer*

Al Downing was born on a small farm in Lenapah, Oklahoma, near the Kansas state line, on January 9, 1940. His father was a sharecropper who enjoyed listening to the *Grand Ole Opry* radio program, exposing his son at an early age to country music. The large family—Al had nine brothers and two sisters—formed their own gospel choir when he was just entering his teen years, performing locally. At about the same time, Al found a piano in a nearby garbage dump; although it had only 40 working keys, he began imitating his favorite artists, including Fats Domino. At age 14 he won a talent contest performing Domino's "Blueberry Hill" in the tiny town of Cotteyville, Kansas. Soon after, he was working as a truck driver, while still pursuing his musical career locally.

In 1957 guitarist Bobby Poe heard Al's Domino imitation and invited him to join his new band. Poe (who was white) figured he could cover the popular white singers of the day, like Elvis and Jerry Lee Lewis, and Downing (who was black) could handle the more soulful hitmakers. The band, originally known as the Rhythm Rockers, was one of the first integrated bands in popular music. Soon, they took the name the Poe Cats, and began recording, working with producer Lelan Rogers, who operated the White Rock label in Dallas. (KENNY ROGERS is his younger sibling.) Al's composition "Down on the Farm," became the band's first and most enduring hit, featuring his energetic vocals. It was licensed by White Rock to the larger Challenge label, which continued to issue the Poe Cats's records through the early 1960s.

Jim Halsey, who was then managing a young rockabilly star named Wanda Jackson, heard the band's first record and invited them to accompany her on her Capitol recordings. The band toured with Jackson for several years, and also appeared on her classic recordings, including "Let's Have a Party," and "In the Middle of a Heartache." They often opened for more mainstream country acts, and Al would oblige the audience with his repertoire of country ballads during band breaks.

Downing continued to appear on releases that were issued both under his and the Poe Cats names through 1964. In 1963 he cut a duet with Little Esther Phillips in Nashville, but it failed to hit big on either R&B or country charts. His last Poe Cats outing, 1964's "Georgia Slop," has won fame among diehard rockabilly fans for its rollicking, good-natured energy.

Downing continued to struggle as a country artist through the 1960s, but then switched to a more soulful sound with "I'll Be Holding On," a minor R&B hit in 1970. In the mid-1970s he even dabbled in disco, although he never reached true star status. In 1978 he returned to his original country roots, signing with Warner Brothers Records. He scored top-20 country hits in 1979 with his songs "Touch Me (I'll Be Your Fool Once More)" and "Mr. Jones," followed by 1980's "Bring It On Home," all his own compositions. However, Warner Brothers was unwilling to bankroll an entire album by Downing. Prejudice still ran deep in Nashville, and it was feared that if his identity as an African American were too widely known, his music would fail to sell. He even had difficulty placing his songs; white music publishers didn't think an African American could write true "country" songs. His last country hit, 1982's "I'll Be Loving You," barely reached the country top 50; it was released on the tiny Tug Boat label, which continues to record Downing.

However, Downing's fame as a rockabilly pioneer gave him a new audience in Europe, where rockabilly has gained greatly in popularity since the mid-1980s. He has toured and performed extensively in Europe since the early 1990s, and he continues to perform everything from Fats Domino–style R&B to country classics. Performance videos and rereleases of his rockabilly work sell strongly to fans of that early country-rock hybrid style.

Drake, Pete (1931–1988) pedal steel guitarist and producer

Roddis Franklin Drake was born in Atlanta, Georgia, on October 8, 1932. He was one of the earliest performers to take up the pedal steel guitar, beginning to play when he was 19 years old. Soon, he was leading a band, the Sons of the South, and performing on radio and in small clubs in his native Georgia. He joined the duo Wilma Lee and Stoney Cooper, coming to Nashville with them in 1959.

After a year and a half struggling to find work, Drake caught the ears of ROY DRUSKY and GEORGE HAMILTON IV, who invited him to perform on their next sessions. Drake's career as a session player took off; it is said that Drake could be heard on two-thirds of *Billboard*'s top 75 country singles throughout the early 1960s. In 1964 he released a solo recording of the pop novelty "Forever," which charted on both pop and country listings.

Drake moved into the studio/production end of the business in the mid-to-late 1960s, and soon became a powerhouse producer. It was his idea to invite Ringo Starr to make an all-country album after hearing the singer's cover of BUCK OWENS's hit "Act Naturally." Drake recorded all of the backgrounds, and then had Starr overdub vocals; the result was arguably Starr's best solo album, *Beaucoups of Blues,* released in 1970. By the early 1980s he was working primarily with older acts, such as B. J. Thomas and Linda Hargrove. Drake died on July 29, 1988.

Draper, Rusty (1923–2003) actor and singer

Farrell Draper was born in Kirksville, Missouri, on January 25, 1923. He earned his nickname thanks to his thick red hair. As a teen he began performing on local radio, eventually working his way west to San Francisco. During the 1950s he worked out of Los Angeles, appearing in western-themed TV shows like *Rawhide,* on the radio hosting a cowboy show, and singing at local clubs. His biggest hits came in 1953 with "Gambler's Guitar," a number-six pop and country hit, and in 1955 with "Shifting, Whispering Sands," which reached number three on the pop charts; both sold more than a million copies. He had other pop hits through 1957.

In the early 1960s Draper moved into mainstream pop-country, scoring a hit in 1963 with WILLIE NELSON's "Nightlife," earning him the nickname "Mr. Nightlife." Draper's last minor hit came in 1980 with a country cover of the song "Harbor Lights," originally recorded by the 1950s doo-wop group the Platters. At that time he began a long battle with heart disease and cancer, which eventually took his life on March 28, 2003.

Drifting Cowboys, The

The backup group that accompanied HANK WILLIAMS on his best-known *Grand Ole Opry* shows and recordings, the Drifting Cowboys became the prototype for hundreds of other honky-tonk bands of the 1950s and beyond.

The core of the group was steel guitarist Don Helms, who had performed with Williams since 1943 when both were still living in Alabama. With the exception of a brief period when Hank starred on the *Louisiana Hayride* radio show, Helms remained with the singer until his death. On early live *Opry* shows, the audience goes wild every time the steel guitar takes a solo. Helms's playing was always tasteful and discreet; he never sought to overwhelm Williams's singing, but rather to accompany it.

Guitarist Bob McNett was from Pennsylvania and had originally accompanied cowgirl sweetheart PATSY MONTANA before he joined Hank in 1949, when the singer was invited to join the *Opry;* fiddler Jerry Rivers came on board at the same time, as did session bass player Hillous Butram. This core group played on all of Williams's classic MGM recordings from the late 1940s and early 1950s, as well as touring with him and appearing on his regular *Grand Ole Opry* spots.

Williams was an alcoholic, and his behavior became increasingly erratic in the early 1950s. This led Butram to jump ship to join HANK SNOW in 1952 (he was replaced by Cedric Rainwater, who had worked in bluegrass bands and also as a session musician), and McNett left soon after, to be replaced by Sammy Pruett. When Williams died, the band disintegrated, with individual members continuing to work as session musicians.

In 1977 the group was reunited thanks to Hillous Butram, who was now working as a music coordinator for movies with "country" themes.

The group first performed in a Lorne Greene film, *That's Country,* leading to a contract with Epic Records, and a hit a year later with a remake of Johnnie Lee Wills's "Ragmop." They continued to perform through 1984, when the group members decided to retire.

Driftwood, Jimmy (1907–1998) *singer and songwriter*

James Corbett Morris, born in Mountain View, Arkansas, on June 21, 1907, first learned music from his family; his uncle gave him a handmade guitar, and he soon mastered fiddle and banjo as well. Jimmy worked his way through high school, occasionally performing at local dances and other gatherings, and became a rural schoolteacher in the late 1930s. He taught for 10 years while working towards his B.A. degree in education at the state teacher's college, located in Conway, Arkansas.

Contacts with folklorists in the 1950s brought Jimmy into contact with the urban folk revival, and he performed at many festivals and concerts. He was signed to RCA in 1958 as a folk singer and issued an album with the academic name of *Newly Discovered Early American Folk Songs.* On this record he recorded his version of "The Battle of New Orleans"; country singer JOHNNY HORTON heard it and released his own version a year later, which became a massive hit. RCA rushed out a second Driftwood album, plus a single version of Jimmy performing his song; this was followed by "Tennessee Stud," which was covered by EDDY ARNOLD for a second hit.

Driftwood continued to perform on the folk revival and country circuits through the early 1960s. He remained devoted to the traditional songs and stories of the Ozarks, and became well known for his playing of the mouthbow (sometimes called "diddley bow"), a single-stringed instrument that is played in a similar manner to the jew's harp (the end of the bow is held up against the player's open jaw, and while strumming vigorously on the string, different notes can be produced by varying the shape of the sound chamber formed by the open mouth).

Driftwood refurbished a barn on his farm near Mountain View, where he continued to perform for weekend visitors through the 1980s. He died at age 91 on July 12, 1998.

Drusky, Roy (b. 1930) *singer and songwriter*

Roy Frank Drusky was born in Atlanta, Georgia, on June 22, 1930. Although his mother was a church pianist who tried to interest him in music, he spent most of his childhood preoccupied with sports. Drusky's interest in country music was born in the navy, where he befriended some shipmates who played together in their own country band. After leaving the service he enrolled in veterinary school in Atlanta, but by 1951 had formed his own band, the Southern Ranch Boys. They were hired to play on a small Decatur, Georgia, radio station, where Drusky also worked as a deejay. After the band dissolved, Drusky began singing at local clubs, and he was signed to Starday Records in the early 1950s. In 1953 he had a hit with "Such a Fool." He was invited to join the *Grand Ole Opry* in 1958, where he remained for more than two decades as a performer.

By the early 1960s Drusky was working out of Minneapolis as a deejay and had signed to Decca Records. His first hits included the self-penned "Alone with You," "Another," and "Three Hearts in a Tangle," all fine honky-tonk ballads. In 1963 he signed with Mercury, producing more hits, varying from the novelty of his first Mercury single, "Peel Me a Nanner," through more country heartache songs that made him famous, like 1969's "Where the Blue and the Lonely Go." His pleasant singing style earned him the nickname "The Perry Como of Country Music."

Drusky's natural propensity for crooning, tied with a change in the country market, led him to be only a minor hit maker in the 1970s. Although he continues to perform on occasion, he is more active today as a songwriter and record producer in Nashville.

DuBois, Tim (b. 1948) *songwriter and manager*

Born on May 4, 1948, DuBois was raised in the small town of Grove, Oklahoma. He took a master's degree in accounting at Oklahoma State University, and after graduation worked as an accountant. Meanwhile, he yearned to be a country songwriter, and penned songs on the side.

Finally he decided to take a shot at making it big in Nashville. He arrived in 1977 and immediately placed his songs with major acts, including the honky-tonk, tongue-in-cheek ballad, "She Got the Goldmine (I Got the Shaft)," recorded by JERRY REED. DuBois then entered the personal management field, establishing a Nashville office for the West Coast firm Fitzgerald-Hartley. His first major signing was the group Restless Heart, in the mid-1980s; he not only signed the band, he groomed them carefully and helped them select material. In the late 1980s he signed VINCE GILL and also began songwriting with him; the two scored a number-one country hit with "When I Call Your Name" in 1992.

In 1989 Arista Records, a pop label based in New York, was looking to open a Nashville office, and tapped DuBois to head the label's efforts. DuBois was an active manager, looking for talent and recognizing potential where even the performers themselves didn't see it. In 1991 he suggested to two singer/songwriters that they might be better off working together than trying to go it alone; the result was the hitmaking duo of BROOKS AND DUNN, still one of the most successful acts around. The band BlackHawk was another DuBois creation that enjoyed several years of success during the 1990s. DuBois also spotted talent in young ALAN JACKSON, quickly signing him after other Nashville labels had turned him down; Jackson has proven to be another durable hit maker.

DuBois was elected president of the board of directors of the Country Music Association in 1996 for a two-year term. Meanwhile, he continued to cowrite songs with many major Nashville songwriters and on his own, often placing them with his acts on Arista. DuBois left Arista in early 2000 to work for Gaylord Entertainment Group, the Nashville-based company that owns the *Grand Ole Opry,* Acuff-Rose publishing, and other entertainment properties.

Dudley, Dave (1928–2003) *guitarist and singer*

Born David Darwin Pedruska, in Spencer, Wisconsin, on May 3, 1928, Dave was given his first guitar by his dad when he was just 11, but baseball was his life throughout his teen years. An arm injury while playing with the Gainesville, Texas, Owls led to his early retirement. He began working as a deejay at a Texas radio station, playing guitar along with the songs, until the station owner encouraged him to perform on his own. He then moved to Iowa and Idaho in the early 1950s, where he continued to perform with a number of groups to limited success. Dudley was struck by a hit-and-run driver when he was loading his guitar into his car in the early 1960s, further sidetracking his career. His luck changed soon after, when he released his ultimate trucker's anthem "Six Days on the Road," on the tiny Soma label in 1963. The song was a crossover hit on both pop and country charts.

He signed with Mercury in the same year, staying with the label for a dozen years and producing 25 country hits. The truck-driving themes continued with odes like "Two Six Packs Away" and "Trucker's Prayer," while he also tried to capture the "God, guts, and guns" conservative country market with his Vietnam War–era waxings of "Mama, Tell Them What We're Fighting For" penned by Tom T. Hall and Kris Kristofferson's "Vietnam Blues."

By the early 1970s he was back to truckin' themes with "Me and My Ole CB," "One AM Alone," and the 1980 hit that listed the contents of every trucker's medicine chest, "Rolaids, Doan's Pills and Preparation H," recorded for the revived Sun label. Dudley was less active in the 1980s and 1990s; he

died of an apparent heart attack at his home in Danbury, Wisconsin, on December 23, 2003.

Duke of Paducah, The (1901–1986)
performer

Benjamin Francis "Whitey" Ford was born in DeSoto, Missouri, on May 12, 1901, and raised by his grandmother in Little Rock, Arkansas. Ford's career is typical of many country musicians of his generation; he moved freely through a variety of styles, from Dixieland jazz, vaudeville pop, cowboy-western, to straight country. At the end of World War I he joined the navy where he learned the banjo, originally playing the tenor (or four-string) banjo in jazz styles. After touring vaudeville with his own dance band, he hooked up with Otto Gray's Oklahoma Cowboys. In the early 1930s he was hired to emcee Gene Autry's radio program on WLS in Chicago, where he acquired his comic persona and new stage name, the Duke of Paducah, with his famous closing line "I'm going to the wagon, these shoes are killin' me." He moved to Cincinnati's *Plantation Party* radio show in the mid-1930s, and then to the new *Renfro Valley* show in 1937.

During World War II, Ford toured various army installations as a comedian/musician, joining the *Grand Ole Opry* after the war ended and remaining a regular until 1959. In the 1950s and 1960s his homespun humor was so popular that he also developed an inspirational talk, called "You Can Lead a Happy Life," which he delivered to sales conventions and at colleges throughout the country. Although he continued to perform into the 1970s, his act changed little over the years. He died on June 20, 1986.

Duncan, Tommy (1911–1967) *singer*

Thomas Elmer Duncan was born in Hillsboro, Texas, on January 11, 1911. A pioneering western swing vocalist, Duncan teamed up with Bob Wills when both were members of the original Light Crust Doughboys in 1932. When Wills left to form his own band a year later, he took Duncan with him, and the two formed the Texas Playboys. It is Duncan's vocals that can be heard on most of Wills's classic recordings, including "San Antonio Rose," "Time Changes Everything," "Mississippi Muddy Water Blues" (adapted from JIMMIE RODGERS), and hundreds of others. When Wills went to the West Coast during World War II, Duncan went with him, but the old friends quarreled, and Wills fired Duncan in 1948. Duncan struck out on his own; his early solo recordings were still in a western swing style, but failed to catch on without Wills's name attached to them. In 1961–62 the duo reunited with some triumphant recordings for Liberty. Duncan died of a heart attack on July 25, 1967.

Earle, Steve (b. 1955) *singer and songwriter*
Born in San Antonio, Texas, on January 17, 1955, Earle came to Nashville in 1974, and began hanging out in local clubs with other displaced Texas singer/songwriters, including Townes Van Zandt and Guy Clark. After a brief move to Mexico in 1980, he returned to his native San Antonio. A year later he was back in Nashville, working as a songwriter and cutting his first demo recordings. He signed with Epic in 1983, releasing five singles, including one minor hit, "Nothin' but You." After being dropped by the label, Earle continued to write, and his songs were covered by some of the older country artists, including JOHNNY CASH and WAYLON JENNINGS.

Earle's 1986 album, *Guitar Town,* was his first release for MCA and seemed to come out of nowhere. Earle combined the sensibility of a Bruce Springsteen or John Cougar Mellencamp as a kind of "people's poet" along with a hard-rockin' attitude. The title hit is his best-known song, although the album's slow ballads, including "My Old Friend the Blues" and "Fearless Heart," are perhaps the true high points. However, Earle had difficulty following up on this success, despite continuing to record and perform through the early 1990s.

Earle made a remarkable comeback beginning in the mid-1990s with the album *Train A-Comin'.* He has produced a series of hard-edged country-rock albums, as well as an unusual collaboration with Del McCoury on an album of bluegrass-style originals, *The Mountain,* in 1999. With 2000's *Transcendental Blues,* Earle revealed bluegrass, rock, country, Celtic, and other musical influences. A year

later, he released *Jerusalem,* a collection of social-protest songs. Earle raised some eyebrows in 2002 with his song "John Walker's Blues," written in the voice of the young American who was captured in Afghanistan, aiding the Al Qaeda rebels who had targeted the United States.

Edwards, Don (b. 1939) *singer*
Although born in Boonton, New Jersey, on March 20, 1939, Edwards achieved fame as a new voice of the Old West. He was raised in rural New Jersey, where his father was a retired vaudevillian. Edwards moved to Texas in 1958, and, three years later, was hired as a performer at the Six Flags Over Texas theme park. In 1964 he cut his first record, "The Young Ranger." By the 1970s he was settled in Fort Worth, where he worked at the White Elephant Saloon. Two nights a week he performed solo, and on weekends he played there with his band, the 7-Bar Cowboys. He has also been a mainstay of the Cowboy Poetry Festival, held in Elko, Nevada, since its inception in 1984. He has since worked the growing cowboy poetry circuit.

Edwards's career was greatly boosted when he was signed to Warner Western Records in the mid-1990s. He recorded four albums for the label, producing the minor hit "West of Yesterday." He also appeared on Nanci Griffiths's Grammy-winning album *Other Voices, Other Rooms,* in 1993, singing a duet with her. In 1998 he was a featured performer in Robert Redford's film *The Horse Whisperer.* That same year Edwards released *My Hero, Gene Autry,* which was recorded live at Autry's 90th-birthday celebration.

Edwards, Stoney (b. 1929) *guitarist and songwriter*

Frenchy "Stoney" Edwards was born in Seminole, Oklahoma, on December 24, 1929. Of Indian, African-American, and Irish descent, Edwards was introduced to country music through his mother's brothers, who all played in a country style, and who encouraged him to listen to the *Grand Ole Opry.* Stoney learned to play guitar, fiddle, and piano by his early teens, playing primarily for his own amusement. After moving around Oklahoma and Texas, in the mid-1950s Stoney moved to the West Coast, where he married and began working in the Bay Area shipyards.

Stoney worked in the shipyards for 15 years, until two freak accidents—carbon monoxide poisoning, followed by a broken back—ended his career as a laborer. He returned to his first love, playing the guitar, and began composing songs in the mold of his idols, HANK WILLIAMS and LEFTY FRIZZELL. Performing at a BOB WILLS benefit concert in 1970, he was spotted by a talent scout for Capitol Records, who signed him to the label. He made his first album in 1971, and two years later had a minor hit with "Hank and Lefty Raised My Soul." His biggest hit came in 1974 with "Daddy Bluegrass," followed a year later by "Mississippi You're on My Mind."

Perhaps because he was of mixed ethnicity in a predominantly white field, or perhaps because his music was strongly influenced by 1950s honky-tonk, Edwards found that his career at Capitol quickly faded. He moved to smaller labels in the late 1970s, with minor success, and then relocated to Texas, where he has continued to perform locally for the last decades.

"El Paso" (1959) *country-folk ballad*

In the late 1950s, there were a number of country hits written in the style of traditional folk ballads; "El Paso" was one of the biggest, charting for half a year, and topping the country charts for seven weeks. The song gave a major boost to its composer MARTY ROBBINS, who also had the hit recording.

Emery, Ralph (b. 1933) *radio and television personality*

Warren Ralph Emery was born in McEwen, Tennessee, on March 10, 1933. He briefly studied at Belmont College in Nashville and also at a local broadcasting school. His first radio job was in tiny Paris, Tennessee, followed by a position in rural Louisiana.

At age 24, back in Nashville and unemployed, Emery applied for a position at the powerful WSM radio station. There was an opening for the grave-yard shift—10 P.M. to 3 A.M.—paying a grand salary of $50 a week. With nothing to lose, Emery encouraged both established stars and up-and-coming acts to stop by, play their records, and sit and chat. The down-home, relaxed atmosphere was greatly appealing, and soon a stop at Emery's show was an important step for record promotion. Plus, because WSM's signal was strong and many other stations were off the air during these hours, Emery's show could be heard in about 38 states—giving him virtually national exposure.

Although not particularly talented as a singer, Emery's popularity landed him a brief moment in the country spotlight. His single "Hello Fool"—an answer record to Faron Young's "Hello Walls"—was a number-four country hit in the early 1960s. He also parlayed his popularity into appearances in a few low-budget films, mostly with country or Nashville themes. Emery also expanded his radio presence with an afternoon show called "Sixteenth Avenue" broadcast from 1966 to 1969, and then launched his first nationally syndicated weekly series, "Pop Goes the Country," which ran eight years, from 1974 to 1982. As payback for his long nighttime service, WSM switched him to the morning drive slot in 1971.

The 1980s saw Emery make a major move into television. He first appeared on the cable network TBS with the *Nashville Alive* show in 1981–82, but it was his next show, the daily *Nashville Now,* broadcast on TNN, that established him as a major presence in this medium. The show ran for about a decade, from 1983 to 1993, with Emery as its host, and soon was attracting a million viewers a day. Emery left the show to start his own syndicated show, *On the Record,* which ran through the mid-1990s.

In 1991 Emery surprised the New York publishing world when his autobiography, *Memories,* became a best seller. Although Emery was virtually unknown outside of country circles, his fans snatched up the book, and this led to a new career as a memoirist. Emery has since written several more volumes, mixing his own life story with stories about the celebrities he has known.

Since the mid-1990s Emery has scaled back his own personal workload to focus on producing specials for cable stations and on occasional radio appearances. He was one of the hosts for the *Grand Ole Opry*'s 75th-birthday celebration in fall 2000 and continues to make local appearances in the Nashville area.

Evans, Sara (b. 1971) *singer*

Born in Boonville, Missouri, on February 5, 1971, Evans was raised on a rural tobacco farm. She began singing with her family bluegrass band at age four and was always the focus of the act. By the time Evans was 10 the family act was billed as "The Sara Evans Show." They traveled by RV to perform at grange halls throughout Missouri. In her early twenties Sara made her way to Nashville to try to establish a career as a singer. Her lucky break came in 1995 when songwriter Harlan Howard heard her singing his "I've Got a Tiger by the Tail" at a demo session. He convinced RCA to sign her.

In 1997 Evans released her first album, *Three Chords and the Truth.* The album was hailed by critics for its honky-tonk authenticity, and Evans's

Sara Evans on the red carpet at the CMA Awards (Raeanne Rubenstein)

vocals were praised as combining the best of LORETTA LYNN and PATSY CLINE. However, despite the accolades, sales were poor. Not surprisingly, Evans's second album, 1998's *No Place That Far,* was a sudden turn toward mainstream pop-country. Although not a major hit, the second album fared far better on the charts, and set the stage for Evans's major breakthrough, 2000's *Born to Fly.* The album spawned several top hits, including the title track and "I Could Not Ask for More." She followed up in 2003 with *Restless,* which had its first hit with the upbeat love song "Perfect."

Everly Brothers, The *performing brothers*
Coming out of a traditional family country-music band, Don (b. Issac Donald Everly, February 1, 1937) and Phil (b. Philip Everly, January 19, 1939) were born in Brownie, Kentucky. The boys got their start when Don was eight and Phil was six, touring and performing with their parents, Ike and Margaret Everly, and playing on the family's local radio show. Ike was a fine blues-style guitarist who was well known in the greater Kentucky region. When Phil graduated from high school, the duo hit the road for Nashville, and Don signed up with Acuff-Rose as a songwriter, penning "Thou Shalt Not Steal" for KITTY WELLS in 1954. Two years later, the brothers recorded a country single for Columbia called "Keep on Loving Me," produced by CHET ATKINS.

A year later they hooked up with Nashville powerhouse producer Wesley Rose, who brought them to Cadence Records and the country songwriting duo FELICE AND BOUDLEAUX BRYANT, and they struck gold with the pair's "Bye Bye Love." Although they were marketed as teen popsters, the Everlys never really shed their country identities, recording 1958's classic *Songs Our Daddy Taught Us,* a country tribute album, right in the midst of their more pop-oriented sessions.

The brothers left Cadence at the height of their popularity for the big bucks offered by Warner Brothers in 1960. Although they lost the songwriting services of the Bryants, they revealed themselves to be talented writers on their own with "(Til I) Kissed You" and "When Will I Be Loved." Their string of good luck ended in 1963 during a tour of England; although it was reported at the time that Don had suffered from a "nervous breakdown," he later admitted that an addiction to prescription pills was the real problem. The brothers struggled, searching for a new identity through the 1960s. During this time their best work was issued on *Roots,* a nod to their country childhood, including a fragment of one of the family's radio shows. They also put out a fine country-pop album, *Pass the Chicken and Listen,* in the early 1970s, produced by Atkins.

In 1973 the duo split up during a performance at Knott's Berry Farm. Don spent most of the next 10 years recording country material in the United States for Hickory and other labels, while Phil went to Europe, where the brothers always had a strong following, to pursue a more pop-oriented career. They reunited in 1983 with the country and pop hit "On the Wings of a Nightingale," written for them by Paul McCartney. Since the late 1980s the duo have reunited for annual tours, including a long-standing engagement in Las Vegas.

Fargo, Donna (b. 1945) *singer and songwriter*
Yvonne Vaughan was born in Mount Airy, North Carolina, on November 10, 1945. The daughter of a big tobacco farmer, she attended college locally, earning a teaching degree, and eventually settled in California to teach. There she met singer/guitarist Stan Silver, who became her biggest booster, her manager, and her husband. He encouraged her to learn the guitar, sing, and write her own material. When she was in her late twenties, she took the stage name of Donna Fargo, recording a single for the Phoenix-based Ramco label; in 1968 she went to Nashville to record the racy (for the time) "Who's Been Sleeping on My Side of the Bed?," which was boycotted by many country stations that thought it too suggestive.

After recording for a number of small labels, Fargo finally achieved a major hit with her "Happiest Girl in the Whole U.S.A.," picked up nationally by Dot Records in 1972, which rocketed to number one on the country charts and earned her a Grammy. The followup was another upbeat anthem, "Funny Face," cementing her image as a well-scrubbed eternal optimist.

Fargo remained with Dot through 1976, when she signed a million-dollar contract with Warner Brothers. The variety of her material increased, ranging from the rocker "Superman" in 1973 to the slightly feminist "A Song with No Music" (1976) that told of the unhappiness of a woman caught in a difficult relationship. In the late 1970s she moved from her own compositions to covering country-pop standards, including "Mockingbird Hill" and "Walk On By." She also landed her own syndicated TV show and appeared to be poised for pop-crossover stardom.

In 1978, however, Fargo learned she had multiple sclerosis. Although she continued to perform into the 1980s, she was increasingly debilitated by her disease. She did manage a comeback hit in 1986, "Woman of the 1980s," which was more progressive than her earlier material in subject matter (it documented the trials and tribulations of five different women struggling with their new roles in a changing world). Fargo has continued to tour through the 1990s, focusing on gospel-tinged material along with her hits. She has also written an inspirational collection available in book form or on her own line of greeting cards.

Fender, Freddy (b. 1937) *singer and actor*
Baldemar G. Huerta was born in San Benito, Texas, on January 4, 1937 to a migrant farmworker family who roamed throughout the Southwest. He took an early interest in the guitar and sang in Spanish. He dropped out of high school at age 16 to join the Marine Corps. At age 19 he began to play local clubs, taking the name "Freddy Fender." With club owner Wayne Duncan, Fender cowrote and recorded "Wasted Days and Wasted Nights," a local hit released nationally on Imperial. In 1960 Fender was convicted on possession of marijuana charges and spent three years in jail. JIMMIE DAVIS, governor of Louisiana and himself a country singer, arranged for his release, with the proviso that he abandon

country music as a career. Fender quickly returned to performing, although his recording career was virtually ended.

In 1974 Huey Meaux, a famous Louisiana-based producer of R&B recordings, produced Fender's most successful recordings. His biggest hit was 1975's "Before the Next Teardrop Falls," sung half in English and half in Spanish, along with a remake of "Wasted Days and Wasted Nights." Fender's first few singles charted on both country and pop charts, although most of the rest of his hits in the late 1970s appealed primarily to a country audience.

Fender spent most of the 1980s pursuing an acting career, achieving his most high-profile role in 1988 in Robert Redford's film *The Milagro Beanfield War*. Late in the decade, he teamed up with long-time bar-band friends Doug Sahm and Augie Meyers, of the Tex-Mex rock band The Sir Douglas Quintet, along with Flaco Jimenez, one of the masters of Tex-Mex accordion, to form the supergroup the Texas Tornados, gaining some success on the country and pop charts. The band performed and recorded together through the 1990s before officially breaking up in 1999.

In 1998 Fender appeared as a member of Los Super Seven, a supergroup of Mexican-American artists put together by David Hidalgo and Cesar Rosas of the rootsy rock group Los Lobos to record an album of traditional Mexican songs. Fender continues to record and tour as a solo artist. After being diagnosed with hepatitis, he underwent a kidney transplant in early 2002. That same year, he released a Spanish-language album under his birth name, *La Música de Baldemar Huerta*.

fiddle

Perhaps the best-known instrument in all of country music, the fiddle is traditional in the music of the British Isles and Appalachian and southwestern America.

Many new listeners wonder what the difference is between the fiddle and the violin. The difference does not lie in the structure of the instrument—although many fiddlers modify their violins in several important ways—but in the style of playing the instrument.

English, Irish, and Scottish immigrants came to the United States in several waves, beginning in the early 18th century and continuing through the 20th century. Each new wave brought its own music, and new, homegrown fiddle styles also developed, particularly in the South and Southwest. Tunes came from the various British traditions but also from minstrel shows and from the popular classical music of the day. There was also a wealth of composers who added an American sound to the fiddle tradition.

Several regional fiddle traditions have been well documented in the United States. Texas has been the home of some of the greatest "show" fiddlers. They have developed a flashy style of playing improvisations on traditional tunes, tinged with jazz and other more modern syncopated dance musics. Texas has a long tradition of virtuoso fiddlers, beginning with Alexander Campbell "Eck" Robertson, usually cited as the first southern fiddler to make a record, in 1922. His version of "Sally Goodin" and "The Brilliancy Medley" set the standard for elaborate and breathtaking variations. Over the years Texas has spawned many other virtuosic fiddlers, so that fancy fiddling in general is known as "Texas" or "contest style."

The fiddle survived as the key melody instrument in both old-time string bands and in the more modern BLUEGRASS band. But its true importance in country music was its role as the main melody instrument on countless Nashville recording sessions, beginning in the early 1950s. All of HANK WILLIAMS's recordings featured a prominent fiddle part played by Tommy Jackson; the bluesy, lonesome sound of Williams's voice was perfectly echoed by the fiddle. Jackson would go on to become a major player in Nashville's so-called A team of session musicians through the 1950s and 1960s. The fiddle was thus established as a must-have instrument on almost any country recording, although it was less prominently featured in "crossover" recordings aimed at the mainstream pop market.

When country musicians began to return to their roots in the early 1980s, it was natural for the fiddler to return to the fore. Meanwhile, young bluegrass and old-time revivalists were learning to play the instrument, mostly through recordings of earlier musicians. One musician who became particularly prominent as both a Nashville session player and as a soloist was Mark O'Connor, who had been a teen bluegrass champion. ALISON KRAUSS has opened a new chapter in bluegrass fiddle history by playing the instrument as leader of her band, Union Station. Prior to her success, the instrument was rarely played by a woman as a bandleader (or even as a backup musician).

Today no reputable country act would tour without a fiddler, although the fiddle player's style may owe as much to electric guitar riffs as it does to traditional fiddle tunes. Amplified instruments and special effects abound; often the fiddle is limited to just an occasional fill here or there. But the fiddler has to be onstage—and very few country artists risk the wrath of the audience by failing to deliver on this account.

Flatt and Scruggs (1948–1969)

Lester Raymond Flatt (b. Duncan's Chapel, Tennessee, June 14, 1914–May 11, 1979) came from a musical family; both of his parents played the banjo in the old-time or frailing style, and he soon learned to play banjo, along with guitar and mandolin. After working in a textile mill and performing semiprofessionally with his wife through the 1930s and early 1940s, Flatt was invited by BILL MONROE to join his new group, the Blue Grass Boys.

Earl Eugene Scruggs (b. Flint Hill, North Carolina, January 6, 1924) also came from a musical family. He took up the banjo at an early age and, inspired by the picking of local banjo whiz Snuffy Jenkins, began playing in a three-finger picked style. He was performing as early as age six with his brothers and had a radio job with the Carolina Wildcats by the time he was 15 years old. During World War II he worked in a textile mill, but by the war's end he hooked up with "Lost" John Miller, who broadcast out of Nashville. When Miller quit touring, Scruggs was hired to join the Monroe band, just after Flatt had come on board.

The Bill Monroe Blue Grass Boys of 1946–48 is a legendary band, in many ways serving as the archetype of all bluegrass bands that followed. Because mandolinist Monroe had a high tenor voice, he switched Flatt to singing lead and playing guitar, with Scruggs prominently featured playing his new style of banjo. When the band began broadcasting on Nashville's *Grand Ole Opry,* listeners were astonished by their power; many couldn't believe that Scruggs was playing a five-string banjo. Their recordings of such Monroe standards as "Blue Moon of Kentucky" and "Molly and Tenbrooks," along with new instrumentals like "Bluegrass Breakdown" that prominently featured Scruggs, were immediate sensations.

Monroe was a difficult taskmaster who worked his band hard for long hours. In 1948 Flatt and Scruggs quit the band. They signed a deal with Mercury Records and took the name the Foggy Mountain Boys after the Carter Family song "Foggy Mountain Top." Flatt and Scruggs's most famous recording of this period is the 1949 instrumental "Foggy Mountain Breakdown," which would be used 18 years later as the theme for the 1967 film *Bonnie and Clyde.*

The group was signed to a radio job in Bristol, Vancouver, where their broadcasts influenced local musicians like the STANLEY BROTHERS and Don Reno to play in the new bluegrass style. They signed with Columbia Records in 1950. One of their first recordings for the new label was 1951's "Earl's Breakdown." By quickly turning the pegs on the banjo, Scruggs was able to drop a note a full pitch after he had struck it. A few years later, he developed special tuners, now known as Scruggs's pegs, to automatically drop or raise a string's pitch.

In 1953 the band signed on with flour maker Martha White, who became their sponsor for many

Earl Scruggs (center, with banjo) and Lester Flatt (with guitar) c. mid-1950s (University of North Carolina, Southern Historical Collection, Southern Folklife Collection, University Archives)

years on the radio, TV, and tours. They were invited to join the *Grand Ole Opry* in 1955, the same year they launched their first syndicated television program. Through the later 1950s they toured widely on the bluegrass circuit.

In the early 1960s Columbia started to market the group to the folk-revival audience. Assigned a younger producer, they began recording songs by Bob Dylan and Pete Seeger, among others. They also were hired to perform the theme for *The*

Beverly Hillbillies TV program, resulting in their first pop hit, 1962's "Ballad of Jed Clampett." They made guest appearances on the show that further promoted the group. Their big break came in 1967 when several of their songs were used in the film *Bonnie and Clyde,* which attracted a hipper, younger audience. However, as their recordings moved increasingly in a pop direction, Flatt became disillusioned with the new sound. Always a traditionalist, he wanted to return to recording the music that had made them famous. Scruggs, on the other hand, had two young sons who played contemporary music, and wanted to broaden his musical horizons. This led to the duo splitting in 1969.

Flatt formed the Nashville Grass, a traditional bluegrass band, which he continued to lead until his death in 1979. Scruggs formed the Earl Scruggs Revue with his sons Randy and Gary, along with Dobroist Josh Graves. By the mid-1970s the band had pretty much run out of steam, and Scruggs went into retirement, performing only on occasion. In 2001 his son Randy produced a new album by the veteran picker, bringing him together with many young Nashville stars. Flatt and Scruggs were inducted into the Country Music Hall of Fame in 1985.

Flying Burrito Brothers, The

The Flying Burrito Brothers were a seminal 1960s country-rock band, featuring Gram Parsons's emotional lead vocals and excellent original songs until he left the group in 1970. After the original lineup dissolved, they remained popular in Europe for years, leading many different lineups to tour through the mid-1980s.

After recording *Sweetheart of the Rodeo,* the Byrds's foray into country rock, Byrds founder Chris Hillman and newcomer Gram Parsons left the band to pursue country rock to its logical conclusions. In forming the Flying Burrito Brothers, they were among the first to incorporate a pedal steel guitar into a pop-rock band (the whining pedal steel being a hallmark of most country recordings of the era).

The original group recorded their debut album, *The Gilded Palace of Sin,* featuring Parson's update of a country honky-tonk ballad, "Sin City." Other notable songs popularized by the band included a countrified cover of "Wild Horses," by the Rolling Stones, the ever-popular "Devil in Disguise," cowritten by Hillman and Parsons and covered by a staple of progressive bluegrass bands through the 1970s, and "Hot Burrito #2 (I'm Your Boy)," a composition by Chris Ethridge and Parsons.

While the group's first album was being made, drummer Jon Corneal left and was replaced by ex-Byrds drummer Michael Clarke; soon after, Ethridge left, replaced by Hillman on bass, with the addition of Bernie Leadon on guitar and vocals. The second album was completed and released as *Burrito Deluxe* in 1970, but arguments among Parsons and the rest of the band led to another shakeup, with Parsons embarking on a solo career and replaced by Rick Roberts. The more-or-less original group released one more album, but it suffered from Parsons's absence.

Further defections came in mid-1971, when Leadon left to form the Eagles and Pete Kleinow also retired; replacements were Al Perkins (pedal steel), Byron Berline (fiddle), Roger Bush (bass), and Kenny Wertz (guitar) as a live touring band. This ensemble lasted until late 1971, when Hillman and Perkins joined ex-Buffalo Springfield leader Stephen Stills to form the short-lived country rock outfit Manassas; the balance of the band, without Roberts, became the nucleus of Country Gazette, a bluegrass-oriented band. Roberts, meanwhile, enlisted yet another group to make a final European tour before forming the rock group Firefall in 1972.

Original members Ethridge and Kleinow revived the "Burrito" name for two mid-1970s Columbia albums, featuring the duo of Gib Guibeau (fiddle) and Gene Parsons (drums; no relation to Gram) along with bassist Joel Scott-Hill. That group held on until the mid-1980s with varying personnel, but none of these later recordings were anywhere near as good as their original albums. Surprisingly, in 1999 Kleinow paired with singer/songwriter John Beland (along with an all-star studio cast) in a revived Flying Burrito Brothers, producing a single album.

"Foggy Mountain Breakdown" (1949)
bluegrass banjo instrumental
This tune was first recorded by FLATT AND SCRUGGS in 1949. It was composed by banjoist Earl Scruggs as a showpiece for the new bluegrass style. The song

was revived in 1967 in the film *Bonnie and Clyde* as its instrumental theme music, introducing it to a new generation. It remains one of the "test pieces" for all would-be bluegrass players.

Foley, Red (1910–1968) *singer*

Clyde Julian Foley was born in Blue Lark, Kentucky, on June 17, 1910. He spent most of his high school and college years on the athletic field, winning numerous awards. He won an amateur singing contest at age 17, and three years later he was hired by country radio producer John Lair to be the vocalist with the WLS *National Barn Dance* radio program. Seven years later, Lair built a new radio show, the *Renfro Valley Barn Dance,* around Foley. Foley became a big star thanks to this radio exposure, which continued through the 1940s on WLS, the *Grand Ole Opry,* and finally, in 1954–61, on the early country-music television program *Ozark Jubilee,* based in Springfield, Missouri.

In 1941 Decca records signed Foley to a lifetime contract. His first recordings were in a sentimental vein, including 1945's "Old Shep" and 1947's "Foggy River." In the early 1950s he showed an interest in rockabilly and bop, laying down "Sugarfoot Rag" with guitarist Hank Garland; the two would make many other rockabilly recordings, including "Birmingham Bounce" in 1950 and the square dance favorite "Alabama Jubilee" in 1951. Foley was also interested in R&B, and he recorded covers of "Shake a Hand" (an early ode to integration originally recorded by Faye Adams) and "Hearts of Stone" (originally by the Charms) in the early 1950s. His biggest hit was 1951's "Peace in the Valley," said to be the first gospel song ever to sell a million copies on disc.

In the 1960s Foley continued to be a popular attraction, and he even appeared for one season on a network TV show, *Mr. Smith Goes to Washington,* costarring with Fess ("Davy Crockett") Parker. Foley died of a heart attack on September 19, 1968, after a performance, one year after he was inducted into the Country Music Hall of Fame.

Ford, Tennessee Ernie (1919–1991) *singer*

Ernest Jennings Ford was born in Bristol, Tennessee, on February 13, 1919, and did not have a particularly rural upbringing; Bristol was a Southern mill town, and Ford sang in the high school choir and played in the school band. When he was 18, he got his first job as an announcer at a local radio station, and then enrolled in the Cincinnati Conservatory of Music for classical music training. After serving in World War II he returned to radio work in Pasadena, California, and began working as a vocalist with Cliffie Stone, a prominent West Coast musician, bandleader, and promoter who quickly took Ford under his wing. As an executive of the newly formed Capitol Records, Stone got Ford his recording contract and went on to manage his lengthy career.

Signed to Capitol Records in 1948, Ford had a number of hits with pseudo-western numbers, beginning with 1949's "Mule Train," "Smokey Mountain Boogie," and "Anticipation Blues," jazzy renderings of pop songs written in the style of country blues and cowboy numbers. A year later he scored big with his own composition "Shotgun Boogie." The hit led to his own network radio show.

In 1955 Ford covered MERLE TRAVIS's "Sixteen Tons," a song about the life of a coal miner that Travis had written in the folk style. Ford's rendition became a massive hit, decked out with a crooning chorus and pop-like instrumental arrangement. Following its success on pop and country charts, Ford had his own TV variety show on NBC, lasting until 1961, besides his regular appearances on a number of other shows, making him a familiar face in American households.

In the early 1960s Ford turned to more conservative material, recording country's first million-selling album in 1963, *Hymns,* the first in a series of religious recordings. Balancing this with remakes of patriotic material like "America the Beautiful," Ford became a leading conservative voice in the country hierarchy. Although he had a chart hit in 1971 with "Happy Songs of Love," Ford's career had pretty much ended by that time, although he could still be heard performing live into the 1980s.

In 1990 he was inducted into the Country Music Hall of Fame. A year later he collapsed at a White House dinner, and he died of liver disease soon after on October 17, 1991.

Forester Sisters, The *performing sisters*

Born in Lookout Mountain, Georgia, to a farmer father and millworker mother, the four daughters— Kathy (January 4, 1955), June (September 22, 1956), Kim (November 4, 1960), and Christy Forester (December 21, 1962)—were early stars at their local church from the mid-1970s. They formed their first band in 1978 to play local clubs while Christy and Kim were still in college and June and Kathy were working as grade-school teachers. A demo tape landed them a contract with Warner Brothers in 1984, and their first hit came a year later, the uptempo "(That's What You Do) When You're in Love." They followed this a year later with the play on words of "Lyin' in His Arms Again," the story of a spunky girl who has cheated on her man (a reversal of the typical country sex roles).

The Foresters' first recordings were produced by Wendy Waldman, who had had a career as a folk-rock singer-songwriter in the 1970s. Waldman supplied them with one of their most moving early hits, 1988's "Letter Home." This simple narrative about a woman who was the high school queen, married young and foolishly, and then was deserted by her husband and left to raise the kids, focuses on issues most traditional country songs avoided.

The Forresters' early 1990s hits continued to emphasize their spunky female point of view. Their recordings took on a more jazzy, almost western swing approach with 1991's scornful "Men," and the not-quite-over-the-hill older woman's anthem, 1992's "I Got a Date," with its playful video. However, a four-year gap followed while the band turned to recording gospel music. Their last country-pop album appeared in 1996 and produced no hits.

Foster and Lloyd *vocal duo*

Typical of mid-1980s country acts, the duo of Radney Foster (b. Del Rio, Texas, July 20, 1959) and Bill Lloyd (b. Bowling Green, Kentucky, December 6, 1955) brought many influences to their music, from country rock sounds inspired by the Eagles to the smooth harmonies of the EVERLY BROTHERS and John Lennon and Paul McCartney of the Beatles, to the honky-tonk blues of HANK WILLIAMS. Their biggest hit was their first single, 1987's "Crazy over You," which combined an intelligent lyric with a solid beat.

Radney Foster went solo in 1992, and Lloyd dropped out of the music scene. Foster's first album featured support from other new country acts, including MARY CHAPIN CARPENTER and John Hiatt. Two further albums followed in the mid-1990s, but Foster was unable to duplicate the earlier success of Foster and Lloyd. After a few years off record, he returned in mid-2001 with a live album, *Are You Ready for the Big Show?* The first single, "Texas in 1880," received some airplay.

Fricke, Janie (b. 1947) *singer*

Janie Marie Fricke (later Frickie) was born in South Whitley, Indiana, on December 19, 1947. Inspired by Joan Baez and Judy Collins, Fricke took up playing the guitar in her teen years. She eventually relocated to Memphis, where she began working as a backup singer for jingles. She made her way to Nashville, where she worked many country sessions as an anonymous vocalist. Fricke was signed by famed producer Billy Sherrill to a solo contract in 1977. Sherrill first asked Fricke to overdub a harmony part on CHARLIE RICH's "On My Knees," giving her her first label credit as a backup singer; the song shot to number one, helping to launch Fricke's career. Her first number-one solo hit was 1982's "Don't Worry 'Bout Me Baby," with backup vocals by soon-to-be new country star RICKY SKAGGS. It was followed that year by "It Ain't Easy Bein' Easy," and her 1983 hit "He's a Heartache (Looking for a Place to Happen)."

Fricke's success lasted through the mid-1980s. She cut one more session as an overdub singer, accompanying MERLE HAGGARD on his number one "A Place to Fall Apart" in 1985. Her last number-one hit came with 1986's "Always Have, Always Will"; at this time, she added an "i" to her last name, because people were always mispronouncing it as "Frick," but then reverted to the normal spelling. After 1989 she ceased recording for Columbia. In 2000 she released her first album in seven years on her own JMF label, aptly titled *Bouncin' Back*.

"Friends in Low Places" (1990) *Garth Brooks hit*

This clever updating of a classic honky-tonk theme is driven by Garth Brooks's excellent comic performance. The song's protagonist is a good old boy who mistakenly gets involved with an uptown girl. The woman's "friends in high places" fail to impress the song's hero, and he ends up leaving her for the happier world of the barroom. The song was given the Country Music Association's "Song of the Year" award.

Frizzell, Lefty (1928–1975) *singer*

William Orville Frizzell was born in Corsicana, Texas, on March 31, 1928, the son of a footloose oil field worker. A common public relations myth was that he gained his nickname "Lefty" thanks to a teenage career as a Golden Gloves boxer; however, Frizzell never actually boxed. He began performing in Dallas and Waco-area honky-tonks covering the hits of his two idols, JIMMIE RODGERS and ERNEST TUBB. His first hit came in 1950 with "If You Got the Money, Honey, I've Got the Time," a classic honky-tonk song. Four records in 1951 all made the country top 10 at the same time. Lefty was poised to be more popular than HANK WILLIAMS,

but then his hits dried up. In 1953 Frizzell moved to Los Angeles and became a regular on the popular TV show *Town Hall Party*.

In the late 1950s Frizzell abandoned his beer-soaked honky-tonk sound to make a number of popular folk-style, story-song records, including 1959's "Long Black Veil" and 1964's "Saginaw, Michigan." Sadly, this was his last hurrah as a charting performer; alcohol took its toll on his recordings and live performances, although he continued to perform until his death on July 19, 1975. By then, he was more or less forgotten by mainstream Nashville, although his recordings would influence the next generation of country performers.

His younger brother, David (b. Corsicana, Texas, September 26, 1941), had several hits in the early 1980s, including several successful duets with singer Shelly West and a few solo recordings.

"The Fugitive" ("I'm a Lonesome Fugitive") (1967) *Merle Haggard's first number-one song*

"The Fugitive" (which became known as "I'm a Lonesome Fugitive") was MERLE HAGGARD's first "signature song." The songwriters were inspired by the hit TV show of the same name, but Haggard made the song a part of his (professional) autobiography. The theme of the lone man who, due to his youthful indiscretions, is condemned to a life of fleeing the law, is supported by the simple arrangement, introduced by a fingerpicked acoustic guitar and the subdued backing track (with just a hint of vocal support on the chorus). But the underlying anger of the man who "would like to settle down/but they won't let me" is projected through the brief, but stabbing electric guitar break (probably played by James Burton), which is briefly reprised as the song fades out. Haggard's "outlaw" stance resonated in the later 1960s/early 1970s work of the country outlaws, including WAYLON JENNINGS and WILLIE NELSON.

Gatlin Brothers, The *performing brothers*

The Gatlin Brothers were a popular three-part harmony group of the 1970s and 1980s. Larry, the eldest brother (b. Lawrence Wayne Gatlin, Seminole, Texas, May 2, 1948; guitar, vocal), was the prime force behind the group and its main songwriter. He was joined in the group by his siblings Steve (b. Steven Daryl Gatling, Olney, Texas, April 4, 1951; guitar, vocal) and Rudy [b. Rudy Michael Gatlin, Olney, Texas, August 20, 1952; bass, vocal). All three brothers performed together as children, beginning in church. This led to a stint as a gospel group on Slim Willet's Abilene-based TV show when they were in their teens; they also recorded a religious album for the tiny Sword & Shield label. Soon after, Larry went into music full time. He first worked with the Imperials, a gospel-harmony outfit out of Las Vegas that accompanied many major country artists, including Elvis Presley. In 1972 DOTTIE WEST encouraged him to move to Nashville, where, a year later, he signed with the Monument label, scoring his first hit in 1976 with his song "Broken Lady."

Meanwhile, brothers Steve and Rudy finished their education and came to Nashville to audition as backup singers for CHARLEY PRIDE; they eventually worked for TAMMY WYNETTE, but left her to rejoin reform their group after Larry's first single hit. Larry continued as a solo act backed by his siblings until 1978, when "I Just Wish You Were Someone I Love" hit number one, credited to "Larry Gatlin with Brothers and Friends." Their next single went to number two as "The Gatlin Brothers Band," and by the end of the year the major labels were pursuing them. They also began appearing on TV variety shows, spreading their appeal well beyond the country audience.

In 1979 the Gatlins scored their next number-one hit, their first for new label Columbia, titled "All the Gold in California." The next three and a half years had their ups and downs as Larry battled alcohol and drug addiction, turning out only a few minor hits. In 1983 they hit number one again with "Houston (Means I'm Closer to You)," although Larry was at a personal low point. This swinging number was an immediate sensation, and was followed by another city ode, "Denver." Then Larry checked himself into drug rehab and finally broke a decade-long pattern of abuse. The Gatlins continued to record for Columbia through 1988, scoring hits with "The Lady Takes the Cowboy Every Time" and "Talkin' to the Moon." They signed with the smaller Universe label in 1988, reflecting the fact that their close harmonies and pop arrangements were losing appeal on the charts.

Still, the Gatlins remain a big draw in Las Vegas and other lounge venues. Larry briefly became a Broadway star playing the lead in *The Will Rogers Follies* in 1992. In 1993 the brothers opened a theater in Branson, Missouri, which became their main performing venue. They have continued to appear there and in vacation spots like Las Vegas over the decade, recording for the small Branson Sound label.

Gayle, Crystal (b. 1951) *singer*

The youngest sister of country star LORETTA LYNN, Brenda Gail Webb was born in Paintsville, Kentucky, on January 9, 1951. She began her career when she was 16, singing backup vocals for her sister and CONWAY TWITTY. Loretta Lynn gave her her stage name, perhaps inspired by the country chain of Krystal hamburger stands. Gayle made her first solo recordings at age 19 with her sister's country weeper "I Cried (The Blue Right out of My Eyes)," but did not crack the country charts again for five years.

Resisting the efforts of Nashville to mold her into a younger version of Loretta Lynn, Gayle finally hooked up with producer Allen Reynolds, who supplied her 1975 hit "Wrong Road Again." Three years later she scored a major pop crossover hit with the lounge favorite, "Don't It Make My Brown Eyes Blue," her best-known recording. She had a few more pop successes in the late 1970s.

In the 1980s Gayle returned to her roots as a country chanteuse, having country hits with a cover of JIMMIE RODGERS's "Miss the Mississippi and You" in 1981 and 1986's "Cry." However, by the late 1980s, when "new country" was in full swing, Gayle's more relaxed vocal style and the mainstream production values of her recordings made her sound decidedly old-fashioned, even to country listeners. Still, she continues to be a steady concert draw and regular performer, although she limits her performances primarily to friendly venues in Branson, Missouri, and Europe.

"Gentle on My Mind" (1967) *first major hit for country singer Glen Campbell*

"Gentle on Mind," was composed by JOHN HARTFORD, an unusual figure on the Nashville songwriting scene, and became GLEN CAMPBELL's first big hit. Hartford was a banjo-playing fan of bluegrass music from Missouri who was influenced by Bob Dylan's mid-1960s stream-of-consciousness songs in composing this song. The music licensing company BMI has said that it is the second most recorded song in their catalog, with more than 800 cover versions. It is also noteworthy for being one of the few major pop hits that lacks a repeated chorus.

Gentry, Bobbie (b. 1944) *singer and songwriter*

Born Roberta Streeter in Chickasaw County, Mississippi, on July 27, 1944, Gentry first learned piano by imitating the sounds she heard in church. The family relocated to Southern California when she was 13, and there she took up a number of other instruments, including guitar, banjo, and bass. While studying philosophy at UCLA, Gentry began performing an occasional club date; her love of music led her to enroll at the Los Angeles Conservatory of Music, and she made a demo tape of her songs that she circulated among local record labels. Los Angeles–based Capitol Records signed her in 1967, and her first record, the self-penned "Ode to Billy Joe," was an immediate sensation on country and pop charts. An album followed, with several more songs inspired by her country childhood, including "Okohona River Bottom Band" and "Chickasaw County Child" (released as a single in 1968). Gentry recorded an album of duets with GLEN CAMPBELL, another Capitol artist, in 1969, scoring hits with "Let It Be Me" and "All I Have to Do Is Dream," both originally recorded by the EVERLY BROTHERS.

Gentry spent the early 1970s performing as a Las Vegas lounge star, while her records virtually disappeared from the charts. Her career was temporarily revived in 1976 when a film based on her famous song was released, but her marriage to songwriter/performer Jim Stafford two years later led to her retirement as a performer, although she remained active in song publishing.

Gibson, Don (1928–2003) *singer and songwriter*

Donald Eugene Gibson was born in Shelby, North Carolina, on April 3, 1928. He was already a fine guitarist during his school days, playing local dances and radio jobs. He signed on with the radio show *Tennessee Barn Dance,* out of Knoxville, in 1946, and began recording soon after. However, Gibson's vocal style didn't mature until he linked up with Nashville producer CHET ATKINS, who signed him to RCA in 1957. For the next seven years the pair produced some of the more listenable of the pop-oriented Nashville recordings. Meanwhile, Gibson's career as a songwriter also took off, with the success of KITTY WELLS's cover of "I Can't Stop Lovin' You" in 1957 (later a hit for RAY CHARLES in 1962) and the posthumous release of "Sweet Dreams" by PATSY CLINE in 1963.

Gibson's own first hit was the double-sided "Oh Lonesome Me" backed with "I Can't Stop Lovin' You" of 1958. That same year, he made his first appearance on the *Grand Ole Opry.* His follow-up hits included further deep-voiced weepers, notably "Blue Blue Day," "Give Myself a Party," and "Lonesome Number One." His last big hit was 1961's "Sea of Heartbreak." In 1964 Gibson gave up his *Grand Ole Opry* membership; as other artists had, he found the demands of playing regularly on the *Opry* restrictive.

Gibson continued to record through the 1960s, as a soloist and in duets with DOTTIE WEST, although an increasing dependence on pills and alcohol slowed his career. He made a comeback in the 1970s, most notably as a duet partner with Sue Thompson, scoring a number-one country hit with "Woman (Sensuous Woman)" in 1972. In 1975 he returned to the *Opry* as a member and scored minor country hits through 1980. Gibson continued to be an attraction on tour and performed on the *Grand Ole Opry* until shortly before his death. In 2001 he was elected into the Country Music Hall of Fame. He died on November 17, 2003.

Gill, Vince (b. 1957) *singer*

Born Vincent Grant Gill in Norman, Oklahoma, on April 12, 1957, Gill was the son of a judge. He began playing bluegrass guitar and banjo in his early teens. He then joined with RICKY SKAGGS in the short-lived progressive bluegrass band Boone Creek. Later he

performed with country-rock outfits including Sundance and the Pure Prairie League, before joining RODNEY CROWELL's backup band, the Cherry Bombs. Although he began recording as a solo artist in 1984, he didn't break through until 1990 with the hit ballad "When I Call Your Name." This led to his induction into the *Grand Ole Opry* a year later.

Gill's greatest chart successes occurred between 1994 and 1996, often with sentimental ballads, including his song written in honor of his father, "Go Rest High on That Mountain" (winner in 1997 of a BMI Most Performed Song Award, along with

Vince Gill performing, 2000 (Raeanne Rubenstein)

his number-one hit of that year, "Pretty Little Adriana"). A popular figure on the music scene, he has scored 14 Grammys out of a total of 30 nominations; his 14 wins put him in a league with Eric Clapton and in front of Michael Jackson and Paul McCartney.

Gilley, Mickey (b. 1936) *singer*

Mickey Leroy Gilley was born on March 9, 1936. His mother was the sister of Jerry Lee Lewis's dad, making them first cousins; Gilley was raised in Lewis's hometown of Ferriday. By 1956 Gilley had moved to Houston, and he began recording for a number of small Texas labels, performing in the style of his more famous cousin. Gilley spent much of the 1950s and 1960s laboring as a local favorite, with an occasional moderate hit, primarily limited to Texas radio. By the early 1970s he had opened his own club, Gilley's Bar, which eight years later would inspire the "urban cowboy" movement, first in an article in *Esquire* magazine, and then in the 1980 film of the same name.

Gilley's career, meanwhile, had ticked upward a little. A local disc jockey asked him to record his composition "She Calls Me Baby," and he backed it with a remake of George Morgan's 1949 hit "Room Full of Roses"; the B side became Gilley's first certifiable hit, leading to a contract with Playboy Records. When the record was reissued by Playboy, it shot to number one in 1974. "I Overlooked an Orchid," Gilley's second single and another flower-themed song, did equally well, and it was followed by a string of recordings, including 1975's "Roll You Like a Wheel" (a duet with ex-Playmate Barbi Benton), 1976's "Don't the Girls All Get Prettier at Closing Time," and 1977's "Honky Tonk Memories."

In 1979 Gilley signed with Epic Records, just in time to cash in on the urban cowboy craze. His remake of the Ben E. King classic "Stand by Me" was featured in the *Urban Cowboy* film, becoming an immediate hit, and was followed by more standard early 1980s country fare, including several number-

one hits, 1980's "True Love Ways," and "That's All That Matters," 1981's "A Headache Tomorrow (Or a Heartache Tonight)," 1982's "Put Your Dreams Away," and 1983's "Fool for Your Love." Gilley himself had one further hit, 1986's "Doo Wah Days," a nostalgic look at 1950s rock. By the end of the 1980s Gilley had faded from the charts in the face of new country music, and his club closed its doors in 1989, although a new Gilley's has been opened in Branson, Missouri.

Gimble, Johnny (b. 1926) *fiddle player*

John Paul Gimble was born near Tyler, Texas, on May 30, 1926. He showed an early talent for music, playing banjo and mandolin. He joined his brothers' group, the Rose City Hipsters, in his early teen years; the band played locally for dances and parties, as well as broadcasting over Tyler's radio station. When he was 17, he was hired to play with the Shelton Brothers, leading to work with JIMMIE DAVIS.

After World War II, western swing master BOB WILLS hired Gimble, originally to play mandolin, although soon his talents as a fiddler showed through. He remained with Wills through the 1950s, and his jazz-influenced fiddling, with its rich tone, became a hallmark of Wills's later recordings. In the 1960s and early 1970s Gimble worked as a Nashville studio musician; he rejoined Wills in 1973 for the Texas Playboys reunion album that was inspired by MERLE HAGGARD's love for western swing; Gimble then performed through the 1970s with several alumni of Wills's band, recording several albums.

From 1979 to 1981 Gimble worked with WILLIE NELSON's touring band. He achieved his greatest chart success accompanying RAY PRICE on the single "One Fiddle, Two Fiddle" drawn from Clint Eastwood's film, *Honkytonk Man* (1982). He has since recorded as a solo artist, leading his own band, Texas Swing, and also worked with various Texas Playboys reunion bands. He has also played as a session musician with new country stars such as

GEORGE STRAIT and older traditionalists such as Merle Haggard. In 1993 his work on MARK O'CONNOR's *Heroes* album garnered him a Grammy nomination, and a year later he won a Grammy for his arrangement of "Redwing" that was featured on Asleep at the Wheel's *A Tribute to Bob Wills and The Texas Playboys* album. Over the last decade, he has hosted "Swing Week" in his native Texas as a workshop for young fiddlers, as well as producing instructional videos.

Girls of the Golden West, The *vocal duo*
Although born in rural Mount Carmel, Illinois, the two Goad sisters—guitarists/vocalists Mildred Fern "Millie" (b. April 11, 1913–May 3, 1993) and Dorothy Laverne "Dolly" (b. December 11, 1915–November 12, 1967)—were raised primarily in midwestern cities, where their father unsuccessfully tried his hand at a variety of occupations. Mama Goad was a talented singer of old-time songs, and it was Dolly who showed the most musical ability. She learned to play guitar early on from her mother. Dolly also was the most interested in a professional career, dragging her 14-year-old sister to an audition for St. Louis's KMOX radio station. They got the job, took the name Girls of the Golden West and changed their last name from Goad to Good; after a period of radio work in Kansas and on the Mexican border-radio station XERA, in 1933 they returned to St. Louis, where they were discovered by scouts for the Chicago-based *National Barn Dance* radio show.

The girls made their first appearance on the *National Barn Dance* in 1934, when they also made their first recordings. They were an immediate sensation, with their sweet harmonies, precision harmonized yodeling, and novelty sound effects (such as imitating vocally the sound of a Hawaiian slide guitar). Their first recording was a remake of Belle Starr's "My Love Is a Rider," which was followed by a number of cowboy numbers, many written by Millie, including "Two Cowgirls on the Lone Prairie" and "Will There Be Any Yodelers in Heaven?" Lucille Overstake, another popular *National Barn Dance* performer, wrote their most popular number, "I Want to Be a Real Cowboy Girl."

The girls left Chicago for New York in 1935, and then relocated two years later to Cincinnati, for the *Midwestern Hayride* program, where they remained into the 1950s. Millie eventually retired to raise a family, but Dolly continued to perform on local radio, hosting a children's show and also a pop hit-parade program.

Glaser Brothers, The *performing brothers*
Siblings Tompall (b. Tom Paul Glaser, September 3, 1933); Chuck (b. Charles Glaser, February 3, 1936), and Jim (b. James William Glaser, December 16, 1937) were born in Spalding, Nebraska, but relocated to Nashville by the late 1950s. Led by Tompall, they first worked as backup singers in Nashville, accompanying MARTY ROBBINS on his hit "El Paso" in 1959 and four years later working with JOHNNY CASH on "Ring of Fire." Brother Jim wrote "Woman, Woman," a hit for the pop group Gary Puckett and the Union Gap in the 1960s. The Glasers began recording as a group in the mid-1960s, taking a break between 1973 and 1979, and having minor hits in 1971 with "Rings" and in 1981 with "Lovin' Her Was Easier (Than Anything I'll Ever Do)." They also became involved in music publishing.

All three pursued solo careers as well, Jim beginning in 1968 and Tompall and Chuck soon after. Tompall became associated with WAYLON JENNINGS and WILLIE NELSON in the mid-1970s, appearing on the famous *Outlaws* anthology album issued by RCA, which gave his career a small boost. He made a couple of commercially unsuccessful LPs for ABC/Dot in the late 1970s. Chuck had his biggest solo hit in 1974 with "Gypsy Queen," but a year later a stroke limited his ability to record and perform.

From 1978 to 1981 the brothers were once again a group, recording for Elektra. They scored some minor hits—particularly with KRIS KRISTOFFERSON's

"Lovin' Her Was Easier (Than Anything I'll Ever Do Again)." However, personal problems again arose, and Jim left the group. He scored his greatest solo successes with 1983's "When You're Not a Lady" and the number-one hit "You're Gettin' to Me Again" in 1984 but couldn't follow up with another hit. Since then, he has performed regularly on the *Grand Ole Opry.*

Tompall made a final solo album in 1986, and then concentrated on working as a producer through the end of the decade. He subsequently sold his studio, and by the late 1990s he was once again on the road, performing in smaller venues at home and in the United Kingdom, where he still has a strong following. After years of acrimony, the brothers no longer speak and so a future reunion is unlikely.

"Goodbye, Earl" (2000) *controversial Dixie Chicks song*

This DIXIE CHICKS song was controversial for a number-one country hit, because it tackled the subject of spousal abuse—although humorously. In the song, Maryanne and Wanda are high school friends; Maryanne leaves for the big city, but Wanda stays home, marrying the abusive Earl. However, Earl hits his wife one too many times, and the girls seek revenge by poisoning him. The song is performed in a lighthearted manner, and the accompanying video—starring actor Dennis Franz as Earl—underscores its tongue-in-cheek comedy. Nonetheless, many country stations refused to play the song.

Gordy, Emory, Jr. (b. 1944) *performer and producer*

Gordy began playing bass in his late teens, and within two years was working professionally in teen popster Tommy Roe's band. A bandmate was Joe South, and South introduced him to the world of the session musician. The two worked steadily in the Atlanta area. In 1970 Gordy relocated to Los Angeles to join Neil Diamond's band, and also worked sessions for Elvis Presley (his bass playing is heard on a number of Presley's later hits, most notably "Burning Love") and Gram Parsons. In 1975 Gordy began touring and recording as a member of EMMYLOU HARRIS's Hot Band, and then in the late 1970s worked as a member of RODNEY CROWELL's group, the Cherry Bombs. In that group he met future country producer Tony Brown and future singing star VINCE GILL.

After Brown relocated to Nashville in the early 1980s, he called on Gordy to come work for him at MCA Records. Gordy became much in demand as a country producer and session artist. While working for MCA, he met label star PATTY LOVELESS, whose records he produced, and then the two married in 1989. He also produced STEVE EARLE's album *Guitar Town* and even worked with bluegrass legend BILL MONROE.

Gordy left MCA in 1996, and he has continued to work as a freelance producer. In early 2001 he oversaw two albums by his wife, including a traditional bluegrass outing called *Mountain Soul* along with a more mainstream commercial album. Also during this time, he worked with veteran country singer GEORGE JONES.

Gosdin, Vern (b. 1934) *singer*

Vernon Gosdin was born in Woodland, Alabama, on August 5, 1934. He performed locally with his brother in a duet act that was inspired by the LOUVIN BROTHERS, whom they heard weekly on the *Grand Ole Opry.* He also sang in a gospel group on local radio station WWOK. By the mid-1960s the brothers had relocated to California, where they were members of the Hillmen, a bluegrass band led by Chris Hillman (who later helped form the Byrds). In 1966 they recorded an album with Gene Clark after he left the Byrds, and another on their own. They had a minor hit with "Hangin' On" in 1967, followed a year later by "Til the End." By 1972 work had dried up, and Gosdin returned to Alabama and abandoned the music business.

Gosdin had a good reputation among 1970s country rockers and was encouraged by EMMYLOU HARRIS to resume his recording career. In 1976–77 he rerecorded his two earlier hits, which both went top 10, and followed them with a series of recordings through the mid-1980s for a variety of labels. He made a comeback in the late 1980s on Columbia with his album *Chiseled in Stone;* while the production is a bit heavy-handed, the title song along with "Who You Gonna Blame It On This Time" are both fine country weepers, made even more compelling by Gosdin's achy vocals. Since then, Gosdin has continued to record and perform, releasing albums on small labels through the 1990s, including a 1995 all-gospel album.

gospel music

Country gospel music, like old-time and bluegrass styles, is the outgrowth of the rich interplay between black and white traditions in the South. It also is a unique product of commercial forces—from song publishing through record production and radio and television broadcasts—that have helped to disseminate new styles and innovations throughout its century-and-a-half existence.

Shape-note singing had been known throughout the original U.S. colonies and was the original "folk" gospel music, taught by traveling singing masters. Each scale tone was represented by a different-shaped note on the staff—a diamond might be "fa," and a square "sol," and so forth. In this way, people who could not read traditional music notation could learn to sing from printed music. By the end of the Civil War, the Ruebush-Kieffer publishing company was founded in Virginia. The firm was the first prolific southern producer of shape-note hymnals, and, more importantly, also established a network of singing schools to teach music to ordinary folk.

The most influential graduate of the Ruebush-Kieffer schools was James D. Vaughan of rural Lawrenceburg, Tennessee. He began his own publishing empire in 1903, and within a decade was dominating the market. Vaughan hit on the happy idea of employing traveling singing groups to promote his books, employing the standard soprano-alto-tenor-bass lineup of barbershop quartets. These groups became popular on their own, and by the early 1920s Vaughan had expanded his empire to include a radio station and a record label. Several of Vaughan's songs became staples of early country acts, ranging from the CARTER FAMILY (who adopted his "No Depression in Heaven") to the Monroe Brothers (who scored a major hit with his "What Would You Give [In Exchange for Your Soul]?").

Country gospel groups became a mainstay of country radio and recording from the late 1920s on. Shows like the *Grand Ole Opry* began to feature their own quartets (most notably, an ex-Vaughan-employee group, the John Daniel Quartet). Groups like the CHUCK WAGON GANG made long careers out of performing gospel material. BILL MONROE was particularly fond of gospel music, and—as the father of bluegrass music—made it a part of the standard bluegrass vocal repertoire.

In 1926 Vaughan's business faced a new competitor in the Stamps-Baxter publishing company. Virgil Oliver Stamps and J. R. Baxter Jr. positioned their songbooks as featuring more "snappy" (ragtime and pop influenced) melodies than Vaughan's more staid publications. The Stamps Quartet, led by Virgil's brother Frank, produced a major hit in this more contemporary mold, "Give the World a Smile Each Day," in 1927, furthering the company's success. Stamps-Baxter became so big that it opened its own printing plant in Dallas, Texas, to meet the demand for the annual songbooks and also to produce customized books for individual groups.

The white gospel quartet tradition was not untouched by the parallel growth of gospel in the black community. Spurred by songwriter Thomas A. Dorsey—previously a blues performer who had recorded as "Georgia Tom"—dozens of black gospel groups had sprung up throughout the South, singing Dorsey's and others' original compositions. Dorsey's songs—most notably "Precious Lord" and "Peace in the Valley" (later a major hit for RED

FOLEY)—became staples of both black and white traditions, and introduced more modern, blues-influenced melodies and themes.

Another major gospel composer and entrepreneur was ALBERT E. BRUMLEY. He combined modern themes with age-old sentiments. His greatest song—"I'll Fly Away"—has become a country and bluegrass standard. It combines an upbeat message with a modern melody and harmonies that wouldn't sound out of place on the pop chart.

Gospel quartets continued to be popular after World War II, although many began to cross over into the pop marketplace. The BLACKWOOD BROTHERS, originally founded in 1934 and briefly employed by Stamps-Baxter, became major hit makers in the early 1950s when they were resident in Memphis, Tennessee, influencing a young singer named Elvis Presley. Presley later emulated their gospel arrangements on his own recordings, using the pop vocal group the JORDANAIRES, a gospel group that had become Presley's number-one choice for vocal accompaniment (although they never totally abandoned their gospel identity). Elvis continued to feature gospel material in his act until his death. Other mainstream country stars would often feature a gospel song as a closing number in their acts, as a way of acknowledging their ties to God and community (two favorites among the country audience).

Gospel-tinged songs have continued to be popular on the country charts, even when they are not overtly religious in content. Such upbeat numbers as Ray Stevens's perennial hit "Everything Is Beautiful" recall gospel sentiments and sound without actually addressing biblical or religious subjects.

Bluegrass gospel has also continued to be popular. Many groups have recorded secular albums with their full band and then cut sacred ones, sometimes omitting some instrumentation that might be associated with the devil's doings (such as fiddles and banjos, strongly associated with dance music—and thus the bane of some religious folks). Some later groups, like Doyle Lawson's Quicksilver, have specialized in country gospel, but most simply featured

it as part of their acts. Ralph Stanley was a major proponent of old-style gospel harmony singing, and made semireligious songs like "Rank Stranger" signature pieces in his act.

By the 1980s and 1990s, religious-tinged material was so much a part of country that the songs continued to pop up on albums and in concerts, and occasionally even become hits. Country gospel also became somewhat outmoded by Christian pop, with singers like Amy Grant taking a more contemporary, mainstream sound to preach a familiar message.

Grand Ole Opry

The *Grand Ole Opry* was not the first country-music radio program, but it became the most popular and the one most closely associated with country music. It helped establish Nashville as a center of country-music recording and also introduced country music to countless listeners over its long existence.

The *Opry* was given its name by announcer GEORGE D. HAY, nicknamed "The Solemn Old Judge." Hay originally worked for Memphis and Chicago radio stations; he had hosted the *Chicago Barn Dance* in 1924 (later called the *National Barn Dance*), which was among the first country-music radio programs (it remained on the air until 1960). He came to the fledgling WSM station, run by Nashville's National Life and Accident Insurance Company (the initials stand for "We Shield Millions"), in early 1925. A program hosted by Hay featuring elderly fiddler Uncle Jimmy Thompson in November 1925 proved the popularity of country music, and a few weeks later the *Grand Ole Opry* was launched.

Early stars of the *Opry* included harmonica-playing DR. HUMPHREY BATE and his Possum Hunters string band; the flamboyant banjoist UNCLE DAVE MACON, who often appeared accompanied by Sam and Kirk McGee; and the blues-tinged harmonica player DEFORD BAILEY. In the mid-1930s the *Opry* launched a booking agency to send its acts on the road; this not only spread the sound of the *Opry* throughout the South and West, it enriched the station, which took a commission on the acts it booked.

The second key figure in the *Opry*'s history was Harry Stone, who was hired to book more modern acts onto the show. In 1931 he brought the Vagabonds, a vocal trio who had previously appeared on Chicago's *National Barn Dance*. Stone would be central in establishing the booking agency, and also in attracting more pop-oriented acts. In the mid-1930s cowboy-style acts such as PEE WEE KING's Golden West Cowboys appeared on the program and, in 1938, a young fiddler/vocalist named ROY ACUFF was invited to join the show. Acuff changed the direction of the *Opry* from being primarily an instrumental broadcast to one focusing on vocals, laying the groundwork for future stars such as EDDY ARNOLD. A year later, the *Opry* joined the NBC "red" network, bringing it to a national audience, and future bluegrass star BILL MONROE joined the cast.

During the 1930s and 1940s, hundreds of similar shows blossomed on local radio stations, giving many country acts their first important exposure. Perhaps the most important radio producer was John Lair, who worked for WLS in Chicago, followed by a stint in Cincinnati, and then, in 1937, created the Renfro Valley Barn Dance, both a tourist attraction in the hills of Kentucky and a popular broadcast, featuring a popular young singer/emcee, RED FOLEY. Lair specialized in packaging bands and singers to fit a specific image, based heavily on a nostalgic (and perhaps exaggerated) sense of what life in the backwoods was like a century earlier.

In 1940 the *Opry* cast was invited to appear in a movie produced by budget studio Republic Pictures. Acuff, young and handsome, was made the lead, but the film also showcased such older stars as Uncle Dave Macon. In the same year, Eddy Arnold joined the show's cast as featured singer with Pee Wee King. In summer 1940 the first *Opry* tent show hit the road, and country comic MINNIE PEARL made her debut on the radio program.

For many years the *Opry* had had various homes. Finally, it found its most famous home in 1943 at Nashville's Ryman Auditorium. This would serve as the home for the *Opry* for 30 years, and still is an important tourist attraction for *Opry* fans.

After World War II, Nashville blossomed as a country music center. Although Victor Records had come on a "field trip" to record country stars in the late 1920s, no permanent studio opened there until 1947, when WSM engineers opened the Castle Studio. In the same year, an ex-*Opry* announcer named Jim Bulleit started his Bullet label. Soon after, RCA opened its Nashville division, hiring CHET ATKINS to be its staff producer.

Meanwhile, the *Opry* was bowing to change. In 1943 ERNEST TUBB shocked the management when he appeared playing an electric guitar; it took several years for this radical departure, along with his honky-tonk repertoire, to find a place on the program. A year later, BOB WILLS's Texas Playboys appeared on the air, the first group allowed to use drums in its act (although the drummer was hidden behind a curtain so the audience wouldn't be shocked). In 1949 a young singing sensation named HANK WILLIAMS popularized the steel guitar on the *Opry*, as well as his blues-tinged repertoire.

George Hay finally retired in 1953, and the *Opry* spent much of the 1950s, 1960s, and early 1970s becoming a bastion of conservative music-making. While new acts continued to be signed, the show became highly predictable. In the 1960s and 1970s the *Opry* had become the voice of conservative America, so much so that when SKEETER DAVIS publicly criticized the Nashville police for brutality from the *Opry* stage, she created a scandal that derailed her career.

In 1973 the old Ryman Auditorium was closed and the *Opry* moved to its current home, Opryland USA. President Richard Nixon, a big fan of country music, appeared at the opening night of the new theater. The 4,400-seat auditorium was built to accommodate large crowds, and it has none of the intimacy of the Ryman. The show increasingly took a manufactured-for-TV look, with its live aspect just incidental to the proceedings. Meanwhile, Opryland blossomed into a major theme park, with rides, hotels, and ancillary attractions. (The amusement park was closed in the mid-1990s, but Opryland remains the home of a large mall and convention center, along with the *Grand Ole Opry* theater.)

Not surprisingly, the new country music of the 1980s and 1990s has helped revitalize the *Opry*. Many new country stars looked to performing on the show as a major career validation. Performers still must be invited to join the *Opry,* and must commit to playing a certain number of Saturdays a year on the show, forgoing more lucrative opportunities on the road. However, increasingly "guests" are allowed to play the show (particularly big hit makers) without committing to full membership. But the tradition of *Opry* membership—with the luster it gives to an act—makes it still one of the most coveted badges of achievement in Nashville.

In fall 2000 a gala 75th-anniversary celebration was held for the *Opry,* including several concerts and a TV broadcast. The *Opry* is now part of Gaylord Entertainment, a major player in Nashville that owns music recording, publishing, and broadcasting properties.

Greene, Jack (b. 1930) *performer*

Born in Maryville, Tennessee, on January 7, 1930, John Henry Greene began his career as an instrumentalist, beginning with the guitar (which he took up at age eight), and then adding bass and drums to his skills. By the time he completed high school, he was living in Atlanta and playing with a number of cowboy-style groups. After a stint in the army in the early 1950s, he returned to Atlanta (via Alaska), playing local clubs with a group called the Peachtree Cowboys. It was there that singer ERNEST TUBB discovered him in the early 1960s, and asked him to join his backup band, the Troubadours.

In the mid-1960s discovering that Greene could sing as well as play, Tubb invited him to contribute vocals to an album track, "The Last Letter," and soon country disc jockeys were requesting more from the smooth-voiced vocalist. He was signed separately to Decca, and under the hand of veteran producer OWEN BRADLEY, cut his first hit, a cover of Dallas Frazier's "There Goes My Everything." Greene's next hit, 1967's "All the Time," led to an engagement as a regular on the *Grand Ole Opry.*

Greene's hitmaking days continued through 1969, with a couple more number-one solo hits and a duet with JEANNIE SEELY, 1969's "Wish I Didn't Have to Miss You." Seely remained with Greene's road show through the early 1980s. His career steadily declined through the 1970s, although he continued to tour and record for Decca/MCA; he later moved to smaller labels in the 1980s.

Greenwood, Lee (b. 1942) *singer and songwriter*

Raised by his grandparents on a chicken farm outside of Sacramento, Melvin Lee Greenwood (b. October 27, 1942) was already playing sax and piano as a youngster in a local band. By 1958 he was performing with local country artist Chester Smith and then playing for Del Reeves, where he served as a backup musician on guitar, banjo, and bass as well as sax. In 1962 he formed a pop-oriented band called Apollo that worked primarily out of Las Vegas. By 1965 the band had signed with the short-lived Paramount Records, under a new name, the Lee Greenwood Affair. The band dissolved without making much of a dent on the pop charts, leaving Greenwood working as a card dealer by day and lounge singer by night.

Larry McFadden, who worked as bandleader for MEL TILLIS, heard Greenwood in Las Vegas in 1979 and urged him to take a more country direction. After a few unsuccessful trips to Nashville to market his demos, Greenwood finally landed a contract in 1981, scoring his first big hit with "It Turns Me Inside Out." Soon he enjoyed a series of ballad hits, including "Ring on Her Finger," "Time on Her Hands," "IOU," "Somebody's Gonna Love You," and "Going, Going Gone." He also penned "The Wind Beneath My Wings" in 1984, a big hit in

England that became a chart-topper stateside for Bette Midler after it was featured in her 1988 film *Beaches.*

Greenwood's best-known hit is his 1985 patriotic ballad "God Bless the U.S.A." Greenwood had less success thereafter, although he continued to tour and record on occasion. "God Bless the U.S.A." took on a life of its own, enjoying revivals on country and pop radio during the Gulf War of 1991–92, and again in 2001 after the September 11 attacks.

Griffin, Rex (1912–1959) *performer and songwriter*

Alsie Griffin was born in Gadsden, Alabama, on August 12, 1912. He began performing professionally as one of many JIMMIE RODGERS imitators, working radio stations throughout the South in the early 1930s. While performing on the air in Birmingham, he gained his stage name, "Rex," because the announcer found "Alsie" impossible to pronounce; Rex also had more of a cowboy ring to it.

In 1935 Griffin was signed to the then-new Decca label, remaining with it for four years. Although none of his recordings were major hits, his own songs quickly entered many singer's repertoires, including 1936's upbeat "Everybody's Trying to Be My Baby" and 1937's classic slow weeper "The Last Letter." This song was supposedly based on a suicide note that Griffin wrote after his wife left him; whether true or not, the stark realism of the lyric had immediate appeal, and the song was covered by countless performers.

In 1939 he recorded a song originated by the southern blackface performer Emmett Miller called "Lovesick Blues." In turn, he taught it to HANK WILLIAMS when the young singer was beginning his career (and often touring as a supporting act for Griffin). Williams later scored big imitating Griffin's vocal style on this number.

Despite a solid start as performer and songwriter, Griffin's career rapidly declined in the 1940s, due to his increasing alcoholism. During this time he was working radio out of Dallas, Texas, but his performances lacked the vitality or quality of his earlier work. By the 1950s he was pretty much forgotten, although his songs continued to live on. Old friend ERNEST TUBB did much to champion his work, while EDDY ARNOLD had a hit with his "Just Call Me Lonesome" in 1955. Griffin died of alcohol-related illness on October 11, 1959.

guitar

The American guitar is a different instrument from its Spanish forebears. Its history has been shaped by a combination of technological advances along with new musical styles.

The common Spanish or so-called classical guitar features a wide fingerboard, gut strings, a slotted peghead, and, most importantly, a fan-shaped bracing system under the instrument's wooden top, giving it a sweet sound; it dates back to the early 19th century. However, the American guitar has its roots in a group of talented Viennese instrument builders who developed a new way of building guitars. Most notably, a German immigrant named Christian Friedrich Martin began making instruments in 1833 in New York City. He moved six years later to Nazareth, Pennsylvania, where the Martin company is still located.

Martin either developed or perfected a new form of bracing called an X-brace. This allowed for greater volume and eventually the introduction of steel strings (fan bracing will not support the increased tension that steel strings create on the face of a guitar). He also redesigned the guitar's body shape, exaggerating the lower bout (or half) of the instrument's body so that it was no longer symmetrical in appearance. By the late 1800s the Martin style had been copied by mass producers like Lyon and Healy in Chicago, and inexpensive guitars were made by the hundreds and sold through mail-order catalogs. In major cities among the middle and upper classes, the instrument became popular among young ladies, and instruction books and pieces written for the instrument in this delicate style (called "parlor guitar," because the instrument was associated with the formal front room of many middle-class homes) proliferated.

It is difficult to point to a specific time period or musician who was responsible for introducing the guitar to country music. Certainly, the instrument had found its way into the backwoods of American society as early as the 1860s. The image of the guitar-toting cowboy is not entirely fiction. Solo guitarists were soon finding a chair in bands; as the guitar entered the traditional banjo-fiddle ensembles of the South, it flattened out modal melodies (because guitars are oriented toward standard, western chordal accompaniment) and also gave the music increased power and drive. Early recording guitarists such as Riley Puckett and, of course, JIMMIE RODGERS helped popularize the instrument as the ideal accompaniment for the solo vocalist.

The second great technological innovation occurred from the 1920s through the 1940s. As a band instrument, the guitar was hampered by its relative lack of carrying power (its ability to be heard among other instruments). Steel strings helped, but didn't answer the problem entirely. Martin developed a new body style it labeled the Dreadnought, after the great battleship (the original Dreadnought model was custom-made by Martin for sale by the Ditson company in the late teens). A squarer and larger-bodied instrument, it was an immediate success among country and bluegrass musicians. Meanwhile, rival guitar makers such as Gibson developed so-called Jumbo bodied guitars, with extra-large bodies. These were highly regarded by cowboy stars such as GENE AUTRY.

Amplified instruments were the next step, although they were slow to win acceptance in country music circles. The first musicians to use amplification were the players of lap steel guitars in western swing bands. To be heard over large brass sections and drums, they had little choice but to turn to amplification. Next, honky-tonk singers such as ERNEST TUBB began using electric guitars to cut through the noisy atmosphere of these tiny bars. Traditionalists were horrified, but could do little to stem the tide of the eventual amplification of all country instruments. CHET ATKINS helped popularize the smooth-sounding, jazz-influenced, hollow-bodied electrified guitar by working with the Gretsch company on designing the Country Gentleman model of the early 1950s; meanwhile, younger players such as BUDDY HOLLY espoused the harder sound of the solid-bodied instruments designed by Leo Fender in the middle years of the decade.

The folk revival of the 1960s brought renewed interest in acoustic instruments, and Martin had its best sales year toward the end of the decade thanks to the popularity of folk-derived music. Today, the line between acoustic and electric instruments has been blurred by the prevalence of built-in pickups on acoustic guitars and the increasing use of effects such as reverb or chorusing that once were limited to electric instruments. Whether acoustic or electric, the guitar remains the primary instrument for all country stars, even if they just carry it as a prop.

Haggard, Merle (b. 1937) *singer and songwriter*

Merle Ronald Haggard was born in Bakersfield, California, on April 6, 1937. Haggard's parents were displaced Oklahoma farmers who had been driven off their land by the ravaging dust storms of the mid-1930s. Like so many of their neighbors, they moved west to California in search of a better way of life. They found living conditions tough there, and jobs few; the family was living in a converted boxcar when Haggard was born. They fared better after Merle's father got a job with the Santa Fe Railroad, but this brief period of prosperity ended with his premature death when Merle was nine.

Haggard attributes his troubled teenage years to his father's passing. He became difficult and unruly, constantly running away from home. He ended up serving time in reform school. When he reached age 17, he served 90 days in prison for stealing. After he was released he was soon in trouble again, and was arrested again after a botched attempt to rob a local restaurant. Haggard spent the next two and a half years in prison. While there, he heard JOHNNY CASH perform, which renewed his interest in country music and his desire to write songs that would reflect his own experiences.

Upon his release in early 1960, Haggard was determined to turn his life around. He began working for his brother, an electrician, while also performing at night in local bars and clubs. In 1963 he was hired by Wynn Stewart to play in his backup band. While Haggard was playing with Stewart, local promoter Fuzzy Owen heard him play and signed him to his Tally record label. Haggard had his first solo hit with "Sing Me a Sad Song," followed by a minor hit with a duet with Bonnie Owens on "Just Between the Two of Us." (Owens was married to BUCK OWENS at the time, although she would soon leave him to marry Haggard and join his road show.) His first top-10 hit, "(My Friends Are Gonna Be) Strangers," came in 1964 and also gave Merle the name for his backup band.

Following this hit, Haggard was signed to Capitol Records. His next hit, "I'm a Lonesome Fugitive," defined the classic Haggard stance: that of a man who had been in trouble with the law, but now, though still subject to temptation, rued his rough and rowdy earlier days. More prison ballads followed, including Haggard's own compositions "Branded Man" and his first number-one hit, "Sing Me Back Home." His 1968 hit, "Mama Tried," told of the difficulty his mother had in raising him and expressed regret for his difficult teenage years. Haggard gained his greatest notoriety for his 1969 recording "Okie from Muskogee," a song that cemented Haggard's position in mainstream conservative country circles.

By the mid-1970s Haggard's life and career were in disarray; his marriage to Bonnie Owens was on the rocks, and he broke with his longtime record label, Capitol, in 1977. He took a brief break from the music business, hinting that he would no longer perform, although he quickly reemerged as a performer and recording artist. He recorded a duet, "The Bull and the Bear," in 1978 with Leona Williams (who also cowrote the song); the two were married soon after. However, the marriage dissolved in 1983.

Haggard's recording career has been more sporadic since the 1980s. He had his greatest success in 1983 when he recorded a duet album with WILLIE NELSON, yielding a number-one hit, the title track, "Pancho and Lefty." Since then, he has had occasional chart hits while continuing to tour. Refusing to follow trends, he stubbornly performs his own brand of country balladry. He has also had a few roles on TV and in films, most notably appearing in Clint Eastwood's *Bronco Billy,* yielding the 1980 hit "Bar Room Buddies," a duet with Eastwood. In 1994 he had his last chart single to date, "In My Next Life"; it only grazed the top 50. The winner of many awards, Haggard was elected to both the Songwriters Hall of Fame in 1977 and the Country Music Hall of Fame in 1994.

Hall, Tom T. (b. 1936) *singer and songwriter*

Born in Olive Hill, Kentucky, on May 25, 1936, Hall is the son of a preacher. He began playing music when he was eight years old on an old Martin guitar that his dad gave him. He hooked up with an older local musician named Clayton Delaney (whom Hall immortalized in his 1971 hit "The Year Clayton Delaney Died"), who impressed the young musician with his stories of his successful band that featured shirts with "puffed sleeves that glowed in the dark." Hall's mother died when he was 11, and three years later his father was hurt in a gun accident. Hall had to quit school and began working in a local garment factory, a job he held for a year and a half.

Hall began his "professional" career when he was 16 as an announcer for a small-time local promoter who had a traveling movie theater mounted on the roof of his car. As an added attraction, Hall put together his first band, the Kentucky Travelers, to perform before the movies were shown. After the band broke up, Hall worked as a disc jockey.

In 1957 Hall joined the army and was stationed in Germany, where he performed over the Armed Forces Radio Network and at clubs. In 1961 he was discharged and returned to radio work, as well as opening a small grocery store. He performed briefly with another band, while moving from station to station as a disc jockey.

Hall's big break came in 1963 when country singer Jimmy Newman recorded his song "DJ for a Day," which went to number one on the country charts. Hall's song "Mad" was a hit for Dave Dudley the next year, encouraging Hall to relocate to Nashville. Hall was not anxious to record himself, but eventually was talked into recording his first single, "I Washed My Face in the Morning Dew," which was a minor 1967 hit.

A banner year for the songwriter followed in 1968. JEANNIE C. RILEY's recording of Hall's "Harper Valley PTA" sold 6 million copies. His own recording career soon took off, beginning with 1969's "A Week in the County Jail," followed by "Old Dogs, Children and Watermelon Wine" and "Ravishing Ruby," both in 1973. He recorded an album of bluegrass standards in the mid-1970s, scoring a hit with Tony Hazard's "Fox on the Run."

After the mid-1970s Hall's popularity waned. He made his last significant recordings to date with banjoist Earl Scruggs in 1982 on the album *The Storyteller and the Banjoman.* Hall has continued to record and perform, signing briefly with Mercury Records in the mid-1990s, but has not enjoyed the same level of success he had in his heyday.

Hamblen, Stuart (1908–1989) *singing cowboy and actor*

Carl Stuart Hamblen was born in Kellyville, Texas, on October 20, 1908. As a child he was introduced to cowboy lore and legend, and participated in amateur rodeo events as a teenager. He enrolled in teacher's college in Abilene, planning a career as a schoolmaster, but soon his love of music swayed him to switch majors.

When Hamblen was 20, he traveled to Camden, New Jersey, where the studios for Victor records were located, becoming one of the first performers to record cowboy material. Soon after, he headed out for Southern California, and soon was performing on the radio, including the *Covered*

Wagon Jubilee. His backup band was a swinging ensemble he called the Beverly Hillbillies (a name later borrowed by TV sitcom producers in the 1960s). His cowboy compositions included the popular "My Mary" and "Texas Plains," both issued in the mid-1930s. In the 1930s and 1940s Hamblen was a popular "heavy" actor, appearing as the bad guy in many of the low-budget westerns that featured white-hatted stars ROY ROGERS and GENE AUTRY.

After World War II, when the cowboy craze gave way to honky-tonk music, Hamblen wrote some of his best-loved songs, including 1949's "But I'll Go Chasin' Women," and "(Remember Me) I'm the One Who Loves You" from a year later, a big hit for ERNEST TUBB. This was an important year in Hamblen's life for another reason: He attended a Billy Graham crusade and was "born again."

Hamblen's biggest 1950s hit was the sentimental "This Old House," issued in 1954; Rosemary Clooney successfully covered it in the same year for the pop charts. A year later, HANK SNOW had a hit with Hamblen's "Mainliner." However, Hamblen was beginning to focus on composing and performing gospel music, including "Open Up Your Heart and Let the Sun Shine In," "Be My Shepherd," and the colorfully titled "When the Lord Picks Up the Phone."

Hamblen married in the 1950s, and he and his wife hosted a Los Angeles–based country-music TV show for a while. He retired from performing during the 1960s, but returned to radio on the invitation of a local station to begin a gospel hour that was eventually given the fanciful title of the *Cowboy Church of the Air*. This show was syndicated and became quite popular in the 1970s, featuring Hamblen's homespun philosophizing. A talented horseman, Hamblen appeared through the 1970s in the annual Rose Bowl parade.

Hamilton, George, IV (b. 1937) *singer and broadcaster*

Born in Matthews, North Carolina, on July 19, 1937, just outside of the commercial center of Winston-Salem, Hamilton first fell in love with country music thanks to the popular cowboy films that were shown at the local movie theaters. He formed a pop-country band in high school, and, through producer Orville Campbell, met famous country songwriter John D. Loudermilk, who gave him his "A Rose and a Baby Ruth" to record in 1956. The song raced up the pop charts and Hamilton became a teen star. For three years he performed with the likes of the EVERLY BROTHERS, BUDDY HOLLY, and Gene Vincent.

After his pop career ended, Hamilton relocated to Nashville in 1959 and signed up with RCA records to record mainstream country material. He had a couple of minor hits between 1959 and 1963, including "If You Don't Know, I Ain't Gonna Tell You," "Ft. Worth, Dallas or Houston," and his number-one country hit, 1963's "Abilene." In the early 1960s he joined the *Grand Ole Opry*, remaining with that program throughout the decade.

In 1965, while touring Canada, Hamilton met young singer/songwriter Gordon Lightfoot, who introduced him to other new Canadian songwriters, including Ian and Sylvia, Leonard Cohen, and Joni Mitchell. Hamilton became a champion of their material, recording several albums devoted to these new folksingers. Although the material, often protest-oriented, did not fare well on the conservative country charts of the day, Hamilton was well received, first in Canada and then in England.

In 1971, tiring of the commercialism of Nashville, Hamilton retired from the *Opry* and moved back to his home state of North Carolina. From there, he began broadcasting a show for Canadian state television, focusing on singers and songwriters from north of the border; this show was syndicated around the world, influencing country music fans in the South Pacific (New Zealand, Australia), the Far East (Hong Kong), and South Africa. Hamilton also continued his touring, being the first country star to perform behind the Iron Curtain, as well as many other far-flung corners of the globe.

In the late 1970s Hamilton tried to revive his stateside career, signing with the Dot label, but he remains primarily known and loved abroad. During the 1980s he switched to performing gospel material, and continues to record and perform this material. His son, George Hamilton V, had a single chart success in 1988 and has toured with his father.

"Happy Trails" (1950) *theme song for Roy Rogers's 1950s-era TV show*

"Happy Trails" was written by ROY ROGERS's partner Dale Evans. The song has become a classic in the cowboy repertoire, covered numerous times, including an unusual cover in the late 1960s by the psychedelic rock group Quicksilver Messenger Service. Rogers and Evans formed the Happy Trails Children's Organization to help abused children.

Harman, Buddy (b. 1928) *drummer*

Murrey M. Harman was born in Nashville, Tennessee, on December 23, 1928. His parents were both amateur musicians. His mother played drums locally with his dad's dance band. Through her, Buddy was able to meet several jazz drummers when they passed through the city, most notably the showmen Buddy Rich (from whom he took his nickname) and Gene Krupa, both early influences. Harman honed his skills in his high school band, and then enlisted in the navy, where he continued to play drums. After his release in 1949, he spent three years in Chicago furthering his drum studies.

Harman returned to Nashville in 1952. Soon he was playing regularly around town, and began working sessions. Two years later, CARL SMITH brought him to the *Grand Ole Opry* as part of his accompanying group; however, Harman was forced to perform behind the curtain (so as not to offend the country audience who objected to drums being used in a "country" band). Soon, though, the *Opry* management allowed Harman to appear onstage, if only with a snare drum. By the late 1950s he had established himself among country producers as a reliable and tasteful drummer through his work with such artists as RAY PRICE. He played on

numerous hit recordings, including JOHNNY CASH's "Ring of Fire," PATSY CLINE's "Crazy," and BRENDA LEE's "I'm Sorry." Soon Harman was also working with the rock artists in Nashville, including the EVERLY BROTHERS, JERRY LEE LEWIS, Dorsey and Johnny Burnette, and Roy Orbison. His work with these stars made him a legend among fans of early rockabilly as well as country.

By the early 1960s Harman was said to be playing 600 sessions a year. He appeared on almost all of Elvis Presley's film soundtrack recordings made after Elvis returned to civilian life in 1959. He also worked with other pop artists, including Simon and Garfunkel and Ringo Starr (the *Beaucoups of Blues* album). Nonetheless, his meat and potatoes continued to be country music, and he worked with dozens of Nashville artists through the 1960s and early 1970s.

Harman has worked less frequently since then, although he continues to perform and record. In 1991 he returned to the *Opry* as house drummer. At last count, he claims to have played on more than 17,000 recordings.

Harris, Emmylou (b. 1947) *singer and songwriter*

Born in Birmingham, Alabama, on April 2, 1947, Harris attended college at the University of North Carolina and formed a folk duo there. In 1969 Harris traveled to New York City's Greenwich Village and recorded her first solo album. In the early 1970s she moved to California and met Gram Parsons, the influential country rocker who had helped transform the Byrds into a more country-oriented group and also founded the FLYING BURRITO BROTHERS. The two became romantically and musically involved, and Harris added harmony vocals to Parsons's solo albums and performances.

After Parsons's death due to a drug overdose, Harris became a champion of country rock. She formed her first backup group, the Angel Band, and had several hits on the country and pop charts

Emmylou Harris, 1975 (Raeanne Rubenstein)

through the 1970s. Changing her backup band's name to the Hot Band in the late 1970s, Harris employed many musicians who would later become well known on their own, including RODNEY CROWELL, RICKY SKAGGS, and VINCE GILL.

Beginning in the 1980s Harris focused on the country audience almost exclusively. She created a country song cycle on her 1985 recording *The Ballad of Sally Rose*. In 1987 she released *Trio* in collaboration with Linda Ronstadt and DOLLY PARTON, yielding her biggest commercial hits. Harris made an abrupt career change in the mid-1990s when she released the album *Wrecking Ball,* returning her to a more mainstream pop-rock

sound. In 2000 Harris released her first album of her own songs, *Red Dirt Girl.*

Hart, Freddie (b. 1926) *songwriter and performer*

Frederick Segrest was born in the small town of Loachapoka, Alabama, on December 21, 1926, one of 15 children. Hart's parents were impoverished sharecroppers. He got started on the wrong road early, running away from home when he was 12 and enlisting in the Marine Corps (by lying about his age) at age 14. He served in the Pacific in World War II. After being released from the service, he took a number of odd jobs on the East Coast, gravitating toward Nashville. Finally Hart relocated to Los Angeles in 1951 in search of a musical career.

His break came two years later in Phoenix, Arizona, where he was working in a cotton mill. He met legendary honky-tonk singer LEFTY FRIZZELL, who admired his songwriting abilities and hired him as a member of his backup band, a position Hart held for 11 years. Frizzell also arranged for Hart's debut recording for Capitol Records, 1952's "Butterfly Love," and also got him a steady job on the *Town Hall Party* radio show, Southern California's answer to the *Grand Ole Opry.*

Hart had more success as a songwriter than performer in the 1950s. CARL SMITH covered his "Loose Talk" in 1955 to earn a solid hit; the song has since been covered more than 50 times. Two years later Hart had a minor hit with "Keys in the Mailbox." PATSY CLINE recorded his "Lovin' in Vain" as the flip side to her smash "I Fall to Pieces," GEORGE JONES had a minor 1964 hit with his "My Tears Are Overdue," and PORTER WAGONER scored a number-three single with 1966's "Skid Row Joe." Yet, Hart's solo career was going downhill, and he moved from label to label throughout the 1960s.

Finally, in 1969, he re-signed with Capitol and released a couple of albums. In 1971 the label was ready to drop him when a disc jockey in Atlanta, Georgia, began playing one of the album tracks,

"Easy Loving," on the radio. The song took off after Capitol had already dropped Hart, but the label hastily renewed his contract after the song made number one. Hart recorded through the 1970s, with his hits coming early in the decade (and featuring his backup band, called the Heartbeats, naturally), including "If You Can't Feel It (It Ain't There)" from 1974, 1975's "The First Time," and 1977's "When Lovers Turn to Strangers."

Capitol dropped Hart in 1979 and he moved on to smaller labels. Although he continued to perform in the 1980s, he has been less active since.

Hawkins, Hawkshaw (1921–1963) *singer*

Harold Franklin Hawkins was born in the river town of Huntington, West Virginia, on December 21, 1921. He won a talent contest as a teen and later performed on local radio in Huntington until he enlisted in the army in 1942. Four years later, after his discharge, he returned home and began performing on the popular *Wheeling Jamboree* radio show and recording for the King label of Cincinnati. His early minor hits included 1949's "I Wasted a Nickel," 1951's "Slow Poke," and the first recording of "Sunny Side of the Mountain," which was to become the theme song for bluegrass singer Jimmy Martin.

Hawkins was signed to RCA in 1955, and became a member of the *Grand Ole Opry* a year later, but the hits just didn't come. It wasn't until 1963, when he recorded Justin Tubb's "Lonesome 7-7203" that he finally had a number-one country hit; but two days after the song charted, on March 5, 1963, Hawkins was tragically killed in the same airplane crash that took the life of PATSY CLINE.

Hay, George D. (1895–1968) *original host of the* Grand Ole Opry

George Dewey Hay (b. Attica, Indiana, November 9, 1895) began his career in real estate, working as a salesman until 1920, when he decided to switch to being a newspaperman. He was hired as a reporter for the Memphis *Commercial Appeal*. The paper branched out into the new field of radio, opening station WMC, where Hay also worked as an editor and announcer. At this station he began to develop his character, calling himself "The Solemn Old Judge" and opening his broadcasts by tooting on "Hushpuckena," his nickname for the steamboat whistle that became his on-air signature. In 1924 Hay was hired away by WLS in Chicago to be the announcer for their popular

George D. Hay at the WSM microphone, c. mid-1930s (Courtesy of Bob Carlin)

National Barn Dance program. He gained national exposure on this program and within a year won a popularity poll as the top radio performer in the United States.

In October 1925 the National Life Insurance Company of Nashville opened a small, 1,000-watt radio station, WSM. Hay joined the new station as an announcer and newsman. On November 28, 1925, he invited local old-time fiddler Uncle Jimmy Thompson to perform on the station, inaugurating a program Hay called the *WSM Barn Dance*. In January 1926 the show was renamed, following a famous quip by Hay. The radio station carried the *NBC Symphony Orchestra* program, picked up from New York. When the *WSM Barn Dance* program followed a symphonic broadcast, Hay said: "You've been up in the clouds with grand opera; now get down to earth with us in a . . . grand ole opry." The name stuck.

Hay was responsible for booking many of the early *Opry* stars, and he did much to bring the best local talent to the station. He was particularly anxious to book Uncle Dave Macon, who was already a well-loved performer in the area. He also introduced to the *Opry* black harmonica player DEFORD BAILEY, the McGee Brothers, the DELMORE BROTHERS, and countless other acts. Hay formed the WSM Artists Bureau in the 1930s, arranging tours for many of the radio performers.

Although Hay continued to be an *Opry* presence until his retirement in 1951, he was less than pleased with the new direction country music was taking at that time. A staunch traditionalist to the end, Hay was unhappy with the new styles, particularly western swing and honky-tonk music. He died on May 8, 1968.

Hayes, Wade (b. 1969) *performer and songwriter*

Hayes was born in Bethel Acres, Oklahoma, on April 20, 1969. His father was a local country performer, and he encouraged his son to take up gui-

tar; by age 14, Wade was playing second guitar in his father's band. In 1992 he traveled to Nashville to establish himself as a working musician, and was quickly hired by JOHNNY LEE. Two years later Wade was simultaneously signed as a songwriter to Sony/Tree music and as an artist to Columbia Records. His debut single, "Old Enough to Know Better," released in fall 1994, was hailed as a return to roots-country sounds, and reached a chart-busting number-one ranking; his second single release, "On A Good Night," also fared well. This led his first album to gold status, and the usual awards and media attention. His label wasted no time releasing followups. However, like many new artists, Hayes did not match his initial success with his second album, although he still managed to score a few moderate hits. His next major hit came from his third album, the playful "The Day She Left Tulsa (In a Chevy)."

Through the 1990s Hayes's career was carefully molded by producers/managers Don Cook and Chick Rains; Rains has also cowritten many of Hayes's hits. His sound is derived largely from the great Bakersfield, California, stars of the 1960s, including more than a nod of the hat to BUCK OWENS and MERLE HAGGARD. Hayes's last minor hit of the 1990s was 1998's "When the Wrong One Loves You Right," a classic honky-tonk weeper. He then took a two-year breather from recording, and also broke with Cook and Rains. In 2000 Hayes returned with a new single, "Up North," released as a teaser for a new album coproduced by Hayes and singer Ronnie Dunn (one-half of the famed duo BROOKS AND DUNN). However, this single and the following album did little to revitalize Hayes's career as a hit maker.

Hee Haw (1969–1993)

Hee Haw was originally a network television variety show featuring country music and humor. Broadcast for two seasons nationally by CBS, the program was hosted by BUCK OWENS and ROY

CLARK, and showcased a wide variety of mainstream country performers. The show's combination of cornball humor and teary-eyed country music dated back to the old-style minstrel and tent shows that had toured the South beginning in the mid-19th century; the quick editing from joke to joke was borrowed from a popular TV series of the day, *Laugh-In*. The network dropped the program after two years, but the producers refused to let it die, taking it into syndication, where it lasted for another two decades.

Set in "kolorful Kornfield Kounty," *Hee Haw* mixed straightforward musical performances with the kind of rube humor that had been entertaining country audiences since the days of the minstrel shows. Add to this a couple of buxom blonds, and you had a surefire formula for long-lasting success. Besides series hosts Clark and Owens, the show featured many regular guests, including banjo-playing comedians Stringbean and GRANDPA JONES; Roni Stoneman, the big-voiced daughter of Ernest "Pop" Stoneman; backwoods comedian/monologist MINNIE PEARL; and even Playboy playmate Barbi Benton. Harmonica player CHARLIE MCCOY served as co-musical director for the original program, ensuring that many fine Nashville session players appeared on the show, along with Buck Owens's regular backup band, the Buckaroos, and the Nashville sound vocal groups the Inspirations and Nashville Addition.

Although it was in many ways a throwback to the old stereotypes of country music as something produced by dim-witted hayseeds, the show did provide valuable exposure for its stars. In 1992 a last-ditch attempt was made to modernize the show, but it finally died as an original production, although it lived on in reruns.

"Hello Darlin'" (1970) *number-one country hit for Conway Twitty*

This tune helped launch CONWAY TWITTY's second career (he had enjoyed some success as a pop/rockabilly singer in the late 1950s–early 1960s).

Written by Twitty and produced by Nashville master Billy Sherrill, the recording appealed both to the core country audience and to mainstream pop fans. In the song a man addresses his ex-lover, expressing his regrets for hurting her and hoping she is happy in her new relationship—while still secretly hoping she'll come back to him someday.

"Hello Walls" (1961) *number-one hit for Faron Young*

Written by WILLIE NELSON, this was a number-one hit for FARON YOUNG in 1961, topping the country charts for an amazing nine weeks. The song became Young's theme song, and it helped establish Nelson as an important songwriter in Nashville.

"Help Me Make It through the Night" (1971) *Kris Kristofferson tune*

Written by KRIS KRISTOFFERSON, this song was a number-one hit for singer Sammi Smith in 1971, remaining at the top of the country charts for three weeks. It eventually went gold, and was named the Country Music Association's "Single of the Year." It was quite controversial for its time, particularly since a female vocalist was singing what amounted to an invitation for a one-night stand. Some country stations banned it, but it heralded a new frankness in country lyrics and helped boost Kristofferson's stature as both performer and songwriter.

Hendricks, Scott (b. 1956) *producer*

Hendricks was born in Clinton, Oklahoma, on July 26, 1956. He attended Oklahoma State University, where he met TIM DUBOIS and future Restless Heart singer Greg Jennings. All three would end up in Nashville, with DuBois and Hendricks producing the group's debut album in 1985. Hendricks was much in demand as a producer through the 1990s, and is said to be responsible for more than 30 number-one country hits. He also groomed new artists, including FAITH HILL, SUZY BOGGUS, and TRACE ADKINS.

In 1995 Hendricks was hired to head the Capitol Nashville label. About a year later he got into a battle with GARTH BROOKS, the label's biggest-selling artist at the time. Brooks saw his sales declining on his newer releases, and he blamed Capitol for poor marketing; Hendricks felt that Brooks was merely maturing from a phenomenon to an artist who was continuing to sell a very respectable number of albums, while not dominating all of the music charts. Brooks held up the release of his album, *Sevens,* because of his anger with Hendricks; in the power struggle, Hendricks was relieved of his position in fall 1997, although he was quickly reassigned to Capitol's sister label, Virgin Nashville (both are part of the EMI conglomerate).

Hendricks got off to a good start at Virgin, signing two of the biggest artists of 2000, Clay Davidson and Chris Cagle. Despite this success, however, the Virgin label was closed in a cost-cutting measure by Capitol in late February 2001.

"Here's a Quarter (Call Someone Who Cares)" (1991) *hit for Travis Tritt*

A number-two hit for TRAVIS TRITT, this song revives a classic honky-tonk theme and style. The song was such a great success that Tritt was often pelted with quarters at his concerts, making him somewhat less than enthusiastic when it came time to sing it.

Herndon, Ty (b. 1962) *singer*

Boyd Ty Herndon was born in Meridian, Mississippi, on May 2, 1962, but raised in Butler, Alabama. He showed musical talent from age five, when he first began playing gospel music on piano. In 1979 he was hired as a singer at Nashville's Opryland theme park, where he worked off and on for the next decade. In Nashville he became a member of the vocal group the Tennessee River Boys;

other members later formed the group DIAMOND RIO. In 1983 he took first-place honors on Ed McMahon's *Star Search* TV show, but it didn't help his career. Reduced to singing jingles while trying to find a label interested in him, he finally left Nashville to try the greener fields of Dallas, Texas. After five years of club performances in Texas, he attracted the attention of producer Doug Johnson, who signed him to Epic Nashville.

Herndon's first single, issued in 1995, was an instant smash, reaching number-one on the country charts and launching his career. Herndon was immediately showered with awards, and he hit the road. However, while touring in June 1995, he was arrested following a bizarre incident in Fort Worth, Texas, and charged with drug possession and indecent exposure. Nevertheless, Herndon bounced back with his second album in 1996. The title track, "Living in a Moment," was another number-one hit, and the fans seemed to have forgiven him. Oddly, it wasn't the 1995 incident that slowed his career, but rather the cooling of the country marketplace in the later 1990s. Although he was still a pleasant-voiced balladeer, his songs were less often heard on the radio and failed to see much action. In 1999 he tried a new tack by releasing the album *Steam,* featuring more hard-rocking numbers, but again failed to stir much chart attention.

"Hey Joe" (1953) *number-one hit for Carl Smith*

"Hey Joe," performed by CARL SMITH, remained on the charts for half a year, topping the country listings for eight weeks. The song was written by FELICE AND BOUDLEAUX BRYANT, who would author many country and early rock hits. It inspired an "answer song" from KITTY WELLS, also called "Hey Joe," and was the basis for MOE BANDY and Joe Stampley's comic mid-1970s hit, "Hey Moe, Hey Joe."

Highway 101   See PAULETTE CARLSON.

Hill, Faith (b. 1967) *singer*

Audrey Faith Perry was born in Jackson, Mississippi, on September 21, 1967, but raised outside Jackson. She began singing at church and local functions. Determined to make it as a singer/songwriter, she moved to Nashville in her late teens, where she was hired by a publishing company in a desk job; this led to work singing on demo recordings, which in turn led to a job as a backup singer for Gary Burr. Burr had a production deal with Warner Brothers, and subsequently produced Hill's first album.

Hill's first single, "Wild One," promoted by a sexy video, shot to number one; the only previous female vocalist to score a number-one hit with her first release was JEANNIE C. RILEY with the sultry "Harper Valley P.T.A." Hill's debut album, *Take Me as I Am*, went gold in 1994, and then reached double platinum. While touring to support the album, she met country singer TIM McGRAW, and the two subsequently wed. Hill scored a minor hit with her duet with McGraw, "It's Your Love," in 1997, and then came back strong in 1998 with her big hit song "This Kiss." Her third album, *Faith*, from which the single was drawn, went platinum in little more than a month after its release.

Hill crossed over from country superstardom to pop diva status in 1999 with the release of her album *Breathe*. The title track became Hill's first platinum seller, topping country pop and adult contemporary charts. The album produced four major hits, including the title track, "The Way You Love Me," and "If My Heart Had Wings."

Hofner, Adolph (1916–2000) *western swing musician*

Born in Moulton, Texas, a small community located between Houston and San Antonio, on June 8, 1916, Adolph Hofner and his brother Emil were raised in a Czech-German family. When he was 10 and his brother eight, the family moved to San Antonio, where both boys were exposed to a variety of musical styles. The first music that really caught their ears was Hawaiian songs; they quickly ordered a mail-order ukulele, which led to lessons on guitar for Adolph and steel guitar for Emil. Along with local musician Simon Garcia, they formed the Hawaiian Serenaders in the late 1920s to play at local picnics and clubs.

In the early 1930s the first western swing records by MILTON BROWN and BOB WILLS were released, and were immediately tremendously successful. The Hofner brothers were bitten by the swing bug, as was another local singer/guitarist, Jimmie Revard. Revard formed his own group, the Oklahoma Playboys (although they were based in Texas) around 1934. He heard Emil playing the steel guitar in a local bar and hired both brothers to join his group. Revard kidded the teenage Emil about his bashfulness around women, which earned him his nickname of "Bash." Revard and his Playboys recorded in fall 1936 in San Antonio, and the brothers played on record, radio, and in local appearances with the group through 1938.

By spring 1938 Adolph was recording for Bluebird as a solo artist while also working locally with Tom Dickey and the Showboys. With the Showboys, he had a hit with Floyd Tillman's song "It Makes No Difference Now." Putting together a full band (including his brother) later in the year, Hofner returned to the studios in October to cut his first swing material. The band had various names; at first just billed as Adolph Hofner and His Boys, they were going to call themselves the Texans until they discovered another band had claimed the name, so they settled on the San Antonians.

From the start the band also played music to appeal to the diverse ethnic groups in the region; it was natural for the Hofners to play Czech waltzes and polkas, but they also performed Spanish-influenced material to appeal to the considerable Hispanic community in Texas. In fact, Hofner's biggest success was the record "Maria Elena," cut in early 1940. He also is credited with cutting the first western swing version of the popular old-time fiddle tune "Cotton-eyed Joe" in 1941.

During World War II, sensitive to anti-German sentiment, Hofner performed under the name of "Dolph." Immediately following the war, like many other western swingers, Hofner and band relocated to Southern California, where many displaced Okies, Arkies, and Texans had moved. Returning to Texas in the early 1950s, Hofner's band gained a radio sponsor, the Pearl Beer company, and so took a new name, the Pearl Wranglers. They toured to promote the local brew and often appeared at local events.

Through the mid-1990s Hofner remained active in his native Texas, mostly recording for the local Sarg label. As his health began to fail, he was forced to stop performing. He died in San Antonio on June 2, 2000, just short of his 84th birthday.

Holly, Buddy (1936–1959) *singer and songwriter*

Clarence Hardin Holley was born in Lubbock, Texas, on September 7, 1936. He was exposed to a wide variety of music in Texas, including western swing, R&B, and country and western. He formed his first musical group in high school with classmate Bob Montgomery, performing as "Buddy and Bob" over the local radio station. When Ferlin Husky and Elvis Presley came to town in 1955, the duo was hired as the opening act, leading to Holly's first record contract. Holly traveled to Nashville to record, but these initial recordings were unsuccessful.

Returning to Lubbock, Holly formed a new group that he named the Crickets. In 1957 the band hooked up with producer Norman Petty who operated an independent studio in Clovis, New Mexico. Over the next two years, Petty oversaw the classic Holly recordings, including hits "That'll Be the Day," "Peggy Sue," "Oh Boy," "Words of Love," and "Not Fade Away." Holly split from the Crickets by the end of 1958, settling in New York and recording more pop-oriented tracks. In 1959 he toured with a new band, featuring bassist WAYLON JENNINGS (whose first single, a cover of the Cajun classic "Jole Blon," had been produced by Holly), and guitarist

Tommy Alsup. It was on this tour that Holly died on February 3, 1959, in the famous plane crash that ended his short career. Holly's recordings were influential on several generations of country and pop performers, ranging from the Beatles to DWIGHT YOAKAM.

Homer and Jethro

Homer (b. Henry D. Haynes, Knoxville, Tennessee, July 27, 1920–August 7, 1971; guitar, vocal) and Jethro (b. Kenneth C. Burns, Knoxville, Tennessee, March 10, 1920–February 4, 1989; mandolin, vocal) were thrown together accidentally in 1936 when auditioning for a talent show for local radio station WNOX in Knoxville. At age 12, mandolinist Jethro was performing with his brother, while guitarist Homer was playing with a trio. The program director heard both groups jamming together backstage, immediately disqualified them from the talent contest, and hired them on the spot to be the house band for the station. For comic relief, Homer and Jethro worked up a few comedy numbers to perform while the band took a break; reaction was so positive that four years later they permanently separated from the group to perform strictly as a parody act.

Homer and Jethro performed at a variety of radio stations between the late 1930s and the late 1950s. In 1947 they had their first country and pop chart hit on RCA Records, a satire of "Baby, It's Cold Outside" featuring young June Carter on vocals. In 1953 they had their biggest chart hit with the satire "Hound Dog in the Winder."

Through the 1950s the duo continued to record satirical singles and albums. They graduated from the backwoods to Las Vegas in the 1960s, while also becoming popular performers on network television. They also got a job promoting Kellogg's Corn Flakes in the mid-1960s.

After Homer's death in 1971, Jethro was inactive for a while. Chicago area singer/songwriter Steve Goodman lured him out of retirement, and he performed on many of Goodman's recordings and toured with him. The bluegrass and acoustic music revivals of the mid-1970s brought renewed interest in his mandolin playing, and Jethro was soon recording solo albums as well as working with jazz instrumentalists such as Joe Venuti. Homer and Jethro were inducted into the Country Music Hall of Fame in 2001.

honky-tonk music

In the days before the jukebox, the honky-tonk—a small bar often located on the outskirts of town—became a center of musical creation. Employing hundreds of small-time performers (many of whom would later become big-time stars), these local watering holes nurtured a new style of music that would become, in the late 1940s and early 1950s, country music's mainstream voice.

Previously, country musicians had performed at local gatherings, often sponsored by schools or churches, and played for a mixed audience including women and children. For this reason, the repertoire tended to emphasize values such as religion, home, and faithfulness to wife and mother. This strong moralistic tone reached its apex in the songs of the brother acts of the 1930s, who popularized songs like "The Sweetest Gift (A Mother's Smile)" and "Make Him a Soldier."

Honky-tonks came to the fore in a response to the lifting of the restrictive national prohibition laws during the early years of the depression. However, because southern towns tended to be conservative, and drinking was still frowned upon, these bars tended to be located either on the outskirts of town or in the no-man's-land between towns. Here, men could gather after work to enjoy a few beers, play pool, and listen to music. The music was often provided by a lone guitar player who often could be barely heard above the racket. For this reason, newly introduced electrified instruments (such as the steel guitar in the 1930s and electric guitars and basses in the 1950s) along with drums became necessary equipment for the small-time country band, along with microphones to amplify vocals.

Besides this change in presentation, the subject matter of church-mother-home was hardly appropriate for a rough bar atmosphere. Songwriters responded by creating lyrics that reflected the realities of honky-tonk life. Songs about drifting husbands, enticed into sin by the "loose women" who gathered in bars, and the subsequent lyin', cheatin', and heartbreak created by their "foolin' around," became standard honky-tonk fare, particularly in the late 1940s. Songs like "Dim Lights, Thick Smoke (And Loud, Loud Music)" celebrate the honky-tonk lifestyle, yet take a moralistic tone, warning against the allure of cheap drinks and equally cheap women. Typically in the world of country music, the "fallen women" were often blamed for dragging down their hapless victims, the hardworking country men.

From about 1948 to 1955, honky-tonk music became the predominant country form, thanks largely to the recordings of HANK WILLIAMS. In songs like "Honky-Tonkin'," he contributed a more upbeat, less moralistically dour view of life in the small bars; his backup combo of crying steel guitar and scratchy fiddle became the model for thousands of honky-tonk bands. The honky-tonk style reached its apex in HANK THOMPSON's 1952 recording of "The Wild Side of Life," another one of those songs that both celebrates and criticizes the honky-tonk life; it inspired the wonderful answer song "It Wasn't God That Made Honky Tonk Angels," which made a major star out of KITTY WELLS.

The coming of the jukebox, which allowed bars to offer music without the need to pay live performers, marked the end of the golden era of the honky-tonk. That and the popularity of younger performers such as Elvis Presley, who launched the brief rockabilly fad (as well as the longer-lasting popularity of white rock and roll), essentially put honky-tonk music in its grave. Still, the musical style continues to have a strong influence on country music today, with the proliferation of local dance halls in some way replacing the original honky-tonks as centers of socializing and live music. And songs like Joe Diffie's "Prop Me Up beside the Jukebox (When I Die)" pay homage to classic honky-tonk.

Hood, Adelyne (1897–1958) *musician and singer*

Born in South Carolina, Hood was a classically trained musician from a genteel southern family when she met singer VERNON DALHART around 1917. Some 10 years later, they joined with country guitarist Carson Robison to make trio recordings, primarily of minstrel-era songs. In 1928 Robison quit, and a year later Hood and Dalhart recorded a series of duets, beginning with their biggest hit, 1929's "Calamity Jane." This highly successful recording led to a series of songs profiling tough western women, on which Hood took the lead with support from Dalhart, quite unusual for a female artist of the day.

In the early 1930s Dalhart and Hood briefly hosted "Barber Shop Chords," a syndicated radio show featuring Hood in the role of a saucy manicurist; in early 1931 they toured England and made some recordings there. The duo continued to work through 1933, and then reunited in about 1938 in upstate New York for radio work and appearances. Meanwhile, in 1936, Hood had begun broadcasting for the NBC network as a folksinger, taking a new name, Betsy White (which she continued to use through the late 1930s when working alone or with Dalhart). She continued to perform on radio through the mid-1940s—originating the Aunt Jemima character for the Quaker Oats Company—but retired when she wed a wealthy Pittsburgian.

Hoosier Hot Shots

The Hoosier Hot Shots got their training portraying country rube characters and playing jazzed-up country music in Ezra Buzzington's touring vaudeville troupe, known as the "Rube Band" or "Rustic Revellers." The four Trietsch brothers—including tenor guitarist Kenny "Rudy" Trietsch and washboard player Paul "Hezzie" Trietsch, along with Paul Trietsch's wife—were all members of this troupe from about 1923 through the company's folding in 1929 due to the depression. Clarinetist "Gabe" Ward had previously led his own group, the Hoosier Melody Five, before also joining with Buzzington in the early 1920s. Buzzington's outfit made one record for Gennett in 1925, including the upbeat "Brown Jug Blues." In about 1927 bass player Frank Kettering joined the troupe, and the four original members of the Hot Shots—now just two Trietsch brothers, Ward, and Kettering—were brought together.

After Buzzington shut down his operation, the four Hot Shots got a nonpaying radio job on WOWO, out of Fort Wayne, Indiana, and scraped along as best as they could. In 1933 they got their big break when they were hired to join the popular WLS *National Barn Dance* out of Chicago. Their combination of rube humor and jazzy novelties made them an immediate success, and they recorded for dozens of small and major labels through the mid-1940s. The group often began each number by asking, "Are you ready, Hezzie?," which also became a popular slang expression.

In 1944 Frank Kettering left the group and was replaced by Gil Taylor, and the group relocated to Hollywood. They had their only country hits in the mid-1940s, and also starred in dozens of western films, providing the comic relief. The group soldiered on through the late 1950s, often playing Las Vegas and other nightclub venues, with various members. They also recorded three albums during the early 1960s folk revival. Ward was the key man holding them together, and continued to perform with various Hot Shots as late as the mid-1970s.

Horton, Johnny (1925–1960) *singer and songwriter*

John LaGale Horton was born in East Los Angeles, California, on April 30, 1925. As a youngster Horton regularly moved between rural Texas, where his father had a small farm, and California. With a spotty education, Johnny eventually finished high school and made a few stabs at college before following one of his older brothers to California in the late 1940s. The brothers rambled between Washington, Florida, and California, before Johnny took a trip to Alaska. In early 1950 Horton was back in Texas, where he was inspired to try a career in music after winning a local talent contest. Back in California by year's end, he was heard by country producer Fabor Robison, who arranged for a record deal and also local radio and TV appearances. One of Horton's "day jobs" was working for a maker of fishing tackle; hence Robison promoted him as the Singing Fisherman. In 1951 Johnny married and relocated to Louisiana in order to appear on the *Louisiana Hayride* radio show. A year later, Robison managed to interest Mercury Records in Horton, but Horton's first big-label release was only a marginal seller.

While playing on the *Hayride,* Horton had befriended HANK WILLIAMS. After Williams died, Horton—whose wife had previously left him— married Williams's widow. His career, though, was quickly going nowhere, and took an even greater blow in 1954 when he parted with manger Robison, who was now more successfully promoting JIM REEVES. Horton left both the *Hayride* and Mercury Records in late 1954, and it seemed his career was over. But then a new force came into his life and career: manager/performer Tillman Franks, who got Horton a contract with Columbia.

Horton's first big hit was the first record he made for Columbia, 1956's "Honky Tonk Man," a song with the upbeat power of rockabilly. A string of hits followed, but then Horton's career took another nosedive from early 1957 to late 1958. Then he bounced back with his first country number-one hit, "When It's Springtime in Alaska." The everpopular "Battle of New Orleans" followed in the same year, leading to a slew of folk-styled ballads, including 1959's "Johnny Reb" and 1960's "Sink the Bismarck" and "North to Alaska."

While enjoying his newfound success, Horton began to have strange premonitions of his own death. Toward the end of 1960, Horton was killed in an automobile accident while en route from Texas

to Nashville. He continued to be a popular country artist even after his death, and his songs have been covered by everyone from Claude King to DWIGHT YOAKAM.

Houston, David (1938–1993) *singer*

Born in Bossier City, Louisiana, on December 9, 1938, Houston came from a distinguished family (his father was a descendant of famous Texan Sam Houston and his mother a descendant of Confederate general Robert E. Lee). He was encouraged in his singing career by a family friend, Gene Austin (who was himself a singing star of the 1920s famous for his recording of the pop classic "My Blue Heaven"). Houston auditioned for the famed *Louisiana Hayride* radio show when he was 12, and was performing as a regular cast member on the show within a few years. While working there, he gained the attention of promoter/musician Tillman Franks, who would play a key role in his career.

After attending a few years of college, Houston returned home to work with his father and brother in their house-building business. Franks called Houston in the early 1960s, asking him if he was interested in recording a new song called "Mountain of Love." Franks supervised the recording, and took it to Epic Records in Nashville, who immediately signed the singer. The song was a big 1963 crossover hit, and Houston followed it with even bigger hits, including 1965's "Livin' in the House of Love" and the song most closely associated with him, 1966's "Almost Persuaded," a classic honky-tonk tale of a man hovering on the edge of cheating on his wife. This song won a Grammy.

A year later Houston was offered a role in a lowbudget film, *Cottonpickin' Chickenpickers,* certainly not one of cinema's finest moments. He continued to turn out the hits through the early 1970s, including two duets with BARBARA MANDRELL, 1970's "After Closin' Time" and 1974's "I Love You, I Love You," plus numerous solo hits. In 1972 he was made a member of the *Grand Ole Opry,* where he performed for 21 years, until his death on November

25, 1993. However, by the mid-1970s his recording career had faded; he bounced from small label to smaller label, scoring a couple of minor hits along the way. Houston continued to tour and perform on the lower end of the country circuit, often accompanied by his manager and friend Franks, who played guitar in his backup band.

Howard, Harlan (1929–2002) songwriter

Although Howard later claimed to have been born in Lexington, Kentucky, he was actually born in Detroit, Michigan, on September 8, 1929. His family hailed from the South and were devoted listeners to WSM's *Grand Ole Opry,* and Howard's first idol was honky-tonk singer ERNEST TUBB. He began composing his own songs at age 12. After completing high school, he joined the air force and was stationed as a paratrooper in Fort Benning, Georgia. He made weekly pilgrimages to Nashville on his days off, and began aspiring to a country music career.

After serving his time in the air force, Howard bummed around the country, eventually ending up in the vibrant music scene in Los Angeles. Howard met Johnny Bond and TEX RITTER, both of whom took an interest in his career and began publishing his songs. He also met and married a young singer named Lulu Grace Johnson (later known as JAN HOWARD). Wynn Stewart was the first person to record a Howard song, "You Took Her Off My Hands," followed by Charlie Walker's classic 1958 recording of "Pick Me Up on Your Way Down," Howard's first major hit.

During the late 1950s and early 1960s, Howard compositions dominated the charts, including 1958's weeper classic "Mommy for a Day," recorded by KITTY WELLS; PATSY CLINE's 1961 hit "I Fall to Pieces" (cowritten with Hank Cochran); 1963's moralistic "Don't Call Me from a Honky Tonk," recorded by Johnny and Jeanie Mosby; "Busted," a hit for JOHNNY CASH on the country charts and Ray Charles on the R&B/pop charts, also in 1963; and "Streets of Baltimore," cowritten with Tompall

Glaser of the GLASER BROTHERS, a 1966 hit for BOBBY BARE.

Howard was more active in the business end of things in the 1970s and 1980s. New country star RODNEY CROWELL lured him out of retirement to cowrite "Somewhere Tonight," a 1987 hit for Highway 101, and Howard had a few other late-career hits, including PATTY LOVELESS's "Blame It on Your Heart." In the later 1990s Howard helped champion the career of newcomer SARA EVANS. He died suddenly at his Nashville home on March 3, 2002.

Howard, Jan (b. 1930) singer

Born in West Plains, Missouri, on March 13, 1930, Lulu Grace Johnson was one of 11 children of an impoverished farm family. She was exposed early to country records and radio, and began performing locally while still in high school. After two failed marriages she moved to Los Angeles in the early 1950s in search of a musical career, where she met up-and-coming songsmith HARLAN HOWARD, whom she soon married. Harlan used her as a demo artist for many of his songs, and soon record executives were as interested in her as an artist as they were in Howard's songs. Through her husband she met and befriended JOHNNY CASH and his wife June Carter Cash, and began touring with their road show.

The Howards relocated to Nashville in 1960 to further both of their careers; Jan signed to Challenge Records, cutting a duet with WYNN STEWART on "Yankee Go Home," followed by a successful solo single on "The One You Slip Around With." In the mid-1960s, she signed with the major label Decca, where she was paired with the smooth-voiced baritone of WHISPERING BILL ANDERSON, beginning with 1966's "I Know You're Married," and continuing for five years with a number of top-10 hits, from 1967's "For Loving You" through 1971's "Dissatisfied." Howard also had solo hits, starting with 1966's "Evil on Your Mind" (a number-five hit written by her husband).

Jan and Harlan divorced in 1967; while previously she had relied on her husband for original material, she now began recording her own songs, beginning with "My Son," written in the form of a letter to her son in Vietnam, who ironically was killed two weeks after the song was released in 1968. Other Jan Howard originals include "It's All Over but the Crying," a 1966 KITTY WELLS hit, and her own playfully titled "Marriage Has Ruined More Good Love Affairs" from 1971. Howard's hit-making dried up by the mid-1970s, and she went into semiretirement. By the late 1980s she was married again and working in real estate.

Husky, Ferlin (b. 1925) *singer and satirist*

Born in Flat River, Missouri, on December 3, 1927, Husky was raised on a farm, where he first heard country music and learned to play the guitar. After serving in the merchant marines, he began working as a country disc jockey, eventually settling in the vibrant country scene that centered in Bakersfield, California. There he was discovered by Cliffie Stone, who was then TENNESSEE ERNIE FORD's manager, and Stone encouraged him to begin performing on his own.

Thinking his name was too rural-sounding, Husky took the stage name of "Terry Preston" on his first recordings. He also portrayed Simon Crum, a backwoods hayseed, as part of his stage act. Initially, it was this comic character that attracted record executives to him, although Husky's first hit, "A Dear John Letter" (1953), was recorded under the Preston persona (in duet with Jean Shepherd; it inspired the follow-up "I'm Sorry John").

Husky had his first minor hit under his own name with the HANK WILLIAMS tribute song "Hank's Song," also in 1953, followed by "I Feel Better All Over" two years later. In 1957 he remade the song "(Since You're) Gone" that he had originally cut as Preston five years earlier, scoring another solid hit, followed by "Fallen Star." A year later, "Simon Crum" had a hit with the novelty number "Country Music Is Here to Stay." Husky also made some wonderful satires of rockabilly and early rock and roll sounds under the Crum name.

Husky hit a dry spell in the early 1960s, but returned to the charts during the period of 1967–75 with middle-of-the-road country sounds, beginning with 1967's "Once" through 1975's "Champagne Ladies and Blue Ribbon Babies," cowritten with Dallas Frazier. Two years later he suffered a stroke and briefly retired from performing. Husky returned to recording in 1984, and four years later he turned to performing gospel music.

"I Am a Man of Constant Sorrow"
(c. 1913) *classic mountain lament*

This song was first recorded by Embry Arthur in 1928. The song was native to Kentucky; banjo playing entertainer Dick Burnett (who made many 78s on his own and in partnership with fiddler Leonard Rutherford), who lived close to the Arthur family farm, published the song in one of his songbooks in 1913, and may have been Embry's source for it. Burnett also claimed to be the song's author, although its lyrics at least have roots in traditional songs of the region. Arthur's recording was a source for traditional singers Sarah Ogan Gunning (who renamed it "Girl of Constant Sorrow") and, eventually, Ralph Stanley of the STANLEY BROTHERS. The song got a considerable boost in 2000 when it was featured in the film *O Brother, Where Art Thou?*, as performed by "The Soggy Bottom Boys" (the film's fictional music group).

"I Can't Stop Loving You" (1963) *Ray Charles hit*

Written in 1958 by country singer DON GIBSON, this song was first covered by KITTY WELLS, who had a country hit with it. But it became a major hit when RAY CHARLES included it on his landmark 1962 album, *Modern Sounds in Country and Western Music.* Charles had made his name as an R&B performer in the mid-1950s, but had always enjoyed country music from his youth in Georgia. This hit appealed both to Charles's R&B fans and to a wider audience, both on the country and mainstream pop charts. The song remained closely associated with Charles throughout his career.

"I Fall to Pieces" (1961) *Patsy Cline's first country number-one hit*

"I Fall to Pieces" is a classic song of the jilted lover who still gets weak in the knees when she sees her ex. PATSY CLINE's languid vocals, perfectly complemented by producer OWEN BRADLEY's slick arrangement, made this a natural crossover record for the country star. The song has been covered numerous times by diverse artists, including Linda Ronstadt, LEE ANN RIMES, and even in a duet by Aaron Neville and TRISHA YEARWOOD.

"If You Got the Money, Honey, I've Got the Time" (1950) *first number-one country hit for singer/songwriter Lefty Frizzell*

This classic honky-tonk song's title has become a cliché pickup line for many a lonesome barfly. Written by LEFTY FRIZZELL and Jim Beck, the song portrays the narrator as living off the largesse of his well-heeled girlfriend (a classic theme in country and blues recordings since the 1920s).

"I'm Moving On" (1950) *honky-tonk ballad that reached number-one in Hank Snow's recording in 1950*

This is the song most closely associated with Snow, and it was one of the first major hits in the new honky-tonk style. It was so popular that it inspired numerous covers, including one by RAY CHARLES that became popular during the early days of the Civil Rights movement, and a parody by the popular country comedy duo HOMER AND JETHRO.

"In the Jailhouse Now" (1928) *song popularized by Jimmie Rodgers*

This song, credited to JIMMIE RODGERS, probably was based on a turn-of-the-century Tin Pan Alley song. Rodgers seems to have made the first recording of it, in 1928; he made a second version (labeled "No. 2") in 1932. It was covered extensively by both white country artists and black blues performers, notably in 1930 by the Memphis String Band. Not all versions feature Rodgers's yodeling refrain. The humorous lyrics link several stories of con men who get their comeuppance and land in jail. WEBB PIERCE's 1955 recording was a major country hit, ranked the third-highest seller of all country releases since *Billboard* began its country charts in 1944. Pierce rerecorded it several times, including a duet version with WILLIE NELSON (who had been a member of Pierce's band in the 1950s) in 1981.

"It Wasn't God Who Made Honky Tonk Angels"   See "WILD SIDE OF LIFE, THE."

"I Walk the Line" (1956) *Johnny Cash's first number-one country and pop hit*

Issued as the B side of "Folsom Prison Blues," which only reached number four on the country chart, "I Walk the Line" introduced JOHNNY CASH's trademark baritone vocals and the unvarying "oom-chicka" accompaniment of the Tennessee Two. Its theme—of a man trying hard to avoid sin while feeling powerfully tempted to "cross the line"—is a classic one for Cash, whose life also teetered on the edge of sin and salvation. The song is not really country and not really rockabilly; Cash's stark rendition has an eerie resonance that fits well with the lyrics' theme.

"I Want to Be a Cowboy's Sweetheart" (1935) *million-selling hit*

Singer PATSY MONTANA made this her signature song. She was the first female country singer to have a million-selling hit, and she paved the way for countless more. Montana proved that a woman could yodel up a storm as well as any man; the song's lyrics matched her strong singing in their assertion that a female could "rope and ride" with the best of them.

Jackson, Alan (b. 1958) *singer*

Born in Newnan, Georgia, on October 17, 1958, Jackson's story is a typical rags-to-riches odyssey that Nashville loves. Marrying young, he worked as a forklift driver while writing songs in his spare time. His wife was his biggest supporter. She urged him to relocate to Nashville, where his first job was in the mailroom of cable's Nashville Network. A chance meeting with GLEN CAMPBELL at the Nashville airport led to a job as a songwriter with Campbell's publisher; the company later sponsored his first tour. In 1989 Jackson released his first album on Arista, featuring nine of his original songs, including his first hit "Here in the Real World." In 1991 his spunky "Don't Rock the Jukebox," a rockabilly number, declared Jackson's allegiance to traditional country sounds.

Jackson's vocal style owes much to his mentor, GEORGE JONES, and the other great 1950s honky-tonk singers. His recordings are tastefully produced in a new country style, and range from old-fashioned weepers to modern dance numbers. His 1993 summer hit, "Chattahootchie," is suited for dancing as well as listening, and the lyrics offer a nostalgic reminiscence of a country youth.

Unlike other early 1990s stars who have faded from the scene, Jackson has continued to produce hits without changing his style much. Although he did not record between 1997 and 1999, he remained active on the road. His earlier hits continued to be aired on radio and country TV, and his style changed little—his 2001 hit, "It's Alright to Be a Redneck," could have been featured on his first album. In late 2001 Jackson released "Where Were You (When the World Stopped Turning)," written and recorded following the 2001 attacks on the World Trade Center and Pentagon.

Alan Jackson in concert (Raeanne Rubenstein)

Jennings, Waylon (1937–2002) *singer*

Born in Littlefield, Texas, on June 15, 1937, Jennings came from a musical family, and was already performing on local radio when he was 12 years old. He got his first work as a disc jockey at the radio station in nearby Lubbock, Texas, where he met pop rocker BUDDY HOLLY. Holly produced his first single, and invited the young singer to be his bass player on what would turn out to be Holly's last tour. Fortunately for Jennings, he elected to remain on the tour bus. The plane crashed, killing Holly and all aboard. Following Holly's death, Jennings continued to work as a disc jockey and recorded in a rockabilly style.

Waylon Jennings, 1975 (Raeanne Rubenstein)

In the mid-1960s Jennings hooked up with producer CHET ATKINS at RCA Records. Although he had some minor country hits, he became unhappy with the way RCA was handling him, and he began introducing different material into his recordings. In 1970 he recorded a couple of songs by a then-unknown writer named KRIS KRISTOFFERSON including "Sunday Morning Coming Down." A year later he released an album titled *Ladies Love Outlaws* featuring more contemporary songs. In 1972 he renegotiated with RCA, gaining artistic control over his recordings, one of the first country artists to achieve this freedom. The first album made under this new contract was 1973's *Honky Tonk Heroes,* featuring Waylon's road band, the Waylors, on a set of hard-driving songs mostly written by Billy Joe Shaver. In 1976 RCA released an anthology album, *The Outlaws,* featuring Jennings and his wife JESSI COLTER along with WILLIE NELSON and Tompall Glaser. It became the definitive collection for this new style of music. In 1978 Jennings recorded a now-classic album of duets with Nelson called *Willie and Waylon.*

Jennings continued to produce hits well into the 1980s. In the mid-1980s he reunited with Kristofferson, JOHNNY CASH, and Nelson for a concept album, *The Highwaymen;* the quartet would release more albums and do various tours through the early 1990s. Jennings's solo recordings also continued through the 1990s. In 2001 Jennings was inducted into the Country Music Hall of Fame. Later that fall, suffering from diabetes, he underwent surgery for the amputation of his foot. On February 13, 2002, Jennings passed away in his home in Chandler, Arizona, from complications of the disease.

Jones, George (b. 1931) *singer*

George Glenn Jones was born in Saratoga, Texas, on September 12, 1931. He began performing honky-tonk material after his discharge from the marines in the early 1950s. In 1954 he hooked up with manager/record producer Harold "Pappy" Daily. Jones's early records showed the influence of HANK

George Jones (University of North Carolina, Southern Historical Collection, Southern Folklife Collection, University Archives)

producer Billy Sherrill. There he recorded a series of hugely successful duets with Wynette, beginning with 1973's "We're Gonna Hold On" and continuing even after their divorce through the '70s. Jones also recorded a number of solo hits, all custom tailored to his legendary status as a heartbroken heavy drinker: most notably 1981's "If Drinking Don't Kill Me (Her Memory Will)" and 1986's "The One I Loved Back Then." In the late 1980s Jones branched out to cut a series of duets with unlikely younger partners, including Linda Ronstadt, Elvis Costello, and James Taylor.

In 1992 Jones was elected to the Country Music Hall of Fame. In 1993 he made yet another comeback (although he's never really gone away) with "I Don't Need Your Rockin' Chair," a good-natured but defiant statement of survival. In 1995 Jones reunited with Wynette for the *One* album and tour; Wynette was very ill by this time, but nonetheless the reunion brought new attention to Jones. A year later, he published his autobiography.

Jones's rough and rowdy ways were not entirely a thing of the past, however; in March 1999 Jones crashed his car into a bridge and was charged with driving under the influence. Luckily for Jones, he was not seriously injured and he returned to recording and performing. In 2001 he released a new album, *The Rock: Stone Cold Country 2001*, which included a duet with GARTH BROOKS on "Beer Run (B Double E Double Are You In?)."

WILLIAMS, although he also briefly jumped on the rockabilly bandwagon. Jones's first big country hits came in the early 1960s with songs drenched in honky-tonk heartache, including 1962's "She Thinks I Still Care." He also recorded his first duets with MELBA MONTGOMERY at this time. Jones continued to record through the 1960s, although he wouldn't break through to become a major country artist for some time.

Jones married TAMMY WYNETTE in 1969, and moved to her label, Epic, in 1971, hooking up with

Jones, Grandpa (1913–1998) *singer*

Louis Marshall Jones was born in Niagra, Kentucky, on October 20, 1913, to a sharecropping family. The youngest of 10 children, he grew up listening to his father's fiddle and mother's accordion. He got his first guitar from his brother, and before he was 15 he was already performing locally for dances and get-togethers.

After moving from farm to farm throughout Jones's early childhood, the family settled in Akron, Ohio, in 1928 where his father hoped to get a job in a tire plant. Marshall, as he was then known, entered a talent contest at the local Keith-Albee Theatre. He hooked up with harmonica player Joe Troyan and the duo began performing on local radio; Jones was billed as "The Young Singer of Old Songs." From there they moved to Cleveland, where they were heard by talent scouts for the radio show *Lum and Abner,* broadcast out of Boston. They were hired to be staff musicians for this popular country-themed radio serial, and it was here that Marshall linked up with country balladeer Bradley Kincaid.

Although he was only 22 at the time, the gruff-voiced Jones already sounded like an elderly back-woodsman. Seeking to cash in on the image, Kincaid outfitted Jones in oversize clothes, old boots, and a comical mustache. Kincaid renamed him "Grandpa" Jones, and from then on the comedian switched to portraying an energetic old-timer. He even switched to playing the banjo, more often associated with old-time music than the guitar.

After touring with Kincaid, Jones had jobs playing on a number of West Virginia–based radio stations. In 1942 he signed on with the *Boone County Jamboree* broadcast out of Cincinnati, where he met the DELMORE BROTHERS and MERLE TRAVIS; they formed the Brown's Ferry Four, which also sometimes featured RED FOLEY. After serving in World War II, Jones returned briefly to Cincinnati, but he felt his talents were not appreciated enough by the radio station there. In 1947 he joined the *Grand Ole Opry,* remaining a favorite performer there for decades. Through the 1950s and 1960s he toured with *Opry* package shows, often accompanied by his wife Ramona. Besides performing traditional mountain songs and energetically playing the banjo, "Grandpa" and Ramona performed the kind of country comedy dialogues that audiences love.

In 1969 Jones signed on with *Hee Haw,* a television program that combined the fast paced editing of *Laugh-In* with old-style country humor. Jones's old-time, cornball humor became a permanent feature of this popular program. His autobiography, *Everybody's Grandpa,* a chatty memoir, appeared in 1984. During the later 1980s and 1990s, Jones was less active as a performer, due to declining health. He died on February 19, 1998.

Jordanaires, The

Formed in 1948 in their hometown of Springfield, Missouri, the Jordanaires first sang in pure barber-shop style. They came to Nashville in the early 1950s, where they emulated the popularity of groups like the Golden Gate Quartet in creating a gospel-harmony hybrid. They began recording spirituals for Decca, backing RED FOLEY on his recording of "Just a Closer Walk with Thee." In 1953 they joined the cast of EDDY ARNOLD's TV show. They also toured with Arnold, performing in 1954 at Memphis's Cotton Carnival, where, supposedly, a still-unknown Elvis Presley first heard them.

The Jordanaires were popular at Nashville sessions, and at Elvis Presley's request, CHET ATKINS, who supervised Elvis's first RCA recordings, called them in to back up the young singer. They provided everything from pop-sounding "ooh wahs" to sophisticated gospel harmonies and even some doo-wop on 1956's "I Was the One" (the B side to "Heartbreak Hotel.") They went on to record many sides with Presley, and are an integral part of the sound of his mid-1950s hits, including "All Shook Up," "A Fool Such as I," "Are You Lonesome Tonight," and "It's Now or Never." Their own solo hit, "Sugaree," was a top-10 country song in 1956.

Hardly a major country artist of the 1950s or 1960s was not associated, at least in the studio, with these smooth vocalists. Such luminaries as PATSY CLINE and MARTY ROBBINS worked with the Jordanaires (along with pop singers such as Steve Lawrence and Julie Andrews). They appear on all of Rick Nelson's classic recordings, as well as on JOHNNY HORTON's late 1950s and early 1960s hits. They also are featured on all 28 of Elvis's film soundtracks.

The Jordanaires continued to work into the 21st century with various different personnel. The group was inducted into the Country Music Hall of Fame in 2001.

Judd, Cledus T. (b. 1964) *singer and satirist*

Barry Poole was born on December 18, 1964, in Crowe Springs, Georgia. He was raised in Alabama and initially worked as a hair stylist. He won a local comedy contest performing satiric versions of rap songs in an Atlanta nightclub in the early 1990s, inspiring him to seek a career as a performer. He moved to Nashville by the mid-1990s, initially signing with an independent label before gaining a contract with Monument/Columbia in 2000. He took his name as an homage to the popular JUDDS duo; his first album was titled *Cledus T. Judd (No Relation)*. Judd's material is straight parodies of major country hits, and he often employs well-known country singers (sometimes the hit's originator) on his own recordings. Judd first broke through with his second release, *I Stoled This Record,* from 1996, which featured parodies of SHANIA TWAIN and other major country stars (Twain even sang on one track). His following albums continued this pattern, although he occasionally branched out into satirizing pop singers like Ricky Martin and also released his own Christmas album (*Cledus Navidad, 2002*). Brooks & Dunn hired him to emcee their popular Neon Circus & Wild West Rodeo in 2001, and a year later he became host of CMT's *Most Wanted Live* program. Recognizing that his material dates very quickly, he released a six-song CD *A Six Pack of Judd* in 2003 so he could remain current.

Judds, The *mother-daughter vocal duo*

Naomi Judd (b. Diana Ellen Judd, Ashland, Kentucky, January 11, 1948; vocals) gave birth to her daughter, Christina Ciminella (later Wynonna Judd), in Ashland, Kentucky, on May 30, 1964. Wynonna's father soon disappeared, and Naomi took her family to California where she tried unsuccessfully to become a model. In the mid-1970s the family returned to Kentucky, where Wynonna began to show her budding talent on the guitar, and mother and daughter began singing together. In 1979 they moved to Nashville, where Naomi pursued a nursing degree while the duo recorded demo tapes on a $30 recorder purchased at Kmart. In 1983 they successfully auditioned for RCA Records, winning a recording contract.

The first Judds recordings were very much in the mold of traditional country harmony singing, and the arrangements emphasized acoustic instruments without too much clutter. Their first number-one hit played off their mother-daughter relationship in "Mama He's Crazy" (1984). A string of hits came in the 1980s, including the sentimental "Grandpa (Tell Me 'Bout the Good Old Days)," the uptempo "Rockin' with the Rhythm of the Rain," and the anthemic "Love Can Build a Bridge." These songs showed the talents of Wynonna as a gutsy lead singer, tempered by her mother's sweet harmonies. As their career grew, their recordings became more heavily produced and their act more elaborate.

The Nashville music world was stunned by the announcement of Naomi's retirement from active performing, due to chronic hepatitis, in 1990; the duo undertook a year-long "farewell tour," culminating in a pay-per-view concert at the end of 1991. Wynonna came out from under her mother's shadow with her first solo album, showing the influence of pop-rock singers, particularly Bonnie Raitt, on her style. Wynonna has continued to release albums, although her later efforts have failed to garner much attention.

"Keep on the Sunnyside" (1928) *upbeat hit song*

An early success for the country trio the CARTER FAMILY, it became one of their best-loved songs. The song expressed a sunny optimism in the face of life's troubles—a topic that appealed to country folk whose living and working conditions were far from ideal. Like many of their recordings, it featured the deep-voiced Sara Carter on lead vocals, with composer A. P. Carter providing bass harmony and their sister-in-law Maybelle contributing tenor harmony on the chorus. Maybelle's lead guitar work, featuring the melody played with a flat pick, was a novelty for its time, and much imitated.

Keith, Toby (b. 1961) *singer and songwriter*

Born on July 8, 1961, in Clinton City, Oklahoma, Keith was a high school football player who worked summers in a rodeo. After graduation he worked on oil rigs. Only when the oil boom began to slow down in the mid-1980s did he take up music, working in a bar band with no name. Although the band was locally successful, Keith continued to divide his time between oil-field work, semipro football, and music. His band released albums and cassettes, and Keith made a few unsuccessful trips to Nashville, but nothing much was happening with his singing career.

In 1988 the group Alabama's former producer, Harold Shedd, heard a tape of Keith's band and flew to Oklahoma City to hear them live. He signed them to a production deal, and produced Keith's self-named debut album in 1992. The album was an immediate success, thanks to its first single, "Should've Been a Cowboy," which hit number one. In short order Keith had hits with the ballad "He Ain't Worth Missing" and the honky-tonk song "A Little Less Talk and a Lot More Action."

Keith followed Shedd to a new label in 1994, but then broke free. He began to coproduce and cowrite much of his material. Keith showed a knack for writing the kind of tongue-in-cheek honky-tonk material that has long been a staple of country music, such as his 1996 hit, "You Ain't Much Fun (Since I Quit Drinkin')." In 1997 he had a hit with a vocal duet with pop star Sting on Sting's song "I'm So Happy I Can't Stop Crying." In 1998 he moved to the new Dreamworks label, which was seeking to establish itself in the country market. He hit big with the title cut of his 1999 album, *How Do You Like Me Now?*, which topped the country charts for five weeks. "You Shouldn't Kiss Me Like This" was the successful follow-up.

Pull My Chain followed in 2001. The lead single, the number-one hit "I'm Just Talking About Tonight," shows Keith's continuing allure. It was followed by "Talk About Me," a country-meets-rap number that ruffled some Nashville feathers but shot up the charts. The album debuted at number one on the country charts. Keith followed in 2002 with *Unleashed*, featuring several hits, including "Courtesy of the Red, White and Blue (The Angry American)," a rabble-rousing response to the September 11th attacks, and the more typical honky-tonk tune "Who's Your Daddy?" A duet with

WILLIE NELSON on "Beer for My Horses" was a third major success from the album.

Kerr, Anita (b. 1927) *singer*

Born Anita Jean Grilli, in Memphis, Tennessee, on October 31, 1927, she began performing as a child vocalist on her mother's Memphis-based radio show, and had her own vocal trio by the time she was in high school. She formed the Anita Kerr Singers in 1949, and signed to Decca in 1951. They appeared on the famed Arthur Godfrey's *Talent Scouts* TV show in 1956. The Anita Kerr Quartet, with Kerr singing lead, Gil Wright (tenor), Dottie Dillard (alto), and Louis Nunley (baritone), worked on countless Nashville sessions. Kerr broke new ground as a Nashville producer, one of the first women to hold this role in country music, working on Skeeter Davis's *End of the World* album. In the later 1960s, she formed a working partnership with poet Rod McKuen for a series of narrated mood albums featuring the Sebastian Strings, as well as leading the Mexicali Singers. Her group was also featured on the *Smothers Brothers' Comedy Hour.* Kerr was less active after the mid-1970s.

Kershaw, Doug (b. 1936) *fiddle player*

Douglas James Kershaw was born in Tiel Ridge, Louisiana, on January 14, 1936. Coming from a musical family, Doug was already fiddling at age eight when he made his professional debut performing with his mother, a talented singer, guitarist, and fiddler, at Lake Arthur, Louisiana's colorfully named Bucket of Blood saloon. Four years later he formed a family band with his brothers Nelson ("Pee Wee") and Russell Lee ("Rusty"; February 2, 1938–October 23, 2001) called the Continental Playboys; they performed on local Lake Charles TV and at bars and social clubs. By 1953 the band was a brother duo, with Rusty and Doug performing on the prestigious *Louisiana Hayride* radio program and recording for a local label.

In 1956 the duo moved to Nashville, where they were signed to the Hickory label. They made recordings in mainstream country, country boogie, early rockabilly, and Cajun styles, scoring their first hit in 1958 with "Hey Sheriff," performed in the close-harmony style of the EVERLY BROTHERS. After that came their biggest successes, 1960's "Louisiana Man" and "Diggy Diggy Lo" in 1961.

The brothers' chart success was short-lived, and by 1964 they had split up musically. Doug continued to work as a session musician through the early 1970s, recording with a diverse assortment of artists, including Earl Scruggs and rockers Grand Funk Railroad. He signed with Warner Brothers in 1969 and recorded several albums that veered from country-rock fusions to mainstream country productions. His most successful recording was 1976's *Ragin' Cajun,* his most roots-oriented outing. Doug's flamboyant performance style made him a favorite as an opening act on the rock circuit as well as on network TV.

Since the mid-1970s Kershaw has continued to record and tour sporadically. He scored his last country hit to date in 1981 with "Hello Woman." In 1988 he cut a duet with HANK WILLIAMS JR. on the novelty "Cajun Baby." In the early 1990s he made a recording with Nashville session fiddler Mark O'Connor, and then later in the decade reappeared on two albums issued by specialty labels.

King, Pee Wee (1914–2000) *accordionist and singer*

Julius Frank Kuczynski was born in Milwaukee, Wisconsin, on February 18, 1914. Julius's father was an emigrant from eastern Europe who played concertina and fiddle at local dances and parties. There was a wealth of different ethnic groups living in and around Milwaukee, including Poles like the Kuczynski family, but also Germans, Swedes, and Italians, as well as Anglo-Americans. Like many regional musicians, King's father played a mix of traditional ethnic dance tunes and the country and square dance tunes that were indigenous to the region. Julius's parents encouraged him to learn the violin ("not the fiddle," he has said, making the distinction between the classical repertoire performed on violin and folk tunes played on the fiddle). In his high school years he bought a secondhand accordion and took the name of "Frankie King" for local performances; he soon had his own radio show out of Racine, Wisconsin, playing popular tunes.

GENE AUTRY is credited with "discovering" King, bringing him to Louisville, Kentucky, to accompany him on his radio show in 1935. Autry had always featured an accordion player in his band, the Log Cabin Boys. It so happened that the other three musicians in the band were also named Frank. Since King was the shortest, he was rechristened "Pee Wee," a name he later legally adopted. When Autry moved to Hollywood in pursuit of a film career, King remained in Louisville, renaming the band the Golden West Cowboys, and continuing his radio program. King soon had his own radio show in Knoxville, and he joined the *Grand Ole Opry* in 1937, appearing on that program through the early 1940s. King's group was the first to perform on the *Opry* with drums, something the traditionalists in the audience bitterly opposed.

During World War II, King toured with his band (then featuring an unknown singer named EDDY ARNOLD), along with comedian MINNIE PEARL, as part of what was called the Camel Caravan, thanks to its sponsors, Camel cigarettes. This outfit toured U.S. military bases, spreading country music. After World War II King resettled in Louisville, where he spent most of the late 1940s and early 1950s. His big hit, "Tennessee Waltz," was cowritten with his new lead vocalist, Redd Stewart, in 1946, but didn't chart until 1948 on the country charts; it was also covered by Cowboy Copas. Patti Page took the song to number one on the pop charts two years later. Through the 1950s King continued to record his own compositions, scoring several modest country hits. He also hosted his own syndicated TV program out of Louisville, which was broadcast nationally in the late 1950s.

King's activities slowed somewhat in the 1960s. He dropped his TV work and cut back on recording, although he still toured extensively through the next decade. His sound and style changed little over the years, a blend of late 1930s pop, with his bouncy accordion playing and upbeat vocals a trademark. In 1969 he retired from performing altogether and became a promoter, packaging and booking minor country acts on the county-fair circuit. He died in early 2000.

"King of the Road" (1965) *singer–songwriter Roger Miller's second number-one country hit*
ROGER MILLER had struggled for success as a songwriter in Nashville beginning in the mid-1950s, making his first recordings in the early 1960s for RCA. It was only after he moved to the West Coast–based Smash label in 1964 that he achieved popular success. Smash promoted him heavily as a novelty singer to the pop and adult contemporary charts as well as a pure country artist. His initial hits came in 1964 with comic novelties including "Dang Me" (number-one country; number-seven pop) and "Chug-A-Lug" (number-three country; number-nine pop). "King of the Road" took the classic theme of rambling and updated it to the modern world of trailer parks and freight trains for what is perhaps Miller's best-remembered song. It has been covered innumerable times, by such varied artists as mainstream country artists and alt-rockers R.E.M.

Krauss, Alison (b. 1971) *fiddle player and singer*
Born in Decatur, Illinois, on July 23, 1971, Krauss won her first fiddle contest at age 10. She was signed to the bluegrass label Rounder when she was 14, and she won her first Grammy when she was 19. Her fourth Rounder album, 1990's *I've Got That Old Feeling*, saw a change in direction, emphasizing her fiddle skills rather than her singing. She had two hits as a singer, "I've Got That Old Feeling" and "Steel Rails." Another innovation was adding Alison Brown to her backup band; this Harvard-educated

banjo player quickly gained a reputation as one of the best modern progressive pickers. However, Brown quickly resumed a solo career after touring briefly with Krauss.

Krauss earned a slew of awards in the early 1990s, including a Country Music Association (CMA) "Single of the Year" award for her hit recording "When You Say Nothing At All," in 1993. She was also invited to join the *Grand Ole Opry* that year, the first bluegrass-oriented act in 29 years to be so honored. In 1995 a retrospective album of

Alison Krauss at the CMA Awards (Raeanne Rubenstein)

hits, *Now That I've Found You,* reached the top 20 on both the country and pop charts, and sold double platinum, propelled by the title cut.

Like other new-bluegrass stars, Krauss found a career boost in 2000 with her inclusion on the soundtrack to the film *O Brother, Where Art Thou?* The album was an unexpected best seller, and Krauss participated in several concerts featuring performers from the film. She has continued to record a mix of contemporary songs with a bluegrass-flavored accompaniment, and has continued to work with her original backing band, Union Station. Through the later 1990s she has released both solo albums and Union Station recordings. In 2000 she added ace Dobro player Jerry Douglas to the group. Early in 2001 she released a new Union Station album, featuring the country hit "The Lucky One." In 2003 Krauss and Union Station were selected by SHANIA TWAIN, perhaps the most popular country vocalist, to accompany her on a network television special.

Kristofferson, Kris (b. 1936) *singer and songwriter*

Born in Brownsville, Texas, on June 22, 1936, Kristofferson was an air force brat who is probably the only country star to ever receive a Rhodes scholarship to attend Oxford University. Kristofferson began performing while living in England, where he recorded as a teen pop singer under the name Kris Carson. In 1960 he joined the army. After his discharge, five years later, he moved to Nashville. He first gained success as a songwriter when ROGER MILLER recorded the first cover version of "Me and Bobby McGee" and JOHNNY CASH covered "Sunday Morning Coming Down," both in 1969. One year later Sammi Smith had a big hit with Kristofferson's "Help Me Make It through the Night," a particularly forthright and controversial love song for the time.

Janis Joplin's cover of "Me and Bobby McGee" just before her tragic death in 1971 helped catapult

Kris Kristofferson, 1975 (Raeanne Rubenstein)

Kristofferson to pop-star status. Two years later Gladys Knight scored a pop hit with her version of "Help Me Make It through the Night." In the same year, Kristofferson wed Rita Coolidge, also a well-known pop singer. The marriage lasted five years and produced two duo albums.

From the late 1970s on, Kristofferson was absorbed with his film career. In the 1980s he did record as one of the Highwaymen, a loose-knit group of old friends and "outlaws" including WILLIE NELSON, Johnny Cash, and WAYLON JENNINGS. Kristofferson made some solo albums in the late 1980s that featured somewhat bitter ruminations on the state of contemporary America, but they failed to make much of an impact on the charts. In the 1990s he cut a few solo albums, including one in 1993 with pop producer Don Was, but was unable to regain much commercial momentum. In 1999 he recut his earlier hits with an all-star supporting cast on the album *The Austin Sessions,* a pleasant enough, if not exactly groundbreaking, release. Kristofferson also made a comeback as an actor in the late 1990s, thanks to his appearance in John Sayles's film *Lone Star.* This led to a few more film roles through 2005.

lang, k. d. (b. 1961) *singer*
Kathryn Dawn Lang was born in Consort, Alberta, Canada, on November 2, 1961. She came to country music thanks to a college dramatic production based on the life of PATSY CLINE; in preparing for the role, she fell in love with Cline's music. She formed her band, the re-clines, in punning homage to her idol, and recorded a successful album of country covers for the Canadian market in 1984. Two years later she won a Nashville contract. Her second Nashville album, *Shadowland,* was produced by the legendary OWEN BRADLEY, who had also worked with Cline. Lang's big breakthrough came with 1989's *Absolute Torch and Twang,* which, as the title suggests, weds her twangy country persona with her aspirations to be a pop diva. A mild stir was created a year later when she threatened to launch an anti-meat-eating campaign, and two years later when she came out as a lesbian in the gay publication *The Advocate.* Her 1992 recording *Ingenue* took her firmly into the area of pop music. Her follow-up albums have been in a modern pop style that has a distinctly retro flavor.

Lee, Brenda (b. 1944) *singer*
Brenda Mae Tarpley was born in Lithonia, Georgia, on December 11, 1944; her stage name is derived from the last syllable of her birth name. Lee was performing on country radio as early as age seven in and around Atlanta. When she was 11, Decca signed her to a contract, and she had her first hit with "Dynamite" a year later, earning her her nickname,

"Little Miss Dynamite." Lee continued to record in the rockabilly mold through the early 1960s, including the novelty Christmas classic, "Rockin' Around the Christmas Tree."

In the early 1960s Lee paired with producer OWEN BRADLEY, who had been nudging country singers such as PATSY CLINE in a more mainstream pop direction. Together the duo produced a string of classic country weepers, including 1960's "I'm Sorry," "Dum Dum" and "Fool No. 1" in 1961, "All Alone Am I" and "Break It to Me Gently" in 1962, and 1963's "Losing You." However, by the mid-1960s, Lee's recordings became increasingly predictable, although the hits continued to come.

Following her last country hit in 1966, Lee made an abortive attempt to break into the Las Vegas/cabaret market by recording more mainstream material. However, she returned to the country fold in the early 1970s, beginning with "If This Is Our Last Time" in 1971 through 1975's "He's My Rock." She recorded more sporadically from the mid-1970s onward, scoring a minor hit in 1984 with "Hallelujah I Love You So," featuring GEORGE JONES and RAY CHARLES. She has since continued to perform, primarily around Nashville. She has also been very active in various charities around her hometown. In 1997 she was inducted into the Country Music Hall of Fame.

Lee, Johnny (b. 1946) *singer*
John Lee Ham was born in Texas City, Texas, north of Galveston on the Gulf Coast, on July 3, 1946.

Raised in rural Alta Loma, Texas, Lee formed his first band in high school, a country-pop outfit called the Roadrunners. He enlisted in the navy and then worked in California after his discharge, eventually returning to Texas, where he hooked up with MICKEY GILLEY, the famous country bar owner and singer, leading Gilley's band when Gilley was out on the road. By the mid-1970s Lee had recorded a number of singles for a variety of small labels, having minor chart hits with "Sometimes," the venerable "Red Sails in the Sunset," and "Country Party."

Gilley's club was selected as the locale for the 1980 film *Urban Cowboy,* and Lee's performance of the theme song, "Looking for Love," gained him a number-one country hit as well as a top-10 pop single. An album was quickly released, with three more tracks hitting the charts. Lee soon graduated from performing in beer-soaked clubs. He moved up to glitzy venues in Las Vegas, often performing with Gilley under the name the Urban Cowboy Band. He made tabloid news when he married TV soap star Charlene Tilton of *Dallas* fame in the early 1980s, a marriage that lasted through mid-decade. After a few more country-pop hits in the early 1980s, Lee faded from the charts. He has nonetheless continued to tour without making any new recordings through the 1990s.

Lewis, Jerry Lee (b. 1935) *singer and piano player*

Jerry Lee Lewis is known, among other monikers, as the "Ferriday Fireball," the original wild man of rockabilly and country. Standard biographies of Lewis divide his career into two parts: his original 1950s hits, in a rockabilly/ pop-rock style, followed by his comebacks in the 1960s, 1970s, and 1980s as a country star. Actually, Lewis has always recorded country songs, often as B sides to his original rock hits, and his sensibility is pure country.

The Lewis family were farmers in rural Ferriday, Louisiana, where Lewis was born on September 29, 1935. Much is made of the fact that Lewis is related to country crooner MICKEY GILLEY and the fallen TV evangelist Jimmy Swaggart (they are his cousins), as if these two men represent polar sides of Lewis's own personality. His musical influences are diverse, from the western swing/ jazz piano stylings of Moon Mullican to the rockin' style of Fats Domino; even the great showman Al Jolson is said to have had an influence on young Lewis. Playing piano since the age of nine, Lewis won a Ted Mack amateur hour show leading to a job at the local Natchez, Mississippi, radio station. After a brief stint at Bible college, he worked his way to the legendary Sun studios headed by Sam Phillips.

At Sun, Lewis first worked as a sideman, backing CARL PERKINS; it was at a Perkins session that he encountered Elvis Presley and JOHNNY CASH in an impromptu jam session where they primarily played old hymn tunes ("the Million Dollar Quartet" sessions). Lewis's first hit was 1957's "Whole Lotta Shakin' Goin' On"; originally, radio stations were wary of the song, fearing its suggestive subtext, but Lewis's wild performance on a Steve Allen TV show catapulted the song—and the star—to fame.

Lewis's rock career came to a grinding halt in 1959 with his scandalous third marriage to a 13-year-old cousin. He struggled through the 1960s, recording in a number of different styles, including his first "pure country" recordings. In the late 1960s and early 1970s, he broke through on the country charts with hits in a honky-tonk style, including "Another Place, Another Time," "What Made Milwaukee Famous (Has Made a Loser out of Me)," and "She Even Woke Me Up to Say Goodbye." In 1978 he made yet another country comeback with the humorous "39 and Holding."

The 1980s brought continuing personal problems, including tax problems (in 1993 the IRS seized Lewis's home for back taxes) and the mysterious murder of his fifth wife. Lewis still continues to perform regularly, particularly in Europe, drawing on both his rock and country repertoires, while making periodic well-publicized comebacks.

"Little Old Log Cabin in the Lane" (1923)
first major country hit

A popular sentimental song of the teens, "Little Old Log Cabin in the Lane" was written by Will S. Hays and made famous by John Carson, a fiddling sign painter from Atlanta, Georgia, who enjoyed local popularity. Local furniture dealer Polk Brockman asked Ralph Peer of OKeh records to record him, and Peer set up a session at Brockman's store. Peer deemed the resulting record—"Little Old Log Cabin in the Lane" backed with "The Old Hen Cackled and the Rooster's Gonna Crow"—so bad that he had it pressed without a label or catalog number, shipping 500 copies to Brockman for local sale. The next day, Brockman reordered and Peer realized he had a hit on his hands. Carson subsequently recorded dozens of sessions for OKeh. The song has been covered by a range of artists, notably BILL MONROE.

See also FIDDLIN' JOHN CARSON.

"Looking for Love" (1980) *theme song for the film* Urban Cowboy

Featured in the movie that brought mechanical bull riding to bars across America, this song was a number-one country hit and top-10 pop success for singer JOHNNY LEE. It represented the height of the "countrypolitan" style, an attempt to sell country songs to fans of middle-of-the-road pop by using light rock arrangements.

Louisiana Hayride

In its heyday second only to the *Grand Ole Opry*, the *Louisiana Hayride* was one of the most influential of all country music radio programs, launching the career of HANK WILLIAMS, among others.

The show was born in 1948 when Dean Upson, one-time member of the Vagabonds and a past talent coordinator for the *Opry*, joined forces with the management of Shreveport, Louisiana's KWKH to break the *Opry* monopoly. With a cast that included the BAILES BROTHERS, Johnnie and Jack,

and KITTY WELLS, the show was given an enormous boost in August 1948 when singer/songwriter Hank Williams joined the roster. Williams, like many after him, stayed little more than a year before moving to the more prestigious *Opry*. Lacking a booking agency (the backbone of the *Opry*'s hold on its acts and a great moneymaker for the station), the *Hayride* was unable to hold onto its talent.

Nonetheless, through the mid-1950s a number of stars got their start on KWKH, including SLIM WHITMAN, WEBB PIERCE, JOHNNY HORTON, and JIM REEVES. In an ironic twist, Hank Williams returned to the *Hayride* in 1952 after he was fired from the *Opry* due to his drunkenness, but by this time his performances were erratic (he died on New Year's Eve 1953). Both Pierce and Reeves served as announcers on the show, which was broadcast nationally over the CBS network in the early 1950s as well as on Armed Forces Radio in Korea.

The *Hayride*'s biggest coup occurred on October 6, 1954, when a young duck-tailed star out of Memphis joined the cast: Elvis Presley. Initially promoted as a country artist, Elvis remained at the *Hayride* for 18 months; he could never find acceptance at the *Opry*. When Elvis left the station in 1956 to sign with RCA as a teen-pop star, the program began its long decline.

Although the *Hayride* continued on the air under its original ownership through 1973, and thereafter through 1987 under new hands, the show never really regained its stature or audience. In 1987 it was briefly reintroduced as a television show, but again made little impact on the country music world.

Louvin Brothers *vocal duo*

Ira (b. Rainesville, Alabama, April 21, 1924–June 20, 1965) and Charlie (b. Jefferson City, Missouri, July 7, 1927) Loudermilk were raised in Henegger, Georgia. The duo began singing from an early age, particularly influenced by traditional balladry, old-time gospel, and the sounds they heard over the radio and on records, particularly acts like the

Ira (left) and Charlie (right) Louvin performing on the
Grand Ole Opry, *c. mid-1950s* (University of North
Carolina, Southern Historical Collection, Southern Folklife
Collection, University Archives)

briefly for MGM and Decca in the late 1940s and
then signed to Capitol in 1951.

The Louvins' hits began in the mid-1950s with "I
Don't Believe You've Met My Baby" and "You're
Running Wild" in 1956. These led to a regular spot
on the *Grand Ole Opry*. They continued to record
successfully through the early 1960s for Capitol.
About half of their albums were gospel recordings.
They also honored their roots on the album *A
Tribute to the Delmore Brothers*.

Ira and Charlie had an increasingly stormy relationship, and Charlie finally broke with his brother
in 1963 to pursue a solo career, beginning with the
hit "I Don't Love You Anymore." Ira continued to
appear with his wife, Florence, who performed
under the stage name of Anne Young; both were
killed in an automobile accident in 1965. In
1970–71 Charlie formed a partnership with vocalist
MELBA MONTGOMERY, who had previously recorded
with Gene Pitney and GEORGE JONES. Charlie continued as a solo artist on the *Opry* and on the road
through the 1990s. In late 2001 following the brothers' induction into the Country Music Hall of Fame,
Charlie was hospitalized due to a serious automobile accident.

Charlie and Ira together are credited with writing some 400 songs, including the perennial standard "When I Stop Dreaming" (covered by
EMMYLOU HARRIS, among many others) and
"Kentucky." Their trademark high-pitched harmonies, with a plaintive sound reminiscent of backwoods gospel music, makes almost all of their
recordings worth hearing, even when they are
awash in syrupy strings. They were one of the few
modern country duos to be able to preserve a true
country sound into the early 1960s.

DELMORE BROTHERS and the BLUE SKY BOYS. They
later adopted the last name Louvin. Their big
break came in 1943 when they won a spot on early-
morning radio in Chattanooga, Tennessee, after
winning a local talent show. By the late 1940s they
had moved to WNOX in Knoxville and the popular
Midday Merry-Go-Round program. They recorded

Loveless, Patty (b. 1958) *singer*

Born Patty Ramey, in Pikeville, Kentucky, on
January 4, 1958, the daughter of a coal miner,
Loveless was first introduced to country music
through her older brother, Roger, who later managed her career. She began performing as a duo with

him at age 12. Roger took her to Nashville two years later, where she was hired to replace her cousin, LORETTA LYNN, in the Wilburn Brothers summer touring show. She toured for several summers with them, and eventually wed their drummer, Terry Lovelace. After her wedding, she went into semi retirement (although she continued to sing rock and pop music locally), leading the life of a house-wife in North Carolina.

Patty returned to Nashville in the mid-1980s after her marriage ended. She changed her stage name to "Loveless" at this time. Her brother intro-duced her to MCA Records and producer Emory

Patty Loveless at the CMA Awards (Raeanne Rubenstein)

Gordy Jr., with whom she has been associated ever since. She has recorded a mix of new country styles by leading singer/songwriters of the Nashville scene. Some of her early hits included the ballad "I Did" from her first album and uptempo, rocking numbers like "Timber I'm Falling in Love" and "I'm That Kind of Girl." Voice troubles waylaid her career in the early 1990s, but she returned triumphantly in 1993 with a hit single, "Blame It on Your Heart," an uptempo, rockabilly-esque number, along with the country swing of "Mister Man on the Moon."

Loveless had a hard time producing hits in the later 1990s, as younger (and more videogenic) female singers came to the fore. Her last major country hits to date, "Lonely Too Long" and "You Can Feel Bad," came in 1995. Nonetheless, she remains a solid concert draw and continues to record critically well-received albums. In 2001 she issued her first acoustic bluegrass album, *Mountain Soul,* joining singers such as DOLLY PARTON and ALISON KRAUSS in a return to bluegrass roots.

"Lovesick Blues" (1949) *Hank Williams' first number-one hit*

"Lovesick Blues" introduced HANK WILLIAMS's sig-nature sound and style, particularly in its yodeling chorus. Despite widespread belief that Williams wrote the song, it was the product of Tin Pan Alley singer/publisher Irving Mills and tunesmith Cliff Friend, and was copyrighted in 1922. Williams learned the song from a 1939 recording by cowboy singer Rex Griffin, who in turn learned it from a 1928 recording by minstrel show performer Emmett Miller (1903–52). Miller's distinctive vocal breaks from normal voice to falsetto were copied by Griffin almost note-for-note, and were possibly also influential on earlier country star, JIMMIE RODGERS. Williams would continue to use this vocal trick throughout his career, in turn influencing dozens of his followers. Williams's recording spent 42 weeks on the country charts, 16 at number one, an incred-ible feat. Its theme of the jilted lover would become a standard for post–World War II honky-tonk songs. The instrumentation of the recording—acoustic rhythm guitar, electric steel guitar, fiddle, bass—is fairly understated, with very few country cues. In following recordings by Williams, the steel guitar would be featured more prominently and become a trademark of his sound.

Lovett, Lyle (b. 1957) *singer and songwriter*

Born on November 1, 1957, and raised in the small town of Klein, Texas (on the northern outskirts of Houston), Lovett formed his musical tastes by a mixture of Texas honky-tonk, BOB WILLS's classic western swing, and the neo-hipster attitude of pop singers such as Tom Waits. Lovett's career was slow getting off the ground, so he worked for a while as an assistant to his mother, who taught courses on motivational training for businesspeople, while he pursued his musical career at local clubs at night. Finally, he raised enough carfare to come to Nashville in the early 1980s and began looking for a recording contract.

Lovett's half-spoken vocals, wordy songs, and unusual looks got him some initial attention, including a recording contract with Curb Records (an MCA affiliate), which produced his first single, "Farther Down the Line," a song that skewed the classic image of the rodeo cowboy. This was followed by further western numbers, including Lovett's only top-10 hit to date, "Cowboy Man." Lovett even titled a song "An Acceptable Level of Ecstasy," addressing issues of upper-class racism.

Lovett hit his stride with his third album, titled *Lyle Lovett and His Large Band,* melding western swing and jazz influences. Oddly enough, this record's minor hit was "Nobody Knows Me (Like My Baby)," a tender, quirky acoustic love song, rich with the kind of hip wordplay that makes Lovett's best compositions so intriguing to his fans.

Lovett's career got an odd boost in 1993 with his surprise marriage to Hollywood starlet Julia Roberts. The marriage was not long-lived, and Lovett's first album following his divorce was widely interpreted as an ode to his lost love. Also in the 1990s Lovett established a movie career, often portraying offbeat characters in films by noted director Robert Altman.

Lovett made a bold move in 1998 by releasing *Step inside the House.* The album consisted only of songs written by other Texas songwriters, including many of his long-time friends and heroes, such as Guy Clark, Townes van Zandt, Walter Hyatt, Robert Earl Keen, and Steve Fromholz. Though critically acclaimed, the album failed to do much on the charts. Still, it showed how closely linked the Texas school of songwriting is. In 2003 he released *My Baby Don't Tolerate,* his first album of original material since 1996, and his first on an independent label.

"Lucille" (1977) *breakthrough hit for Kenny Rogers*

"Lucille" established KENNY ROGERS as a hit maker on both country and adult contemporary charts. It topped the country charts for two weeks, and was named the Country Music Association's "Song of the Year." The song tells a classic story of a honky-tonk angel who seeks solace in the bottom of a whiskey glass. She entices the song's narrator, but he's shocked when her husband shows up, ruing the fact that she's abandoned him and her children. The narrator eventually leaves with Lucille, but is unable to stay with her because of the haunting memory of how she has betrayed her husband. Despite the song's rather silly narrative, Rogers's convincing performance and the song's mainstream pop accompaniment made it a major hit.

Lynn, Loretta (b. 1935) *singer and songwriter*

One of country music's pioneering female performers and songwriters, Lynn has a classic country voice that is perfectly suited to her blunt lyrics that always reflect a woman's point of view. Perhaps the only country singer who has taken on a wide variety of issues, from birth control to the Vietnam

War to spousal abuse, Lynn has made an important contribution to widening the subject matter and audience for country music.

Loretta Webb was born in a small coal-mining community, Butcher Hollow, Kentucky, on April 14, 1935. When she was 13, she married Oliver "Mooney" Lynn, who later became her manager. The couple relocated to Washington State, where Lynn raised four children while she began performing her own material. Her first single, "I'm A Honky Tonk Girl," in the classic barroom mold, was released in 1960 on the tiny Zero label. It brought her to the attention of OWEN BRADLEY, the legendary producer who had worked with PATSY CLINE.

Lynn's early 1960s recordings showed the influence of KITTY WELLS in their brash lyrics of lovin' and losin'. Soon, however, her vocal style softened and her original material turned to unusual (for the time) topics, including "Don't Come Home a-Drinkin' (With Lovin' on Your Mind)," "You Ain't Woman Enough (to Steal My Man)," and "The Pill," a song in support of birth control. All of the songs were written from a woman's point of view; although their sound was classic honky-tonk, their message was unusually liberated for the mid-1960s and early 1970s. This heavy dose of reality in a medium that seemed to thrive on fantasy pointed the direction for many of the more progressive songwriters of the 1970s and 1980s. Lynn's autobiographical song "COAL MINER'S DAUGHTER" (1970), perfectly expressed the pride and anguish of growing up dirt poor in the mountains.

The early 1970s also saw Lynn teamed with CONWAY TWITTY on a series of successful duets, including "After the Fire Is Gone" and "Louisiana Woman, Mississippi Man." Her autobiography, published in the mid-1970s, was instrumental not only in cementing her image as a true country woman, but in reasserting country music's roots at a time when many acts were trying to cross over onto the pop and rock charts. Sadly, the success inspired by her autobiography and the subsequent film of her life seems to have encouraged Lynn in the 1980s and early 1990s to move in a more mainstream direction. She less frequently wrote her own material, and the material selected for her was weak. Her live show leaned heavily on her early hits, and her many fans seemed content to hear her perform the same repertory of well-known numbers.

In 1988 Lynn was elected to the Country Music Hall of Fame. From 1990 to 1996 she withdrew from performing in order to nurse her ailing husband, who finally succumbed to diabetes in August 1996. She returned to performing on a limited basis thereafter, although she has also suffered from time to time with health problems of her own. In 2000 she released her first new album in more than five years on the small Audium label. A second autobiographical volume, *Still Woman Enough*, appeared in 2002. A year later she was awarded a Kennedy Center Honor. In 2004 she issued her first new album of original material in many years, entitled *Van Lear Rose*, working with rocker Jack White of the White Stripes.

![m](musical notation showing the letter m on a staff)

Macon, Uncle Dave (1870–1952) *banjoist*

David Harrison Macon was born outside Nashville, in Smart Station, Tennessee, on October 7, 1870, but the family soon relocated to the big city, where his father operated a hotel located on Nashville's main street. When Macon was a teenager, his father was killed in a brawl outside of the hotel, and his mother opened a rest stop for stage coaches in rural Readyville. As a young man, Dave began playing the banjo as a hobby, meanwhile establishing his own freight-carting business, using mule-drawn wagons. However, after several successful decades, the coming of engine-driven trucks began to threaten Macon's business. In his fifties he decided he could not adapt to new times, and let his business go.

Throughout this period Macon had continued to play the banjo, mostly to amuse his customers and family. In the early 1920s, while visiting a Nashville barbershop, Macon was playing for customers when he was heard by a scout for Loew's vaudeville houses. Macon was soon performing onstage, and in early 1924 he made his first recordings. A year later he was invited to be the second member of WSM's *Barn Dance* program in Nashville, which would soon be renamed the *Grand Ole Opry.*

Macon was an exceptionally talented musician, but his ability to perform stunts—such as playing the banjo while swinging the instrument between his legs and other tricks that he learned through years of informal entertaining—was what really won over his audiences. Macon's hearty vocals, good humor, and energetic banjo playing influenced an entire generation of musicians, including Stringbean and GRANDPA JONES. He recorded hundreds of 78s, often accompanied by the talented McGee brothers and fiddler Sid Harkreader, going under the name the Fruit Jar Drinkers (moonshine—illegal liquor—was often dispensed in used fruit jars, hence the name). In the 1940s and early 1950s he was often accompanied by his son, Dorris, in *Opry* appearances.

Uncle Dave Macon in the WSM Grand Ole Opry *studios, c. 1930s* (Courtesy of BenCar Archives)

Macon's repertoire, like those of other early country performers, was made up of a mix of traditional songs and dance tunes, sentimental and popular songs of the late 19th and early 20th centuries, and his own offbeat adaptations of these songs along with original compositions. Macon's presentation of his material showed the influence of years of performing on the tent-show circuit; his recordings often began and ended with a lusty shout of "Hot dog!" Macon's biting social commentary is illustrated in songs like "In and Around Nashville," in which he criticizes, among other things, women who chew gum and wear "knee-high" skirts. One of his popular songs, "The Cumberland Mountain Deer Chase," was transformed in the 1950s by Pete Seeger into a long story-song for children that he called "The Cumberland Mountain Bear Hunt." Macon died on March 22, 1952, in Nashville.

Maddox, Rose (1925–1998) *singer*

Roselea Arbana Brogdon was born in Boaz, Alabama, on August 15, 1925. Her family, like many other southerners and westerners who had previously worked on farms, emigrated to Southern California in search of a better way of life in the early 1930s. Her five older brothers had a western/cowboy style band, which performed at local rodeos and parties. In 1937 the group was approached by a Modesto, California, radio station to put on a cowboy music show, with the stipulation that they have a female singer. Twelve-year-old Rose was enlisted, and the group was christened the Maddox Brothers and Rose.

The band temporarily broke up due to World War II, but regrouped in the late 1940s, signing with Southern California's Four Star label and producing a series of high-energy recordings that melded western swing with early honky-tonk. Rose's big-throated vocals were ably accompanied by the band, along with her brothers' good-natured horseplay. The group's biggest hit was a 1946 cover of Woody Guthrie's "Philadelphia Lawyer," introducing the song to the country repertoire. In 1951 the group

was signed to Columbia. However, the label saw more potential in Rose's more serious side, and began playing down their antics on the recordings. The band was featured on the popular *Louisiana Hayride* radio program in the early 1950s, and continued to record and perform through 1957.

Rose switched to Capitol Records in 1959 as a solo artist, and continued to have hits through the early 1960s with her gutsy recordings of "Down, Down, Down," "Sing a Little Song of Heartache," and duets with BUCK OWENS, another Southern California–based Capitol star, notably on the classic "Mental Cruelty." In 1963 bluegrass star BILL MONROE suggested to Capitol that Rose's style was perfectly suited to his style of music. Since the folk revival was then in full swing, the label decided to release an album of Rose singing bluegrass standards. This album would become a collector's item a decade later, during the bluegrass revival, and helped launch an entirely new career for Maddox. After a period of inactivity from the mid-1960s through the mid-1970s, she returned as a bluegrass vocalist, recording a number of records for folk revival labels and performing on the bluegrass circuit. However, a number of heart attacks slowed her down, and she retired from performing in the early 1990s, although she made one last album in 1996. She died of kidney failure on April 5, 1998.

Mainer, J. E. (1898–1971) *bandleader*

Joseph Emmett Mainer (b. Weaverville, North Carolina, July 20, 1898) and his younger brother, banjo player Wade (b. April 21, 1907) were both cotton mill workers who began working semiprofessionally in the late 1920s as musicians. In 1934 they were hired by WBT, in Charlotte, North Carolina, and formed their first band, a quartet originally known as the Crazy Mountaineers. A year later they were signed to Bluebird and made their first recordings, including their 1935 hit, "Maple on the Hill." The Mountaineers existed in various forms through the 1930s. At times Wade and J. E. would split, each leading his own Mountaineers, while at other times they came back together. Wade formed his own group, the Sons of the Mountaineers, in 1937, scoring a hit with "Sparkling Blue Eyes" two years later.

After a period of inactivity during World War II, both brothers turned up again in the late 1940s as recording stars on the King label. Toward the end of the decade, folklorist Alan Lomax "discovered" Mainer's band, recording them for two large musical projects he was producing at that time. This led to renewed interest in the group, and some bookings on the folk revival and bluegrass circuits. Later, in the 1960s, Wade was leading a more bluegrass-oriented outfit, while J. E. was in semiretirement, repairing fiddles. J. E. Mainer died on June 12, 1971.

"Make the World Go Away" (1965) *Eddy Arnold's comeback hit*

With this song EDDY ARNOLD returned to hit-making in the mid-1960s after a fallow period that had started in the late 1950s. Recorded with a lush pop arrangement, "Make the World Go Away" is often cited as an example of the excesses of the Nashville sound of the 1960s. Country artists were eager to cross over to the pop charts, and the country audience had little taste for the more traditional instrumentation or themes of earlier times. The song was first recorded for the country audience by RAY PRICE in 1963, but was best known in Arnold's hit version. It was probably the most successful composition by Hank Cochran, who began his career playing rockabilly with Eddie Cochran (no relation) in the 1950s and had some success as a country songwriter and singer in the 1960s.

"Mama He's Crazy" (1984) *first number-one hit for the Judds*

This song launched the career of the JUDDS. Written by Kenny O'Dell, the song plays on the title/chorus line (her new-found love isn't really crazy; he's crazy for her!) The simple, perky tune and the Judds's excellent harmony work made this an instant classic.

"Mamas Don't Let Your Babies Grow Up to Be Cowboys" (1978) *number-one hit for Waylon Jennings and Willie Nelson*

This song topped the country charts for four weeks in 1978 after being recorded by WAYLON JENNINGS and WILLIE NELSON. The song playfully warns parents against the dangers of the cowboy life, as opposed to the lifestyles of "doctors, and lawyers, and such." The song was written by Ed and Patsy Bruce; Ed had a long career, beginning as a rockabilly singer in the 1950s and then recording as a country singer-songwriter from the 1960s through the 1980s.

mandolin

The mandolin, an instrument originally of Neapolitan origin, has become a key voice in bluegrass and country music. Its odyssey into country music is a typical American story of experimentation and innovation.

It is an eight-stringed instrument, tuned like a fiddle, that originally was made with a bowl-shaped back, like a lute. In the late 19th century, American musical instrument designer Orville Gibson came up with a new idea: a carved-body instrument that would emulate the design of the great violins. The back of the instrument had a slight arch, but sat more comfortably against the player's body. Gibson came up with two basic designs, one a pear-shaped instrument with a sweet sound that he called his "A" series, and the other a fancier design with scrolls and points that he called the Florentine or "F" model. Mandolin clubs sprang up on college campuses and in small towns, many organized by the Gibson company. Just after World War I an inexpensive "Army and Navy" model was introduced specifically for sale at military bases. Other makers—notably mass-marketers Lyon and Healy—entered the fray, and soon mandolins were readily available and inexpensive.

The mandolin's first popularity came in the so-called brother acts of the 1930s, although there had been a couple of mandolin players in earlier string

Gibson F-4 mandolin, c. mid-1920s (George Gruhn, Gruhn Guitars)

high-powered, and flashy. After the band broke up, Bill formed his first Blue Grass Boys and became the pioneer of bluegrass-style mandolin. For this reason, most bluegrass pickers prefer the F-series Gibson instrument, the one most closely associated with Monroe, and dozens of companies have copied the design.

The mandolin enjoyed another resurgence in popularity in the 1970s when a group of former bluegrass players took it into a blend of new acoustic and jazz music. David Grisman pioneered what he called "Dawg music," performing in a quintet with two mandolins; soon others were forming similar outfits. Earlier pickers like Tiny Moore (who had played for BOB WILLS) and Jethro Burns (one half of the famed HOMER AND JETHRO comedy act) gained new popularity as masters of a jazz style of picking. The mandolin, which was rarely heard on country recordings outside of bluegrass records, enjoyed new popularity thanks to session work by Grisman and others. Most recently, Sam Bush (an original member of New Grass Revival) has been Nashville's busiest session picker.

Mandrell, Barbara (b. 1948) *singer*

Born in Houston, Texas, on December 25, 1948, Barbara Ann Mandrell came from a musical family. Although born in Texas, she was raised in Southern California. She began playing with the family band at a young age, and was adept at a number of instruments, particularly the pedal steel guitar. When Mandrell was 11, she was already playing the instrument in Las Vegas shows, and two years later she toured with JOHNNY CASH. After a minor hit as a vocalist on "Queen for a Day," released by the small Mosrite label, Mandrell and her family moved to Nashville, where she was signed by Columbia in 1969. She failed to achieve major success until signing with ABC/Dot in the mid-1970s, scoring hits with 1977's "Married (But Not to Each Other)" and "Sleeping Single in a Double Bed," a number-one hit in 1978. Mandrell continued to be a major star in the early 1980s, thanks to the increased exposure

bands. The sweet-voiced instrument, perfect for playing short melodic fills, became a favorite after it was popularized by such duos as the BLUE SKY BOYS. Then, in the mid-1930s, a new brother act hit the radio: the Monroe Brothers. BILL MONROE played a Gibson F-5, the fanciest of the Florentine mandolins introduced in the 1920s, which had a biting sound; his melodic parts were intricate, of a network variety program that she hosted with her sisters, Irlene and Louise.

Barbara's life and career were dealt a severe blow in 1984 when she was involved in a head-on collision with another car, leading to a long period of hospitalization and some doubts about her ability to recover. However, she came back a year later with the hit "Angels in Your Arms," although her popularity on the country charts was already eroding with the influx of new country stars. Through the mid-1990s Mandrell continued to draw sizable audiences to shows in Las Vegas and Branson, Missouri, but her chart-topping days were over. In 1997 she gave a well-publicized farewell show, saying she wished to focus on her acting career.

Mandrell, Louise (b. 1954)

Louise Mandrell was born in Corpus Christi, Texas, on July 13, 1954, and played fiddle and bass in the family band. In 1978 she signed as a solo act to Epic, and a year later married country singer R. C. Bannon, with whom she had her first major hit, the duet "Reunited." The pair signed to RCA in 1981, and Louise continued to have solo hits with "Where There's Smoke There's Fire." Beginning in 1983 she appeared with her sisters BARBARA MANDRELL and Irlene Mandrell on network TV, spawning hits with "Save Me" and "Too Hot to Sleep." Louise's last major charting song to date was 1984's "I'm Not through Loving You Yet." Louise's career slowed after the Mandrell sisters' TV show was canceled.

"Man, I Feel Like a Woman" (2001) *major country, pop, and adult contemporary hit for Shania Twain*

This song was promoted with a clever video in which SHANIA TWAIN was accompanied by a group of hunky men on guitars, a direct response to an earlier pop video by singer Robert Palmer for the song "Simply Irresistible" in which he was surrounded by a similar band of good-looking women. Twain wrote the song with her husband, producer Robert "Mutt" Lange, who specializes in mainstream pop, so it's not surprising that this—and their many other hits—have sold well beyond the country audience.

Maphis, Joe (1921–1986) *guitarist*

Otis Wilson Maphis was born in Suffolk, Virginia, on May 12, 1921. Raised in Cumberland, Maryland, Joe began performing with his father in the family band, the Railsplitters, in 1932. Not content to simply play chord accompaniments to the band's uptempo readings of traditional square dance tunes, Maphis developed his unique approach to finger-picking the melody. When he was 17, Maphis went professional, eventually performing on country radio shows such as Chicago's *National Barn Dance*. He took up the newly introduced electric guitar in 1947, and in the same year hooked up with vocalist Rose Lee (b. Baltimore, Maryland, 1922), who was to become his musical partner and, five years later, his wife. The duo wrote a honky-tonk classic, "Dim Lights, Thick Smoke (And Loud, Loud Music)," still one of the favorites of this genre. In 1952 they were invited to star on the Southern California–based *Town Hall Party* TV program.

In 1954 Maphis became one of the first performers in any musical style to play a twin-necked guitar, recording the classic "Fire on the Strings," his adaptation of a country fiddle standard, "Fire on the Mountain." He also began performing as a session musician on mandolin, banjo, and guitar, as well as recording and performing with the other great country guitarist of the day, MERLE TRAVIS. Maphis's distinctive picking can be heard on the early pop hits of Ricky Nelson, as well as on theme songs for TV's *Bonanza* and *The FBI*.

Maphis and his wife continued to record through the 1980s. He also encouraged his young niece, BARBARA MANDRELL, another talented instrumentalist, to enter country music as a profession. Always a heavy smoker, Maphis succumbed to lung cancer on June 27, 1986. Sons Dale and Jody carried forward his sound as Nashville session men.

Martin, Grady (1929–2001) *guitarist and fiddle player*

Thomas Grady Martin was born in Chapel Hill, Tennessee, on January 17, 1929. Martin played fiddle and guitar as a youngster; he debuted on the *Grand Ole Opry* as a fiddler at age 17, two years after moving to Nashville from his small hometown. However, he would become famous as one of Nashville's leading session guitarists. He cut the jazzy guitar instrumental "Chattanooga Shoeshine Boy" on his own in the late 1940s, and then moved into a steady stream of session work, beginning with HANK WILLIAMS and continuing with most of the big-name country acts through the 1970s.

Martin was a member of the group of studio musicians who worked under the guidance of producer CHET ATKINS, including pianist FLOYD CRAMER. Like Cramer he developed a pleasant, adaptable, middle-of-the-road style. In 1979 he joined WILLIE NELSON's road band, with which he performed for the next 16 years. In 1995 he retired from performing, and he died on December 3, 2001.

Massey, Louise, and the Westerners

Victoria Louise Massey was born in Hart County, Texas, on August 2, 1902. The Massey family relocated when her father purchased a farm in New Mexico in 1914. The entire family—father, mother, and eight children—were musically inclined. Louise's dad was an old-style western fiddler, and Louise herself was a talented pianist and vocalist. Louise married bass player Milt Mabie in 1919, and he quickly became a member of the group. The Massey family band began performing on the local vaudeville circuit in the early 1920s, and then began longer tours across the United States and Canada. The elder Massey finally retired, exhausted by life on the road. The rest of the band settled into a five-year stint on KMBC radio out of Kansas City, Missouri, which led to a network broadcast on the station's parent network, CBS. In 1933 a talent scout for the WLS *Barn Dance,* out of Chicago, heard the group and signed them to this influential show.

The center of attention of the band was the glamorous Louise who, besides providing lead vocals, was also something of a fashion plate, wearing Spanish-style costumes for their "south of the border" numbers and pioneering sequined cowboy suits for herself and members of the band, while she wore satin boots. The group, now known as Louise Massey and the Westerners, moved east to broadcast out of New York for a couple of years, before returning to Chicago and then going to Hollywood to appear in the low-budget cowboy film *Where the Buffalo Roam,* starring TEX RITTER.

Like most of the cowboy bands of the day, the group played a wide range of material, mostly filtered through a soft pop sound. Besides the obligatory cowboy and sentimental numbers, they played dance music as varied as fiddle tunes, eastern European polkas, waltzes, and schottisches, novelty numbers, ragtime, light jazz, and even an occasionally jazzed up traditional mountain song. Louise wrote many of the group's hits, including their early 1934 disc "When the White Azaleas Start Blooming," featuring her honey-voiced vocals, and their biggest number, 1941's "My Adobe Hacienda," which would become a crossover country and pop hit after World War II. Other major hits for the group were 1939's "South of the Border (Down Mexico Way)" and "I Only Want a Buddy (Not a Sweetheart)."

In 1948 Louise and her husband Milt retired to New Mexico. Her brother Curt went to Hollywood, where he would gain fame as the writer of two memorable TV themes, for *The Beverly Hillbillies* and its spinoff series, *Petticoat Junction.* (He also sang the *Petticoat Junction* theme song.) Louise died on June 22, 1983.

Mattea, Kathy (b. 1959) *singer*

Born in Cross Lanes, West Virginia (southwest of Charleston), on June 21, 1959, Mattea began playing music in her teens, and she joined a bluegrass band while a student at the state college. She left college to move to Nashville, where she got a job as a tour guide at the Country Music Hall of Fame and did occasional work as a backup and demo vocalist. She was signed to Mercury in 1983, but failed to produce any hits until three years later, when she scored big with a cover of Nanci Griffith's song "Love at the Five and Dime." She enjoyed several more hits through the 1980s, including the modern-day truck drivin' song "Eighteen Wheels and a Dozen Roses" (1988), "Come from the Heart" and "Burnin' Old Heart" (1989), and "She Came from Fort Worth" (1990). Mattea suffered from vocal-cord problems in 1992, and to date has not achieved great chart success since then.

McBride, Martina (b. 1966) *singer*

Martina Mariea Schiff was born in Sharon, Kansas, a small farming community near the Oklahoma border, on July 29, 1966. Her father, Daryl Schiff, led the family in a band called the Schiffters, which featured Martina on lead vocals and keyboards. They played at local clubs, benefits, and parties through Martina's high school years in 1984.

Martina briefly attended community college while continuing to work as a singer with local bands. Through one of her bands she met John McBride, a native of Wichita who owned a rehearsal studio and worked as a sound engineer. The two married in 1988, and they relocated to Nashville in search of careers. In late 1991 Martina was signed to RCA Nashville. Her first album and single releases were not terribly successful, but her career took off in 1993 with her second album, *The Way That I Am,* buoyed by the hit, "My Baby Loves Me." McBride enjoyed minor hits through the 1990s, but broke out to greater success with her 1999 album *Emotion,* featuring the ballad "I Love You," which spent five weeks at number one on the country charts and won McBride a Grammy nomination for best country song. As part of a hits album in 2001, she released a new single "When God-Fearin' Women Get the Blues," promoted through a clever video. Further hits followed, including the number-one hit "Blessed." She won the Best Female Vocalist award from the Academy of Country Music in 2002 and 2003.

McCall, C. W. (b. 1928) *monologuist*

William Fries was born in Audubon, Iowa, on November 15, 1928. A fine-arts major at the University of Iowa, Fries took a job after graduation in advertising. In the early 1970s he created the character of C. W. McCall for an ad campaign for a local bakery. His spoken monologues touting the goodness of old-time baked products soon were drawing lots of attention on local radio; in 1974 he adapted the routine successfully to his first record, "The Old Home Filler-Up and Keep on A-Truckin' Cafe." It was his first commercial hit. Follow-up monologues included "Wolf Creek Pass," "Classified," "Black Bear Road," and his biggest hit, 1975's "Convoy." McCall continued to churn out minor hits, including 1976's "There Won't Be No Country Music (There Won't Be No Rock 'n' Roll)" and the comic novelty "Crispy Critters," followed a year later by "Roses for Mama." In 1982 he was elected mayor of the small Colorado town of Ouray, and retired from both advertising and music, although he attempted a comeback in 1990.

McClinton, O. B. (1942–1987) *guitarist and songwriter*

Obie Burnett McClinton was born in Senatobia, Mississippi, on April 25, 1942. The son of an African-American reverend in rural Mississippi, O. B. was exposed early on to country radio. He particularly favored the bluesy sounds of HANK WILLIAMS. At 17, he ran away from home and landed in Memphis, where he got his first guitar. After working odd jobs in the big city, he returned to Mississippi to attend Rust College on a choral scholarship, performing with the a cappella choir there. In 1966, after graduation, he returned to Memphis and worked as a disc jockey for a while, and then enrolled in the air force at the end of the year. He appeared in several talent shows, where he was discovered by the owner of Memphis's Goldwax records, Quinton Claunch. His songs became popular among many Memphis-based soul artists, and he attracted the attention of Stax Records executive

Al Bell in the early 1970s, who signed him to Stax's country label, Enterprise.

O. B.'s first hit was 1972's "Don't Let the Green Grass Fool You," followed by a version of the MERLE HAGGARD classic "Okie from Muskogee" remade as "Obie from Senatobia." He had a 1974 hit with "Something Better," and then, a year later, after Stax folded, he moved to several other labels before landing at Epic, where he was produced by country producer Buddy Killen, who had discovered Joe Tex. O. B.'s Epic hits included the 1978 single "Hello, This Is Anna." He moved to the smaller Sunbird label in the early 1980s, and then the even smaller Moonshine label for a minor hit with 1984's "Honky Tonk Tan," before being diagnosed with cancer. The disease took his life on September 23, 1987.

McCoy, Charlie (b. 1941) *harmonica player and singer*

Charles Ray McCoy was born in Oak Hill, West Virginia, on March 28, 1941. He began playing the harmonica at age eight and had some music training in his teen years as both a vocalist and arranger. In the late 1950s he began performing on both rock and country circuits as a backup artist; MEL TILLIS heard him playing at a local club and introduced him to his Nashville agent, who brought McCoy to the country-music capital, where he began playing sessions, tours, and the *Grand Ole Opry* radio show. He also gained a great deal of exposure playing in country star Stonewall Jackson's touring band.

In the early 1960s McCoy signed a contract as a vocalist. Not much success resulted, although he did have a minor hit in 1961 with "Cherry Berry Wine." He subsequently led his own pop-rock lounge group in Nashville, the Escorts, and also played sessions with various artists, appearing prominently on Roy Orbison's single "Candy Man." Thanks to his playing, the harmonica was established as a must-have instrument on hundreds of Nashville recordings.

McCoy was much in demand as a studio musician through the 1960s, impressing folk rocker Bob Dylan, who used him on his *Blonde on Blonde* and *Nashville Skyline* sessions. This led to work with other pop stars interested in the country sound, including Ringo Starr, Joan Baez, and Elvis Presley. McCoy joined with the Nashville-based supergroup Area Code 615, and his harmonica playing was featured on their instrumental hit "Stone Fox Chase."

In 1972 McCoy's solo recording of "Today I Started Loving You Again," originally recorded as an album track four years earlier, started getting airplay on country radio, and it was followed by a series of covers, including HANK WILLIAMS's "I'm So Lonesome I Could Cry" and the perennial bluegrass fiddle-festival favorite "Orange Blossom Special." He recorded "Boogie Woogie" with the country-rock group Barefoot Jerry in 1974, and in the early 1980s formed a partnership with Laney Hicks that produced minor hits, 1981's "Until the Night" and 1983's "The State of Our Union." McCoy served as musical director for the country comedy TV show *Hee Haw* from 1977 until 1996.

McDaniel, Mel (b. 1942) *singer and songwriter*

Born in Checotah, Oklahoma, on September 9, 1942, McDaniel began his career as a rocker. He briefly moved to Nashville, then went to Alaska, where he worked as a lounge singer, and finally returned to Nashville, where he performed at the Holiday Inn while pursuing a songwriting career. His big break came in 1976 when his comic novelty "Roll Your Own" was covered by Commander Cody and His Lost Planet Airmen, Hoyt Axton, and Arlo Guthrie. This led to a contract with Capitol Records, and a minor hit with a cover version of "Have a Dream on Me" in 1976, followed by a couple more minor successes through the late 1970s.

In the early 1980s McDaniel's luck took a turn for the better. His 1981 releases "Louisiana Saturday Night" and "Right in the Palm of Your Hand" were major successes, followed by a number of top-20 hits through the mid-1980s. He was made a *Grand Ole Opry* member in 1986, but since then he has had few major hits.

McDonald, Skeets (1915–1968) *singer*

Enos William McDonald was born on a small farm near Greenway, Arkansas, on October 1, 1915. He moved to Michigan with his family in 1932, where he formed his first band, the Lonesome Cowboys, specializing in a blend of country, pop, and jazz. They performed on Michigan radio through the early 1940s, until McDonald was drafted into the army in 1943. He revived the band in 1946, and then made a couple of solo recordings, including "Please Daddy Don't Go to War" in 1950. McDonald was hired as lead singer for the Michigan-based group Johnny White and His Rhythm Riders soon after, returning to an uptempo country-boogie sound with a couple of minor hits, including "Mean and Evil Blues" and "The Tattooed Lady."

By 1952 McDonald was living in Los Angeles and signed to Capitol Records, where he had his biggest hit with his own composition, "Don't Let the Stars Get in Your Eyes." By the mid-1950s he had jumped on the rockabilly bandwagon, recording the novelty hit "You Ought to See Grandma Rock and Roll." He was signed as a country act to Columbia in the early 1960s, having minor hits in the mid-1960s with "Call Me Mr. Brown" and "You Took Her off My Hands," both in the pop-country style then popular. McDonald died of a heart attack on March 31, 1968.

McEnery, Red River Dave (1914–2002) *singer*

McEnery was born in San Antonio, Texas, on December 15, 1914. After performing throughout the South on a variety of small radio stations, McEnery hit it big when he moved to New York City in the late 1930s. Before returning to his native Texas, he released his recording of "Amelia Earhart's Last Flight" in 1941, the first in a long string of topical songs based on current events. After the war, he appeared in a couple of low-budget westerns, including 1948's *Swing in the Saddle.*

McEnery's career faded in the 1950s, but brightened again in the early 1960s with "The Ballad of Francis Gary Powers," recounting the story of the shooting down of the famous spy plane pilot over Russia. He followed this with such perishable topical numbers as "The Flight of Apollo Eleven" and even "The Ballad of Patty Hearst." In his later years, Dave was more of a personality than a performer, well known for his long white hair and pointy goatee, gold-colored boots, and glittering, Nudie-styled cowboy suits. He died on January 15, 2002.

McEntire, Reba (b. 1954) *actress and singer*

Born in Chockie, Oklahoma, on March 28, 1954, McEntire comes from an authentic rodeo family; her grandfather was a celebrity on the national rodeo circuit, and her father was a talented roper. Her brother, Pake, and two sisters, Alice and Susie, all performed in rodeos, as did young Reba, and the four formed a family singing group, scoring a local hit in 1971 with a ballad memorializing their grandfather, "The Ballad of John McEntire." Country star Red Steagall heard Reba sing the national anthem at the National Rodeo Finals in Oklahoma City in 1974 and invited her to come to Nashville to make a demo. Reba, her mother, and Pake all ended up in Nashville, and both Pake and Reba made their first albums in late 1975.

Reba's first recordings were in a traditional style, and although they forecast the new country trends of the next decade, they failed to find much chart action. In the late 1970s and early 1980s she finally began to see some chart action, covering PATSY CLINE's "Sweet Dreams" and "A Poor Man's Roses"; McEntire's first number-one record came in 1983 with "Can't Even Get the Blues." This launched a series of hits through the decade.

In 1987 McEntire divorced her first husband. Two years later she wed her steel guitarist and road manager, Narvel Blackstock. The duo began building McEntire's empire, taking over the responsibility of managing and booking her act, working with the record company and producers to shape her image, and even becoming involved in the nuts and bolts of song publishing and transporting equipment for tours. She also began to pursue an acting career, landing some minor TV roles in miniseries and movies, but her best acting remained in her videos in which she continued to project a feisty, down-home, lovable personality.

The 1990s saw McEntire continue to be a strong concert draw, while her recordings consistently sold well. In 1999, celebrating her 40 millionth record sold, the Recording Industry of America named her "Female Country Artist of the Century." In 2001 McEntire made a splash when she appeared on Broadway in the revival of Irving Berlin's *Annie Get Your Gun,* showing that her perky performance style translated well to the musical stage. That fall, her own sitcom premiered on the WB network.

McGraw, Tim (b. 1967) *singer*

Timothy Samuel McGraw was born in Delhi, Louisiana (near the Mississippi border), on May 1, 1967. He descends from baseball royalty: his father, Tug McGraw, had an affair with his mother, a fact that was not revealed to McGraw until he was a teen. To that point, he was raised as "Tim Smith," the unassuming son of a trucker. McGraw at first focused on a possible sports career, but a knee injury in college sidelined his goal, and he turned to music and the guitar. Arriving in Nashville in 1989, he scuffled around until Tug arranged for a friend at Curb Records to listen to his son's audition tape, and McGraw was signed to the label in 1991.

After releasing a debut album in 1992 that saw little action, McGraw leapt to prominence with the release of 1994's aptly titled *Not a Moment Too Soon.* The best-selling country album of the year, it yielded two gold singles ("Indian Outlaw" and "Don't Take the Girl") in less than three months, a feat not yet beaten as of 2005. The hits kept coming with his third album release, *All I Want,* in 1995. On this album McGraw balanced romantic ballads (the title track) with more uptempo rockers ("I Like It, I Love It"). Following its release, McGraw made a summer tour, selecting up-and-coming country singer FAITH HILL as his opening act. A romance blossomed, and the two were wed in 1996.

Tim McGraw and Faith Hill backstage at the CMA Awards (Raeanne Rubenstein)

Cashing in on their romantic attachment, McGraw and Hill released their first vocal duet, "It's Your Love," which was the lead release from McGraw's fourth album, 1997's *Everywhere.* The song spent six weeks in the number-one spot, a *Billboard* record, and launched further McGraw mania. McGraw also coproduced singer JO DEE MESSINA's first album that year, launching her career.

In 1999 McGraw released his next album, *A Place in the Sun,* which continued the formula of bad-boy uptempo numbers and tearful ballads, producing five hit singles, including two number-one hits ("Please Remember Me" and "Something Like That"). The album debuted at number one on both pop and country charts. McGraw issued a *Greatest Hits* set in 2000. Another duet with Hill—"Let's Make Love"—brought McGraw his first Grammy. McGraw released *Set This Circus Down* in April 2001, featuring the lead single, "Grown Men Don't Cry," a tearful weeper. By the turn of the 21st century, McGraw had sold more than 19 million albums and nearly 5 million singles, eclipsing GARTH BROOKS as the biggest male name in country music.

"Me and Bobby McGee" (1969) *influential song by Kris Kristofferson*

Although not a major hit in its initial recording by ROGER MILLER, "Me and Bobby McGee" represents a landmark in the transition from 1960s to 1970s country music. It was the first charting song written by new songwriter KRIS KRISTOFFERSON, who soon would provide major hits for JOHNNY CASH ("Sunday Morning Going Down") and Sammi Smith ("Help Me Make It through the Night"). Kristofferson was the first of a new generation of songwriters influenced by Bob Dylan and rock music, bringing a contemporary edge to country music. Although not a great hit for Miller, the song was an enormous (albeit posthumous) success in 1971 for pop star Janis Joplin, her sole number-one hit. It remains Kristofferson's best-known song.

Messina, Jo Dee (b. 1970) *singer*

Hailing from Holliston, Massachusetts, where she was born on August 25, 1970, Messina began her career at age 13 at the local Holiday Inn, belting out "Stand by Your Man." As an older teen she formed her own country band, which gained some popularity around New England. At age 20 she moved to Nashville to try to make it as a singer. She became a regular at a local bar showcase, the Pink Elephant, winning a prize that gained her a radio job in Kentucky. Meanwhile, a young producer named Byron Gallimore was developing his own new artist, TIM MCGRAW. Hearing Messina, he signed

her to a development deal. Gallimore brought her to Curb Records in 1995.

In 1996 Messina's debut album was released, yielding two hits, the uptempo number-one hit "Heads Carolina, Tails California" and the number-five hit "We're Not in Kansas Anymore." It took Messina two years to produce a follow-up, but her next album, *I'm Alright,* produced several hits, including the number four "Bye Bye" and the number-two title track. In 1999 she won the Horizon Award for best new artist from the Country Music Association, and *Billboard* named her the most-played female artist of the year.

In 2000 Messina released *Burn,* a pop-influenced collection that launched her as a pop, as well as country, superstar. The album's first single, "That's the Way," held the number-one spot for four weeks, earning her her first Grammy nomination for Best Female Country Performance. The album produced three more hits, including a duet with McGraw on "Bring on the Rain." A Christmas album followed in 2002, and then a greatest hits collection a year later.

Miller, Roger (1936–1992) *singer and songwriter*

Roger Dean Miller was born in Fort Worth, Texas, on January 2, 1936. Although born in a large city, Miller grew up in tiny Erick, Oklahoma. His father died when he was an infant, and Miller was raised by his aunt and uncle, who had a small cotton-and-chicken farm there. Like many other future country stars, Miller was exposed to the music through the radio, and also through a relative, country comic Sheb Wooley.

After completing the eighth grade, Miller worked as a ranch hand and small-time rodeo star for several years before enlisting in the army during the Korean War. By this time he was an adept guitarist who could also play the fiddle, banjo, piano, and drums. After the war Miller traveled to Nashville for an audition at RCA Records. Although Miller's initial audition was not successful, he did eventually get session and band work, playing the fiddle for comedian MINNIE PEARL and joining FARON YOUNG's backup band as a drummer.

In the late 1950s Miller began achieving success as a songwriter, first with "Invitation to the Blues," covered by RAY PRICE (with whom he played as a backup musician) and, later, pop crooner Patti Page. Further Miller-penned hits included "Half a Mind" for ERNEST TUBB and "Billy Bayou" for JIM REEVES. Miller had his first hit as a performer with 1961's "When Two Worlds Collide," which he cowrote with BILL ANDERSON.

Miller was still frustrated, however, with Nashville's failure to take him seriously as a solo act, so he relocated to Hollywood in 1963. There he signed with the MGM subsidiary Smash Records. It was at this label that he had his biggest success, including his first two novelty songs, 1964's "Chug-a-Lug" and the perennial favorite "Dang Me." His most productive year was 1965, when he had the monster hit "King of the Road" as well as "Engine Engine No. 9" and "Kansas City Star." Smash, a label more oriented toward pop than country, successfully marketed Miller as a pop star, and his songs reached number one on the pop charts but settled only in the top 10 on the country charts. In 1966 pop singer Andy Williams had a big hit with Miller's "In the Summertime."

Miller's career went into eclipse from the late 1960s through the mid-1980s. His big comeback came in the mid-1980s with the Broadway hit *Big River,* a musical based on Mark Twain's *Adventures of Huckleberry Finn,* which he scored. Miller's good-humored country songs were a perfect fit for this light musical, and his success on the Broadway stage brought renewed interest in his country music career. Sadly, Miller died soon after on October 25, 1992.

Milsap, Ronnie (b. 1943) *singer*

Milsap was born in Robbinsville, North Carolina, near the Tennessee border, on January 16, 1943. Blind from birth, he was a musical prodigy, becoming proficient on several instruments by the time he

was 10 years old. In high school he formed his first group, and decided to pursue music full time. He performed with blues rocker J. J. Cale before going out on his own, recording his first singles for the Scepter label in an R&B style. In 1969 he settled in Nashville and began writing and performing in a mainstream country style.

Although he had some minor hits, Milsap's career didn't really take off until he signed with RCA Records in 1973. From 1975's "Day Dreams about Night Things," Milsap scored major hits through the mid-1980s, primarily focusing on smooth ballads. Perhaps his biggest crossover pop/country hits were 1981's "(There's) No Gettin' Over Me" and "I Wouldn't Have Missed It for the World," and his 1982 remake of Chuck Jackson's 1962 hit, "Any Day Now." However, Milsap's recording career went into decline by the mid-1980s, although he continues to be a strong concert draw.

Monroe, Bill (1911–1996) *mandolinist and bandleader*

Justifiably known as the "Father of Bluegrass Music," mandolinist Bill Monroe was a highly influential composer, vocalist, and instrumentalist. He was born William Smith Monroe in Rosine, Kentucky, on September 13, 1911, the youngest in a family of farmers and musicians. His elder brother Charlie played guitar and another brother, Birch, played the fiddle. Because he was the youngest by a wide gap (Charlie, the next in line, was eight years older), and also because of poor eyesight, Monroe grew up a shy loner who sought refuge in his music.

Charlie and Birch left home to search for employment in the North in the mid-1920s, settling in East Chicago, Indiana. Bill joined them there when he was 18 years old and stayed for five years. They worked in the local oil refineries by day, while playing music at nights and on weekends. In 1934 Chicago radio station WLS offered them full-time employment; Birch quit the group, but Charlie and Bill continued as the Monroe Brothers. They relocated to the Carolinas in 1935, performing on radio out of Greenville and Charlotte sponsored by Texas Crystals, a popular over-the-counter home remedy.

In 1936 Bluebird Records (a division of RCA Victor) made the brothers' first recordings. They recorded traditional songs and hymns, including their first hit, "What Would You Give (In Exchange for Your Soul)." Their recording of the folk standard "Nine Pound Hammer (Roll On Buddy)" was widely imitated, and shows how they could take a traditional song and modernize and energize it. Charlie's laconic delivery was a good foil to his brother's highly charged tenor vocals, and their records and radio appearances were very successful.

The brothers split up in 1938. A year later, with his new group, known as the Blue Grass Boys, Bill auditioned for legendary *Grand Ole Opry* announcer GEORGE D. HAY, who hired him on the spot; Monroe's first performance on the *Opry* was of the JIMMIE RODGERS classic that he made his own, "Mule Skinner Blues." During 1945–46 Monroe's greatest band was assembled, featuring Lester Flatt as lead vocalist and guitarist and Earl Scruggs on banjo. (See FLATT AND SCRUGGS.) The group recorded some of Monroe's first compositions, including the classic "Blue Moon of Kentucky," "Footprints in the Snow," and "Will You Be Loving Another Man?" They also recorded fine instrumentals, with "Bluegrass Breakdown" introducing Earl Scruggs's new banjo style, which would be the model for all bluegrass banjo playing to come. The group's Columbia recordings made between 1946 and 1948, along with their appearances on the *Opry* and on the road, made them legends in their own time.

Flatt and Scruggs left the band to form their own group in 1948. Monroe continued to lead bands through the 1950s, scoring hits on the country charts. He composed a series of high-powered instrumentals featuring his mandolin playing, including "Rawhide" and "Roanoke." He also composed his homage to his fiddling uncle, "Uncle Pen," which has become a bluegrass standard. By the mid-to-late 1950s, Monroe was experimenting with a twin fiddle sound, composing the instrumental "Scotland" using one fiddle as a drone to try to cap-

ture the modal sound of the traditional music that was at the roots of his Appalachian heritage.

In the early 1960s Monroe linked up with Ralph Rinzler, a young mandolinist who became his connection to the folk revival. Rinzler encouraged Monroe's label, Decca, to reissue his 1950s recordings and also acted as Monroe's agent, booking him into many prestigious folk festivals. By the late 1960s and early 1970s, Monroe was an established legend in the bluegrass and country worlds. Fiddler Kenny Baker, who had originally played with Monroe in the late 1950s and early 1960s, became a fixture in the band from 1967 through the early 1980s. Bill's son James Monroe, born in 1941, was also often featured in the band on bass and vocals, although he also formed his own group, the Midnight Ramblers. New country star RICKY SKAGGS, who got his start in bluegrass, did much to revive Monroe's songs for a new audience, as well as featuring Monroe in his video "Country Boy" and on his recordings. Monroe continued to perform until shortly before his death on September 3, 1996.

Bill's brother Charlie (b. Rosine, Kentucky, July 4, 1903–September 27, 1975) had a less successful career after the brothers split in 1938. He formed his own band that eventually took the name of the Kentucky Pardners, recording, working radio, and touring through 1957. He made a few further appearances, coming out of retirement in 1972 to perform on the bluegrass circuit until his death.

Montana, Patsy (1908–1996) *singer, fiddle player, and yodeler*

Rubye Blevins was born in Jessieville, Arkansas, near Hot Springs, on October 30, 1908. A talented fiddler, vocalist, and yodeler, she originally partnered with JIMMIE DAVIS in the early 1930s before joining the Prairie Ramblers, a four-piece western band featured on Chicago's *WLS Barn Dance* program. Their 1935 recording of "I Want to Be a Cowboy's Sweetheart" was Montana's million-selling signature song, and lay the groundwork for the success of women in country music after World

War II. She remained with the Ramblers through 1941, recording sporadically through the 1940s as a soloist and appearing on radio on the ABC network program *Wake Up and Smile* right after World War II. Montana retired from active recording and performing in the 1950s, although she continued to appear occasionally through the 1980s. She died on May 3, 1996.

Montgomery, Melba (b. 1938) *singer*

Born in Iron City, Tennessee, on October 14, 1938, but raised in rural Alabama, Montgomery was introduced to music as a young girl by her father, who taught singing at her hometown's Methodist church, as well as playing fiddle and guitar at local parties. Along with her brothers, she formed a family harmony band that performed at fairs, talent contests, and local charity events.

In the late 1950s Montgomery relocated to Nashville in search of a singing career, and she won a talent contest in 1958 sponsored by WSM, the home station of the *Grand Ole Opry*. One of the judges was ROY ACUFF, who added her to his road show. In 1962 she broke with Acuff, and a year later was linked with GEORGE JONES for a series of successful duets, beginning with "We Must Have Been out of Our Minds" and followed in 1964 by "Let's Invite Them Over." She continued to record and perform with Jones until 1967, although she also made solo recordings with some success, including 1963's "Hall of Shame," as well as dueting with other pop and country stars, including Gene Pitney in 1966.

In the early 1970s Montgomery moved to Capitol Records, where she was paired with producer Pete Drake and singing partner Charlie Louvin (of the LOUVIN BROTHERS). When Drake was invited to start a country division for the folk rock label Elektra Records in 1973, he took Montgomery with him, and she scored her biggest solo hits with him, including the 1974 number-one cover of HARLAN HOWARD's "No Change." By 1977 the hits had dried up, but Montgomery continued to record for small-

er labels into the early 1980s, scoring only sporadic success. She reunited with Charlie Louvin for some recordings in the early 1990s.

Montgomery Gentry

Baritone vocalist Eddie Montgomery (b. Gerald Edward Montgomery, Danville, Kentucky, September 30, 1963) is the younger brother of country star John Michael Montgomery; he met lead vocalist Troy Lee Gentry (b. Lexington, Kentucky, April 5, 1967) while both were working in bar bands around Lexington, Kentucky. They both ended up in John Michael's backup band, working with him until he achieved enough success to go solo. Gentry then tried to make it as a solo artist. He won a Jim Beam talent contest in 1994, which earned him a slot as an opening act for several country headliners, but didn't lead to a recording deal. He turned to Lexington with Montgomery soon after, and the pair soldiered on as a duo, first calling themselves Deuce, and then combining their two last names. A showcase performance attracted the attention of Columbia Records, which signed them in the late 1990s.

The duo is often compared with southern rockers such as CHARLIE DANIELS, the Allman Brothers, and Lynyrd Skynyrd; they rock harder than BROOKS AND DUNN, although their music could be seen as an extension of that successful pair's bootscootin' sound. Their association with southern rock is furthered by their choice of backup musicians on record, which includes a number of Allman Brothers–associated musicians, including keyboardist Chuck Leavell. Montgomery Gentry is made more distinctive thanks to their unusual vocal stylings; Gentry has a sweet, high tenor, which Montgomery complements with an earthy, sometimes raspy, baritone. They also are known for their energetic stage show and dress; Montgomery is particularly flamboyant, with his all-black suit, featuring a long-tailed coat, and wide-brimmed black hat. He wields the microphone like a weapon.

Montgomery Gentry showing off their duds at the CMA Awards (Raeanne Rubenstein)

Their first album, *Tattoos and Scars,* produced two top five hits, "Lonely and Gone" and "All Night Long," which featured Charlie Daniels. Their success was noted by the Country Music Association, which named them "Duo of the Year" in 2000, ending the eight-year dominance of this category by Brooks and Dunn. Montgomery Gentry continued to produce hits with their next two releases, 2000's *Carryin' On* (the number-two hit "She Couldn't Change Me"), and 2002's *My Town,* whose title track reached number five. The classic barroom rocker "Hell Yeah" followed as a major hit, propelled by a successful video portraying the duo performing in a rowdy roadhouse.

Morgan, George (1924–1975) *singer*

George Thomas Morgan was born in Waverly, Tennessee, on June 28, 1924, but spent his high school years in rural Ohio. After graduation, he worked part time as a performer while holding day jobs in truck driving and sales. After World War II he was hired as a regular vocalist on Wheeling, West Virginia's WWVA *Jamboree* radio program, which won him the attention of Columbia Records. In 1947 Columbia released his first recording, his self-penned schmaltz classic, "Candy Kisses," which raced to number one. He became a member of the *Grand Ole Opry* in 1949, and had a few lesser follow-up hits with the equally sentimental "Rainbow in My Heart," "Room Full of Roses," and "Cry-Baby Heart."

Although he continued to be popular on radio and in personal appearances, Jones would never again equal his early hit-making days. By the mid-1960s Columbia had dropped him, and he moved to Starday. By the early 1970s he was moving from label to label. He scored a minor hit with 1973's "Red Rose From the Blue Side of Town" on MCA. In 1975, while working on the roof of his house, he suffered from a heart attack, and he died soon after, on July 7, 1975.

His daughter, Lorrie (b. Loretta Lynn Morgan, Nashville, Tennessee, June 27, 1960), enjoyed success as a country balladeer in the early 1990s. After touring as a backup singer for George Jones, she joined the *Grand Ole Opry* in 1984. In 1987 she met new country singer KEITH WHITLEY backstage, and he became her second husband. Whitley was a heavy drinker, however, and he died of alcohol poisoning two years later. After his death Lorrie was propelled to country stardom with the weeper "Dear Me," which seemed to reflect her turbulent life. Morgan enjoyed her greatest success in the early 1990s, including her 1992 hits "Watch Me" and "Something in Red." Further number-one hits came in 1993 with the brassy "What Part of No" and her final number one, 1995's "I Didn't Know My Own Strength." However, her star faded after that. She wed singer Sammy Kershaw in the late 1990s; the couple produced a duet album in 2001.

Morris, Gary (b. 1948) *singer and actor*

Born in Fort Worth, Texas, on December 7, 1948, Morris got his musical start in the church choir before forming a pop country trio in high school; after graduation, the threesome successfully auditioned for a job in a Denver country music club, where they performed for several years. Morris returned to Texas in the early 1970s. Through his agent, Morris was asked to perform at rallies during Jimmy Carter's 1976 presidential bid; this led to a performance at the White House in 1978, followed by some demo recordings for MCA, and then a contract with Warner Brothers in 1980.

Morris's greatest success came in the early-to-mid-1980s, beginning with 1981's "Headed for a Heartache," through 1983's "Velvet Chains," and then a string of number one hits beginning with "Baby Bye Bye" in 1985 and its follow-up, the R&B-flavored "I'll Never Stop Loving You." In 1984 Morris appeared in an off-Broadway play, costarring with Linda Ronstadt in an updated version of Puccini's *La Bohème;* he asked Ronstadt to record "Makin' Up for Lost Time," a song he cowrote with Dave Loggins, as a duet with him. She was signed to another label, so the record was eventually made with his labelmate CRYSTAL GAYLE. It became a number-one hit in 1986. Although Gayle had recorded her part separately from Morris and had never met him, the success of this song led a year later to them recording an entire album of duets.

Morris's TV career blossomed in 1986 when he was hired to portray a blind country singer in several episodes of ABC's soap *Dynasty II: The Colbys;* he premiered on the show his last number-one single to date, 1987's "Leave Me Lonely," from his album *Plain Brown Wrapper,* a more simplified, roots-oriented effort than his earlier Nashville pop work. Later that year, he appeared in the Broadway production of *Les Miserables.* Although he continues to perform on the *Grand Ole Opry* and to tour, his country recording career faded out in the late 1980s.

"Mountain Music" (1982) *Alabama's best-known song*

One of a string of 20 number-one country hits released by the popular country harmony group ALABAMA between 1980 and 1986, its anthemic chorus made it a fan favorite for concert sing-alongs. Its combination of nostalgia for an imagined country past, uptempo pop beat, and attractive harmony vocals made it irresistible.

"Move It on Over" (1947) *Hank Williams's first chart hit*

Although not a number-one hit, this was the first song by HANK WILLIAMS to make the *Billboard* country chart. It reached number four, and so was an auspicious beginning. Typical of Williams's honky-tonk roots, the song is an upbeat dance number about a man locked out of his house for having cheated on his mate. The song has been covered numerous times, including versions by Johnnie and Jack, Buddy Alan, BOXCAR WILLIE, and George Thorogood and the Destroyers.

Mullican, Moon (1909–1967) *piano player*

Aubrey Wilson Mullican was born near Corrigan, Texas, on March 29, 1909. Raised in a religious household, Mullican began his keyboard career playing on the family's pump organ, although his secular bluesy style was not pleasing to his fundamentalist family. Around age 21, he worked his way to the Houston area, where he played piano in several unsavory nightspots, earning the nickname "Moon" because he worked all night and slept all day. He soon was leading his own band, performing throughout Louisiana and Texas, and by the end of the 1930s was also working with several prominent western swing ensembles, most notably one led by swinging fiddler Cliff Bruner, as well as performing on radio out of Beaumont. In 1939 he made his way to Hollywood to appear in the film

Village Barn Dance and began performing in the Los Angeles area.

Returning to Texas in the 1940s, Mullican continued to perform as well as opening his own night-clubs in Beaumont and Port Arthur. His big break on the country charts came in 1947 with his cover of the Cajun classic "Jole Blon" on the King label, called "New Jolie Blon." He had a series of hits on King with folk and boogie numbers, including a cover of Lead Belly's "Goodnight Irene" (later popularized by the folk revival group the Weavers) and his own "Cherokee Boogie," cowritten with W. C. Redbird.

Mullican stayed with King through 1956, although his hits pretty much dried up in the early 1950s. His recordings featured many of the greatest hillbilly jazz pickers, including steel guitarist Speedy West and guitarist Jimmy Bryant, running the gamut from weepers to upbeat country to full-fledged rock and roll. When he signed with Decca and came under the hands of producer OWEN BRADLEY, the quality of his recordings suffered greatly, because Bradley tried to mold him into just another mainstream Nashville act. (Bradley later admitted that he just didn't know what to do with Mullican.) Mullican continued to broadcast and perform through the 1960s. He died of a heart attack on January 1, 1967.

Murphey, Michael Martin (b. 1945) *singer and songwriter*

Born in Dallas, Texas, on March 13, 1945, Murphey was educated at UCLA and quickly became part of the burgeoning California folk-rock scene in the later 1960s. He was a member of the country rock band the Lewis and Clark Expedition, which enjoyed minor success on the pop charts. His songs were recorded by diverse Southern California groups, including the NITTY GRITTY DIRT BAND and TV's the Monkees.

Murphey returned to Texas in 1971. He scored his first hit with "Geronimo's Cadillac" in 1972, an Indian-rights anthem. Four years later he had his biggest successes on the pop-rock charts with "Wildfire" and "Carolina in the Pines," followed by the country hits "Cherokee Fiddle" and "A Mansion on the Hill" in 1977. In 1978 he settled on a ranch in Taos, New Mexico.

In the 1980s Murphey charted primarily as a country singer/songwriter, beginning in 1982 with "What's Forever For," and scoring a number of other hits, including "Will It Be Love by Morning," "I'm Gonna Miss You, Girl," and "Talkin' to the Wrong Man." In 1990 Murphey recorded his first all-cowboy-song album, including such venerable old chestnuts as "Home on the Range," "When the Work's All Done This Fall," and "Old Chisholm Trail," combined with newer hippie cowboy anthems such as Ian Tyson's "Cowboy Pride." This album was the first in a trilogy of cowboy-style releases for Murphey. Murphey has also recorded his own epic-length songs, including one that is seven minutes long. Murphey has been the moving force behind West Fest, a cowboy song and story gathering held annually.

Murray, Anne (b. 1945) *singer*

Murray was born on June 20, 1945, and raised in the Canadian coal mining and fishing village of Springhill, Nova Scotia, where she heard country music on the local radio station. She began singing pop and folk music in high school and continued to perform in local clubs while attending teacher's college. From 1966 to 1970 Murray performed on a local TV show, *Sing Along Jubilee.* She was signed to the Canadian division of Capitol Records in 1969; its U.S. counterpart picked up her single "Snowbird," which became a gold record in 1970. It took three years for Murray, now living and recording in Los Angeles, to return to the charts; in 1974 she scored her first major hit, "He Thinks I Still Care," which established her as a country star. Murray briefly retired in the mid-1970s, but returned to great chart success by decade's end, scoring hits in 1978 with "You Needed Me" and a number-one country hit, "I Fall in Love Again." "Could I Have This Dance?" was featured in the 1980 film *Urban Cowboy*. Murray gained further attention with her 1983 hit "A Little Good News," which pleased such political conservatives as then-vice president George Bush, who quoted from its lyrics during campaign speeches.

In 1986 Murray scored another country number one with "Now and Forever (You and Me)." However, a move toward mainstream pop led to a decline in her country audience. Murray had one final hit in 1990, "Feed This Fire," a surprise top-10 country hit, and then performed primarily on the country fair and Las Vegas circuit. In the later 1990s she turned to performing religious and inspirational material.

Nashville sound

In an attempt to broaden the appeal of country music, several producers—mostly notably CHET ATKINS and OWEN BRADLEY—developed a more pop-oriented style of recording that almost completely eliminated traditional country instrumentation and reoriented the careers of country or honky-tonk singers to a more commercial, middle-of-the-road repertoire of pop ballads (for men) and tearjerkers (for women).

In the mid-1950s some young Nashville-based musicians were embarrassed by the "old-fashioned" musical styles and hillbilly routines employed by older acts. They thought the clichéd image of the fiddle-sawing, banjo-banging backwoodsman was holding back country music; many were more interested in playing jazz than country; they felt jazz was a more progressive musical style. A leader of this movement was Chet Atkins, whose elder brother was a talented jazz guitarist and who himself had a great love for the chamber-style jazz that was popular in the 1950s. An informal group of musicians began jamming with Atkins at the Carousel Club in Nashville to play modern jazz, including pianist Floyd Cramer, sax master Boots Randolph, bassist Bob Moore, and drummer Buddy Harman. Because Atkins was working as assistant head of A&R at RCA (he became head of the country division in 1957), the leading Nashville studio, he was in a position to hire these musicians for session work; Cramer was particularly popular, playing piano on hundreds of sessions, including accompanying Elvis Presley on such classics as

"Heartbreak Hotel." Along with this "modern," light-jazz-style instrumentation, Atkins introduced vocal choruses, particularly with the JORDANAIRES and the ANITA KERR Singers, again to soften the rough edges of country recordings.

In a similar move, producer Owen Bradley worked through the 1950s at Decca to change country music into a more popular style. His biggest achievement was in molding the career of singer PATSY CLINE, who started out as a big-lunged honky tonker but was transformed into the kind of dreamy pop chanteuse who could appeal to a broad audience. Cline hated the more pop-oriented material, but her icy, gliding vocals became the model for hundreds of country singers to come.

Nashville had become a professional music-making center by the early 1960s. The local session musicians prided themselves on their ability to accompany anybody, and thus to sound like nobody. Although some developed a distinctive style (such as Cramer's "slip-note" piano playing), the emphasis was on a homogenized, one-sound-fits-all style that was bound to take the character out of the music. Plus, with the advent of large music publishing houses (beginning with Acuff-Rose), Nashville became the Tin Pan Alley of the South. Unlike folk and rock, in which the trend was for songwriters to perform their own material, in country the music was still dominated by "professionals" who carefully molded the music to fit the often conservative audience.

Naturally, as country instrumentation was eliminated, so, too, was the repertoire watered down until country acts were playing the same kind of bland mainstream pop that dominated the charts of the 1950s and early 1960s. Although Atkins always argued that the Nashville sound was a compromise, a way of preserving country music during a time when its popularity was in decline, in retrospect it did little to preserve traditional country styles. It was up to a select band of pioneers—such as BILL MONROE in bluegrass or the renegade rockabilly stars CARL PERKINS and JERRY LEE LEWIS—to keep the true spirit of country alive during the dark days of the Nashville sound.

The Nashville sound eventually matured into the 1970s phenomenon known as countrypolitan, and middle-of-the-road pop music flooded the country charts.

National Barn Dance

National Barn Dance was the first successful country-music radio program, beating the *Grand Ole Opry* to the airwaves by a year. The *National Barn Dance* was most successful in the 1930s and spawned a slew of talented performers.

The first show was broadcast on April 19, 1924, over Sears, Roebuck & Company's Chicago-based station, WLS (named for Sears's slogan, "World's Largest Store"). The first program was an experiment, and simply featured a fiddler and square-dance caller, recreating a Saturday-night "barn dance." Listener reaction was very positive, and the show was off and running; one of its first announcers was GEORGE D. HAY, later the founding genius behind the *Grand Ole Opry*.

The show expanded to more than five hours by the late 1920s. Sears sold the station in 1928 to Burridge D. Butler, owner of an agricultural newspaper, *The Prairie Farmer*. The show became a cornerstone of the station's broadcast, reflecting Butler's down-home philosophy and conservative Midwestern values. In 1931 he was able to increase the station's power to 50,000 watts, which effectively meant its signal blanketed the entire U.S. Midwest.

Two years later the NBC "Blue" network picked up national syndication rights. The newly introduced medicine Alka-Seltzer was the show's first sponsor, and it soon became as successful as the fiddlers, comedians, and singers. Star names of the 1930s included cowboy crooners GENE AUTRY, RED FOLEY, and PATSY MONTANA; comic novelty act the Hoosier Hot Shots; and more traditional singers, such as Lulu Belle and Scotty. The show had a more contemporary sound in its heyday than did the *Opry;* this made it tremendously successful for a while, but when tastes changed, listeners also left. The brains behind the show's 1930s success was performer/producer John Lair, who left (along with popular star RED FOLEY) to found the *Renfro Valley Barn Dance* in 1937.

For a period from 1946 through 1949, the show had no sponsor and dropped off of national radio. It picked up a new sponsor in 1949, and continued on the national airwaves through WLS's sale in 1960, when the station was converted to a teen-pop format. The cast moved to competitor WGN soon after, and a companion syndicated TV show went on the air in 1964. However, by 1971 the *National Barn Dance* was no more, a victim of changing tastes.

The *National Barn Dance* was never able to grow beyond its success in the 1930s promoting smooth-voiced cowboy acts. Unlike the *Grand Ole Opry,* which grew into a multimillion-dollar business, the owners of the *National Barn Dance* did not expand their empire into other areas, such as music publishing or tourism. Furthermore, after World War II Chicago ceased to be a center of country-music performance, while Nashville rose to become the music's capital.

Nelson, Willie (b. 1933) *singer and songwriter*

Born in Abbot, Texas (north of Waco), on April 30, 1933, Nelson was the son of a rural farmer. He began performing while still in high school. He served in the air force until 1952, and then worked in Texas and briefly in Vancouver, Washington, as both a performer and country disc jockey. After publishing his first song, he moved to Nashville, where he joined RAY PRICE, working as bassist in Price's backup band, the Cherokee Cowboys. Nelson's first success was as a songwriter, penning such number-one country classics as "Crazy" for PATSY CLINE and "Hello Walls" for FARON YOUNG, both in 1961.

Willie Nelson (left) and Lyle Lovett celebrate their Texas kinship. (Raeanne Rubenstein)

Nelson signed to Liberty and then to RCA Records in the 1960s as a solo artist, but his unique style was ill-suited to the typical Nashville productions of the day. When his house burned down in 1970, he moved to Austin, Texas, turning his back on the country-music community. Influenced by younger performers who also were weary of the Nashville sound, including KRIS KRISTOFFERSON and WAYLON JENNINGS, Nelson began to experiment with writing song cycles, or groups of related songs, that were issued on a series of seminal albums, including 1973's *Shotgun Willie*, 1974's *Phases and Stages* (telling the story of the breakup of a relationship from both the man's and woman's perspective), and 1975's landmark *Red Headed Stranger*, a romantic story set in the 19th-century West. Nelson was given artistic control over his recordings, and he pared down his sound, often to just his own vocals and guitars, as on his first hit, a cover of Fred Rose's "Blue Eyes Crying in the Rain" from the *Red Headed Stranger* concept album (1975).

RCA gave the outlaw movement a strong push when it released the compilation album *Wanted: The Outlaws* in 1976, featuring Nelson, Jennings, Jessi Colter (then Jennings's wife), and Tompall Glaser. In typical contrary fashion, Willie followed this success with *Stardust,* an album of covers of 1930s and 1940s pop standards. He proved what country audiences long knew; that there was a strong following for these pop songs among country-music fans.

Through the late 1970s and early 1980s Willie performed as a soloist and in duets with Jennings, Leon Russell, MERLE HAGGARD, and in an informal group, the Highwaymen, with JOHNNY CASH, Kristofferson, and Jennings. A brief movie career also developed, including a remake of the classic 1932s film *Impromptu*, about a classical musician's love affair with his student, improbably reset in the world of country music as *Honeysuckle Rose* (1980, yielding the hit "On the Road Again," which has become a theme song for Nelson), and a TV version of *Red Headed Stranger* (1987).

When the IRS presented Nelson with a huge bill for unpaid taxes, he recorded two solo albums that featured just him and his guitar performing his "old songs" and then marketed them directly through late-night TV ads; the proceeds were used to pay off the government. He returned to more mainstream recording on his 60th birthday with a new album produced by mainstream pop producer Don Was and a TV special. Nelson continued to record through the 1990s. He moved to Island Records in 1996 and worked with a variety of producers (including Daniel Lanois, who had jump-started Bob Dylan's career), as well as producing more theme albums, including another collection of standards and an album of blues covers. In 2002 he released *The Great Divide* on Lost Highway (a division of Mercury Records), featuring duets with various other pop, rock, and country stars, including Kid Rock and Sheryl Crow. The first single, "Mendocino County Line," a duet with LEE ANN WOMACK, was Nelson's first charting record in some time; it was followed by an even bigger hit, "Beer for My Horses," a duet with TOBY KEITH.

Newman, Jimmy "C" (b. 1927) *performer*

Newman was born in Big Mamou, Louisiana, on August 27, 1927, to a Cajun family. He began performing in the Lake Charles area, already focusing on the mix of country and traditional Cajun dance numbers that would become his trademark. Beginning in 1949, he recorded for several small local labels and quickly gained a strong regional following. Hired for the popular *Louisiana Hayride* radio program, he was then signed to Dot, where he had a rockin' country hit with "Cry, Cry, Cry" (1954). He was invited to join the *Grand Ole Opry* in 1956, and had his biggest country-pop hit a year later with "A Fallen Star." Newman remains a performing member of the *Opry*.

After a couple of lackluster years at MGM, Newman returned to the country charts under the hands of producer OWEN BRADLEY at Decca Records, beginning with 1961's "Alligator Man" (playing off

his Cajun heritage) and the half-spoken record "Bayou Talk." In 1962 he recorded *Folk Songs of the Bayou Country* to appeal to the growing audience for folk music; this featured many songs sung in his native Cajun French, and wonderful instrumentation by noted Cajun fiddler Rufus Thibodeaux and "Shorty" LeBlanc on accordion.

In the mid-1970s Newman returned to his roots with a new band called Cajun Country. Although no longer a strong chart presence, he continues to record and perform, mostly focusing on traditional material.

Nickel Creek

Like many bluegrass groups, Nickel Creek is a family affair. Raised in Southern California, both the Watkins and Thiele family were local patrons at a Carlsbad pizzeria that featured the newgrass band Bluegrass Etc., associated with well-known fiddler Byrone Berline. The young Sara Watkins (fiddle), Shawn Watkins (guitar), and Chris Thiele (mandolin) began studying with band members, and a local promoter, recognizing their talent—and youthful good looks—encouraged them to hit the road, taking along Chris's father, Scott, on bass. They hit the bluegrass trail, playing festivals big and small and garnering an audience among the traditional music set. They also garnered awards, particularly Thiele, who became a noted mandolin player and began working as a session player in Nashville, recording his own solo albums, and working with DOLLY PARTON.

They met ALISON KRAUSS, then 19, and herself a young prodigy on the bluegrass circuit. Krauss became the band's unofficial fourth member and advocate, promoting them as the next wave in bluegrass acoustic music. Signed to the Sugar Hill label in 1999, Nickel Creek released their debut album in 2000, which led to great media attention. Discreetly dropping the elder Thiele, the band was showcased on video and special programs on CMT (Country Music Television) and also named one of five "Music Innovators of the Millennium" by *Time* magazine. Their debut self-titled album was also nominated for a Grammy Award. Its lead single, "Reasons Why," was number one on the Americana chart; the follow-up, "When You Come Back Down," was a major hit in 2001 on the country charts and in heavy rotation on CMT. The group proved equally successful on their 2002 album *This Side,* which spawned hits with the title track and "The Smoothie Song." The latter reached number one on the adult alternative charts, a first for an instrumental recording. The album was certified gold in fall 2003.

Nitty Gritty Dirt Band, The

The Nitty Gritty Dirt Band was a California country rock band that crossed over into being a pure country band in the mid-1970s. Based in the California folk-rock community, the original band members—guitarist Jeff Hanna (b. Detroit, Michigan, July 11, 1957); banjo player John McEuen (b. Oakland, California, December 19, 1945); and drummer Jimmy Fadden (b. Long Beach, California, March 9, 1948)—wed the sensibilities of a traditional jug band with an electric folk sound. They initially scored hits with the late 1960s pop song "Buy for Me the Rain" and a remake of a 1910s standard, "The Teddy Bear's Picnic." They disbanded in the late 1960s only to reform in 1971, with new member Jimmy Ibbotson (b. Philadelphia, Pennsylvania, January 21, 1947). The new band scored its biggest pop hits with country rock versions of "Mr. Bojangles" and Mike Nesmith's "Some of Shelly's Blues."

In 1973 the band organized sessions in Nashville that brought together traditional country stars (Earl Scruggs, Maybelle Carter, Jimmy Martin, MERLE TRAVIS, and Doc Watson) to perform a set of country standards. The result was a landmark three-album set, *Will the Circle Be Unbroken?,* which helped popularize these country stars among rock audiences, as well as elevating the Nitty Gritty Dirt Band into heroes of both the country and rock communities.

By the mid-1970s mandolin player Les Thompson had left and the band was performing country-rock material under the name the Dirt Band. Now a quartet, they continued to try to appeal to both their rock and country constituencies. They reached the bottom of the top 10 with their 1979 recording "An American Dream."

By the 1980s the "Nitty Gritty" was back in their name, and they were recording as a pure new country act with the addition of new member, keyboard player Bob Carpenter (b. Philadelphia, Pennsylvania, December 26, 1946). They scored a number of hits, performing a combination of original songs and Nashville songwriters' products, with just a hint of traditional style. In 1984 they had their first country number one with RODNEY CROWELL's "Long Hard Road (The Sharecropper's Dream)." In 1985–86, in time for their 20th anniversary, they hit number one again with "Modern Day Romance," cowritten by Kix Brooks (later of BROOKS AND DUNN).

In 1987 McEuen left the band to pursue a solo career; he was briefly replaced by banjoist Bernie Leadon (one of the founding members of the Eagles), but in 1989 the Nitty Gritty Dirt Band was again reduced to a quartet. They remained a foursome through 1999, when Ibbotson also left the band. A followup to the famous *Will the Circle Be Unbroken* was released in 1989, with a cast drawing on more contemporary country figures (ROSANNE CASH, John Hiatt, and others), although it was not a landmark effort like the first set. That same year, the band produced a streak of top-10 country singles, solidifying their position as more consistent hit makers than in the past.

The band's final decade saw them touring and producing a handful of albums, although without the success they had enjoyed on the country charts in the 1980s. In 2001 Ibbotson and McEuen rejoined the band for a series of reunion concerts. A third version of *Will the Circle Be Unbroken* was released in 2002, this time featuring a mix of older (Doc Watson, JOHNNY CASH) and younger (EMMYLOU HARRIS, ALISON KRAUSS) performers.

Noack, Eddie (1930–1978) *singer, songwriter, and music publisher*

Born in Houston, on April 29, 1930, Armond Noack studied English and journalism in college. An amateur musician, he won a talent contest in 1947 at the Texas Theatre, leading to local radio work, and, two years later, to a contract with the local Gold Star label. His first success was a cover of the pop hit "Gentlemen Prefer Blondes," but he soon was label hopping. He scored his next big country hit in 1951 with "Too Hot to Handle," on the TNT label; this led to a contract with the Nashville-based Starday label that ran through the mid-1950s. In 1958 he moved to HAROLD "PAPPY" DAILY's "D" label, recording rockabilly and teen pop under the pseudonym of Tommy Wood, and enjoying another minor country success under his own name with "Have Blues Will Travel." He soon became active in Daily's music publishing operation, and retired from performing in the early 1960s to focus on the business side of Nashville.

During the 1950s Noack's songs were covered by many mainstream country acts following HANK SNOW's success with "These Hands," including honky-tonkers ERNEST TUBB and GEORGE JONES. Jones covered many of Noack's songs in the early 1960s, including "Barbara Joy," "No Blues Is Good News," and "For Better or Worse."

Noack attempted several comebacks as a recording artist from the late 1960s until his death. Perhaps his most interesting recording was *Remembering Jimmie Rodgers,* which featured sparse, acoustic instrumentation (unusual for the time) in a program of material that had all been made famous by the Singing Brakeman. His recordings were issued by a variety of tiny labels in the United States and abroad, but with little success. After Noack's death, his earlier recordings were rediscovered, particularly among country rock and rockabilly fans.

Norma Jean (b. 1938) *singer*

Norma Jean Beasler was born in Welliston, Oklahoma, on January 30, 1938. Beasler began singing on the radio when she was 13 years old, and was touring as a vocalist with various western swing bands two years later. She made her way to Nashville where she hooked up, emotionally and professionally, with PORTER WAGONER, who molded her "just folks" image. She recorded a number of brassy songs, including her first hit, 1964's suggestive "Let's Go All the Way." In 1967 her first working-class anthem, "Heaven Help the Working Girl (In a World That's Run by Men)," was released. After parting with Wagoner, she recorded a concept album, *I Guess That Comes from Being Poor,* featuring hokey crowd-pleasers like "The Lord Must Have Loved the Poor Folks (He Made So Many of Them)."

After her marriage to a fellow Oklahoman, Norma Jean retired from the music business between 1974 and 1984. She returned to Nashville in 1984, and has since performed her old hits as a nostalgia act.

Oak Ridge Boys, The *pop-country vocal group*
Tracing their roots to a gospel quartet that performed in and around the Oak Ridge, Tennessee, nuclear facility, the group went through many personnel changes from its founding in the late 1940s to today.

Original founder Walter Fowler was a country singer/songwriter who crossed over into gospel music and promotion; he founded the Oak Ridge Quartet in 1948. Fowler was a member of the Georgia Clodhoppers, a country gospel quartet based in Oak Ridge, Tennessee, in the late 1940s. Inspired by the success of EDDY ARNOLD, Fowler recorded as a soloist for Decca and King, writing and performing such sentimental country favorites as "I'm Sending You Red Roses" and "That's How Much I Love You Baby." The Clodhoppers eventually took the more elegant Oak Ridge Quartet name, but Fowler left the band by the early 1950s to become a gospel music promoter.

The Oak Ridge boys soldiered on through the 1960s, and the lineup stabilized by the mid-1970s. All of the group's members were educated musicians, and they all had long histories in other gospel or pop vocal groups. Lead singer and guitarist Duane Allen (b. Taylortown, Texas, April 29, 1943), who joined in 1966, had a music degree from East Texas State and had previously sung baritone in a popular group, the Southernaires. Tenor Joe Bonsall (b. May 18, 1948), a native of Philadelphia and an Oak Ridge Boy since 1973, performed with many local streetcorner harmony groups, as well as dancing regularly on Dick Clark's *American Bandstand*

TV show. Baritone Bill Golden (b. William Lee Golden, Brewton, Alabama, January 12, 1939), who joined in 1964, had performed with his sister as a country duo in his native Alabama and had also worked in a paper mill. Distinctive bass singer Richard Sterban (b. Camden, New Jersey, April 24, 1943), who came to the group in 1972, had performed with gospel groups the Keystone Quartet and the Stamps (who recorded and toured with Elvis Presley).

The Oak Ridge Quartet, as they were known in their gospel incarnation, were successful gospel recording artists and performers by the mid-1970s. However, they longed to cross over to the more lucrative pop market. Their first break came when they were invited to provide vocal backups on Paul Simon's mid-1970s hit "Slip Slidin' Away." They were then signed to ABC in 1977, and also began performing at upscale venues in Vegas, opening for Roy Clark. Mainstream hits came through the early 1980s, along with dozens of TV appearances on variety shows and dramatic parts on country-oriented shows like *The Dukes of Hazzard*. Among their better-known recordings is 1981's huge seller "Elvira" (with the distinctive "oom-papa-mow-mow" bass line borrowed from an early 1960s teen-pop hit), the patriotic "American Made" from 1983, 1985's cover of the Staple Singers' gospel favorite "Touch a Hand, Make a Friend," and 1988's "Gonna Take a Lot of River," featuring new lead singer Steve Sanders (b. Richland, Georgia, September 17, 1952–June 10, 1998). (William Lee Golden had been forced out of the band in 1987 and subsequently sued the group for $40 million.) Sanders left in 1995 and was replaced by Golden; subsequently, in 1998, Sanders committed suicide. The Oak Ridge Boys continued to tour and record sporadically through the decade's end.

"Ode to Billie Joe" (1967) *major pop and country hit in 1967*

The first single released by BOBBIE GENTRY, and her most famous song, it was written by Gentry herself, which was unusual for a female country singer at that time. The "mystery" of exactly what Billy Joe threw off the Tallahatchie Bridge made the song a cult item, while Gentry's delivery seemed to put more meaning in the lyrics than perhaps were there. The supposed racy content of the song probably resulted in less country airplay than it would have otherwise garnered; nevertheless, the single went gold, selling more than a million copies. A movie based on the song was made in 1976, showing the enduring appeal of the unanswered questions raised by the lyric.

"Okie from Muskogee" (1969) *number-one hit for Merle Haggard*

MERLE HAGGARD was inspired when his drummer Eddie Burris spotted a road sign for the town of Muskogee during a tour through Oklahoma; the drummer commented, "I bet the citizens of Muskogee don't smoke marijuana." Haggard made Muskogee a symbol of middle America and its values. The song inspired numerous parodies, including one by Patrick Sky (which changed the refrain to "Love me . . . or I'll punch you in the mouth"), and the Youngbloods' "Hippie from Olema #5." The song became a conservative anthem, and Haggard has said he feels his message was misinterpreted, although he followed "Okie" with the equally conservative "The Fightin' Side of Me," full of old-time American bravado, and began hanging out with President Nixon.

"On the Other Hand" (1986) *first number-one hit for Randy Travis*

RANDY TRAVIS did much to revive the classic honky-tonk style of the 1950s during the new country movement of the 1980s. The song plays off the meaning of its title: "on the one hand" the singer is attracted to the unnamed woman who lures him to sin, but he wears a wedding ring on "the other hand," which reminds him he should not stray.

"On the Road Again" (1980) *theme for the film* Honeysuckle Rose

Written and sung by WILLIE NELSON, this song served as the theme for the film *Honeysuckle Rose,* the first feature with Nelson in a starring role. It hit number one on the country charts, and became a signature song for Nelson, who seems to tour almost constantly. He often closes his concerts with it.

Oslin, K. T. (b. 1941) *singer*

Born in rural Arkansas, Oslin (b. Kay Toinette Oslin, Crossett, Arkansas, May 25, 1941) relocated with her family first to Mobile, Alabama, and then to the Houston area. In 1962, she formed a folk trio with singer/songwriter Guy Clark and local radio producer Chuck Jones. She moved to Los Angeles soon after, and switched to theatrical singing, touring with the road company of *Hello Dolly!,* ending up in New York City in 1966. She worked at honing her songwriting skills, which by the mid-1970s began to attract some attention in the music publishing world. A brief period recording for Elektra in 1981–82 as "Kay T. Oslin" failed to produce hits, and she spent the next few years doing commercial work.

Finally, in 1987, Oslin signed with RCA in Nashville, scoring a hit with her own "80s Ladies," an ode to her generation of women, who had "burned our bras and burned our dinners." A series of spunky country chart-toppers followed, including "Didn't Expect It to Go Down This Way" and her 1990 number-one hit, "Come Next Monday."

Through the 1990s, Oslin was less active. In 1999 she released an album of covers playfully titled *My Roots Are Showing*. Five years later she attempted a comeback with an album of pop numbers produced by Maverick's head Raul Malo.

Osmond, Marie (b. 1959) *singer*

The youngest daughter in the well-known pop music clan from Utah, Marie Osmond (b. Ogden, Utah, October 13, 1959) had a brief career as a country singer. Whiz producer Mike Curb had shaped pop careers for Osmond brothers Donny and "Little Jimmy"; in search of another star, he turned to the Osmond matriarch and asked her if 13-year-old Marie had any talent. Curb hooked her up with veteran ex-rockabilly star Sonny James, who produced her first number-one success, a cover of the 1960 Anita Bryant hit, "Paper Roses," which Osmond cut in 1973; not only was it a number-one country hit, it hit number five on the pop charts. As a teen Marie joined with her brother Donny to perform pop material on the Las Vegas lounge-club circuit, and the duo had their own variety TV show from 1976 to 1979. Osmond's career faded thereafter, although she had a few more country hits in the mid-1980s.

Owens, Bonnie (b. 1932) *singer*

Originally from a dirt-poor Oklahoma family, Bonnie Owens (b. Bonnie Campbell, Blanchard, Oklahoma, October 1, 1932) picked cotton as a child to help her family survive. The family relocated to Arizona when she was a young teenager. She got her first job in Mesa, Arizona, working on the *Buck and Britt* radio show, where she met future husband BUCK OWENS. The twosome worked for a while in a touring country band, eventually making their way to new country mecca Bakersfield, California, in the mid-1950s, where Bonnie was hired to sing on the locally broadcast *Trading Post* TV show. Their marriage soon dissolved, and Bonnie's mother came west to care for Bonnie's two

children while Bonnie began building her career as a solo artist. She had her first local hit in the early 1960s with "Dear John Letter," released on the tiny Marvel label, as well as her tribute song to PATSY CLINE, "Missing on a Mountain."

In the early 1960s she befriended an up-and-coming country singer named MERLE HAGGARD, and the two began making demo recordings together, attracting the attention of local producer/record label owner Fuzzy Owen (no relation to Buck). Owen signed Bonnie and Merle to his Tally label, and Bonnie had solo hits with 1963's "Daddy Doesn't Live Here Anymore," a classic weeper, and the more feisty "Don't Take Advantage of Me" in 1964; also in 1964 Bonnie and Merle scored a big hit with "Just Between the Two of Us," leading to a contract with Capitol Records for them both; a year later, they wed.

Bonnie had a couple more hits through the 1960s as a solo artist, but retired from performing in 1970, at least on her own. Although she divorced Haggard in 1975, by the early 1980s she was singing in his backup band as well as managing his business affairs.

One of Bonnie's sons from her marriage to Buck Owens is Buddy Allan, who has had some success as a solo country performer, as well as performing with his dad in the early 1970s.

Owens, Buck (b. 1929) *singer/bandleader*

Originally from Texas, Buck Owens (b. Alvis Edgar Owens Jr., Sherman, Texas, August 12, 1929) was the son of a sharecropper, born in relative impoverishment. The family moved to Arizona in search of a better standard of living, but to little avail, and Buck had to leave school after the ninth grade to help support his family. Already a talented musician playing both mandolin and guitar, he was performing on local radio in Mesa, Arizona, when he was just 16; he met future wife Bonnie Campbell Owens there and married her a year later.

In 1951 he relocated to Bakersfield, California, which was a center of California's country-music community in the 1950s, thanks to its military base. He formed his first band there, as well as working as a guitarist on numerous country and poprock sessions. Owens also recorded some rockabilly tunes under the name of "Corky Jones." Local country star Tommy Collins gave Owens his first big break in the mid-1950s, when he hired him to be lead guitarist in his band and featured him on many of his early hits. Owens formed his own band, the Buckaroos, in the late 1950s, but signed to Capitol as a solo performer.

Owens's first hit was "Second Fiddle," followed by "Under Your Spell Again" in 1959, "Excuse Me, I Think I've Got a Heartache" in 1960, and "Fooling Around" in 1961. From the first, Owens established himself as a purveyor of upbeat, honky-tonk material. Owens was rarely off the charts in the 1960s, including wonderful hits such as 1963's "Act Naturally," "I've Got a Tiger by the Tail" and "Buckaroo" (1965), "Waitin' in Your Welfare Line"

(1966), and 1969's "Tall Dark Stranger." He also made some fine duet recordings in the early 1960s with a western-swing-turned-bluegrass vocalist, Rose Maddox.

In 1969 Owens was hired to cohost a new country music TV show called *Hee Haw*. The success of the show made Buck one of the most instantly identifiable of all country stars. However, by this time the quality of his recordings had declined. By the early 1980s he was focusing on his business interests and had retired from music making. Then, in the mid-1980s, new country star DWIGHT YOAKAM took Owens's characteristic 1960s sound and reintroduced it to a new generation of listeners. Owens rerecorded "Act Naturally" as a duet with Ringo Starr (who popularized the song with the Beatles), and cut a duet with Yoakam, as well as continuing to perform live dates. In 1996 he was given his rightful spot in the Country Music Hall of Fame.

Paisley, Brad (b. 1972) *singer and songwriter*
Paisley was born on October 28, 1972, in rural Glen Dale, West Virginia, in the Ohio River valley. His grandfather was a railroad worker and amateur guitarist who gave Brad his first guitar when he was eight years old. Within two years, Paisley was performing at local parties and functions, and at age 12 he was heard by a scout from WWVA radio, out of Wheeling. He invited Paisley to appear on the station's popular *Jamboree U.S.A.* country show, and the young performer was so well received he remained with the show for the next eight years. Paisley initially enrolled in college locally but, encouraged by his adviser, he transferred to the music business program at Nashville's Belmont College. On graduation, he was signed as a writer by the publishing arm of EMI. He also cut demos of his own songs, which caught the attention of a producer at Arista Records, who signed him in 1998.

Paisley's first single, 1999's "He Didn't Have to Be," was an immediate hit, reaching number one on the charts and inspiring strong sales for his debut album, *Who Needs Pictures,* which eventually went platinum. He was invited to perform on the *Grand Ole Opry* in mid-1999, and became a member two years later. He also was showered with awards, including the CMA Horizon Award in 2000 for Best New Artist. In 2002 Paisley followed up his initial success with *Part II.* The album had major hits with the tongue-in-cheek honky-tonk song "I'm Gonna Miss Her (The Fishing Song)," promoted through a clever video, "Wrapped Around," and "I Wish You'd

Stay." Paisley quickly followed up with a third offering, *Mud on the Tires,* a year later, with the initial hit "Celebrity" spoofing his newfound fame.

Brad Paisley clowning with his hero, "Whispering" Bill Anderson (Raeanne Rubenstein)

Parton, Dolly (b. 1946) *singer and songwriter*

The fourth of 12 children, born on January 19, 1946, in rural Locust Ridge, Tennessee, Dolly Rebecca Parton made her first recordings in 1959 for Goldband; in 1964 she traveled to Nashville. She signed with Monument Records and scored her first hit, "Dumb Blonde," in 1967. That same year, she joined forces with country legend PORTER WAGONER, a savvy businessman who ran a large country revue. He recorded a string of duets with Parton, beginning with a cover of Tom Paxton's "Last Thing on My Mind," which helped launch her career.

Dolly's solo recordings on RCA in the late 1960s and early 1970s established her as a sensitive singer/songwriter who could reflect on her own rural heritage. In songs like 1971's "Coat of Many Colors," she honored the memory of her mother, who made her a patchwork coat out of fabric remnants. In 1974 Parton permanently split from Wagoner, and her songs began to be covered by folk-rock artists from Linda Ronstadt ("I Will Always Love You," later a 1992–93 number-one hit for pop singer Whitney Houston) and Maria Muldaur ("My Tennessee Mountain Home"). This encouraged Parton to attempt her own crossover recordings for the pop charts, beginning with the bouncy 1977 hit "Here You Come Again."

In 1980 Parton's everywoman persona was successfully exploited in the working-class feminist movie *9 to 5;* her title song for the film was a pop and country hit. This success led to a decade of minor and major film roles, plus continued recordings in a pop-country vein. A longtime friendship with Linda Ronstadt and EMMYLOU HARRIS resulted in the 1987 album *Trio* and a minor hit in their cover of Phil Spector's "To Know Him Is to Love Him." In 1989, in an attempt to return to her roots, she recorded a more country-oriented album called *White Limozeen* produced by new country star RICKY SKAGGS, an artistic accomplishment if not a great chart success. Parton also showed savvy as a businesswoman, opening her own theme park, Dollywood, to celebrate Tennessee mountain crafts and culture.

In 1993 Parton partnered with LORETTA LYNN and TAMMY WYNETTE for the *Honky Tonk Angels* album, a nice collection that showed all three were still in fine voice (despite Wynette's failing health). Parton continued to record mainstream country through the later 1990s, without enjoying much success. In 1999 Parton was finally recognized by the country world by being elected into the Country Music Hall of Fame. That same year, she issued an album accompanied by a bluegrass band, working with a new bluegrass star, ALISON KRAUSS. Parton followed up in 2001 with a second all-acoustic, bluegrass album, setting yet another new course for her career. The song "Shine" from the second album saw some airplay, and its accompanying video was popular on CMT (Country Music Television).

Dolly's sister Stella (b. 1949) also had some minor country hits in the mid-1970s.

Paycheck, Johnny (1938–2003) *performer and songwriter*

Born Donald Eugene Lytle in Greenfield, Ohio, on May 31, 1938, he began playing guitar and bass as a teenager, as well as writing countrified songs. At age 15 he left home and enlisted in the navy; he was released in 1959 and moved to Nashville. He began working as a bass player in PORTER WAGONER's Wagonmasters backup band, followed by stints with other singers. He also took up steel guitar. In the early 1960s, he cut some rockabilly-styled sides under the name of Donny Young.

By the mid-1960s he returned to performing and writing country material, and was signed to Mercury in 1965 when he took his new stage name, Johnny Paycheck. He had a couple of modest hits in the mid-1960s, including "A-11" in 1965 and "Heartbreak Tennessee" in 1966, as well as writing hits for TAMMY WYNETTE ("Apartment No. 9") and RAY PRICE ("Touch My Heart"). However, by the late 1960s Paycheck's career was derailed by his increasing dependence on alcohol and drugs.

Famed producer Billy Sherrill gave Paycheck a chance at making a comeback in the early 1970s, and he scored a couple of hits with the Sherrill-produced "Song and Dance Man" in 1974 and "I Don't Love Her Anymore" a year later. In 1977 he was back on the charts with "I'm the Only Hell (Mama Ever Raised)" and the DAVID ALLAN COE–penned "Take This Job (And Shove It)," his sole country number-one hit, and the song most closely associated with him to date. That same year, he was awarded a Career Achievement Award by the Country Music Association.

Paycheck teamed up with GEORGE JONES in 1979 for a series of successful duets, beginning with a countrified cover of Chuck Berry's classic "Maybelline." The duo produced a rockin' album with the tongue-in-cheek title of *Double Trouble*. Next he teamed with another country legend, MERLE HAGGARD, for a duet, "I Can't Hold Myself in Line," a 1981 hit. After many years spent fighting alcoholism, Paycheck was convicted on an aggravated assault charge following a barroom brawl in his native Ohio and sentenced to a nine-and-a-half-year prison sentence in 1985, a case that he appealed until 1989, when he finally was sent to prison (he was paroled after two years). While appealing his case, Paycheck scored a hit with the ballad "Old Violin" in 1987.

After his release from prison in 1991, Paycheck performed primarily in Branson, Missouri, and recorded occasionally for small labels. He also changed the spelling of his name to "PayCheck." In the late 1990s he was seriously ill with emphysema. He died on February 19, 2003.

"Peace in the Valley" (1951) *first million-selling hit for singer Red Foley*

This song is said to be the first gospel number to sell more than a million records. It reached number five on the country, jukebox, and disc jockey charts on its original release. The song has been covered countless times, particularly by Elvis Presley.

Pearl, Minnie (1912–1996) *performer*

Sarah Ophelia Colley (b. October 25, 1912) was raised in an educated family in Centerville, Tennessee. She was exposed to classical music and literature (and only vaguely aware of the country music around her); her mother, known as "Aunt Fannie" Colley, led a book circle and played organ at the local church. The young Colley aspired to be an actress and attended Ward-Belmont College in Nashville, where she also showed talent as a dancer.

A very young and demure Minnie Pearl, before she attached a tag-sale label to her country hat (University of North Carolina, Southern Historical Collection, Southern Folklife Collection, University Archives)

After graduation and teaching dance locally, Colley was hired to be a dramatic coach for a small company in Atlanta that specialized in sending directors out into small southern towns to mount amateur productions. She worked at this job for five years. She began performing monologues portraying a rural woman named "Minnie Pearl" as a way of raising interest in the plays that she was directing. In the late 1930s her father died and she returned to her hometown to take care of her ailing mother. Asked to entertain a local bankers' meeting, she revived her hayseed character, taking as the character's hometown a nearby railroad crossing named Grinder's Switch. One of the bankers recommended that she audition for the *Grand Ole Opry*. She did; they liked her act but were concerned that some of their rural listeners might be offended by it. Her first broadcast was scheduled well after the prime listening time, at 11:05; their fears were groundless, however, because Pearl soon became one of the *Opry*'s most popular attractions. Made a permanent member in 1940, she continued to perform until 1991, when she suffered a massive stroke. She spent her last years in a nursing home, and she died on March 4, 1996.

The Pearl persona—complete with a flowered hat with a dangling price tag and a thrift-store cotton-print dress—along with her signature greeting of "How-dee" are instantly recognizable even by people who rarely listen to country music. Her typical monologue was made up of corny old jokes, set as "true" events from the little town of Grinder's Switch; this trick of incorporating dusty old jokes into supposedly real stories was appropriated by later performers such as Garrison Keillor, whose monologues are set as "news" from his fictional hometown of Lake Wobegon.

pedal steel guitar

The steel guitar has its roots in the lap-played Hawaiian styles of the 1920s. It's called a steel guitar because the player uses a steel bar to note the strings, not because the body of the instrument is made of steel, although some do have metal bodies.

Originally, standard guitars were adapted for lap playing by raising the nut (giving a higher action) and lowering the frets. However, because the sound hole was facing up, rather than out, it was difficult to produce an instrument that could be easily heard, particularly in a band setting.

In a search for greater volume, instrument builders like the Dopyera brothers introduced models with built-in resonators, marketed as National steel guitars and later as Dobros. In the mid-1930s electric amplification came in, and players like Leon McAuliffe and Bob Dunn in western swing ensembles began playing electrified instruments for greater volume and a cutting, hard-edged sound. In the late 1940s the amplified steel guitar became a part of honky-tonk ensembles, thanks to the radio appearances and recordings of HANK WILLIAMS, whose backup band featured the instrument. The bluesy sounds that could be created on the pedal steel were a perfect accompaniment to the sad and lonesome music that Williams made.

With amplification, there was no longer a necessity for the guitar to have a large and bulky body that had to be balanced on the player's lap. One of the first innovations was the electrified instrument nicknamed the "frypan"; this tiny-bodied instrument was easily transportable and sat comfortably on a player's lap, but it still had all the power that amplification offered. Later, musicians began mounting these instruments on legs.

Because lap players work with open tunings, it is often necessary to retune their instruments many times during a performance, a time-consuming annoyance. Someone came up with the idea of mounting two separate necks on a stand, each tuned to a common, but different, open chord, to alleviate this problem. More strings were added, again to expand the range of the instrument. Eventually, ancillary pedals and levers were added to the instrument, giving the player greater control over volume, retuning individual notes, and other special effects.

One of the first country musicians to embrace the pedal steel was Speedy West, who began using the instrument in 1948. His wide-ranging session work on the West Coast helped popularize the instrument among other players. In the mid-1950s Buddy Emmons began playing with popular singer "LITTLE" JIMMY DICKENS, and Emmons also became a leading innovator in instrument design and manufacture when he founded the Sho-Bud company. His partner in the company was Bud Isaacs, another innovative player, whose appearance on WEBB PIERCE's recording "Slowly" in 1953 is generally credited with introducing the modern pedal steel sound to country music. Isaacs also served as a consultant to Gibson during the 1950s in the development of their early pedal steel guitars. By the early 1960s the pedal steel was firmly established on Nashville recordings, despite the fact that other traditional instruments such as fiddles and banjos had been eliminated by producers working in the new Nashville sound.

When country-rock groups were first formed in the late 1960s, the pedal steel was eagerly embraced by a new generation. Gram Parsons's first country rock outfit, the International Submarine Band, featured a young steel player named J. D. Maness, whose style was widely copied. The group Poco centered on steel player Rusty Young, the Flying Burrito Brothers featured "Sneaky" Pete Kleinow, and Mike Nesmith's First National Band had Red Rhodes. These groups eliminated the excesses of the Nashville sound, but kept the pedal steel as a vital link to country's past.

The 1970s saw a revival of interest in the pedal steel's ancestors, including the Dobro and earlier electrified steel instruments. But the pedal steel continues to be used in most major country stars' backup bands, while individual players have evolved diverse styles of performance.

Perkins, Carl (1932–1998) *guitarist and songwriter*

Born Carl Lee Perkins on April 3, 1932, to a poor farming family living in Tiptonville, Tennessee, Perkins was exposed to music from youth. His father was an avid fan of the *Grand Ole Opry,* and it was one of the few radio shows he would allow to be played on the family's radio. A second important influence was a black sharecropper who played guitar in a rural, fingerpicking blues style.

After World War II the family relocated to Bemis, Tennessee, where Carl's uncles were working in a cotton mill. They settled in their first home with electricity, and soon Carl was practicing on a second-hand electric Harmony guitar in the attic. In the early 1950s Carl talked his brothers Jay and Clayton into forming a country trio, and they began performing in local honky-tonks as the Perkins Brothers. After a while, it became clear to Carl that the group would need drums if they were to provide a danceable beat. After a trial drummer joined in 1953, Clayton brought on board schoolmate W. S. "Fluke" Holland, who had a keen appreciation for R&B music as well as country. Carl, meanwhile, was moving the music in an uptempo direction to suit dancing, thus forming the seeds of rockabilly. At the same time they were playing honky-tonks at night, the brothers worked by day in a local bakery.

In 1954 Carl Perkins heard Elvis Presley's recording of "Blue Moon of Kentucky" on the radio and realized that someone else was experimenting with uptempo country music. He took his brothers to Memphis in search of Sun Records, which recorded Presley, and met legendary producer Sam Phillips. After recording a few country numbers, Perkins performed "Gone, Gone, Gone," which featured a rocking beat. This was his first recording in his new R&B-influenced style. In late 1955 Perkins returned to the studio, recording two rockabilly numbers: "Blue Suede Shoes" and "Honey Don't." "Blue Suede Shoes" established Perkins's reputation, making him a star. However, Perkins's new success was short-lived. While driving the brothers to New York for a taping of Perry Como's TV show in early 1956, their manager fell asleep at the wheel, and all three Perkins brothers were injured.

By 1957 Perkins was a has-been at Sun. Two newer artists, JOHNNY CASH and JERRY LEE LEWIS, were successful on the country and rock charts, respectively, and Perkins was all but ignored by Phillips. Columbia Records signed the frustrated singer in 1957, and the following year he began issuing teen-oriented pop, including "Pink Pedal Pushers" and "Pop Let Me Have the Car." Tragedy beset Carl's life when his brother Jay died of a brain tumor in 1958; Perkins and his other brother both became alcoholics (Clayton eventually died of alcoholism); drummer W. S. Holland quit the group in early 1959.

In the early 1960s Perkins was disillusioned with the music business; dropped by Columbia in 1963, he recorded country material briefly for Decca before being dropped again. He went into retirement for a while, until early in 1964 he was approached to tour England with rock and roll legend Chuck Berry. Perkins was surprised to discover that he was venerated in England, particularly by a young guitarist named George Harrison, who had learned many licks off of Perkins's recordings. The Beatles's recordings of Perkins's songs—including "Honey Don't," "Matchbox," and "Everybody Wants to Be My Baby"—revitalized Perkins's career in Europe, where he quickly became a favorite touring artist.

In the late 1960s Perkins was a featured artist in Johnny Cash's touring group. He wrote the nostalgic 1968 country hit "Daddy Sang Bass" for Cash, about a backwoods country band. He recorded a comeback album with the rock revivalists NRBQ in 1979, producing a minor hit with "Restless," and then recorded sporadically through the 1980s, primarily in Europe, mixing country and early rock. In 1986 he reunited with Cash and Roy Orbison for the *Class of '55* album, an attempt to recapture the glory days of Memphis. He continued to perform and record into the 1990s, although he was slowed by a series of strokes, which eventually took his life on January 19, 1998.

Pierce, Webb (1921–1991) *singer and songwriter*
Born in rural West Monroe, Louisiana, on August 8, 1921, Pierce began playing guitar as a teenager. After World War II he traveled to Shreveport, then Louisiana's center of country music, thanks to the popular *Louisiana Hayride* radio program that orig-

inated there. After a couple of unsuccessful years Pierce finally attracted the attention of Horace Logan, the program's producer, and was hired to join its cast in the early 1950s.

Webb had made recordings as a vocalist with Tillman Franks's band, and then was signed on his own to a small local label. In 1951 he moved to major label Decca, where he had his first hit, "Wondering," followed quickly by the number-one record "Back Street Affair." Between 1952 and 1958 all of his releases made the country top 10; in 1952 he left the *Louisiana Hayride* to join the more prestigious *Grand Ole Opry*. Some of Pierce's best-known recordings include classic barroom numbers such as 1953's "I'm Walking the Dog," "That's Me Without You," and "There Stands the Glass," 1954's uptempo "More and More" and the classic "Slowly," 1956's "Teenage Boogie," a cover of the Everly Brothers' "Bye Bye Love" and "Honky Tonk Song" from 1957, and two songs cowritten with MEL TILLIS, 1958's "Tupelo County Jail" and 1959's "A Thousand Miles Ago."

Although he was no longer dominating the charts, Pierce continued to produce solid hits through the mid-1960s, including 1961's "Sweet Lips," 1962's "Crazy Wild Desire" (also cowritten with Tillis), and his last major hit, 1964's "Memory Number 1." In the mid-1960s Pierce switched his attention to the business end of publishing and promoting. Although he continued to record for Decca/MCA through the mid-1970s, Pierce's hits became fewer and fewer after the mid-1960s. In 1977 he moved to the tiny Plantation label, and then semiretired, although he was lured out of retirement for a duet session with country outlaw WILLIE NELSON in a 1982 remake of Pierce's 1955 recording of "In the Jailhouse Now." Pierce died of pancreatic cancer on February 24, 1991. In 2001 Pierce was inducted into the Country Music Hall of Fame.

"Pistol Packin' Mama" (1944) *country hit*
Composed by Al Dexter, this song was successfully covered for the pop and country charts by the Andrews Sisters with Bing Crosby (1944). Its theme

of a strong-willed western woman forecast the success of Irving Berlin's show *Annie Get Your Gun*, which opened on Broadway two years later.

Price, Ray (b. 1926) *singer*

Ray Noble Price was born in rural Perryville, Texas, on January 12, 1926, and raised on a small farm. The family relocated to Dallas when Price was a teenager. He began performing locally there. After serving in the marines in World War II, he began performing on Abilene radio, taking the name of "The Cherokee Cowboy." In 1949 Price was invited to join Dallas's prestigious *Big D Jamboree* radio show. This led to one release on the small Nashville-based Bullet label. In Nashville in 1951, he met his idol, HANK WILLIAMS, with whom he briefly lived and toured. At the same time, he signed to Columbia, achieving his first hit with 1952's "Talk to Your Heart."

After Williams's death, Price began performing with the Drifting Cowboys, Hank's old backup band, which he enlarged into a new group by the mid-1950s that he called the Cherokee Cowboys. Price created a stir in Nashville by including a drummer in his group (for years, drums were forbidden on the *Grand Ole Opry*'s stage). In these early recordings, Price used the drummer and rhythm section to create what is now known as the shuffle beat, which became a standard for country music recording.

Price's first big hits were 1954's "I'll Be There" and his signature tune, "Release Me," which has become a country classic. From that point, he was rarely off the charts. A list of Price's 1950s and 1960s hits reads like an encyclopedia of country standards: 1956's "Crazy Arms," 1958's "City Lights," 1959's "Heartaches by the Number," 1963's "Make the World Go Away," 1965's "The Other Woman," 1970's "For the Good Times" (written by a then relatively unknown songwriter named KRIS KRISTOFFERSON), and 1973's "You're the Best Thing that Ever Happened to Me," all released by Columbia.

Price recorded less in the later 1970s, but he returned in 1980 with an excellent duet album made with WILLIE NELSON, which spawned a hit with their cover of Bob Wills's classic "Faded Love." Price has recorded sporadically since then, mostly for small labels, while performing at his own theater in Branson, Missouri.

Pride, Charley (b. 1938) *guitarist and singer*

Pride was born in Sledge, Mississippi (near the Arkansas border), on March 18, 1938, one of 11 children to poor tenant farmers. Like many other black families in rural Mississippi, they made their living picking cotton. Early on, Pride became a fan of country radio, particularly emulating the bluesy sounds of HANK WILLIAMS, and taught himself the guitar. After serving in the military, Pride began a career as a minor-league baseball player, working as a bar singer in his off-hours. Country star Red Sovine heard Pride signing in a bar in Montana in 1963, and recommended that he come to Nashville to audition for RCA. A year later Pride was signed to the label.

Pride's recording career had early success. His first single, "The Snakes Crawl at Night," was an immediate top-10 country hit. It was followed by another hit, "Just Between You and Me." His label placed little emphasis on Pride's racial identity, and audiences did not seem to mind that he was a lone black star among a white (and relatively conservative) group of performers.

Pride enjoyed his greatest success in the late 1960s and early 1970s, winning numerous Grammy Awards, CMA honors, and gold records. In addition to the standard songs of lovin' and losin', Pride also was a popular gospel recording artist, bringing the same smooth, pop delivery to his gospel recordings that he did to his songs of heartache.

A longtime resident of Dallas, Pride retired from performing in the 1980s, although he continues to record sporadically, issuing a couple of albums late in the decade for the small 16th Avenue label. In 1993 he enjoyed a brief comeback with the single "Just for the Love of It."

Rabbitt, Eddie (1944–1998) *singer and songwriter*

Rabbitt was born on November 27, 1944, in Brooklyn, New York, to an Irish fiddler father. Rabbitt won an amateur contest while still a high school student, and landed a radio job broadcasting live from a Paterson, New Jersey, bar. This led to further work in local clubs in the New York City and northern New Jersey area. In the early 1970s Rabbitt relocated to Nashville in search of a career as a performer. He placed a few of his songs with other performers, and then signed with Elektra Records as a performer in 1974.

Eddie had a couple of hits in the mid-1970s, mostly written or cowritten by him ("Drinking My Baby off My Mind," "Two Dollars in the Jukebox," "We Can't Go On Living Like This"). In 1979 he was asked to perform the title song for Clint Eastwood's comic western, *Every Which Way but Loose*. This led to another movie job, singing the title song for *Roadie* in 1980, called "Driving My Life Away"; this was Rabbitt's first crossover hit.

In the early 1980s the good-looking, smooth-singing star was rarely off the pop and country charts. He had a series of hits with the pop rock songs "I Love a Rainy Night," "Step by Step," and "Someone Could Lose a Heart Tonight," all in 1981. From the mid-1980s on, Rabbitt's career as pop crooner faded, even as he continued to tour and perform for his loyal country fans. His life was cut short by cancer on May 7, 1998.

railroad songs

The railroad played a key role in opening up rural America to outside influences between the mid-19th century and first decades of the 20th century. It also became the subject of many country songs, as did the workers who manned the trains.

In the early days of railroading, when timetables were at best approximations and national time zones not clearly established, train accidents caused by two trains being on the same track at the same time (but heading in opposite directions) were frighteningly common. In the sentimental literature of the day, as well as in song, the "honest trainman" who stayed with his train even as it hurtled into another locomotive became a hero, like the captain who bravely goes down with his ship. One of the most popular of these sentimental stories was retold in "The Wreck of the Old 97," a song that told the story of a tragic train derailment. Its most famous recording was by VERNON DALHART. It became country music's first million-selling hit on its release in 1924.

The image of the trainman was so beloved in country culture that one of the first great country stars, JIMMIE RODGERS, was promoted as "the singing brakeman." Rodgers had indeed worked on the trains, but when he began performing, he dressed in fancy clothes and horn-rimmed glasses, looking very much like a recent college graduate. When he was signed to Victor Records, one of his first publicity shots showed him in full railroader's regalia, including striped overalls and hat. It was important for the label's publicity department to establish Rodgers as "one of the folks," and clearly his well-

acts like the Monroe Brothers and Bill Boyd's Cowboy Ramblers.

Although Nashville had long been the home of the *Grand Ole Opry,* little recording was done there during the height of the 78 era. However, after World War II, RCA (the inheritor of the Victor label) established itself in Nashville, and Columbia, Decca, and other labels soon followed. The availability of talented songwriters, musicians, and music publishers—and its central location in the South—made the city an ideal place to record country music. Nashville also gave birth to several independent studios and labels, notably Bullet Records, founded in 1946 by WSM announcer Jim Bulleit. In 1949 the label also established Nashville's first pressing plant.

The major labels were the ones that made Nashville the center of country recording. Victor was dominated in the 1950s by A&R man Steve Sholes and his studio cohort, guitarist CHET ATKINS. From EDDY ARNOLD in the late 1940s through Elvis Presley in the mid-1950s, RCA's major hit-making acts were managed out of Nashville. In 1957 they opened their own studio, which was run by Chet Atkins through the 1960s. RCA continued to be a major player in the country market, albeit aimed at the more conservative end of the spectrum, through the mid-1970s. The 1980s saw some notable new country successes, including the JUDDS, VINCE GILL, and CLINT BLACK. In 1986 the label was purchased by the German media conglomerate Bertelsmann. It rechristened the country division RCA Nashville in the 1990s; later in the decade, Arista's Nashville division, another part of the Bertelsmann empire, was folded into RCA.

Columbia Records, in its modern form, came together in 1938 when CBS radio purchased American Record Corporation (ARC), itself a conglomeration of smaller labels, many marketed through five-and-ten stores. Popular acts like BOB WILLS, cowboy crooner GENE AUTRY, and ROY ACUFF were among ARC's assets that Columbia inherited. Under the new regime, country recordings were

Eck Robertson from the Victor catalog at the time of his first recording in 1922 (University of North Carolina, Southern Historical Collection, Southern Folklife Collection, University Archives)

first issued on subsidiary labels, including Vocalion (in the later 1930s) and Okeh (in the early-through-mid-1940s). From 1945 Columbia featured its country acts on the main label. A&R man Don Law had the greatest influence on Columbia's country roster during the postwar era, serving as head of country at the label from 1952 to 1967. New acts developed under his reign included CARL SMITH, LEFTY FRIZZELL, MARTY ROBBINS, and RAY PRICE, as well as bluegrass stars FLATT AND SCRUGGS. In 1953 the company formed the Epic subsidiary, but it did not expand the label into Nashville until 1963. Producer Billy Sherrill brought Epic's country line to its highest level of success from the late 1960s through the mid-1970s with such acts as TAMMY WYNETTE, CHARLIE RICH, and GEORGE JONES. In 1987 Columbia, Epic, and the remaining associated labels were purchased by Japanese consumer-electronics giant Sony. Since then, both the Epic and Columbia labels have been continued, both featuring contemporary Nashville artists.

Decca has also continued to be a major player, although the Decca name disappeared in 1973. After World War II Paul Cohen, then working for the firm in Cincinnati, took over Decca's country roster, and oversaw its growth in the late 1940s and 1950s with artists ranging from BILL MONROE to KITTY WELLS and BRENDA LEE; he also secured the distribution rights to PATSY CLINE's recordings (she had been under contract to the independent Four Star label). From 1949 Cohen employed producer OWEN BRADLEY, who operated out of his own studio. Bradley put together a house band that helped form the smooth jazz-and-pop-influenced Nashville sound. In 1958 Bradley took over as head of Decca's country operations and remained there until 1976. During his heyday in the 1960s, Bradley brought LORETTA LYNN, "WHISPERING" BILL ANDERSON, and CONWAY TWITTY, among many others, to the label. In 1962 the label was absorbed into the MCA corporation, which continued to use the Decca name until 1973. In 1979 further country artists were brought to MCA with the purchase of ABC/Dot. The label was reinvigorated in the 1980s, first under the leadership of Jimmy Bowen and then Tony Brown, both ex-musicians. New artists, including REBA MCENTIRE, PATTY LOVELESS, MARTY STUART, and VINCE GILL were all key to the label's growth. In 1990 MCA was purchased by a Japanese electronics manufacturer, Matsushita Electric Industrial. Brown continued through the 1990s, developing more hit makers, including TRISHA YEARWOOD, Mark Collie, and Tracy Byrd.

The major labels of Nashville were not the only important outlets for country music in the late 1940s and 1950s. A number of independent labels—often operated by ex-country promoters and/or record-plant owners—helped introduce new acts and document changes in country and early rock and roll. Cincinnati's King Records, operated by the colorful, cigar-chomping Syd Nathan, took advantage of the popularity of a local radio show, *Boone County Jamboree* to find talented performers for its roster. In 1943 MERLE TRAVIS and GRANDPA JONES were among the first to record for the label, quickly followed by acts like the DELMORE BROTHERS and Moon Mullican. Country promoters Harold "Pappy" Daily and Jack Starnes Jr. founded the Starday label in Houston, Texas, in the early 1950s; among their greatest discoveries was singer George Jones. In the mid-1950s the label briefly had a distribution/production deal with Mercury Records, which wanted to expand into the country market.

Mercury was founded in Chicago in 1945 as an outgrowth of a record-pressing business. Early country artists included Flatt and Scruggs, signed in 1948, and Carl Story. In the early 1950s JOHNNY HORTON was added to the roster. After the Starday deal ended, George Jones remained with Mercury, helping to lay the foundation for its growth in the 1960s and 1970s. Taken over by Phillips International, a Dutch electronics giant, in 1961, the country roster grew, particularly in the Smash subsidiary label, which featured successful country satirist ROGER MILLER and rocker-turned-country star JERRY LEE LEWIS on its list. A&R man Shelby Singleton was an important part of the label's 1960s success, and his cohort, Jerry Kennedy, helped continue the label's growth into the 1970s with TOM T. HALL and the STATLER BROTHERS. In 1971 Phillips was absorbed into PolyGram, a large Dutch record conglomerate; a year later, the country catalog of MGM Records was added to the list. (MGM was founded in 1947, and its most famous artist was HANK WILLIAMS.) Mercury's 1980s stars included KATHY MATTEA and JOHNNY CASH (after he was dropped in the mid-1980s by his longtime label, Columbia). BILLY RAY CYRUS was the label's biggest name in the early 1990s. A product of very successful promotion and hype, Cyrus quickly faded from the scene. However, SHANIA TWAIN helped bring the label back into contention by the decade's end.

Sam Phillips, the famous recording engineer who founded Sun Records and subsequently discovered Elvis Presley, recorded many country artists during their rockabilly phase in the 1950s. Among his most notable signings were Johnny Cash, Jerry Lee Lewis, CARL PERKINS, and CHARLIE RICH, along with dozens of lesser-known names. He also gave producer/engineers Jack Clement and Billy Sherrill their starts in the business. Sun was sold to eccentric promoter/record executive Shelby Singleton in 1969. Singleton continued to reissue and license Sun material through the later 1990s.

Three other country independents were Hickory Records, founded in 1953 by ROY ACUFF, Wesley Rose, and FRED ROSE as a means of expanding their very successful Acuff-Rose publishing empire; Monument Records—best remembered for its recordings of Roy Orbison—was founded by Fred Foster in Washington, D.C. (and named for the Washington monument); and Dot Records, founded by record store owner Randy Wood in 1950.

On the West Coast, where a new form of country was developing thanks to the influx of Texans, Oklahomas, and other displaced southwesterners during the depression and continuing after World War II, a number of small labels thrived. These included Abbott and Fabor Records, run by Fabor Robison, a country promoter; and Four Star, originally an R&B label that soon focused on country. Four Star was controlled by the notoriously tight-fisted entrepreneur Bill McCall and producer Don Pierce. The biggest was Capitol Records, founded in 1942 to record pop material. However, that same year the label signed TEX RITTER, recognizing the popularity of western music in Southern California. In 1951 Ken Nelson came on board to manage the country list, and he began building an impressive roster, including FARON YOUNG, FERLIN

HUSKY, and Jean Shepherd. In 1955 Capitol was purchased by the British EMI conglomerate. During the 1960s the leading Capitol country acts were BUCK OWENS and MERLE HAGGARD. The label was West Coast–oriented until Nelson's retirement in 1976, when the country division turned its focus to Nashville. The label focused on pop country in the later 1970s and early 1980s, with such artists as ANNE MURRAY. However, the label took a big jump into new country in 1989 with the signing of GARTH BROOKS.

The folk revival also saw the birth of several labels, beginning in 1947 with Moses Asch and his Folkways family of labels. Operating on a shoestring budget with the goal of recording all types of musical expression, Asch created a model that many others would emulate. Arhoolie, Folk Lyric, and Folk Legacy were the first to follow in Asch's footsteps in the late 1950s and early 1960s; the early 1970s brought his most important imitator, the Rounder collective. All of these labels issued bluegrass music, among other folk styles, and were instrumental in building the folk revival. County Records, founded by record collector/old-time country fan Dave Freeman in 1963, was another Folkways-inspired label that began reissuing old 78 rpm recordings but then recorded contemporary bluegrass groups; the spinoff Sugar Hill label, founded in 1978 by Freeman and Barry Poss, has since become a major player in acoustic country and bluegrass.

Bluegrass fans have formed specialty labels for their music. Most notable is Charles R. Freeland, who in 1959 formed Rebel Records in suburban Washington, D.C., to document the thriving bluegrass scene there. In the later 1960s, many prominent traditional bluegrass bands—including Ralph Stanley and the Country Gentlemen—along with newer groups like the Seldom Scene were recording for Rebel. In 1979 the label was sold to County Records, and it continues to operate under the Rebel name. Freeland has continued to issue recordings under his own Freeland label. Smaller labels, including Old Homestead, Puritan, Vetco, and many others, have released recordings aimed at the bluegrass market over the years.

Reed, Jerry (b. 1937) *guitarist and songwriter*

Born Jerry Reed Hubbard on March 20, 1937, to a mill-working family in Atlanta, Georgia, Reed took up the guitar as a youngster, and he was a talented picker by the time he reached his teenage years. A friend of the family introduced him to publisher/producer Bill Lowery in 1955, when Jerry was 16, and he was signed to a recording contract with the Los Angeles–based Capitol label. His biggest success, however, came as a songwriter when Gene Vincent had a hit in 1956 with his song "Crazy Legs."

After serving for two years in the army, Reed settled in Nashville, signing to Columbia and having minor hits with the instrumental "Hully Gully Guitars" and a cover of Lead Belly's perennial folk classic "Goodnight Irene." However, Reed's real success came as a session player, backing country and pop acts. CHET ATKINS, another talented guitar player, signed him to RCA in 1965, and he had his first major hit two years later with "Guitar Man," which was quickly covered by another RCA act, Elvis Presley (Presley also covered Reed's comic song "U.S. Male"). Reed continued to score hits through the early 1970s, most notably with his unique blend of cajun, rock, and country on 1970's "Amos Moses," his first number-one country hit and a significant pop hit as well. Reed's last solid country hit was 1971's cover of the HANK SNOW classic, "I'm Movin' On." As an instrumentalist he produced his best later work, particularly in several duet albums with Chet Atkins.

Reed pursued an acting career beginning in 1974 with the Burt Reynolds country flick *W. W. and the Dixie Dance Kings;* he continued to work with Reynolds in many of his light comedies, including the popular *Smokey and the Bandit* pictures. He had his last number-one hit in 1982 with the comic novelty number "She Got the Goldmine (I Got the Shaft)." Reed has made several abortive comebacks over the last 20 years, with little success, although he continues to be a popular act on the road.

Reeves, Jim (1923–1964) *singer and songwriter*

James Travis Reeves (b. Galloway, Texas, August 20, 1923) came from a single-parent household, with his mother working as a field hand after the death of his father. He showed an early interest in music and was given a guitar by a construction worker friend of the family when he was five years old. He made his first radio broadcast at age nine in Shreveport.

Reeves developed an interest in baseball during his high school years, and was signed to the St. Louis Cardinals because of his pitching skills. However, he injured his ankle in 1947, ending his career. At about the same time as his injury, Reeves met his future wife, Mary White, a schoolteacher who encouraged him to seek a career in music. Jim landed a job as an announcer at a local radio station, thanks to his baritone voice, which carried well over the air. In 1949 he made a few recordings for a small Houston-based label, and by 1951–52 he was announcing for KWKH, the Shreveport, Louisiana, station that hosted a well-known country radio program, the *Louisiana Hayride.* It was while performing on the *Louisiana Hayride* that he was heard by Fabor Robison of Abbott Records, who immediately signed him.

Reeves's first country hit, "Mexican Joe," came out in 1953. In 1955 he joined the *Grand Ole Opry* and signed with RCA, hitting immediately with "Yonder Comes a Sucker." In 1957 he scored his first crossover hit on the pop charts with "Four Walls," leading to many TV appearances. From 1960 to his untimely death on July 31, 1964, in an airplane crash, Reeves was rarely off the charts, beginning with "I'm Getting Better" in 1960, 1962's "Adios Amigo," 1963's "Is This Me?," and his last single released while he was still alive, "Welcome to My World." After his death, Reeves's wife arranged for his unissued material to be released, and his popularity grew from the first posthumous single, 1964's

"I Guess I'm Crazy" through 1970's "Angels Don't Lie" to 1979's "How I Miss You Tonight."

"Rhinestone Cowboy" (1975)
Glen Campbell's biggest country hit

This song came during a career comeback for GLEN CAMPBELL in the mid-1970s. Campbell's first period of success was as a pop singer and TV personality in the mid-to-late 1960s, when he had a number of hits, mostly written by pop songwriter Jimmy Webb. His career then slumped, but "Rhinestone Cowboy" brought him back to prominence. The song perfectly reflects in sound and theme the mid-1970s "countrypolitan" movement, when country stars like Campbell and KENNY ROGERS, among others, were trying hard to cross over to the mainstream pop audience.

Rich, Charlie (1932–1995) *piano player and singer*

The son of a heavy-drinking farmer and a fundamentalist mother, Charlie Rich (b. Colt, Arkansas, December 14, 1932) was greatly influenced by jazz and blues as a young musician. Unlike many other country performers, he studied music in college. He joined the air force and was stationed in Oklahoma,

Charlie Rich, 1975 (Raeanne Rubenstein)

where he formed his first semiprofessional group, the Velvetones, a jazz/blues combo; his future wife Margaret was the group's lead vocalist. After leaving the air force, Rich returned to West Memphis, Arkansas, to help his father work his cotton farm. While performing with Bill Justis's band there, Rich was invited to audition for Sun Records. Rich performed as a session pianist on many late 1950s Sun recordings, and scored his first solo hit with 1959's "Lonely Weekends."

Rich struggled in the early to mid-1960s to find his sound, moving from the boogie-woogie-influenced "Big Boss Man" of 1963 to the country novelty of "Mohair Sam." In 1968 he was signed to Epic, a major label, and assigned to producer Billy Sherrill. It took five years for Rich and Sherrill to hit a winning formula, but they hit it big in the period 1973–75 with such songs as "Behind Closed Doors," "The Most Beautiful Girl in the World," "A Very Special Love Song," and "Every Time You Touch Me." Rich spent the late 1970s and early 1980s label hopping. Although he continued to have hits, most notably 1979's "I'll Wake You Up When I Get Home," his days of chart-topping success were over. Rich died from a blood clot in the lung at age 62 on July 25, 1995.

Riley, Jeannie C. (b. 1945) *singer*

Jeanne Caroline Stephenson was born on October 19, 1945, in the small town of Anson, Texas. Her father worked as an auto mechanic and her mother was a fundamentalist Christian. Jeanne began singing locally while still a teenager, and married a gas station attendant, Mickey Riley, when she was 17. In 1966 they moved from Texas to Nashville, where she worked as a secretary in the music industry while making demo recordings on the side. She was hired by famed producer Shelby Singleton to launch his new country label, Plantation, and immediately scored a number-one hit with "Harper Valley P.T.A." in 1968. It would be her most successful recording.

With her sexy stage presence and smooth vocals, Riley scored a couple of follow-up hits,

including 1968's "The Girl Most Likely," 1969's "There Never was a Time," 1970's "Country Girl," and 1971's "Good Enough to Be Your Wife," before moving to MGM and lesser stardom. She broke up with her husband in 1970 and continued to record occasionally through the mid-1970s, when she became a born-again Christian and gave up secular music. She continues to record and perform as a gospel artist.

Rimes, LeAnn (b. 1982) *singer*

Margaret LeAnn Rimes was born in Jackson, Mississippi, on August 28, 1982. Rimes was starstruck from an early age, and her parents, particularly her father, Wilbur, became driving forces behind her career. At age seven she was a two-time *Star Search* winner and was also performing regularly in the Dallas, Texas, area. At age 11 she cut her first album for the small Nor Va Jak label. Two years later she signed with Nashville's Curb Records. Although her first single, 1996's "Blue," attracted a great deal of attention, it only reached number 10; nonetheless, her fans drove her first album (also called *Blue*) to number one, and her third single "One Way Ticket (Because I Can)" brought her to the top of the country singles chart as well.

Rushing to cash in on Rimes's newfound fame, Curb repackaged some earlier recordings, along with a new remake of "Unchained Melody," for her first 1997 album, *The Early Years*. It debuted at number one but was a disappointment to fans looking for new material. Later that year, Rimes released *You Light Up My Life: Inspirational Songs*, composed primarily of light pop hits from the 1970s, along with a few standards. The album was the first to achieve the triple crown of opening at number one on the pop, country, and contemporary Christian *Billboard* charts. It also produced the number-one hit "How Do I Live (Without You)," a Diane Warren composition, which held the top position for a record-breaking 69 weeks in 1997–98. The single went triple platinum, placing Rimes in a rarefied club along with pop singer Whitney

LeAnn Rimes (Raeanne Rubenstein)

(he produced it before his falling-out with his daughter). It featured "Looking through Your Eyes," used in the animated film *The Quest for Camelot*. Like her previous album, it moved LeAnn more toward mainstream pop than country, and some fans were perturbed. To appease her country base, she released a self-titled album in 1999 that consisted entirely of country covers, mostly classics from the 1950s and 1960s. However, it failed to produce chart hits. Veering back to pop, she cut a duet with Elton John, called "Written in the Stars," drawn from John's score for the Broadway show *Aida*, which was a major hit. That same year, she was one of the divas on VH1's special *Divas Live*, cementing her position as a pop singer.

In 2000 Rimes appeared in the film *Coyote Ugly*, recording four Diane Warren–penned songs for it, including the hit "Can't Fight the Moonlight." Rimes followed with "I Need You," taken from the television miniseries "Jesus." In 2001 she hosted the Academy of Country Music awards in her new hometown, Los Angeles. In fall 2001 Rimes also sought to be released from her contract with Curb Records, saying that she was underage when she was signed to the label. After settling, she released *Twisted Angel*, her most pop-oriented album yet, in 2002, with the hit "Life Goes On."

Houston as the only artists to achieve such a distinction in any musical genre. In 1997 Rimes won two Grammy Awards, including Best New Artist.

Also in 1997, Rimes's parents' pending divorce took a toll. Her father, who had produced her first three albums, was cut out of the picture, and LeAnn and her mother moved to Nashville. A protracted court battle has ensued between Rimes and her father, with suits and countersuits continuing through the early 2000s.

In 1998 she released *Sittin' on Top of the World*, a heavy-handed pop album produced by her father

Ritter, Tex (1904–1974) *singing cowboy*
Woodward Maurice Ritter was born on January 12, 1904, in Nederland, Texas, where his parents owned a 400-acre ranch. He was a true cowboy, raised amid cattle roundups and ranch hands. Ritter was introduced to cowboy songs at the University of Texas, where folklorist J. Frank Dobie was collecting and teaching the material. Ritter began performing this material on radio in Houston in 1929, and traveled to New York in 1931 to act in the play *Green Grow the Lilacs;* during scene changes, he performed his cowboy ballads, becoming an immediate sensation. He remained on the East Coast for five years, performing on New York radio stations and giving lecture-concerts in which he introduced "authentic" cowboy

material to his audiences. He also made his first records for the budget label ARC in 1934.

In 1936 Ritter traveled to Hollywood to cash in on the singing-cowboy craze in the movies. Although his films suffered from low budgets, they often featured good music, including 1940's *Take Me Back to Oklahoma,* featuring western swing veteran BOB WILLS as the second lead. After 1943 Johnny Bond became Ritter's bandleader on film, often appearing with him. All in all, between 1936 and 1945 he made more than 60 films. In 1942, after unsuccessfully recording for ARC and Decca, Ritter was signed to the fledgling Capitol label as their first country act, and recorded a combination of traditional folk songs ("Boll Weevil," "Rye Whiskey"), sentimental ditties ("There's a New Moon over My Shoulder"), and patriotic odes ("Gold Star in the Window").

Ritter's biggest break came in 1952 when he recorded the theme song for the high-class western film *High Noon.* Although he didn't appear in the film, it gave a considerable boost to his career. He served as host of the popular *Town Hall Party* TV program, along with his friend Johnny Bond, furthering his exposure to a country audience. By the late 1950s and early 1960s, Ritter was working as a straight country act, scoring his biggest hit with 1961's unabashedly sentimental "I Dreamed of a Hillbilly Heaven." In 1958 he became involved with the movement to form the Country Music Association (CMA), and was elected its president in 1963. In 1965 he joined the *Grand Ole Opry.*

In the late 1960s Ritter attempted to enter politics, running without success for a Tennessee senatorial seat in 1970. He served as narrator for the 1971 *Thank You, Mr. President* album, featuring various conservative country performers crooning in honor of President Richard Nixon. His son, John Ritter, gained great popularity in the 1970s as the star of the TV sitcom *Three's Company.* Tex Ritter died on January 2, 1974.

Tex Ritter, c. 1950 (University of North Carolina, Southern Historical Collection, Southern Folklife Collection, University Archives)

Robbins, Marty (1925–1982) *singer and songwriter*

Raised in the small town of Glendale, Arizona, Martin David Robinson (b. September 6, 1925) was particularly close to his grandfather, a retired medicine-show performer known as "Texas" Bob Heckle. Heckle was immersed in cowboy lore, much of which he shared with his young grandson. Saturday matinees featuring GENE AUTRY filled out Robbins's cowboy education, and he soon was playing a second-hand guitar given to him by his older sister.

When he was 12, he relocated with his family to urban Phoenix, where Marty attended high school.

He enlisted in the navy in 1944, and was stationed in the Pacific. At this time he began to write original songs and perform them for his fellow soldiers. On his return to Phoenix after the war, Robbins drifted from job to job, while beginning to perform locally in clubs and bars at night. He took the name "Marty Robbins" because it sounded a little more western than his real name.

By the early 1950s Marty was performing on local radio station KPHO, hosting his own *Western Caravan* show. "LITTLE" JIMMY DICKENS was a guest on the show, and was so impressed that he recommended that his label, Columbia, sign Robbins. Robbins released his first single for Columbia in 1952, "Love Me or Leave Me Alone," and a year later joined the *Grand Ole Opry,* where he remained a member for 29 years until his death. Two months after his first *Opry* appearance, Robbins scored his first top-10 country hit, "I'll Go On Alone." For the next two years Robbins struggled to place his songs on the country charts.

His big break came in 1956 with "Singing the Blues," followed a year later by "Knee Deep in the Blues," "The Story of My Life," and "A White Sport Coat (and a Pink Carnation)." These jazzy country numbers, with Marty's peppy, smooth vocals, not only scored big on the country charts, but also helped him break into the pop charts. He continued in this pop-influenced vein through the 1950s, turning out 1958's "She Was Only Seventeen" and "Stairway of Love."

Robbins's career took a western swing with his appearance in the 1958 film *Buffalo Gun,* along with other country stars WEBB PIERCE and CARL SMITH. He recorded his classic album of western story songs, *Gunfighter Ballads and Trail Songs,* a year later. It contained several hits, including "Big Iron" and "El Paso," a song that would become closely associated with him. "El Paso" topped both country and pop charts, gaining the first Grammy Award ever given to a country song. Robbins followed it with "Big Iron," and "Battle of the Alamo."

Robbins continued to be a force on the country charts through the 1960s. He toured extensively throughout the United States and Canada, but the hits started to thin out by the end of the decade. His most distinctive recording of this time was 1968's "I Walk Alone," another blues-tinged number in the vein of his earlier hits. In 1969 he suffered the first in a series of massive heart attacks.

Robbins had a quick recovery, and began the 1970s with a major hit, "My Woman, My Woman, My Wife." Through the decade, Robbins turned out a few further hits, mostly under the hand of seasoned producer Billy Sherrill. "El Paso City," a 1976 release, was a follow-up to his earlier hit, filled with references to his best-loved song. "El Paso City" and "Among My Souvenirs," were his last country number-one hits. In the 1970s Robbins suffered several injuries while pursuing his hobby of stock-car racing. In 1981 he suffered a second heart attack, recovering to make a comeback a year later with his last release, "Some Memories Just Won't Die," which proved prophetic in 1982, when Robbins suffered a final major heart attack on December 2, dying six days later.

rockabilly

Literally the wedding of rock and roll with "hillbilly" or country music, rockabilly is a limited style, but one that was highly influential in the mid-1950s. Elvis's first Sun studio recordings are firmly rooted in the rockabilly style. Indeed, it was Elvis's success that helped nail down rockabilly's basic sound: a single guitar playing jazzy riffs, a heavy, slapped bass, and frantic, pounding drums. Countless country stars jumped on the rockabilly bandwagon, some producing one or two classic sides while others faded into obscurity. The most successful were the Burnette brothers, Johnny and Dorsey, who led the Rockabilly Trio.

Perhaps the greatest rockabilly star was CARL PERKINS. His blends of high-energy country sounds with R&B and blues made him an innovative composer and performer. From the sassy attitude of "Blue Suede Shoes" to his cover of Blind Lemon Jefferson's classic "Matchbox," Perkins defined the rockabilly sound and attitude. While some would also place JERRY LEE LEWIS in the style, his music mixed many other elements into the stew, including the jazz tinges of western swing piano and the intensity of country gospel.

Perkins's and Lewis's success led many other country acts to jump on the rockabilly bandwagon, sometimes for single recordings, sometimes for a few years of ceaseless searching for hits. The style was dismissed by older country performers, who felt it represented a sellout to teen-pop trends. Country comedian FERLIN HUSKY took on the pseudonym of "Simon Crum" to record some humorous satires of rockabilly's excesses.

Rockabilly's powerful style—including simple instrumentation, basic riffs, and primal lyrics—appealed strongly to post-punk audiences in the late 1970s, particularly in Europe, when the style was revived and many pioneering figures returned to the stage. Newer groups such as the Stray Cats picked up on a rockabilly sensibility, enjoying some success in the late 1970s, but like so many others they eventually found the style rather limiting. Today, elements of the rockabilly sound can be heard in new country music, particularly the heavy backbeat and slapped bass, but no star centers his or her act solely on the rockabilly style.

Jimmie Rodgers in his most famous pose, dressed in full "Singing Brakeman" regalia, c. 1929 (University of North Carolina, Southern Historical Collection, Southern Folklife Collection, University Archives)

Rodgers, Jimmie (1897–1933) *singer*

James Charles Rodgers was born in Meridian, Mississippi, on September 8, 1897. The son of a railroad man, Rodgers worked as a brakeman until tuberculosis cut short his career in 1924. He began performing as a singer and guitarist, working at local tent shows and on the vaudeville circuit. By the mid-1920s he was leading a band called the Teneva Ramblers, which specialized in the popular music of the day. In 1927 Rodgers and the group auditioned for famed country producer Ralph Peer, who was on a talent-scouting trip in Bristol, Tennessee/Virginia. Rodgers was signed as a solo act to Victor Records.

Rodgers's recordings enjoyed immediate success; his first, "Blue Yodel," sold a million copies, and many of his recordings have remained in print, in one form or another, for the past six decades. Rodgers had major hits with such songs as "In the Jailhouse Now," a vaudeville favorite that, thanks to his recording, would become a country standard, and "Waiting for a Train." He also recorded with a wide variety of accompanists, even including jazz trumpeter Louis Armstrong. Victor successfully marketed his recordings by promoting Rodgers as "The Singing Brakeman" (the name of a short motion picture in which Rodgers appeared in 1929) and "America's Blue Yodeler." Most of his recordings featured Rodgers's distinctive yodeling, a combination of the traditional Swiss vocal style influenced by the blues singing of African Americans.

Plagued by tuberculosis, Rodgers performed and toured as widely as possible, but made his greatest impact through his recordings. He made his last recordings in New York in 1933; two days after this final session, he died in his New York hotel room on May 26, 1933. The death of Jimmie Rodgers only added to his legendary status; like HANK WILLIAMS and Elvis Presley after him, Rodgers became a larger-than-life performer after his death, with record sales continuing unabated for six decades.

duet with DOTTIE WEST on "Every Time Two Fools Collide," solidifying his position as a country music star. Later that same year, he scored on his own with "The Gambler," which has become his best-loved country song (and also inspired a made-for-TV movie two years later). In 1979 he had another hit with "You Decorated My Life." A year later came a duet with popster Kim Carnes on "Don't Fall in Love with a Dreamer" and Lionel Richie's ballad, "Lady."

After scaling the heights of mainstream pop, Rogers spent most of the 1980s performing for country audiences. He also took to acting, mostly in made-for-TV movies, and primarily in parts that

Rogers, Kenny (b. 1938) *singer*

Rogers was born on August 21, 1938, in relative poverty in Houston, Texas. He had his first exposure to music in the church choir, and then took up the guitar, teaching himself to play chords. He often got together with another neighborhood kid, pianist MICKEY GILLEY, to perform the latest pop hits. In high school Kenny formed the Scholars, a rockabilly outfit, and signed as a soloist with a local label. After a brief try at college, he joined a light jazz trio. He relocated to Los Angeles in 1966, hooking up with the folk group the New Christy Minstrels, and made some recordings as a soloist for Mercury that same year.

Along with fellow Minstrel Mike Settle, he formed the folk-tinged pop vocal group the First Edition, scoring a major pop hit with 1967's "Just Dropped In (to See What Condition My Condition Was In)." Other hits, in a more country vein, followed, including "Ruby (Don't Take Your Love to Town)" and the folk anthem "Reuben James." The First Edition remained together under Rogers's leadership until 1975, when he embarked on a solo career.

The late 1970s were golden years for Rogers, beginning in 1977 with his monster hit "Lucille," which established him as a star on both country and pop charts. He followed it in 1978 with a hit

Kenny Rogers gives a thumbs-up at Fan Fair.
(Raeanne Rubenstein)

are tailor-made for his personality. His career as a singer slowed considerably in the 1990s; in 1998 he formed his own label to release his new recordings and reissue his classic material.

Rogers, Roy (1911–1998) *singing cowboy*

The son of migrant farmworkers, Leonard Franklin Slye (born in Duck Run, Ohio, on November 5, 1911) came to California in 1930 to work as a fruit picker. He began performing with a number of western bands, founding his own group, the Sons of the Pioneers, in 1934. Their big break came when they supported GENE AUTRY in his 1935 epic *Tumbling Tumbleweeds*. Slye decided he could be a singing cowboy, too, and took the names Dick Weston and then Roy Rogers. He began starring in B-grade westerns in 1938 and, four years later when Autry went off to fight in World War II, became the leading U.S. cowboy star.

In 1947 he wed Dale Evans (b. Frances Smith, Uvalde, Texas, 1912–2001), a pop singer who had appeared in many of his westerns and would continue to work with him through the rest of his career. From the 1950s through Rogers's death, the pair worked on radio, films, and TV, and Roy has also pursued business interests, including a franchise of fast-food restaurants. His best-known song is his theme song, "Happy Trails." Rogers and Evans founded their own museum in their hometown of Victorville, California, where you can visit the stuffed remains of Roy's favorite horse, Trigger. Rogers is the only country performer elected to the Country Music Hall of Fame in two capacities, as a member of the Sons of the Pioneers in 1980, and again for his solo work in 1988. He died on July 6, 1998.

Rose, Fred (1898–1954) **and Wesley Rose** (1918–1990) *father-and-son managing and producing team*

Born in Evansville, Indiana, on August 24, 1898, Fred Rose was a pioneering publisher, songwriter, and producer in country music. His son Wesley built his empire in partnership with ROY ACUFF into one of the powerhouses of the Nashville music establishment.

The elder Rose began his career as a Chicago-area pianist, initially recording jazz for the Brunswick record label and piano rolls for QRS. In Chicago he wrote many songs for the big-throated chanteuse Sophie Tucker, including her signature tune, "Red Hot Mama," " 'Deed I Do," and "Honestly and Truly." After working in Paul Whiteman's band for a while, he joined CBS Radio as a house producer in Chicago and then relocated to the West Coast, where he hooked up with up-and-coming cowpoke star Gene Autry. Rose composed his major hit, "Be Honest with Me."

Anticipating the market for country music, Rose moved to Nashville where he was hired as staff pianist for WSM, home of the *Grand Ole Opry*, and quickly befriended a young fiddler/singer named Roy Acuff. Recognizing the value of the acts that he was managing and producing, he formed a partnership with Acuff in 1942 to form Acuff-Rose music publishing. He also was instrumental in the forming of Broadcast Music International (BMI) as an alternative to the more conservative ASCAP (American Society of Composers, Authors, and Publishers), which was uninterested in representing country or blues composers.

His son Wesley (b. Chicago, Illinois, February 11, 1918–April 26, 1990) was trained as an accountant and worked for Standard Oil before joining the family business in 1945. Fred left the business to take a more active hand in managing his last great discovery, HANK WILLIAMS, for whom he composed "Kaw-Liga." Other popular Rose compositions include "Blue Eyes Crying in the Rain" (revived by Willie Nelson), "Tears on My Pillow," "A Mansion on the Hill," and "Settin' the Woods on Fire." After his father's death on December 1, 1958, Wesley discovered and helped build the career of such acts as the EVERLY BROTHERS. In the late 1950s he founded with Acuff the Hickory record label, which became the home for many important country acts in the early 1960s.

"Rose Garden" (1970) *1970 hit for Lynn Anderson*

This was one of the first country songs to cross over to success on the pop charts. It was prominently featured as the theme song for a popular film, *I Never Promised You a Rose Garden,* released that year. Although recorded by LYNN ANDERSON, a country performer, its accompaniment was in the style of other pop recordings of the day, which is why it enjoyed such wide appeal. Later, it became a cult favorite among alternative rock bands, and was covered by such groups as Suicide Machines and 10,000 Maniacs.

rube/hillbilly humor

The stereotypical image of the "hick from the sticks" is a long-lasting one in American culture, and it has been exploited by generations of country music entertainers. This condescending attitude to poor southerners was reinforced by years of stereotyped images through minstrel shows, tent shows, and finally vaudeville through the beginning of the 20th century. Early country performers often adopted the role of the "hillbilly" in deference to the common image that folk performers had among more "sophisticated" people, like recording company executives and northerners in general. A professional musician, Al Hopkins, who led a popular string band in the mid-1920s that broadcast and performed in such urban centers as Washington, D.C., and New York City as well as their southern base, dubbed his band the "Hill Billies" when recording executive Ralph Peer asked him what to call the group.

Humorous skits—supposedly recreating real backwoods events like fiddling contests, picnics, and other get-togethers—were very popular during the mid-1920s. Sometimes skits would be issued on a set of 78 rpm records, as a means of selling more records (to hear the end, you had to buy five or more discs). Gid Tanner, himself an old tent-show performer, and his Skillet Lickers specialized in these skits, and many other string bands were

encouraged to record similar material. Backcountry activities such as fox hunting and bootlegging were popular topics for these records.

Almost every performing country band from the 1920s onward featured at least one "rube" comedian among its members. Perhaps as a holdover from minstrel shows, this comedian was often a banjo player (like GRANDPA JONES, who at the beginning of his career was a young man bedecked in white false whiskers, wig, and tattered coveralls; eventually he aged into the part). UNCLE DAVE MACON was another former tent-show performer; he performed tricks onstage like dancing and playing the banjo at the same time, holding the instrument between his legs while playing it, and other eye-catching routines. Although he recorded and performed everything from Victorian sentimental songs to topical numbers, he is best remembered for his humorous songs and his shouted "Hot Dog!" when completing a particularly satisfying performance.

Not all performers were full-time comedians. Often a musician will carry two identities in a country or bluegrass band: one his "serious" role as musician, the other his "comic" role, interacting between numbers with the band's leader. Thus Dobroist Buck Graves of the 1950s-era FLATT and SCRUGGS band would become "Uncle Josh" when it was time for a little horseplay on stage. This not only saved the band having extra (and costly) personnel, but also gave the performer another means of drawing attention to himself and could further his career.

Besides musicians, rube comics have come forward who specialize simply in delivering monologues. The most famous in country music is MINNIE PEARL, but there have been many more who specialized in delivering mock sermons, "news" from the backwoods (as Pearl did), or other comic material. However, making a living as a full-time comedian is harder, and Pearl was somewhat unique in her ability to survive without adding music or songs to her act. Pearl was a major influence on Garrison Keillor; her monologues on the *Grand Ole Opry* (and the *Opry* itself) were highly

Riders in the Sky, c. 1980 (Courtesy of Rounder Records)

influential on the development of his popular *Prairie Home Companion* radio series of the last three decades.

After World War II the country comedy tradition was carried forward in a more sophisticated way. The duo HOMER and JETHRO introduced song satire into their act, taking popular country numbers and reworking them for humorous effect. Although they dressed in typical hayseed costumes, they had an appeal as nightclub performers, being as competent playing pop and jazz instrumentals as they were playing their normal comic songs. They were rubes that winked at the audience, sharing the fact that they weren't as stupid as they appeared. In the 1960s ROGER MILLER took up the mantle of country comic song, drawing on age-old humorous themes, such as drinking moonshine ("Chug-a-Lug") and countrified speech ("Dang Me").

The later 1960s saw the institutionalization of country humor in the television show *HEE HAW*. Although many southerners were embarrassed by it—and it had only a two-year network run—the show remained in syndication for two decades. Despite the fast pace borrowed from the contemporary hit comedy show *Laugh-In*, *Hee Haw* was really just an updated minstrel show without the blackface, but with the same mix of sentiment, song, and cornpone humor.

Because of the stigma attached to rube humor—and the Civil Rights movement that made blackface humor also politically incorrect—very few performers have tried to revive either the white or black traditions of this style of comedy. When bluegrass became newly popular among urban performers in the 1970s, many older bands dropped the rube comedy from their repertoire, recognizing that while it appealed to their traditional audience, it did not go over as well with the college-educated crowds they were now drawing.

A few of the young groups tried to revive the humor tradition. The band Hot Rize even formed an alter ego band, Red Knuckles and the Trailblazers, to perform honky-tonk music as both an homage to and a humorous change of pace for their stage show. That group became so popular that it issued its own separate album. Sometimes contemporary groups seem to combine humor and affection in their revival of older styles; Riders in the Sky are a winking tribute to cowboy acts of the 1930s and 1940s, and the character of Ranger Doug, taken by bandleader Doug Green, for example, is somewhat of a comic alter ego.

"Rudolph, the Red-Nosed Reindeer"
(1949) *number-one country hit for Gene Autry*
This song has become a Christmas standard, and the story of the outcast reindeer has been adapted several times for children's cartoons and books. Autry also wrote and originally recorded "Here Comes Santa Claus" (1947) and "Frosty the Snow Man" (1950).

"San Antonio Rose" (1938/1940) *Bob Wills hit*
This song launched the popularity of western swing, as well as the career of bandleader/fiddler BOB WILLS. It became a theme song for him and his band, The Texas Playboys. The original version was a jazzy instrumental that sold so well that Wills's producer asked him to add lyrics to it. The result was issued as "New San Antonio Rose" in 1940 with a great lead vocal by the band's singer Tommy Duncan. Wills quipped that the song's success took him "from hamburgers to steak."

"Satisfied Mind, A" (1955) *Porter Wagoner hit*
PORTER WAGONER's second single, "A Satisfied Mind," was a major country hit, topping the country charts for four weeks, as well as the pop chart. It remained on the country charts for an astounding 33 weeks. The song's lyric promotes the familiar belief that wealth can't buy happiness.

Sawyer Brown
Sawyer Brown came together as backup musicians for singer Don King. Vocalist Mark Miller and keyboard player Gregg "Hobie" Hubbard were friends from high school in Florida. Guitarist Bobby Randall and bassist Jim Schloten were from Michigan. Drummer "Curley" Joe Smyth had previously played percussion with the Maine Symphony. While working for King, they were impressed by the commercial success of ALABAMA; after leaving King's employ, they formed a band, giving it a similar regional name, Savannah, in hopes of attracting similar success.

The group soon took the name of Sawyer Brown (the names of two roads that cross in Nashville), and got their first break in 1984 when they won first prize on *Star Search*. The prize was a recording contract, and the boys immediately scored with 1985's "Step that Step," written by Miller, their second single and a number-one hit. They followed with more fluffy upbeat numbers, including "Betty's Bein' Bad" and a remake of GEORGE JONES's "The Race Is On." Their road show featured smoke bombs, twirling lights, and jazzy costumes, reflecting their arena-rock leanings, paving the way for similar theatrics from later country acts such as GARTH BROOKS.

In the early 1990s, recognizing that new country was making their meld of Alabama's and Exile's rock sound passé, the group remade itself in the boot-scootin' mode of a good-time honky-tonk band. It turned out that they could produce watered-down western swing in an attractive manner. Miller continued his Mick Jagger-esque stage antics, particularly in their video for "The Boys and Me," an unabashed retro rocker. The band's popularity declined in the later half of the decade, although they continued to record and tour.

Seely, Jeannie (b. 1940) *singer*
The daughter of a steelworker and sometime farmer, Marilyn Jeanne Seely (b. Titusville, Pennsylvania, July 6, 1940) was performing locally by age 11, when

183

she sang on local radio; five years later, she was regularly featured on a country TV show out of Erie. After graduating high school, she enrolled in night school to learn banking while working as a secretary by day. With three friends, she left Pennsylvania to cross the United States in 1961. She ended up in Beverly Hills, where she worked briefly in a bank before taking a job as secretary at Liberty Records. There she met a young country guitarist named Hank Cochran. She began writing songs (R&B singer Irma Thomas had a hit with her "Anyone Who Knows What Love Is" in 1964), worked as a disc jockey, and recorded for the tiny Challenge label. Cochran urged her to follow him to Nashville for a career in country music.

Arriving in Nashville in 1965, Seely went into the studio with Cochran, who wrote and produced her first big hit, "Don't Touch Me," a sultry backroom ballad that was a 1966 Grammy Award winner. The couple married, and Seely continued to produce hits between 1966 and 1969, as well as appearing on the *Grand Ole Opry*, causing a stir because she refused to appear in the frilly gingham dress of the stereotypical country girl; instead she wore a fashionable miniskirt. In the late 1960s she performed several hit duets with singer Jack Greene, including "Wish I Didn't Have to Miss You," as well as appearing in his road show.

In the early 1970s, Seely returned to the charts, thanks to her association with country outlaw WILLIE NELSON and friends. She had hits with her reworking of traditional folk ballads, changing "Can I Sleep in Your Barn Tonight Mister?" into "Can I Sleep in Your Arms," while the southern lament "Come All You Fair and Tender Ladies" was transformed into the bouncy "Lucky Ladies." By the late 1970s Seely was recording more spicy material, like "Take Me to Bed," showing how much country music had changed.

Seely dropped off the country charts in the 1980s and turned her attention to appearing in regional theater productions of popular musicals and publishing a volume of her saucy aphorisms, while still appearing on the *Grand Ole Opry*.

Shelton, Ricky Van (b. 1952) *singer*

Born January 12, 1952, in Danville, Virginia, but raised in rural Grit, Shelton was first more interested in rock and roll than country music, although he did sing in the small church choir where he was raised. His brother Ronnie played mandolin and had his own bluegrass country band, and he encouraged his younger sibling to take up country music. Shelton remained in his hometown into his early twenties, working as a pipefitter by day and a musician at night. Then his wife got a job as a corporate personnel director in Nashville, and the two moved to the country-music capital.

Shelton worked on demos in his basement while performing at nights in a small club called the Nashville Palace, where he met another country hopeful who was working there washing dishes—RANDY TRAVIS. Shelton's wife befriended the wife of a *Nashville Tennessean* reporter, who brought one of his demo tapes to Columbia producer Steve Buckingham, and Buckingham signed the artist in 1986. A year later, Shelton had his first hit with his first of many covers, "Somebody Lied," originally recorded by CONWAY TWITTY two years previously. His follow-up hits came from even further back in the country music songbook, including Harlan Howard's "Life Turned Her That Way" (a hit for Mel Tillis in the 1960s), "Statue of a Fool" (a pop song recorded by Jack Greene in 1969), and 1989's "From a Jack to a King," which was originally written and recorded by Ned Miller in 1963. In the early 1990s Shelton had a hit covering Elvis's "Wear My Ring around Your Neck" that was featured in the film *Honeymoon in Vegas.*

Shelton came to a crossroads in his personal life in 1991, when his wife confronted him after years of enduring his heavy drinking and womanizing. He underwent a "born-again" experience in 1992, and released a gospel album and a series of inspirational children's books. It took Shelton several years to return to more secular material, and he lost his standing on the country charts. In the later 1990s he attempted to return to his more mainstream material, and despite failing to produce many hits, he continues to be a fairly good draw on the country concert circuit.

Shenandoah

This group originated as the informal house band of Muscle Shoals, Alabama's, MGM Club, where they all worked as session musicians and songwriters. Leader Marty Raybon worked a day job as a bricklayer with his father; the duo also played together in a family bluegrass band. Raybon began hunting for a record deal, finally hooking up with Robert Byrne at CBS, who offered to hire Raybon if he brought along his backup group. It was Byrne who gave them the name Shenandoah.

On the group's first album, Byrne tried to mold their sound into mainstream country pop; it was a commercial failure. But the group came back with a more roots-oriented second disc, producing their first hits, "The Church on Cumberland Road" and "Sunday in the South." However, their breakthrough into widespread popularity brought legal difficulties in 1991, when three other bands—from Kentucky, Nevada, and Massachusetts—sued the group, claiming that they had prior rights to the "Shenandoah" name. The lawsuit bankrupted the band by the end of the year, and they were dropped by CBS.

In 1992 the group had settled the various lawsuits (making the argument that, after all, they had not chosen the name, but it was given to them by CBS so therefore they couldn't be accused of stealing it). Moving to RCA, Shenandoah scored new hits with "Rock My Baby" and "(Your Leavin's Been) A Long Time Comin'." The band began 1993 with the hit "If Bubba Can Dance" and the humorous "Janie Baker's Love Slave." They moved to Capitol Records in 1994.

Shenandoah scored their last major hit in 1995, with "Somewhere in the Vicinity of the Heart" featuring guest vocalist ALISON KRAUSS. A 1996 album of remakes of their earlier hits showed the band treading water, and then they took a four-year recording hiatus. Their most recent album, the grandly titled *2000,* was issued on the small Free Falls label.

"She Thinks I Still Care" (1962) *first number-one country hit for singer George Jones*

"She Thinks I Still Care" is a classic honky-tonk ballad and song of denial. The narrator goes through a list of reasons that "she thinks I still care," ("Just because I asked a friend about her . . ."), the irony being that the more he says he doesn't care, the more the listener—and implicitly the singer—knows that he does. The song has been covered many times, including a version by Elvis Presley.

"Six Days on the Road" (1963) *a number-two country hit for newcomer Dave Dudley*

This song was originally issued on the tiny Soma label. It created the 1960s craze for truck-driving songs, portraying the truck driver as a heroic loner, battling fatigue, long hauls, and loneliness to make it back home again. The song was equally embraced by country singers and the young country rockers of the late 1960s, who had their own vision of the freedom of life on the road.

"Sixteen Tons" (1955) *Merle Travis hit*

Written by MERLE TRAVIS, this song tells of the hard life he witnessed among his coal mining family and neighbors in his native Kentucky. First recorded by Travis in 1947 for his album *Folk Songs of the Hills,* it was covered eight years later by TENNESSEE ERNIE FORD and hit number one on the country charts, holding this position for an amazing 10 weeks; Ford's recording was also a major pop hit. Ford's signature finger-snapping, which occurs at the end of each chorus, became an aural trademark of this recording. The song has been often covered and parodied; one of the best parodies was recorded by comedian Mickey Katz in his "Sixteen Tons (of Kosher Salami)," which resets the song in a Jewish delicatessen.

Skaggs, Ricky (b. 1954) *singer and bluegrass musician*
Skaggs was born near Cordell, Kentucky, on July 18, 1954. A multi-instrumentalist, Skaggs began his career while still in high school with his friend Keith Whitley, performing mandolin and guitar duets in a traditional style derived from country's brother acts. The duo was particularly enamored of the STANLEY BROTHERS' sound, and they soon found themselves performing as members of Ralph Stanley's band. Poor pay and a grueling touring schedule led to Skaggs's retirement and brief employment as an electric-company worker in a suburban Washington power plant. There, he began performing with a later version of the progressive bluegrass band the Country Gentlemen.

In the early 1970s Skaggs joined briefly with J. D. Crowe's groundbreaking bluegrass ensemble, the New South, along with ace guitarist/vocalist Tony Rice. Determined to modernize and popularize the bluegrass sound, he formed his own progressive band, Boone Creek, with Dobro player Jerry Douglas, who has appeared on many of Skaggs's recordings, and singer/guitarist Terry Baucom. By the late 1970s Skaggs was working as a backup musician for EMMYLOU HARRIS, helping mold her new traditional approach on landmark albums such as *Roses in the Snow*.

Blessed with a unique high tenor voice, Skaggs recorded his first solo album in a contemporary country vein for the bluegrass label Sugar Hill. At the same time he made a duet album with Rice featuring just their guitar and mandolin and vocal harmonies in an homage to the 1930s country sound. He was quickly signed to Epic, and had a string of hits in the early 1980s with his unique adaptations of bluegrass and country standards of the 1950s. In fact, his cover of BILL MONROE's "Uncle Pen" in 1984 was the first bluegrass song to hit number one on the country charts since 1949. He also was one of the first new country artists to tour Europe, scoring great success in England where he performed with diverse artists such as Elvis Costello and Nick Lowe.

The mid-1980s found Skaggs moving toward a more pop-country sound, but basically he stuck close to his country roots in choice of material and performance. He married country vocalist Sharon White of the Whites, and produced some of their successful recordings of the 1980s. He returned to his bluegrass/country swing roots as a member of Mark O'Connor's New Nashville Cats band, which featured another crossover artist from bluegrass, VINCE GILL. After watching his mainstream country career peter out, Skaggs renounced commercial country in the mid-1990s and formed a new band, Kentucky Thunder. Recording on his own Skaggs Family label, he has returned to playing acoustic bluegrass music. He oversaw a tribute album to Bill Monroe in 2000, aptly titled *Big Mon*. He continues to tour with his own band.

"Slipping Around" (1949) *number-one hit*
A 1949 hit for pop singer Margaret Whiting and cowboy star Jimmy Wakely, this song is notable because it was among the first to openly discuss a husband cheating on his wife. This was then a fairly racy topic for country music, and the fact that the song was so successful encouraged others to write more honestly about the ups-and-downs of romantic relationships. The song inspired a follow-up hit, "I'll Never Slip Around Again," which reached number two just two months after the release of the original.

"Slowly" (1954) *major hit for Webb Pierce*
WEBB PIERCE's "Slowly" topped the country charts for an incredible 17 weeks. It also did fairly well on the jukebox, best-seller, and disc jockey charts. Cowritten with Nashville session man Tommy Hill, the song's lyrics originally rued a lost love, but Pierce changed them because he felt women in his audience preferred upbeat love songs. Pierce's recording was also noteworthy for Bud Isaac's pedal steel guitar part; it helped popularize the sound of the "crying" steel guitar, which became a must-have for many country recordings.

Smith, Carl (b. 1927) *singer*

Smith (b. March 15, 1927) came from Maynardville, Tennessee, (the same town that gave country music ROY ACUFF), and Smith's sound was originally heavily influenced by Acuff, as well as by EDDY ARNOLD. Smith got his first break on radio station WROL in Knoxville after World War II, and then was hired for the WSM morning show in Nashville in 1950. This led to a contract with Columbia Records, and his first hit with 1951's "Let's Live a Little." Through the 1950s Smith produced myriad hits, mostly barroom classics like "Loose Talk," "Hey Joe," "Kisses Don't Lie," and "If Teardrops Were Pennies." His mid-1950s band, known as the Tunesmiths, featured the steel guitar of Johnny Sibert and the bass-twangy guitar of Sammy Pruett (who had previously played with HANK WILLIAMS's Drifting Cowboys). Smith was also one of the first bandleaders to feature drums, which were still controversial in country music; his drummer Buddy Harman later became a leading Nashville session man.

Smith combined a honky-tonk attitude with flashy western garb, as well as borrowing a few choice songs from the western repertoire, including Bob Wills's classic "Time Changes Everything." In 1952 Smith wed June Carter, and performed with the Carter Sisters and their famous mother, Maybelle. The two produced a daughter, Carlene, who became a well-known country rocker (performing under the name Carlene Carter) in the late 1980s and early 1990s. (See CARTER FAMILY.)

By the late 1950s Smith had jumped on another big country bandwagon, capitalizing on the popularity of pseudo folk songs sung in a melodramatic style with his last big hit, 1959's "Ten Thousand Drums," telling a revolutionary war story. In 1957 he married his second wife, Goldie Hill (who also had a minor career as a country singer), and settled down on a large horse farm. Although he continued to record for Columbia through 1974, and then made some more recordings for the smaller Hickory label in the mid-1970s, he never achieved the same chart success he had had in the 1950s, and eventually he gave up performing to focus on his home life.

Smith, Connie (b. 1941) *singer*

Born Constance June Meador, in Elkhart, Indiana, on August 14, 1941, to an abusive father in a large household (she was one of 13 siblings), Smith led a troubled young life, culminating in a nervous breakdown at the end of her teenage years. By 1963 she had settled into being a rural housewife when she won a talent contest in Ohio, attracting the attention of *Grand Ole Opry* star BILL ANDERSON, who recommended her to RCA. She made her first recordings under the guidance of producer Bob Ferguson in 1964, including her first hit "Once a Day," a weepy love song that Anderson had written for her.

Through the 1960s and early 1970s, Smith was idolized as a pretty young lady who had the ability to pour her heart out through her vocal cords. She made a specialty of singing songs of loneliness and desolation, scoring hits from 1966's "The Hurtin's All Over (Me)" through 1972's "Just for What I Am." She also toured widely with many other country stars, and appeared in a couple of budget country films of the day, including *Road to Nashville, Las Vegas Hillbillies,* and *Second Fiddle to a Steel Guitar.*

Two failed marriages and a general dissatisfaction with the marketing of female country stars led Smith to become increasingly dissatisfied with her career. In 1972 she wed for a third time, and began incorporating more gospel music into her act; she and her husband became evangelists, and by the turn of the decade Smith had retired from performing, except for her weekly spot on the *Grand Ole Opry* where she continued to share her gospel beliefs.

Through the 1980s and the 1990s, Smith continued to perform regularly on the *Opry.* From the mid-1980s through the mid-1990s, Smith only performed gospel music. But in 1997 she wed the much younger new country performer MARTY STUART. A year later, she returned to secular material on an album produced by her new husband, including many songs that they wrote together.

"Smoke! Smoke! Smoke! (That Cigarette)" (1947) *honky-tonk anthem*

The Capitol label's first million-selling single, Tex Williams's recording of "Smoke! Smoke! Smoke! (That Cigarette)" is a classic honky-tonk anthem. Written by guitar whiz MERLE TRAVIS (Tex Williams rewrote one verse that he felt was too risqué for the country radio of the day, earning cowriter credit), the upbeat song gently satirizes the common barroom dweller's (and traveling musician's) addiction. Travis also recorded his own version, as did Phil Harris. Ironically, Williams died of cancer in 1985, unable to give up his two-pack-a-day habit.

Snow, Hank (1914–1999) *guitarist and singer*

Born Clarence Eugene Snow in Liverpool, Nova Scotia, Canada, on May 9, 1914, Snow left home when he was 12 to take a job as a cabin boy on a freighter. An early love of country recording star JIMMIE RODGERS and American cowboy legends led him to take up the guitar, and he was soon a proficient performer, getting his first break at age 19 when he was hired by the local radio station. He was signed to RCA in Canada in 1936, recording two of his own songs that were closely modeled after Rodgers's recordings. He nicknamed himself "The Yodeling Ranger," combining Rodgers's famous yodeling persona with that of the heroic Canadian mounted police; later he changed his nickname to "The Singing Ranger" in recognition of the end of the yodeling fad. Through the 1930s, Snow continued to work in Canada, gaining the attention of American country performers who passed through the local clubs.

One of these performers, ERNEST TUBB, convinced the *Grand Ole Opry* to hire Snow in 1950. Meanwhile, Snow's 1949 recording of the sentimental "Marriage Vow" was a minor hit, followed by his classic "I'm Movin' On" and "Golden Rocket" in

1950. Both were million-sellers, establishing his career. Snow produced myriad hits through the 1950s for RCA, including "Rhumba Boogie," "I Don't Hurt Anymore," "A Fool Such As I" (later covered in an up-tempo version by Elvis Presley), "Ninety Miles an Hour (Down a Deadend Street)," and many more. Snow's recordings were remarkably simple productions, highlighting his fine singing voice that had equal appeal to mainstream and country audiences. In 1953 Snow was a prime mover behind establishing Jimmie Rodgers Memorial Day in Rodgers's hometown, Meridian, Mississippi, acknowledging his considerable debt to the earlier singer. Toward the end of the decade, he began recording theme albums, particularly of railroad songs (again reflecting his love of the songs of Jimmie Rodgers).

Although Snow continued to work through the 1960s, 1970s, and 1980s, his last big hit was 1962's "I've Been Everywhere," a novelty song featuring a jaw-breaking list of towns that Snow supposedly had visited. He last made the charts in 1973 with "Hello Love" (later the theme song of Garrison Keillor's *A Prairie Home Companion*). A staunch traditionalist, Snow became increasingly conservative as time went by. He remained a popular performer on the *Opry* and on tour, despite his lack of recording success. Snow also became involved in raising money for abused children, a cause close to his heart because he had been abused as a youth.

In 1981 RCA dropped Snow from its roster after a distinguished 45-year recording career. Snow was understandably enraged by the move, and RCA, in retaliation, kept his recordings unavailable in the United States for many years, although by the late 1980s they had relented. In 1994 Snow published his autobiography, *The Hank Snow Story*. He suffered from a major respiratory infection in 1997, but recovered sufficiently to return to limited performing. He died on December 19, 1999, of heart failure.

Snow's son, Jimmie Rodgers Snow, had a few minor country hits of his own before becoming an evangelist.

"Soldier's Joy" (c. 1750) *fiddle standard*

A classic British fiddle tune known originally as "The King's Head," this tune migrated to the United States where it became a standard among Southern fiddle players. It has been widely performed and recorded.

Sons of the Pioneers *cowboy vocal group*

Originally formed as the Pioneer Trio with Leonard Slye, Bob Nolan, and Tim Spencer, they became the Sons of the Pioneers around 1934 in Southern California with the addition of the talented Farr Brothers on guitar and fiddle. With a swinging, jazzy sound, and pop-flavored three-part harmonies, the Sons of the Pioneers were an immediate sensation on stage and screen. The lead vocalist, Slye, became better known as ROY ROGERS, going solo by 1937 as a recording artist and actor; the core group of Nolan, Spencer, and the Farrs stuck together through the early 1950s with various additional members. Nolan was a virtual one-man hit machine, creating such classic cowboy songs as "Cool Water," the band's unofficial theme song, "Tumbling Tumbleweeds," and the immortal "A Cowboy Has to Sing"; Spencer was also a prolific songwriter, turning out "Cigarettes, Whiskey, and Wild Women," "Careless Kisses," and "Roomful of Roses." The Sons of the Pioneers popularized smooth, harmonized vocals and showy yodeling, and performed cowboyesque rope tricks and other novelties in their stage show.

The group originally recorded for Decca and Columbia before World War II, and then began a long association with RCA Victor that lasted from the early 1940s through the late 1960s. By the early 1950s, RCA was covering their bases by having the Sons of the Pioneers record with such pop singers as Perry Como, the Fontaine Sisters, and the Three Sons; on a handful of sides, they even accompanied opera star Ezio Pinza on some novelty recordings.

By the mid-1950s the powerhouse vocal/songwriting team of Nolan and Spencer was gone, but by then the group had a life of its own. By adding new vocalists and musicians as the years went by, they carefully re-created their past hits in a patented style. Unlike their early 1950s recordings in which RCA sought to modernize their style, their later recordings through the end of the 1960s emphasized their original style, albeit in a slicked-up style. Spencer died in 1974 and Nolan died six years later, but the Sons of the Pioneers have gone on, performing winters in Las Vegas and summers in Branson, Missouri.

Sprague, Carl T. (1895–1979) *cowboy singer*

Born on May 10, 1895, and raised on a ranch in south Texas, near the small town of Alvin, Sprague learned most of his cowboy material from a singing uncle. However, he did not intend to pursue a musical career; instead, he attended Texas A&M University, studying physical education. Hearing VERNON DALHART's successful folk song recordings for Victor, he realized a similar market might exist for the songs he had learned as a youth. He traveled to New York, and in 1925 recorded "When the Work's All Done This Fall" for Victor, the first major hit in the cowboy style. He had two more sessions for Victor in 1926 and 1927, recording many songs that would later enter the repertoire of the singing cowboys of the 1930s. However, Sprague never performed as a professional; instead, he pursued singing as a hobby, while working as an athletics coach at Texas A&M.

During the folk revival of the 1960s, Sprague was rediscovered and again performed his cowboy material, recording an album of western songs for the German Bear Family label in 1972. He died on February 19, 1979.

"Stand by Your Man" (1968) *classic for Tammy Wynette*

Along with MERLE HAGGARD's "Okie from Muskogee," "Stand by Your Man" is a classic of late 1960s country conservatism. While stars like LORETTA LYNN scolded their cheatin' husbands,

TAMMY WYNETTE's song urged women to accept the wayward sins of their husbands because "after all, he's just a man." Yet despite its conservative message, Wynette's full-throttle delivery of the song and its anthemic chorus seemed to suggest that the women held more power in their marriages than the song's lyrics implied. The fact that producer Billy Sherrill, who closely shaped Wynette's image and sound, shared writing credit may indicate that he had a hand in molding its passive message. The song was an enormous success on the country charts, becoming the biggest-selling single recorded by a female country star to its date. During the women's liberation movement of the 1970s, the song was widely attacked for its message, which only increased its popularity among Wynette's country audience. The phrase "stand by your man" entered American culture, notably when President Bill Clinton was accused of cheating on his wife, Hillary, during the 1992 presidential campaign. She stated, "I'm not a 'stand-by-your man' woman." Soon after, Hillary apologized for what seemed to be an attack on "family values." Later still, during the 1999 Monica Lewinsky scandal, many would recall this remark when Hilary appeared to "stand by" her man.

Ralph Stanley of the Stanley Brothers in the late 1970s (Larry Sandberg)

Stanley Brothers, the *bluegrass performers* Carter Glen Stanley (August 27, 1925–December 1, 1966) and Ralph Edmond Stanley (b. February 25, 1927) Stanley were raised in rural western Virginia, in the small town of McClure, where their mother was an old-time banjo player. Both sons began playing the banjo, learning traditional songs like "Little Birdie" in the drop-thumb or clawhammer style. Carter switched to guitar after Ralph became proficient on banjo, and the duo began performing locally. Their first professional work came after World War II with Roy Sykes and the Blue Ridge Boys in 1946; one year later, they left the band, along with mandolinist "Pee Wee" (Darrell) Lambert, to form the Clinch Mountain Boys. It was about this time that they heard the legendary per-

formances of BILL MONROE's Bluegrass Boys, and Ralph adopted the finger-picking style of Earl Scruggs to his banjo playing. The Stanleys were hired to perform on the radio in Bristol, Tennessee/Virginia, and made their first recordings for the tiny Rich-R-Tone label.

In 1949 they relocated to take a radio job in Raleigh, North Carolina, where the Columbia talent scout Art Satherley heard them and signed them to that label. The Stanleys recorded for Columbia for three years, featuring their breathtaking traditional harmonies on traditional mountain ballads and

Carter Stanley's compositions in a traditional vein, including the classic "White Dove" and "A Vision of Mother." In 1952 guitarist/vocalist George Shuffler joined the group. A talented flatpicker, he would be featured prominently as a soloist in the band for the next decade.

Carter took a job as lead vocalist for Bill Monroe's band briefly in 1952, recording the lead vocals on Monroe's own "Uncle Pen" and the honky-tonk song "Sugar Coated Love." The brothers reunited in 1953. They signed to Mercury, remained with the label through 1958, and then recorded for King/Starday until Carter's death. By this time they had solidified their sound around lead guitar and banjo. Carter's expressive lead vocals were perfectly complimented by Ralph's unearthly high mountain tenor and Shuffler's more modern-sounding harmonies.

In the late 1950s and early 1960s the market for bluegrass music was fairly small, so the Stanleys relocated to Florida for the winters, hosting a radio program as well as recording for smaller local labels. The folk revival in the 1960s helped revive the Stanleys' popularity, and they toured the revival circuit and in Europe. Carter's life was cut short by alcoholism in 1966, and for a while it seemed as if the band would fold.

However, Ralph emerged as an important bandleader by the decade's end. He first enlisted vocalist Larry Sparks to fill Carter's shoes, and Sparks went on to be one of the 1970s' most important progressive bluegrass performers. Then Ralph hired the more traditional Roy Lee Centers, who sounded eerily like Carter. The band signed with Rebel Records, and was popular both on the revival and traditional bluegrass circuits. Centers was murdered in 1974, but he was soon replaced in the band by two high school–age musicians whom the elder banjo player had discovered: mandolinist RICKY SKAGGS and guitarist Keith Whitley. Stanley helped launch their careers in bluegrass and later in the new traditional Nashville music.

Through the mid-1990s the Stanley band centered on Ralph's banjo, the showy fiddling of Curly Ray Cline, and the bass playing of Jack Cooke, usually augmented by a young guitarist/vocalist and mandolinist. Since then Cline has retired but Cooke has continued with the group into the 21st century. Despite the variability in the talents of the lead vocalists, the sound of Stanley's music remains virtually unchanged. Ralph Stanley's contribution and influence on Nashville's new country stars was finally acknowledged by the recent release of a two-CD set on which he performs with Ricky Skaggs, VINCE GILL, and other new Nashvillians.

Ralph Stanley's career was given a major boost by the 2000 film *O Brother, Where Art Thou?* On the soundtrack, Stanley is prominently featured singing an a cappella version of the song "O Death." That same year, he was made a member of the *Grand Ole Opry*. In 2001 Stanley recorded a solo album for Columbia, produced by T-Bone Burnett (who also oversaw the *O Brother* soundtrack), and has since continued to record with and lead his band.

Starr, Kay (b. 1922) *singer*

Born Katheryn LaVern Starks, in Dougherty, Oklahoma, Starr was raised in Dallas, where at age nine she already had her own 15-minute daily radio show. Her prematurely husky voice won her many fans, and she began performing as a teenager with the popular western swing bands of the day, including Bill Boyd's Cowboy Ramblers and one of the later lineups of the Light Crust Doughboys. In the late 1930s her family moved to Memphis, where Starr again found a big audience for her powerful delivery.

Starr spent the war years traveling to different army bases to perform; she came down with a severe case of laryngitis due to the overuse of her voice and exposure to cold on army transport planes. The result was an even sexier, growling delivery that made her a postwar sensation. She first hit it big in 1950 with "Bonaparte's Retreat," written for her by Wynn Stewart and PEE WEE KING, followed in the same year by her duet with TENNESSEE ERNIE FORD on "I'll Never Be Free." She crossed over onto the pop charts with her big-throated delivery of 1952's "Wheel of Fortune" and "Side By Side" (1953); the latter was one of the first recordings to feature a double-tracked vocal.

In 1955 Starr moved to RCA, where she began recording pop-oriented material, including the hit "Rock and Roll Waltz." After a few hitless years, she came back to the country charts with 1961's "Foolin' Around" and 1962's "Four Walls." She continued to record country material through the 1970s. In the 1990s she returned on the oldies circuit performing with veterans Helen O'Connell and Margaret Whiting as "3 Girls 3."

Statler Brothers, The

Not really brothers or named Statler, the Statler Brothers have been one of the most popular of the smooth-harmony vocal groups in country music for more than 30 years.

Originally forming in 1955 as a church-based trio in Staunton, Virginia, around tenor vocalist Lew DeWitt (b. Roanoke, Virginia, March 8, 1938–August 15, 1990), baritone Phil Balsley (b. Augusta County, Virginia, August 8, 1939), and bass singer Harold Reid (b. Augusta County, Virginia, August 31, 1939), the group was first called the Kingsmen. In 1960 Harold's younger brother Don (b. Staunton, Virginia, June 5, 1945) joined as lead vocalist, and the group signed on with JOHNNY CASH's road show; they're featured on Cash's recording of CARL PERKINS's classic "Daddy Sang Bass." Soon after, they changed their name to the Statler Brothers, taking their surname from a Massachusetts-based manufacturer of facial tissues.

In 1964 the Statlers signed with Columbia Records, and had their first hit with the DeWitt-penned "Flowers on the Wall" a year later. Follow-up hits included 1967's "Ruthless" and the corny "You Can't Have Your Kate and Edith Too," although Columbia didn't do much to promote their career. In 1970 the Statlers switched to Mercury and had their first solid hit with the

crossover success "Bed of Roses." Many of their 1970s hits were written by the brothers Reid, including 1972's nostalgic "Class of '57," the sentimental tear-jerkers "I'll Go to My Grave Loving You" from 1975 and their first number-one single, "Do You Know You Are My Sunshine" from 1978, and the humorous "How to Be a Country Star" from 1979. Recalling their roots as a gospel quartet, they also recorded religious albums, including two albums based on the Old and New Testaments that were released in 1975.

In 1981 the group founded the Statler Complex in their base of Staunton, Virginia, which includes a museum showing their many awards and memorabilia. Around this time, cofounder Lew DeWitt was forced to retire due to continuing problems from Crohn's disease; he died in 1990. His replacement was Jimmy Fortune (b. Newport News, Virginia, March 11, 1955), who contributed many of the brothers' 1980s hits, including "Elizabeth" from 1984, and "My Only Love" and "Too Much on My Heart" from a year later.

Although the Statlers have fallen off the charts, they remain immensely popular in such places as Nashville and Branson. For many years they hosted their own variety show on TNN; it was the top-rated show on that cable network for seven years. However, when CBS purchased TNN in 1999, the show was canceled. Their brand of smooth, church-oriented harmonies and mixture of sentimental and humorous material made them one of the most popular—and lasting—of all country quartets. However, citing the pressures of continuing to tour, the group announced that 2002 would be their last year as performers.

"Still" (1962) *crossover pop hit for Bill Anderson*
BILL ANDERSON's second number-one country hit and his only crossover pop hit, "Still" is a country weeper that combines a sung chorus with a maudlin recitation, in which Anderson laments the loss of his one true love. He vows that he loves her still despite the fact that she left him.

Strait, George (b. 1952) *singer and songwriter*
The son of a junior high school teacher who also raised cattle on the side, Strait (b. Poteet, Texas, May 18, 1952) began, as most musicians of his generation did, playing rock and pop music. He eloped with his high school sweetheart, and soon after joined the army. The army sent him to Hawaii, where he began performing country music, perhaps to remind himself of home. Returning to the family farm, he began performing locally with the group Ace in the Hole, and recorded for the tiny D label out of Houston. He hit Nashville in the late 1970s, but failed to find a contract until 1981, when he signed with MCA.

George Strait onstage (Raeanne Rubenstein)

His first album, *Strait Country,* established his signature southwestern sound. His sound recalled the best of the early 1950s honky-tonkers, including HANK THOMPSON, RAY PRICE, and FARON YOUNG. Strait also scored a number-six hit with his first single, "Unwound." He continued to hit it big through the 1980s, covering Bob Wills's classic "Right or Wrong" and Whitey Shafer's "Does Fort Worth Ever Cross Your Mind?" His novelty hit "All My Ex's Live in Texas," even got some pop radio play.

Beginning in the early 1990s, George recorded more slick, "urban" country material, such as "Ocean Front Property." He gave an unaffected, straightforward performance in the 1992 film *Pure Country,* which garnered him critical praise. His 1995 career retrospective, the four-CD *Strait out of the Box,* was a huge seller, and his follow-up album, *Blue Clear Sky,* debuted at number one on the country chart and number seven on the pop chart, an unusual feat even for a new Nashville artist; the title track was a major hit. He continued to produce big hits through the decade's end, including the amusing "Murder on Music Row," a duet with ALAN JACKSON. Strait's track record is amazing; only three out of his 61 career singles have failed to chart in the country top 10.

Street, Mel (1933–1978) *singer and songwriter*
Born King Malachi Street in Grundy, Virginia, on October 21, 1933, Street began his career as a hobby by performing on local radio, while working for many years in the construction and auto paint and repair businesses. By the late 1960s, he had his own TV show in rural Bluefield, West Virginia, and in 1970 he made his first recording for the tiny Tandem label. The B side of this single, "Borrowed Angel," his own composition, slowly gained momentum on the charts, finally hitting the top 10 when it was reissued by Royal American records in 1972. Despite the success of this hit, and the follow-up "Lovin' on Back Streets," Street was ignored by the major labels until four years later, when he signed with Polydor. Polydor had the clout to properly promote him, and

he had several more hits over the next two years, including 1978's top 10 "If I Had a Cheatin' Heart." However, he committed suicide on his birthday in the same year.

Street's emphasis on the traditional honky-tonk sound was undoubtedly ahead of his time. He was one of the first younger artists to appreciate the achievements of George Jones and other then-forgotten stars of the 1950s and early 1960s. He also was among the first to record songs by younger artists like EDDIE RABBITT and EARL THOMAS CONLEY, who would later become hit makers on their own.

Stringbean (1915–1973) banjo player

David Akeman, known professionally as "Stringbean," was born in Annville, Kentucky, in the foothills of the Appalachian Mountains, on June 17, 1915. His father was a traditional banjo player, and his son followed in his footsteps when he made his own first instrument at age 12. He began performing in the Lexington, Kentucky, area, landing a radio job when he was 18 as a member of Cy Roger's Lonesome Pine Fiddlers. Like most country groups at the time, the Lonesome Pine Fiddlers prominently featured a country rube comedian as part of their act; the gangly, six-foot-two-inch banjo player seemed a perfect candidate to take this role. Akeman was given the nickname "Stringbean" because of his long, lean appearance.

In the late 1930s Stringbean joined Charlie Monroe's band, again taking the comic role. At about the same time, Charlie's brother BILL MONROE was forming the first incarnation of his first Blue Grass Boys, and he hired Stringbean away from his brother to be the comedian and banjo player in his new outfit. Stringbean's main role was as a stage comedian; his style did not fit in with even this early version of the Blue Grass Boys, a swinging outfit propelled by Monroe's high-powered mandolin playing. (His banjo playing can barely be heard on Monroe's recordings.) Stringbean would be replaced in the mid-1940s by the innovative banjoist Earl Scruggs.

In the late 1940s Stringbean embarked on a solo career as a comic and banjo player in the tradition of UNCLE DAVE MACON (he later recorded a tribute album to the elder banjo player). He was a well-loved member of the *Grand Ole Opry* for more than 25 years. His career got a boost in the late 1960s when the popular TV show *Hee Haw* was first broadcast; he was an original cast member whose style fit in perfectly with the hayseed humor of the program.

Stringbean was murdered along with his wife when the pair encountered burglars robbing their home after returning from a performance at the *Opry* on November 10, 1973.

Stuart, Marty (b. 1958) guitarist and mandolin player

Born in Philadelphia, Mississippi, on September 30, 1958, Stuart was a child prodigy mandolinist and guitar player who performed with Lester Flatt and other traditional bluegrass artists before he became a new country star. Stuart's Nashville-based recordings of the late 1980s and early 1990s show a strong rockabilly influence, including the twangy guitar sound that is a trademark of early rock.

Stuart began performing professionally at age 12 as a member of Lester Flatt's Nashville Grass. After Flatt's death, he worked with JOHNNY CASH and Bob Dylan, recording his first solo album for Sugar Hill, a bluegrass label, in 1982. Stuart jumped on the new country bandwagon in 1986, signing with MCA, but didn't achieve success until his breakthrough single of 1991, "That's Country," and his duet with TRAVIS TRITT on his self-penned "This One's Gonna Hurt You," very much in the tradition of honky-tonk weepers. In 1993 he was made a member of the *Grand Ole Opry*.

Stuart's hit-making days slowed in the second half of the 1990s. An avid photographer, he published an interesting collection of his photos, and also began producing other artists. In 1997 he wed country crooner CONNIE SMITH. He is a great collector of country memorabilia and has contributed to the collection of the Country Music Foundation and Hall of Fame. He served as the president of the foundation's board from 1998 to 2001. His 1999 album *The Pilgrim* featured an instrumental version of the traditional song "John Henry" that won a Grammy Award in 2000. In 2001 he scored the Billy Bob Thornton film *All the Pretty Horses,* which led to him producing an album with Thornton. In 2003 Stuart moved to Columbia Records and released *Country Music,* featuring a duet with MERLE HAGGARD on "Farmer's Blues."

Supernaw, Doug (b. 1960) *singer and songwriter*

Supernaw, the son of a research scientist, was born in Bryan, Texas, on September 26, 1960, and raised in Houston. He began singing and writing his own songs in high school, but his main interest was golf. However, after a brief stab at making it as a professional golfer, he discovered he couldn't handle a club well enough to succeed. By the late 1970s Supernaw was working in a cover band in Florida, and then, during the early 1980s, he spent some time working on an oil rig off the Texas coast. Later in the decade, he went to Nashville, where he gained a job as a staff songwriter for one of the many country publishers but labored without much success as a performer.

In 1991 Supernaw returned to Texas and soon formed his own band. He was signed to RCA in 1992 and released his first album in 1993. He had two hits, the self-penned "Reno" and "I Don't Call Him Daddy," a classic country weeper about the plight of a stepchild. Soon after the album's release, Supernaw was involved in two major accidents (one a head-on collision), and his first marriage fell into ruins. Although his first album went gold, Supernaw's follow-up album failed to do much business. In 1995 Supernaw moved to Giant Records, finally returning to the top 10 with the love song "Not Enough Hours in the Night." However, he continued to be dogged by controversy, thanks to the single "What'll You Do About Me," about a one-night stand gone wrong. Supernaw's career sagged in the later 1990s, although he continued to be popular on the rodeo and NASCAR circuit. In 1999 he released *Fadin' Renegade,* which continued the combination of tear-jerking ballads with up-tempo rockers.

"Swingin' " (1983) *number-one hit for John Anderson*

This song remained on the charts for 12 weeks and sold more than a million copies. The song was among the greatest successes of JOHN ANDERSON's career, and was named the Country Music Association's Single of the Year. Cowritten by Anderson with Lionel Delmore, the song is full of country clichés—fried chicken, chocolate pie, and porch-swing courtship. The "swingin' " in the title is a play on words for the porch swing, the "swingin' " feeling of falling in love and the jazzy "swing" of the tune.

"Take This Job and Shove It" (1977)
rebel-rousing anthem sung by Johnny Paycheck
"Take This Job and Shove It" perfectly expressed working people's attitude to the grinding monotony of many a low-wage job. The song was a number-one country hit, and loosely inspired the film of the same name released in 1981. Paycheck's straight-ahead message was controversial for country radio in the early 1980s, although the song would be viewed as rather tame today.

"Talk about Me" (2001) *major hit for singer Toby Keith*
"Talk about Me" combines a country sensibility with a semi-rapped verse. Keith's playful personality was showcased in a clever video in which he portrayed several henpecked characters, all trying to get a word in edgewise with their chatty girl-friends. The song represented a comeback for its writer, Bobby Braddock, whose last major hit was "D-I-V-O-R-C-E," which he cowrote for TAMMY WYNETTE in 1968.

"Tennessee Waltz" (1948) *number-three country, juke box, and best-seller hit for Pee Wee King*
King cowrote this waltz-ballad with Redd Stewart, who at the time was lead vocalist in King's band, the Golden West Cowboys. The song was initially recorded and released in 1946 but took two years to chart; it was subsequently a major pop crossover hit in 1950 for Patti Page. In 1965 it was made the state song of Tennessee. It is said to have been recorded in more than 500 different versions.

"T for Texas (Blue Yodel Number One)"
the best known of Jimmie Rodgers's "blue yodels"
"T for Texas" is a simple three-line blues incorporating many standard verses found in dozens of folk songs. JIMMIE RODGERS's mournful vocal and simple guitar accompaniment made it a classic, and his version has been covered countless times, including a version by southern rockers Lynyrd Skynyrd and new country singer DWIGHT YOAKAM. Rodgers himself used the same melody for many more "blue yodels," which were often assembled from folk sources.

Thompson, Hank (b. 1925) *singer*
Henry William Thompson was born in Waco, Texas, on September 3, 1925. He began as a teenage performer on local radio under the name of "Hank the Hired Hand," as well as recording for the tiny, local Globe label. These sides were so successful that they led TEX RITTER to recommend him to California-based Capitol Records. Capitol signed him in 1948, and he remained with that label for eighteen years. His backup band, the Brazos Valley Boys, was a good western swing outfit; on records and tours, they were often augmented by the legendary Capitol session guitarist MERLE TRAVIS. Lyrically, Thompson focused on women, booze, and heartbreak, classic honky-tonk themes.

Thompson's first big hit was "Humpty Dumpty Heart" from 1948; he followed this with many classics, including 1952's "Wild Side of Life." In the mid-1950s he helped promote singer Wanda Jackson by featuring her in his live shows and in recordings.

In the early 1960s, impressed by the success of big band vocalist Louis Prima, who had established a successful career in Las Vegas, Thompson began regularly performing there. He recorded a fine live album there in 1961. After leaving Capitol in 1966, Thompson roamed among labels for a while, and began performing mostly with session musicians. Thompson continues to record and perform, and is most active around Fort Worth, his current home. He was elected into the Country Music Hall of Fame in 1989. In 2000 he issued the impressive album *Seven Decades*.

Tillis, Mel (b. 1932) *guitarist and singer*

Born in Tampa, Florida, on August 8, 1932, Lonnie Melvin Tillis was raised in the small town of Pahokee, on the eastern shore of Lake Okeechobee, where he learned to play the guitar. After serving in the air force in the early 1950s and spending two years in college, Tillis went to Nashville in search of a career as a singer. Webb Pierce liked his material, and he recorded Tillis's "I'm Tired" in 1957. The duo cowrote "I Ain't Never" soon after, and also recorded a duet together in 1963, the humorous "How Come Your Dog Don't Bite Nobody but Me." Tillis was signed to Columbia Records, but he scored only minor hits there, beginning with 1958's sentimental "The Violet and the Rose."

Tillis's next big break came in 1963 when Bobby Bare had a monster hit with his "Detroit City." Tillis

Mel Tillis picnics with some fans in 1975. (Raeanne Rubenstein)

signed with Kapp Records, and had his first solo hit with 1965's "Stateside." Two years later came a monster hit, Howard Harlan's classic weeper ballad "Life Turned Her That Way." (the song would be covered by Ricky Van Shelton in 1987.) As a songwriter, Tillis had another hit with KENNY ROGERS and the First Edition's cover of his "Ruby (Don't Take Your Love to Town)."

Tillis began the 1970s on MGM, recording a fine combination of honky-tonk songs and weepers, including 1971's "The Arms of a Fool" and "Brand New Mister Me," a remake of "Sawmill" in 1973 (which he had originally cut for Columbia in 1959), "Midnight Me and the Blues" in 1974, and "The Woman in the Back of My Mind" in 1975. He then switched to MCA, where his recordings took a decided turn toward country pop after one last fine honky-tonk number, "Good Woman Blues" in 1976.

Tillis switched to Elektra in 1980, recorded an album of duets with Nancy Sinatra in 1981, and then returned to MCA for a couple of minor hits, including 1983's "In the Middle of the Night" and 1984's "New Patches." Although he fell off the charts in the early 1980s, Tillis has remained a popular performer on the road and on TV, and operates his own theater in new-country haven Branson, Missouri. His daughter PAM TILLIS is one of new country's finest singers; the pair recorded their first duet in 2001.

Tillis, Pam (b. 1957) *singer and songwriter*

The daughter of MEL TILLIS, Pam Tillis was born in Plant City, Florida, on July 24, 1957. She was raised in Nashville, during the height of her father's popularity. After singing in a variety of styles from R&B to pop, Tillis renewed her interest in country music in the early 1980s, thanks to the many new singers and songwriters who were settling in Nashville. In 1986 Tillis formed "Twang Night," a mock-country revue that celebrated Nashville's honky-tonk glories while building her reputation as a new country songwriter. In the late 1980s her songs were covered by the trio of Parton-Ronstadt-Harris ("Those

Memories"), Highway 101 ("Someone Else's Troubles Now"), and Judy Rodman ("Goin' to Work"). Tillis recorded on her own for Warner Brothers, but she didn't chart until switching to Arista in 1990.

Tillis's early 1990s hits include 1991's romantic, steamy love ballad "Maybe It Was Memphis," 1992's "Shake the Sugartree," and her 1993 tongue-in-cheek "Cleopatra (Queen of Denial)," in which Tillis created the ultimate suffering country female. In 1994 she scored with the Tex-Mex number-one hit, "*Mi Vida Loca* (My Crazy Life)" and a cover of "When You Walk In the Room." However, the second half of the decade saw fewer charting hits, although she continued to record and tour. In August 2000 Tillis was made a member of the *Grand Ole Opry*. A year later, she released her first new album since 1999, hoping to regain her chart momentum; it also included her first recorded duet with her father.

Tippin, Aaron (b. 1958) *singer and songwriter*

Although born in Pensacola, Florida, on July 3, 1958, Tippin was raised in rural South Carolina, where he dreamed of becoming a commercial pilot. He obtained his pilot's license when he was 15 and began studying so he could be certified to fly large commercial jets. Music was strictly a sideline at this time, but when the early 1980s brought the energy crisis and recession, Tippin realized that his future as a pilot was limited. Discouraged by the failure of his marriage, he took a job in a cotton mill and temporarily abandoned music.

However, in 1985 Tippin moved to Nashville, and he was hired as a staff writer by Acuff-Rose music publishers. After recording demos and writing songs, he was signed by RCA in 1990, producing an immediate sensation with his first single, "You've Got to Stand for Something," released in the wake of the Gulf War. This patriotic song set the stage for future Tippin hits that celebrated the ordinary man, including "Trim Yourself to Fit the World" and "Working Man's Ph.D."

Like many other early 1990s country stars, Tippin had trouble sustaining his hit-making years. In 1998 he left RCA for Lyric Street/Hollywood Records. Also like other 1990s survivors, Tippin was able to revive his career beginning in the new century. He scored big in 2000 with the tough-sounding single "Kiss This," which propelled his album *People Like Us* to gold status. Tippin's career was revived in autumn 2001 with the release of the patriotic "Where the Stars and Stripes and the Eagles Fly," in the wake of the terrorist attacks on the country. Like fellow country artist ALAN JACKSON, Tippin was quick to record and release a number to ride the wave of patriotism.

Travis, Merle (1917–1983) *guitarist and songwriter*

Merle Travis was born in Rosewood, Kentucky, on November 29, 1917. Travis's father was a banjo player who taught him to play the instrument in a two-finger-picked style that was common in the upper South in the 1920s and 1930s. When Merle switched to the guitar, he adapted this picking style to the new instrument, playing the bass strings with his thumb while using a flat pick on the upper strings. He dampened the strings with the heel of his hand as he strummed, giving a "choked" sound to his music. This technique has come to be known as "Travis picking," and it was highly influential on the next generation of country guitar players, including CHET ATKINS, Doc Watson, and scores of others.

In the mid-1930s Travis briefly joined fiddler Clayton McMichen's jazzy band the Georgia Wildcats, but was soon hired by Cincinnati's *Boone County Jamboree,* a popular radio program. He worked on the show for a decade as a soloist and accompanist, performing with GRANDPA JONES and the DELMORE BROTHERS in the informal group known as the Brown's Ferry Four (named after the Delmore Brothers' big hit, "Brown's Ferry Blues"). The group recorded in various configurations for the fledgling Cincinnati-based King label, which

would in the early 1950s become a leader in country and R&B recordings.

During the last two years of World War II, Travis served in the military. Then he returned to civilian life and settled in Southern California, where he worked with several of the transplanted western swing bands that were based there. He signed to another new label, Capitol Records, and had his first solo hits with his own compositions, the honky-tonkin' "Divorce Me C.O.D.," "So, Round, So Firm, So Fully Packed," "Sweet Temptation," and the tongue-in-cheek "Smoke, Smoke, Smoke (That Cigarette)," which was written for and recorded by Tex Williams. In 1947 he cut an album called *Folk Songs of the Hills,* which included his own compositions in a folk style based on his memories of the tough life of the coal miners in his native Kentucky. Two of these songs, "Dark as a Dungeon" and "Sixteen Tons" have become standards in the folk and country repertoires, the latter thanks to TENNESSEE ERNIE FORD's 1955 hit cover version.

In the 1950s Travis experimented with developing a solid-body electric guitar; instrument makers Paul Bigsby and Leo Fender both worked on Travis's design, which eventually led to the mass production of the instruments that would become the lead voice in rock-and-roll ensembles. The electric instrument that Travis often played suited his picking style, which emphasized a percussive, rhythmic chop while downplaying the natural "ringing" sound of the acoustic instrument.

Through the 1950s and 1960s Travis worked both as a soloist and session artist, although he never regained the popularity of his late 1940s recordings. He was invited to participate in the NITTY GRITTY DIRT BAND's all-star country tribute album, *Will the Circle Be Unbroken,* in 1971, which helped to revive his career as a performer. After that recording, he made a few more albums with Chet Atkins and Joe Maphis, as well as returning to his western swing roots on an album featuring many alumni of Bob Wills's bands. His 1981 album, *Travis Pickin',* was a Grammy nominee. He died in Nashville on October 20, 1983.

Travis, Randy (b. 1959) *guitarist and singer*

Born Randy Bruce Traywick, in Marshville, North Carolina, on May 4, 1959, Travis was exposed early to the classic country recordings through his father, who was a major country fan. Randy began playing guitar at age eight and was performing as a duo with his brother six years later at local clubs. When he was 16, he ran away from home. He won a talent contest in Charlotte, which led to his discovery by local bar owner Lib Hatcher, the manager who would support his career for seven years before he hit it big (later, they married).

Performing under the name Randy Ray, he came to Nashville with Hatcher at age 23. He soon took the stage name of Travis in honor of legendary country singer/guitarist MERLE TRAVIS. Randy was quickly signed to Warner Brothers and recorded the classic *Storms of Life* album. Randy's hits from this album have the sly edge of the best of country music; "On the Other Hand" tells the story of a married man wavering on the edge of an affair, but who keeps being reminded of his marital status by the ring he wears on the other hand. "Digging Up Bones" tells of a man who keeps digging up the bones of his failed relationship; the humor is perfectly paired with Randy's deadpan delivery.

Randy scored numerous hits through the mid-1990s, but few were as adventurous as his first recordings. Travis's career cooled as newer stars dominated the charts. He went hitless through the period, and was dropped by Warner Brothers in 1995. Travis made a couple of appearances in made-for-TV films and guest starred on some TV series. In 1997 he signed with the new Dreamworks label, and in 1998 scored his first chart topper in four years with "Out of My Bones." In 2000 Warner Brothers released his first gospel album; Travis has continued to record in this style through the early years of the new century.

Trick Pony *vocal trio*

Trick Pony, a neo-rockabilly band, was originally formed in 1996. The Atlanta-born guitarist Keith Burns had previously worked as a backup musician on the road with JOE DIFFIE and penned Diffie's hit "Whole Lotta Gone" from 1996. The Raleigh, North Carolina, native Ira Dean was previously employed as a bassist with TANYA TUCKER's road show. Lead vocalist/guitarist Heidi Newfield was a singer/songwriter who had come to Nashville in the mid-1990s looking for success as a solo artist when she hooked up with the other two. The group worked up an exciting stage act, complete with flashing headlights mounted in Dean's upright bass, and Newfield's sex appeal.

All of this excitement was successfully captured in the band's first video, the arch "Pour Me," a neo-rockabilly tune, cowritten by the band members. It starts out as a woman's lament for her lost love, until we realize that "poor me" actually means "pour me . . . another shot of whiskey." Newfield's energetic, good-natured performance, the catchy hook, and sprightly three-part harmonies made the song a video hit that also worked its way up the music charts. Trick Pony followed with another hit, "On a Night Like This," a more conventional country pop ballad. In 2002 *On a Mission came* out; the title track was a minor hit, but otherwise the album was less successful than their debut, despite the group's strong performances.

Tritt, Travis (b. 1963) *performer and songwriter*

Coming from a middle-class background in Marietta, Georgia, Tritt (b. February 9, 1963) had his first exposure to music in the church choir. He taught himself guitar when he was eight and wrote his first song at age 14. Like many of today's country artists, he was influenced by mid-1970s folk rock as well as by pure country, learning songs by groups such as the Eagles (he sang an Eagles song on a 1993 fund-raising album of Eagles songs released by new country artists).

After high school Tritt labored for four years on a loading dock, working his way up to a manager's position while still performing part time in local clubs. He was heard by Danny Davenport, a Georgia-based talent scout for Warner Brothers, who was as much interested in his songwriting abilities as his performing skills. They worked together for two years crafting demo tapes for the label, leading to the release of Tritt's first album, 1990's *Country Club,* which yielded four hit singles, including the number-one country hit "Help Me Hold On."

Tritt's career really took off with his second album, released in 1991. It contained the barroom anthems "Here's a Quarter (Call Someone Who Cares)" and "The Whiskey Ain't Working Anymore," (the latter a duet with new country star MARTY STUART). Fans took to throwing quarters at Tritt while he performed, which made him quickly drop his signature song from his concerts for fear of suffering injuries from the flying change!

In 1992 Tritt was inducted into the *Grand Ole Opry,* and he remains the youngest member of this venerable institution. He toured with Stuart while at the same time gaining exposure thanks to agent Ken Kragen through the placement of his songs in movies, including the theme song for *My Cousin Vinny* ("Bible Belt," a collaboration with the country rockers Little Feat) and a cover of Elvis Presley's "Burnin' Love" for *Honeymoon in Vegas.* In 1993 Tritt appeared with another Kragen client, grizzled country crooner Kenny Rogers, in a TV movie, *Rio Diablo.*

Tritt's 1993 successes include the topical "Lord Have Mercy on the Working Man," with a clever video showing how the "honest, ordinary citizen" is ignored by the media and politicians; and the barhopper's anthem "T-R-O-U-B-L-E," the title track of his third album. In 1994 he released the platinum-charting album *Ten Feet Tall and Bulletproof,* as well as his autobiography, which had the same name. It spawned the number-one hit "Foolish Pride," and marked Tritt's greatest success on both country and pop charts. A year later, his *Greatest Hits* package arrived, and also sold strongly.

After a dry period in the mid-to-late 1990s, Tritt left Warner Brothers and signed with Columbia. He returned in summer 2001 when his song "It's a Great Day to Be Alive" reached number two on the country charts; "Modern Day Bonnie and Clyde" was another major hit for Tritt in early 2002.

truck-driving songs

Three subjects have become stereotypes of country songwriting: mothers, prison, and trucks. The image of the lone trucker blazing a path through the wilderness has replaced the cowboy in American folklore as the last hero of the blacktop frontier. An explosion of songwriting in the early 1960s through the CB radio craze of the 1970s helped fuel this myth into an entire subgenre of country music.

Western swing bandleader Cliff Bruner's 1939 recording of "Truck Driver Blues," with a vocal by Moon Mullican, is generally credited with being the first truckin' ode on wax. "Truck Drivin' Man," the best-loved and most often parodied song of the open road, first appeared on a recording by Terry Fell in 1954. However, the song that spurred the movement was DAVE DUDLEY's 1963 hit, "Six Days on the Road." Jimmy Martin leapt on the truckin' bandwagon with his "Widow Maker" in 1964, Dick Curless followed with his 1965 hit, "Tombstone Every Mile," and traditional bluegrassers Jim and Jesse scored a surprise 1967 hit with "Diesel on My Tail." Two small bluegrass/country labels, Starday and King, fueled the truck-drivin' song mania, releasing several albums with colorful names like *Super Slab Hits, Truckin' On, Forty Miles of Bad Road,* and *Diesel Smoke, Dangerous Curves* and equally colorful covers featuring big rigs, burly drivers, and the gals they love.

Many of these songs incorporated the sentimentality of earlier country odes celebrating the railroad engineer. The engineer who bravely piloted his train (even staying at his post through a gruesome train wreck) was replaced in the new trucker songs by the image of the brave, honest truck driver, who sometimes had to give his own life to save another. A subgenre of trucking recitations is stories supposedly told by the rig masters themselves about the difficulties of life on the road; a classic in this style is "The Man behind the Wheel."

The 1970s brought a new facet to the truck rage: the CB (citizen's band) radio, with its own special jargon. The biggest song to celebrate the new wave of CB outlaws was C.W. McCall's hit "Convoy." More recently, ALABAMA has had hits with "Roll On (Eighteen Wheeler)," and the trucker has been turned into a romantic softie in KATHY MATTEA's 1988 hit "Eighteen Wheels and a Dozen Roses."

Tubb, Ernest (1919–1984) *singer*

Born in the small town of Crisp, Texas (south of Dallas), on February 9, 1914, Tubb had no ambition to be a country singer until he heard the recordings of JIMMIE RODGERS. So determined was he to emulate Rodgers's style that he sought out the singer's widow, who gave him her blessing to perform the "blue yodeler's" material. From the mid-1930s through the early 1940s, Tubb honed his style, beginning as a pure Jimmie Rodgers imitator but slowly transforming himself into a more modern honky-tonk singer. Undoubtedly, his experience performing in many small barrooms across Texas helped shape his newer sound, which relied on amplified instruments to cut through the noise, while choosing songs that expressed classic barroom sentiments.

The real change came with his signing to Decca Records in 1940, and his enormous hit, one year later, with the loping "Walking the Floor over You," a quintessential honky-tonk anthem that was to become his lifelong theme song, and perhaps the first country recording to feature electric guitar lead. Tubb's bone-dry delivery wed with the chunky rhythm of the backup band made this recording a country classic. During World War II, Tubb migrated to Hollywood, where he appeared in several of the era's low-budget cowboy films and even recorded with pop music's the Andrews Sisters.

Tubb made his most influential recordings and radio appearances in the late 1940s and early-to-mid-1950s with his band the Texas Troubadours, always featuring electric lead guitar. He nurtured the talents of several guitarists, including Fay "Smitty" Smith, Eddie Tudor, Jimmie Short, Butterball Paige, and, later, Billy Byrd and Leon Rhodes, as well as steel guitarists Buddy Charlton and the legendary Buddy Emmons. Tubb introduced the electric guitar to the *Grand Ole Opry* when he became a member in 1943; four years later, he opened his record store down the street from the Ryman Auditorium, and for many years hosted WSM's *Midnight Jamboree* radio show, broadcast immediately following the *Opry,* from his store. (When Opryland opened, a replica of his store was opened in the park to simulate the original.)

From the early 1960s onward, Tubb coasted on his living legend status. His stripped-down sound was augmented on recordings, while the quality of his singing suffered. Although he continued to perform until two years before his death in 1984, his recording career all but ended in 1975 when he left Decca. He died in Nasville on September 6, 1984.

Tubb was followed on the *Opry* by his son, singer/songwriter Justin (b. San Antonio, Texas, August 20, 1935–January 24, 1998). Best known as the author of "Lonesome 7-7203," a 1963 hit for Hawkshaw Hawkins, Justin was active as a recording star and member of the *Opry* from 1955 until his death. His father was an innovator, but Justin took a conservative tack, fighting for the pure honky-tonk sound during the 1970s when "countrypolitan" ruled the airwaves. While he continued to appear on the *Opry,* the younger Tubb made few recordings during his final 20 years. He died of an aneurysm.

Tucker, Tanya (b. 1958) *singer*

Tucker was born in Seminole, Texas, on October 10, 1958, but raised in Phoenix, Arizona. Her father was a starstruck country-music fan who was determined to make his daughter a hit. He pushed her onstage whenever a country act came to town. When she reached nine years old, he was convinced he had star material on his hands, so he financed a trip to Nashville. After several unsuccessful attempts, her demo tape landed in the hands of ace country producer Billy Sherrill, who signed her at age 13 to Columbia. She immediately hit with the slightly suggestive "Delta Dawn" and "Would You Lay with Me (in a Field of Stone)." Tucker was immediately successful at playing up her sexy-but-sweet image.

By the end of the 1970s, as she reached her late teen years, Tucker's career took a detour into an ill-advised attempt to cross over into pop/rock with the album *T.N.T.* The early 1980s brought duets with her then-beau GLEN CAMPBELL in a more mainstream country style. After struggling to find a style, she returned in the mid-1980s to traditional country and honky-tonk sounds.

While Tucker continues to record in a variety of styles, from sentimental ballads to hard-edged country rock, her best material continues to play on her image of a good girl gone (slightly) bad. Her 1992 hit, "It's a Little Too Late" is a classic honky-tonk number that also catered to the craze for country dances. Tucker is one of the few female country stars who could get away with singing this type of song, which would more typically be given to a male artist because of its implicit sexuality. She is able to communicate a nonthreatening good humor to her audience that allows her to cross the line just a little bit beyond what might be otherwise acceptable for a country "lady."

The later 1990s were more difficult for Tucker on the charts, but her touring activity went unabated. Her last chart single to date was 1997's "Little Things," a top-10 country hit. That same year she published her autobiography, *Nickel Dreams,* which was a best seller. She has yet to produce a follow-up album, but continues to be active on the road.

"Tumbling Tumbleweeds" (1948) *hit for*
Sons of the Pioneers
This western-style song was first successfully recorded by the SONS OF THE PIONEERS for Decca in 1934. Group member Bob Nolan also wrote the classics "Cool Water" and "A Cowboy Has to Sing." "Tumblin' Tumbleweeds" was the title song for a

1935 GENE AUTRY film, and Autry's version was a major hit that year, making it a western standard. The Sons of the Pioneers rerecorded it in 1948 for another chart hit.

Twain, Shania (b. 1965) *singer*
Born Eileen Edwards, in the small backwoods town of Timmins, Ontario, on August 28, 1965, Twain began singing at age three, winning talent shows from the age of eight, and performing locally and on national television from her early teen years. She trained professionally in Toronto as a Broadway-style singer/dancer/performer. She began performing at the resort town of Deerhurst after her mother and stepfather were killed in an automobile accident. She had started singing Vegas-style material, but she decided to jump on the country bandwagon and came to Nashville in 1991.

Twain was quickly signed to Mercury Records, hitting it big with her sexy video presence on her first single, "Whose Bed Have Your Boots Been Under." The self-titled album produced more hits, including "Any Man of Mine" and "(If You're Not in It for Love) I'm out of Here." All of the songs were marked by a spunky forthrightness in their lyrics that appealed strongly to women, while the sexy underpinning—and basically romantic and nonthreatening message—made the songs attractive to men. The album eventually went nine times platinum and remained on the charts for nearly 200 weeks.

The album teamed her with pop-rock producer Robert "Mutt" Lange, who coauthored many of her hits and was soon her husband. The duo returned big time with Twain's 1997 album, *Come On Over.* Although a "country" album in name, it was really mainstream pop in the style of singers like Gloria Estefan or Celine Dion. The album was a monster seller, producing many top hits, including the big ballads "You're Still the One" and "From This Moment" (recorded as a duet with Bryan White on the album, but released as a solo single), to the spunky "That Don't Impress Me Much," "Don't Be

Shania Twain in concert (Raeanne Rubenstein)

music in late 2002 with the album *Up*. In an unusual move, the CD was released in three versions. American buyers received two CDs, one mixed for the country market, the other for pop; Europeans received a unique mix of their own, plus the pop mix. The album's first single, "I'm Gonna Getcha," was an immediate number-one hit on country and pop charts. It was followed by more top hits, including "Forever and for Always" and "She's Not Just a Pretty Face."

Twitty, Conway (1933–1993) *singer*

Harold Jenkins was born on September 1, 1933, in the small riverfront town of Friars Point, Mississippi. His father was a ferryboat captain who operated a tug between Friars Point and Helena, Arkansas. His father gave him his first rudimentary guitar lessons; young Jenkins had his own country band performing on Helena radio by the time he was 10 years old. He cited two important influences from his earliest years: the jukebox at the local honky-tonk, and the singing at the African-American church across the cotton fields from his home. "I would sit on the ditch bank and listen to them sing for two or three hours," he recalled. "I'd be singing right along." Like many of his contemporaries, he would wed black and white musical influences in his mature works.

As a teenager Jenkins dreamed of being a professional baseball player; he was talented enough to get an invitation to join the Philadelphia Phillies. He also contemplated a career as a minister. Both plans were put aside when he received his draft notice in the mid-1950s. While he was in the army, he continued to perform country music. Meanwhile, another country artist, Elvis Presley, was recording his first big hits in a new style: rockabilly.

On Jenkins's return from service, he heard the first Elvis recordings and, inspired by Elvis's success, he decided to adapt the new rockabilly sound. He decided that, if he was going to be a rock star, he needed a rock star's name. Looking on a map, he hit on the names of two local towns: Twitty, Texas, and

Stupid," and "Man! I Feel Like a Woman," which subsequently was used in an advertising campaign by Revlon featuring Twain. The album has broken all records, selling more than 18 million copies to date, spawning eight hit singles, and becoming by *Billboard*'s estimation the best-selling recording by a female artist of all time, in any genre.

Twain took some recording time off after promoting her second megaselling hit through tours and TV appearances in 1998 and 1999. She gave birth to her first child in 2001. Twain returned to

Conway, Arkansas. He called his band the Twitty Birds. (Later, when he achieved success as a country star, he made his home into a theme park, aptly called Twitty City.)

Twitty's first big hit, a million-seller on the pop chart, came in 1958 with "It's Only Make Believe," which he cowrote. A number of rockabilly/teen-pop singles followed on MGM, including 1960's hit "Lonely Blue Boy." His success won him the attention of Hollywood, and, like Elvis, he appeared in a number of forgettable low-budget movies performing his music, including the memorably titled *Sex Kittens Go to College* and *Platinum High.* But after the Beatles broke through the charts in 1964, Conway's pop career fizzled.

After an abortive attempt to be a mainstream pop crooner, he relocated to Oklahoma City and formed a new country band, the Lonely Blue Boys. Legendary Decca producer OWEN BRADLEY signed him to the label, where he remained for many years. After appearing on his own local TV show, Twitty relocated to Nashville, where, by the end of the 1960s, he was a major star. His first big country hit came in 1970 with "Hello Darlin' " and was followed by further charting singles through the decade. Most of his best songs were on the classic country concerns of lovin', leavin', and being lonely, from the humorous ("Tight Fittin' Jeans") to the sentimental ("After All the Good Is Gone").

At this time he began a successful collaboration with singer LORETTA LYNN. Their duets included sexually suggestive numbers that initially upset mainstream country disc jockeys. Their first hit, 1971's "After the Fire Is Gone" reflected a typical Twitty concern: a relationship on the skids. Other numbers celebrated regional identity ("Louisiana Woman, Mississippi Man") and downhome humor ("You're the Reason Our Kids Are Ugly").

In the 1980s and early 1990s, he rarely charted as he had in the past, but continued to perform most months of the year, while his home became a kind of landmark shrine for country-music fans. He had just finished playing a date in Branson, Missouri, in 1993 when he collapsed due to a ruptured blood vessel; he died soon after, on June 5, 1993.

"Uncle Pen" (1950) *standard bluegrass number*
BILL MONROE wrote this song in honor of his fiddle-playing uncle, Pendleton Vandiver, with whom he had lived as a teenager. The song incorporates parts of traditional Kentucky fiddle tunes that Pen played. Guitarist Jimmy Martin sang lead on the original recording. It has become a bluegrass standard, and was a top-20 country hit for PORTER WAGONER in 1956 and a number-one hit for RICKY SKAGGS in 1984.

Urban, Keith (b. 1967) *guitarist and songwriter*
Although born in New Zealand on October 26, 1967, Urban was raised in Australia, where his parents exposed him to country-music recordings. A high school friend introduced him to the guitar work of Mark Knopfler of Dire Straits, and Urban's blend of rock-flavored solos with country themes was born. In the later 1990s he formed his first group in Australia and recorded an album there, which was very successful. In 1998 he came to Nashville, and, a year later, signed with Capitol. His blond good looks and mix of up-tempo rock numbers with tearful ballads, made him an immediate sensation. Besides earning the normal award nominations, he also scored hits with "It's a Love Thing," a sensitive rocker that Urban cowrote with Monty Powell, "Where the Black Top Ends," a country retro-rocker composed by Steve Wariner, "Your Everything," a ballad, and "But for the Grace of God," cowritten with the Go-Go's Charlotte Caffrey and Jane Wiedlin. Urban even recorded a collaboration with hip-hop producer Stevie J., which he describes as "hip-hop meets banjos." In 2002 he released his second album, *Golden Road,* which duplicated the general mix of material and style of his first hits. It spawned the number-one hits "Somebody Like You" and "Who Wouldn't Want to Be Me?"

"Wabash Cannonball" (1936) *major country hit for Roy Acuff*

Drawn from ROY ACUFF's first recording session, this song was one of many country hits celebrating famous railroad trains, beginning with "The Wreck of the Old 97." The sound of a moving train is cleverly mimicked on the Dobro, played by band member "Bashful Brother" Oswald.

Wagoner, Porter (b. 1927) *singer and television personality*

The son of a Midwest farmer, Porter Wagoner was born near West Plains, Missouri, on August 12, 1927. He was exposed to country radio from an early age and soon was singing and playing along with his favorite songs. When he was 14, he was hired as a clerk at a West Plains market, where he often entertained customers with his music. The store owner decided that Wagoner's music was good for business, so he sponsored him on a 15-minute radio show on the local station. By the late 1940s Wagoner's show was attracting regional attention, and in 1951 he was booked to perform on the radio station in the capital city of Springfield. A year later, he signed with RCA Victor records.

Coincidentally, RED FOLEY was establishing his *Ozark Jamboree* television program at about this time to originate from Springfield. He took Wagoner under his wing and by the mid-1950s made him a star of the program. This led to Wagoner's first hit, "Satisfied Mind," in 1955. His first gospel recording, "What Would You Do (If Jesus Came to Your House)," followed a year later. In 1957 he was invited to join the *Grand Ole Opry,* and he relocated to Nashville. Soon after, Porter formed his backup band, known as the Wagonmasters.

Wagoner's career would continue to alternate pop country songs and gospel numbers for more than 20 years. His best-known hit was 1965's "Green, Green Grass of Home," which also made a major showing on the pop charts. Other notable Wagoner songs include "I've Enjoyed as Much of This as I Can Stand" (1963), "Skid Row Joe" (1966), and "Be Proud of Your Man" (1968), all expressing typical country sentiments.

In 1960 Wagoner began his syndicated television program in Nashville. Starting with just 18 stations, the program grew to be one of the most popular in syndication, with more than 100 outlets in the early 1970s. Wagoner introduced singer Norma Jean in the early 1960s as his partner, and then, in 1967, gave DOLLY PARTON her first career exposure. Parton and Wagoner charted with the duet "Last Thing on My Mind," a Tom Paxton folk-revival standard, and continued to work and record together through 1974. Wagoner felt that he deserved the credit for Parton's later success, and he resented her attempts to establish herself as a solo act in the early 1970s; Parton, on her side, felt stifled by what she viewed as Wagoner's old-fashioned musical ideas, and eventually broke off from him. A series of lawsuits followed, and Wagoner's career faded while Parton made the crossover into mainstream pop and movie-star status.

Although Wagoner continued to produce minor hits into the early 1980s, his pop-style vocals were something of an anachronism in the new Nashville. After dropping him in 1981, RCA dug in the vaults to find unissued Porter-and-Dolly material, and this, along with his more recent solo recordings, kept his fans reasonably happy. Like many country performers before him, Wagoner discovered that his core fans were slow to abandon him, so he has been able to continue touring and performing while his recordings continue to sell. In 2000 he issued his first new album in some years on the small Shell Point label, and another CD followed in 2002.

Walker, Clay (b. 1969) *guitarist and singer*

Ernest Clayton Walker, born in Beaumont, Texas, on August 19, 1969, had strong musical roots; his grandfather was a semiprofessional country singer, and both his father and uncle played guitar, although neither made a living out of music. Walker began playing guitar at age nine, and then continued his lessons in high school, where he met another soon-to-be country star, TRACY BYRD. Walker began pursuing music as a profession at age 16, attending college to study business so he could better manage his career.

In 1992 he signed with Giant Records. Walker's first single, "What's It to You," released in July 1993, was an immediate number-one hit. More hits followed through mid-decade, including an eventual total of 11 number-one hits, following a predictable pattern of alternating up-tempo dance numbers with more heartfelt ballads. His first album produced two other number ones, "Live until I Die" and "Dreaming with My Eyes Open." His second album, released in 1994, contained "If I Could Make A Living," the rocking title track, and "This Woman and This Man," the tearful ballad. A classic honky-tonk number, "Who Needs You Baby," came out in 1995, juxtaposed with the ballad "Hypnotize the Moon." In 1999 he scored another number-one hit with "The Chain of Love." Each of his first four albums went platinum. In 2000 Giant Records was

closed, and Walker moved to parent company Warner Brothers. In early 2001 he released his seventh album, *Say No More.* In 2003 he released another album, *A Few Questions,* this one on RCA.

In 1996 Walker was diagnosed with multiple sclerosis. Although the disease didn't slow him down, he did become active in raising awareness about the disease and its treatment. Walker has continued to tour and perform on the usual country music rodeo, race car, and sports circuits.

"Walking the Floor over You" (1941)
honky-tonk ballad

ERNEST TUBB's "Walking the Floor over You" set the mold for postwar honky-tonk ballads. The loping beat, electric guitar, and lovelorn lyrics provided the theme and basic sound for a generation of barroom singers. It was an immediate sensation, selling more than 400,000 copies in its first year, and eventually selling more than a million copies in its original version. The song became Tubb's signature piece, and he would revisit it countless times on disc and thousands of times in concert. It has been covered dozens of times over the years, notably by Bing Crosby (1942), Pat Boone (1958), GLEN CAMPBELL (1963), GEORGE HAMILTON IV (1965), ASLEEP AT THE WHEEL (1989), and many more.

Wariner, Steve (b. 1954) *singer*

Steven Noel Wariner was born in Indianapolis, Indiana, on December 25, 1954. He was inspired to play guitar by his father, who had his own amateur country band. The younger Wariner began performing while still in high school; after finishing his schooling, he worked as a bass player for DOTTIE WEST for three years, followed by two and a half years with Bob Luman before signing as a solo artist to RCA in 1977. His first release, the self-composed "I'm Already Taken," was a minor hit for him, and later was covered by CONWAY TWITTY. Through the late 1970s and early 1980s, Wariner did not perform much of his own material, and his releases were bathed in a pop-country backup that really wasn't suited to him. However, he did manage to break through in 1982 with the number-one hit "All Roads Lead to You."

It was in the mid-1980s, when he changed to more progressive producers, that he finally hit his stride, beginning with a remake of "Lonely Women Make Good Lovers" in 1984, and his first number one since 1982, "Some Fools Never Learn" (1985). Wariner cowrote his next hit, "You Can Dream of Me" (1986), which had a pop/contemporary sound. This success led to an invitation to write a new theme song for TV's *Who's the Boss*. Wariner continued to move in a pop rock direction, as on 1987's

Steve Wariner and Keith Urban backstage (Raeanne Rubenstein)

"Small Town Girl." After a couple more pop hits, Wariner scored a hit in 1989 with the countrified "Where Did I Go Wrong?," his second self-written number-one song. This was followed by his jazzy "I Got Dreams," which featured Wariner's scat singing (a novelty for a country recording).

In the early 1990s Wariner enjoyed further hits, including 1992's number-one song "The Tips of My Fingers" and "Like a River to the Sea" (1993). His 15th album, *Drive,* came in 1993. It had a more hard-rocking sound and scored a top-10 hit with "If I Didn't Love You." Wariner then took a three-year recording break, returning with *No More Mr. Nice Guy,* an all-instrumental album featuring a band of super pickers. This was, to say the least, an unusual move for a country pop singer, and the album sold poorly. Wariner was made a member of the *Grand Ole Opry* in 1996.

Wariner came roaring back by returning to big-lunged balladry. He cut a duet with new country singer/instrumentalist Anita Cochran on "What If I Said" in 1998, which made number one, followed by his own major hit, the weeper "Holes in the Floor of Heaven." Signed to a new label, Wariner released *Burnin' the Roadhouse Down,* which scored well on both country and pop charts. His following two albums through the end of the 20th century were in a similar mold.

weeper

A weeper is a song dripping with heavy sentiments, often dealing with romantic loss, death, or betrayal. Sentimental songs have long been favorites in country circles. Songs of orphaned children, lost mothers, betrayed lovers, train wrecks, coal-mining disasters, flood, fire, and famine seem to win the hearts and ears of country audiences, no matter what the decade. Perhaps because life in the rural South was so difficult— poverty, disease, and little opportunity for improvement were facts of life— the country audience gravitated toward music that had a strong "blue" or sad component. The very first country hit—VERNON DALHART's recording of

"The Wreck of the Old 97"—falls squarely in this category; despite an upbeat tune, the song tells of an unmitigated disaster, a train wreck that took the lives of the devoted engineer and his colleagues. Other classic weepers of the early country era include many of the BLUE SKY BOYS' hit recordings, as well as many classics by the CARTER FAMILY. ("Bury Me Beneath the Willow" tells of an unrequited lover's request to be buried "under the weeping willow tree" so that "maybe then she'll think of me.")

In the period after World War II, when honky-tonks became centers of hard drinkin' and hell raisin', a new crop of weepers arose. HANK WILLIAMS's "Your Cheatin' Heart" is a typical song in the new style; its weepy content is matched by the "crying" sound of the steel guitar and Williams's very emotional delivery. Often the songs tell of a young man who is lured to his doom by a "honky-tonk angel," a loose woman who hangs out at a bar hoping to ensnare and lead astray the dedicated, hard-working country boy (needless to say, this stretched the truth, because many young men were looking for trouble in the bars). HANK THOMPSON's "Wild Side of Life" is a classic of this genre, and it inspired the first great weeper sung by a female, KITTY WELLS's answer song, "It Wasn't God Who Made Honky Tonk Angels," which finally presented the woman's point of view.

The 1960s saw the weeper formula become largely a female domain. Stronger female vocalists, like TAMMY WYNETTE, had hits with ballads like "Stand by Your Man," but songs like Wynette's "D-I-V-O-R-C-E," telling of the painful breakdown of a marriage that a mother tries to hide from the prying ears of her child, are more typical of the woman's repertory of the period.

Although no-holds-barred weepers are not as often heard today, the tradition lives on in various guises, ranging from the upbeat ("Forever and Ever Amen" by RANDY TRAVIS, with its vow of eternal love verging on the bathetic) to songs mixed with mid-1970s singer/songwriter sensibility ("The River" by Garth Brooks), to big-throated pop ballads like Lorrie Morgan's "Something in Red" or LEE ANNE WOMACK's "I Hope You Dance."

"Welcome to My World" (1964) *Jim Reeves's last single*

This song was the last single released by singer JIM REEVES before his tragic death, and for that reason it is closely associated with him. It reached number two on the country charts, remaining at the second slot for two weeks but totaling an astounding 26 weeks.

Wells, Kitty (b. 1919) *singer*

Muriel Deason was born in Nashville, Tennessee, on August 30, 1919. She began performing on local radio with her sisters and a cousin as the Deason Sisters in 1936. A year later, she wed Johnnie Wright, a talented musician. Soon after, she began performing with Johnny and with her sister-in-law, Louise Wright, as Johnnie Wright and the Harmony Girls. In 1939 Johnnie added Jack Anglin (who had married Louise) to the band to form the Tennessee Hillbillies (later the Tennessee Mountain Boys). In 1942 Jack was drafted, so Johnny began performing with his wife as a duo; at this time, he christened her "Kitty Wells," taking her stage name from the folk ballad "Sweet Kitty Wells." After the war Jack reunited with Johnny to form the popular country duo Johnnie and Jack. In 1947 they joined radio station KWKH, becoming members of the new *Louisiana Hayride* show on that station the next year, which made their reputation and won them a contract with RCA.

In 1949 Kitty began recording gospel numbers backed by Johnnie and Jack's band, with little success. Meanwhile, the duo's recordings sold well. Semiretired from music as a housewife, she was lured back into the studio for one more try at recording in 1952. Paul Cohen, a Decca label executive, wanted her to record a woman's answer song to the immensely popular HANK THOMPSON song "Wild Side of Life." The result, "It Wasn't God Who

Made Honky Tonk Angels," rightfully asserted that men had to share the blame for the "fallen women" who frequented the rough-and-tumble backwoods bars. The song shot up the country charts, making Wells's reputation. Through the 1950s and 1960s Wells proved she was no one-hit wonder. On solo recordings ("I Can't Stop Loving You," "Mommy for a Day," "Heartbreak U.S.A."), and duets with Red Foley ("One by One," "As Long As I Live") she honed her image as the gutsy good girl (sometimes gone wrong).

Although Wells continued to record from the mid-1960s through the 1970s, her major hit-making years were over. She continued to tour and perform for her loyal fans with her longtime husband, appearing occasionally on the *Grand Ole Opry,* and the duo operate their own museum near their suburban Nashville home. She was elected to the Country Music Hall of Fame in 1976, and won a Grammy Award for lifetime achievement in 1991, only the third country performer and the first woman to that date to be so honored.

West, Dottie (1932–1991) *singer and songwriter*

Born on October 11, 1932, and raised in a tiny farm community near McMinnville, Tennessee, Dorothy Marie Marsh West was inspired to become a musician by her fiddling father. She made her debut on local radio when she was 12, although she had not yet decided to make music a career. She enrolled at Tennessee Technical College, where she began performing with steel guitarist Bill West on radio and at dances; the couple were married in 1953, and they relocated to the Cleveland, Ohio, area. Dottie appeared on Ohio's *Landmark Jamboree,* a Western-style TV show, during the 1950s, as well as performing with singer Kathy Dearth, also known as Kathy Dee, as the Kay-Dots, a vocal duo who blended country harmonies with pop material.

In 1958 Dottie began traveling to Nashville on weekends, securing a recording contract with the bluegrass-oriented Starday label a year later, and

then with the jazz label Atlantic. She moved permanently to Nashville in 1961, and had her first big break in 1963 when JIM REEVES had a hit with her song "Is This Me?"; the pair teamed up for the 1964 hit "Love Is No Excuse." She was signed to RCA and producer CHET ATKINS, who produced her first hit, the self-written "Here Comes My Baby," a year later, leading to her membership in the *Grand Ole Opry.* This was followed by other hits in the typical Nashville sound of the day, including 1966's "Would You Hold It against Me?" and "Paper Mansions" from a year later.

West continued to focus on songs of heartbreak and loss. She even recorded a theme album in 1966 called *Suffer Time,* chronicling, in the words of the liner notes, the story of "an eternal loser"! West produced some classic weepers, including 1968's "If You Go Away"; two original songs, the 1969 hit "Clinging to My Baby's Hand" and 1970's "The Cold Hand of Fate"; and 1971's "Once You Were Mine" and "Six Weeks Every Summer."

West's popularity as a singer and songwriter reached its height in 1973 when she was invited by Coca-Cola to write a series of jingles; one of them, "Country Sunshine," became a big hit that year. Her solo hits came more sporadically after the mid-1970s, although she still managed a couple of number ones, including "A Lesson in Leavin' " in 1980 and "Are You Happy Baby" and "What Are We Doin' in Love" in 1981, the latter an uncredited duet with KENNY ROGERS.

At the same time, West became a popular duet partner, first singing with Jim Reeves, Justin Tubb, and then DON GIBSON, before forming a very successful partnership with Kenny Rogers. West and Rogers recorded several racy titles between 1978 and 1981. However, West's career slowed in the 1980s, culminating in the foreclosure of her Nashville mansion in 1990 and a bankruptcy filing and public auction in 1991. She had a couple of failed marriages (she had divorced original husband Bill West in 1972 to marry several younger musicians and associates in succession). Just as she was about to make a comeback, West was killed in an automobile accident on her way to the *Grand Ole Opry* on September 4, 1991.

Her daughter Shelly West was a popular country singer, performing in duet with her then husband David Frizzell and also as a solo artist, enjoying her greatest period of popularity in the early through mid-1980s.

western swing

Western swing is a unique combination of string band music with jazz styles. It was born in the Texas-Oklahoma region in the late 1920s. There, musicians were influenced by blues and jazz recordings, as well as early pop crooners, to form an amalgam of traditional country sounds with a swinging accompaniment.

The band credited with creating this sound was the Light Crust Doughboys in 1931–32, featuring fiddler BOB WILLS and vocalist Milton Brown. Soon, Wills and Brown formed their own bands. Although Brown's band was in many ways better than Wills's, it was short-lived (Brown died in the mid-1930s following an automobile accident); meanwhile, Wills's band grew into a full jazz ensemble, with a large horn section and the crooning vocals of Tommy Duncan. The band's instrumentation also included smooth steel guitar, ragtime-influenced piano, and often twin harmony fiddling. Wills's repertoire was made up of popular songs, blues, traditional fiddle tunes (often jazzed up), and big-band standards.

A second wave of western swing came in the late 1940s in Southern California, where many western musicians had settled after the war to appear in the countless cowboy films that the lesser Hollywood studios (particularly Republic) were busily churning out. Wills's postwar band returned to the stripped-down sound of his original unit, now featuring electric guitar, steel guitar, and even electric mandolin (played by Tiny Moore), with various vocalists (Wills had fired Duncan in 1948 in a fit of anger). Another popular California-based band was led by SPADE COOLEY.

The 1950s and 1960s were lean times for the music. But then, in early 1970s, new, young bands began playing the music, such as ASLEEP AT THE WHEEL, introducing a new generation to the western swing sound. Meanwhile, country superstar MERLE HAGGARD recorded an album in homage to Wills's music, and then brought the star out of retirement for his famous last session in 1973. A slew of reissues of early recordings in the 1970s, 1980s, and 1990s have made even the lesser-known bands famous once again.

White, Bryan (b. 1974) *singer and songwriter*
Bryan Shelton White was born in Lawton, Oklahoma, on February 17, 1974. Both of his parents were professional musicians: his father sang country music and his mother performed R&B, and they encouraged Bryan to begin playing drums at age five. Bryan didn't switch to guitar or write a song until he was 17, but that didn't stop him from moving to Nashville in 1992 to seek fame and fortune. He found it in 1994; his first two singles did moderately well, but then came two number-one hits, "Someone Else's Star" and "Rebecca Lynn." His second album fared even better, yielding the ballad "I'm Not Supposed to Love You Anymore." In 1999 he cut a duet with SHANIA TWAIN, "From This Moment On," for her tremendously successful album, *Come On Over,* although the mega-selling single version had his vocal stripped out. White has also frequently collaborated with guitarist/singer STEVE WARINER.

Whitley, Keith (1955–1989) *singer*
Born on July 1, 1955, in Sandy Hook, Kentucky, Whitley began performing at a young age, working on local radio by the time he was nine. Along with his high school buddy RICKY SKAGGS, he developed a love of the traditional music of the STANLEY BROTHERS. The two formed a duo that so impressed Ralph Stanley that he asked them to join his band in 1971. Whitley remained with Stanley for six years as

lead vocalist and then performed with J. D. Crowe in his progressive bluegrass band, the New South, from 1977 to 1982. A year later Whitley moved to Nashville and was signed to RCA, becoming one of the first new traditionalists to record.

Unlike Skaggs, who kept one foot in traditional country, Whitley wholeheartedly embraced more mainstream Nashville sounds. He wed Lorrie Morgan, daughter of the well-known country singer GEORGE MORGAN; she would achieve her greatest success as a performer after Whitley's death. His first hit came in 1986 with "Miami, My Amy," which reached number 14 on the country charts, followed two years later by his first number one, "Don't Close Your Eyes" from Whitley's third album, the first that he coproduced and the first that he felt really reflected his sound. The same album produced two other hits, "When You Say Nothing at All," (later a hit for ALISON KRAUSS), as well as "I'm No Stranger to the Rain," which wasn't released until early 1989. Already suffering from bouts of alcoholism, Whitley was found dead at home on May 9, 1989. His death made him something of a country-music martyr, like many other artists who die young, helping propel his posthumous hits "I Wonder Do You Think of Me" shortly after his death and "I'm over You" a year later to the top of the charts.

Whitman, Slim (b. 1924) *singer*

Otis Dewey Whitman Jr. was born in Tampa, Florida, on January 20, 1924. Beginning as a professional baseball player, Whitman began singing in local bars in the late 1940s to augment his income. This led to a contract with RCA in 1949, where he scored moderate success with western numbers such as "Casting My Lasso in the Sky." In 1952 he was signed to Imperial, where he immediately scored with "Indian Love Call," an old pop chestnut that had previously been a hit for Jeanette MacDonald and Nelson Eddy. Whitman's high tenor voice, augmented by frequent yodeling on this record, was a novelty on country and pop charts. He continued to

record pop songs with a western theme through the mid-1950s. Whitman remained popular in Europe through the following decades, although he was little remembered at home.

"Wild Side of Life, The" (1952) *classic honky-tonk song and Hank Thompson's biggest hit*

Considered one of the classic honky-tonk songs, "The Wild Side of Life" was HANK THOMPSON's biggest country hit. Its most famous line, the opening of the chorus—"I didn't know God made honky tonk angels"—inspired a famous answer song, "It Wasn't God Who Made Honky Tonk Angels" (1952) that launched the career of KITTY WELLS. Thompson's song blames the "honky-tonk angel" for returning to her partying ways, abandoning her true love for the "gay night life." Wells's response states that if it wasn't for male barflys luring women into sin, there wouldn't be any "honky-tonk angels." Thompson's version has been covered by numerous country artists, and even rocker Rod Stewart has recorded the song.

Williams, Don (b. 1939) *singer and songwriter*

The son of an automobile mechanic, Williams was born in Floydada, Texas, on May 27, 1939. He was taught guitar by his mother, and began playing as a teenager in the rocking country styles that were popular at the time. After finishing high school and serving in the army, Williams began performing as a duo with a friend named Lofton Kline; they hooked up with another local performer, Susan Taylor, to form the Pozo Seco Singers in 1964. A year later, they broke through on the pop charts with "Time." The group remained together until 1971, with a few more minor pop hits.

Williams followed Taylor to Nashville to work as a songwriter in support of her nascent solo career in the early 1970s. There he hooked up with producer Allen Reynolds, who worked for noted recording engineer/performer Jack Clement. Clement had just formed his own JMI label, and he quickly signed

Williams. Williams had minor hits with his first two releases, but then hit it big with 1974's "We Should Be Together," leading to a contract with ABC/Dot and his first number one, "I Wouldn't Want to Live If You Didn't Love Me."

The hit-making continued through the 1970s, all the songs characterized by simple productions emphasizing Williams's laid-back vocalizing. His resonant baritone voice led him to be compared with JIM REEVES and, like another country hit maker of the era, KENNY ROGERS, Williams managed somehow to combine pop styling with enough country sentiments to appeal to a fairly broad audience. Other typical Williams hits include the bathetically romantic "Til the Rivers All Run Dry," cowritten with Wayland Holyfield, from 1976, 1977's "I'm Just a Country Boy," which became a signature tune for the singer, 1979's upbeat anthem "Tulsa Time" (which was covered by Eric Clapton a year later for the pop charts), and his biggest seller, 1980's "I Believe in You."

The 1980s saw Williams's career slow, although he continued to turn out records in his patented style. After a successful duet with EMMYLOU HARRIS on "If I Needed You" in 1981, he released "Lord, I Hope This Day Is Good," a 1982 number-one country record. This was followed by 1983's "If Hollywood Don't Need You," given a boost by its references to such celebrities as Burt Reynolds, with whom Williams had worked in the films *W. W. and the Dixie Dancekings* and *Smokey and the Bandit II.* His sound changed slightly in 1984 with "That's the Thing About Love," which featured light sax playing by Jim Horn.

Williams retired for a while in the mid-1980s due to continuing back trouble, but returned to recording again for Capitol in 1986. His last number one came that year with "Heartbeat in the Darkness," cowritten by Amazing Rhythm Aces vocalist Russell Smith. It was an unusual song for Williams, with its slight R&B flavor, but he managed to mold it into his distinctive laid-back style. Williams switched to RCA in 1989, and had a number-two hit a year later with "Back in My Younger Days." In early 1992 he

scored his last top-10 country hit to date, "Lord Have Mercy on a Country Boy." Dedicated to life on his farm near Nashville, Williams continues to perform and record on occasion, although his hit-making days seem to be over. His last album of new material to date appeared in 1998.

Williams, Hank (1923–1953) *singer and songwriter*

King Hiram Hank Williams was born in rural Mount Olive, Alabama, on September 17, 1923. Williams's family were poor dirt farmers who relocated to metropolitan Greenville, where Williams first heard the blues performed by street singer Rufe Payne; as with many other white country artists, Williams's life was changed by this exposure to black traditional music. Around 1937 the family relocated to Montgomery, where Williams made his first public appearance. This led to a regular spot on local radio. He formed his first band, the Drifting Cowboys, a name that he would use for his backup band throughout his career. He also composed "Six More Miles (to the Graveyard)," a blues that for the first time showed his unique sense of gallows humor.

He spent the war years in Mobile, Alabama, shipyards. He returned to music with a new band, featuring a young female singer, Audrey Sheppard Guy, who was to become his first wife (and mother of HANK WILLIAMS JR.). Williams signed with Nashville power-broker FRED ROSE in 1946; Rose became the mastermind behind Williams's successful career. After a brief stint with the small Sterling label, Williams signed with MGM in 1947, charting with his first release, the bluesy and ballsy "Move It On Over," and his first honky-tonk anthem, "Honky Tonkin." Williams could even transform religious material into his own unique style, making a hit out of his own "I Saw the Light." In August 1948 Williams was invited to join the prestigious *Louisiana Hayride* radio program, second only to the *Grand Ole Opry* in popularity among rural listeners. This spread his sound throughout the

Southwest, and helped propel his cover of the 1920s novelty number "Lovesick Blues" into a number-one country hit in 1949. An invitation to join the *Opry* followed, elevating Williams to the heights of country stardom.

Despite his increasing dependence on alcohol and painkillers, Williams continued to turn out major country hits through the remaining three years of his life. The savvy Rose also peddled Williams's songs to more mainstream performers, so that his "Cold, Cold Heart" was a hit for Tony Bennett, "Hey Good Lookin' " scored for Frankie Laine, and Jo Stafford made a hit out of the cajun novelty number "Jambalaya."

By mid-1952 hard drinking and drug use caught up with Williams. He was expelled from the *Opry*, and his marriage ended in divorce. He quickly remarried in a lavish ceremony, but his life was soon over. He died in the back of a car on the way to a performance on New Year's Day in 1953. As often happens, his death propelled his final recordings, "Your Cheatin' Heart" and the novelty "Kaw-Liga," to the top of the country charts.

As with many other performers who die young, Williams's death cast a long shadow. His recordings have been in print continuously since his death, and they remain staples on jukeboxes across the country.

Williams, Hank, Jr. (b. 1949) *singer and songwriter*

Randall Hank Williams was born in Shreveport, Louisiana, on May 26, 1949, the son of country star HANK WILLIAMS. Williams's career initially was shaped by his manipulative mother, Audrey, who hoped to make him into a junior version of his famous father. Even though she had separated from Hank Senior before his death (and he had remarried), Audrey carried a torch for him, using his fame to further her own singing career. Hank Junior was featured in her road shows, always performing his daddy's material. Meanwhile, Hank Senior's old record label MGM encouraged the younger Williams to record letter-perfect renditions of his father's songs.

By the late 1960s Williams was bridling at his mother's management of his career and the limitations of being a clone of his father. He had a number of hits in which he commented on his strange situation, including 1966's "Standing in the Shadows (of a Very Famous Man)." He also began to write songs in a plain-spoken, straightforward style, and befriended the Nashville outlaws, including WILLIE NELSON and WAYLON JENNINGS, who were seeking to return country music to its pure roots. In 1974 Williams left Nashville to live in Alabama, recording his breakthrough album, *Hank Williams Jr. and Friends,* featuring country rockers such as CHARLIE DANIELS. The album shocked his record label while it announced his new freedom from the slick Nashville sound. In 1977 Williams's transformation was completed when he switched from his father's label to Warner Brothers, which marketed him as a hell-raisin' country rocker.

Williams had many hits for Warner Brothers, particularly in the late 1970s and early 1980s, starting with 1978's "I Fought the Law" and capped by his "All My Rowdy Friends (Have Settled Down)" single and video in 1981, which featured Hank joined by country, rock, and blues musicians. Hank cultivated a born-to-boogie image. By the late 1980s the "unstoppable party" sound was beginning to wear thin, and Williams seemed to be searching for a new direction. One of his strangest career moves was the 1990 "duet" with his dead father in the video and single "There's a Tear in My Beer," in which, through overdubbing and computer editing, Hank Junior was able to sing and perform along with his long-gone dad. This was followed by the alcohol-drenched "Hotel Whiskey," a duet with new country star CLINT BLACK.

Williams spent most of the second half of the 1990s coasting on his reputation. In 1999 his first new studio album in three years, *Stormy,* was released, with songs that seemed to parody Hank's once rowdy image. In 2003 he performed with rapper Kid Rock for the CMT "Crossroads" series.

Wills, Bob (1905–1975) *bandleader, fiddle player, and songwriter*

Born in Kosse, Texas, on March 6, 1905, Wills was the son of an old-time fiddler and cotton farmer, who introduced his son to the traditional fiddle tunes of the Southwest. At this time Wills also heard black field workers singing in the cotton fields, and so his youth was equally influenced by the traditional hollers and blues that they performed, as well as the jazz sounds newly introduced on records and radio. By 1932 Wills, a passable old-time fiddler himself, was a member of the Fort Worth–based Light Crust Doughboys, a band sponsored by Burrus Mills, makers of Light Crust Dough, which featured Milton Brown, the other seminal name in western swing, as vocalist. By 1934 Wills had his own band, the Texas Playboys, based in Tulsa, and a year later they gained a recording contract with Brunswick Records.

Wills's new band was defined by two distinctive elements: the newly introduced electric "steel" guitar and the smooth vocalizing of singer Tommy Duncan. Steel guitarist Leon McAuliffe (b. Houston, 1917–88) was responsible for the group's big hit, "Steel Guitar Rag"; his burbling solos were a trademark of the early Wills recordings, and he was often introduced by Wills's high falsetto shout of "Take it away, Leon." Duncan blended a mainstream

Bob Wills (to the right of the microphone, holding fiddle) and an early version of the Texas Playboys (University of North Carolina, Southern Historical Collection, Southern Folklife Collection, University Archives)

sensibility with an affinity for the blues of JIMMIE RODGERS. The band also featured the fine boogie-influenced piano playing of Al Stricklin and a loping bass-and-drum rhythm section that predicted the shuffle beat of later country boogie outfits. By the end of the 1930s the group had grown to include a large brass section, rivaling the popular big bands of the day in size and sound.

World War II spelled the end of the big bands of the 1930s, and Wills turned to working with a smaller outfit in his new home, Southern California (he had moved there to appear in a number of forgettable D-grade Hollywood westerns). Singer Tommy Duncan was expelled from the band in 1948, and was replaced by a series of lead vocalists, male and female, who were similarly modern in their approach. Wills's pared-down band made an excellent series of recordings for MGM in the late 1940s and early 1950s that in many ways was more exciting than his big-band sides of the late 1930s.

Wills continued to work and record sporadically through the 1950s and 1960s, most notably recording two reunion albums with singer Tommy Duncan in 1961–62. Championed by country performer MERLE HAGGARD, who made a tribute album to Wills in 1970, he came out of semiretirement to supervise one last session just before his stroke in 1973. He died two years later on May 13, 1975.

Different Texas Playboys continued to perform in the 1970s and 1980s, one band led by Leon McAuliffe, and another led by Wills's brother, Johnnie Lee (September 2, 1912–October 25, 1984), who recorded the original version of "Rag Mop" in 1950 (later a hit for the Mills Brothers). Another brother, Billy Jack (February 26, 1926–March 2, 1991), worked as a drummer, bassist, and vocalist for Bob's band before forming his own group in 1949 (along with mandolinist Tiny Moore) known as Billy Jack Wills and the Western Swing Band. They had the most progressive sound of any of the western bands, with a jazz and R&B bent that was rarely heard in western swing; the group folded in 1954 when its members rejoined Bob Wills's ensemble.

Wills was also a talented songwriter. His most notable composition was "San Antonio Rose," although he also transformed several traditional fiddle tunes ("Liza Jane," "Ida Red," and others) into swinging pop confections.

"Will the Circle Be Unbroken?" (1933)
country song

Written by A. P. Carter and recorded by him with the CARTER FAMILY, this song is based on a popular southern hymn. It has become one of the best-known of all country songs, and it was used as the title track for the 1971 collaboration between country stars the NITTY GRITTY DIRT BAND, along with two subsequent follow-up collections.

Womack, Lee Ann (b. 1966) *singer*

Born in Jacksonville, Texas, on August 19, 1966, Womack was exposed to country music at an early age, thanks to her father, who worked as the local high school principal by day and as a country disc jockey by night. As a teen she began singing and writing her own songs, drawn on country styles. When she was 17 she enrolled at South Plains College in Levelland, Texas, one of the few—if not the only—colleges to offer degrees in bluegrass and country music. While attending school, she joined the college's performing group, Country Caravan, appearing with them on tours of the South and West.

At age 20 she moved to Nashville to enroll at Belmont University, where she studied music business. She married songwriter/instrumentalist Jason Sellers, who was touring with VINCE GILL at the time (the couple would later divorce). She also landed a brief internship at MCA Records. Performing at local showcases, she first landed a songwriting contract in 1995, working for Tree Music. She cowrote several songs with various Tree staff members, including Bill Anderson, who recorded one of their compositions. She also befriended many new traditionalists in Nashville, including RICKY SKAGGS (who also employed her husband in his band).

Lee Ann Womack at the CMA Awards (Raeanne Rubenstein)

In 1996 she was signed to the Decca label, a part of MCA. Her solo debut single was the very traditional country song "Never Again, Again." Although it charted only in the country top 40, the song was hailed as a return to roots country, and Womack was favorably compared to DOLLY PARTON and TAMMY WYNETTE, among others. Womack's career was launched with her second single, "The Fool," which leapt to number two on the country charts.

Womack followed up in 1998 with her second album, *Some Things I Know.* Combining classic country weepers with more upbeat pseudo–western swing romps, the album produced more hits for the singer, most notably "A Little Past Little Rock." Womack also began recording songs by some of the more progressive Nashville songwriters, including husband-and-wife team Buddy and Julie Miller, as well as older new-country icons like Rodney Crowell.

However, Womack's big break came in fall 2000 with the release of her third album, *I Hope You Dance.* The song became a phenomenal hit, shooting to number one. Its upbeat message had strong appeal, and soon the single and album went gold, then the album went platinum. Womack was invited to sing the title song at a concert in December 2000 at the Nobel Prize festivities in Sweden, and followed that in January 2001 with an appearance at one of the Young People's inaugural concerts for President Bush. This success was quickly followed by her next single, "Ashes by Now," a song written by Rodney Crowell and originally recorded in a much different version by him in 1980.

"Would You Lay with Me (In a Field of Stone)" (1974) *controversial tune*

Young teen TANYA TUCKER caused considerable controversy by recording this song, written by David Allen Coe. Many radio stations banned the recording, fearing backlash for both its indirect but powerful sexual content and Tucker's sultry delivery. Tame by today's country music standards, the song was nonetheless a breakthrough, with its success ensuring that country music would soon be open to more explicit lyrics.

"Wreck of the Old 97, The" (c. 1903) *classic railroad ballad*

"The Wreck of the Old 97," a classic railroad disaster ballad, is generally recognized as the first major country hit record, and it is the song that launched VERNON DALHART's career as a country singer. It was originally recorded by the rough-hewn Virginia guitarist/vocalist Henry Whitter and his partner, blind fiddler G. B. Grayson, for OKeh in 1923, under the name "The Wreck on the Southern Old 97." Victor suggested to Dalhart, who had previously recorded everything from pop songs to light operatic selections, that he cover the song. Dalhart's version is said to have sold more than 5 million copies, establishing the fact that there was a large audience for country music.

"Wreck on the Highway" (1942) *major hit for Roy Acuff*

This is one of the songs most closely associated with ROY ACUFF. It is also known as "I Didn't Hear Nobody Pray," the first line of the song's chorus. The sobbing Dobro part forecast the sound of the pedal steel guitar that would sweep country recordings in the 1950s.

Wynette, Tammy (1942–1998) *singer*

Virginia Wynette Pugh was born near Tupelo, Mississippi, on May 5, 1942. Raised by her grandparents in rural Mississippi, Wynette showed early musical talent, learning to play several instruments as well as singing. She joined her mother in Birmingham, Alabama, during her teen years, and was married for the first time at age 17; the marriage ended by the time she was 20. Wynette worked as a beautician during the day and a club singer at night to support her three children. Local success led to a regular featured slot on the *Country Boy Eddy* TV show.

Wynette came to Nashville in the mid-1960s in search of a career. She auditioned for several labels while working as a singer and song plugger. Ace producer Billy Sherrill recognized her potential and signed her to Epic, where she had an immediate hit with 1966's "Apartment Number 9," followed by the racy (for the time) "Your Good Girl's Gonna Go Bad." Wynette's good-girl-on-the-edge-of-going-bad image was underscored in a series of hits, including "I Don't Wanna Play House" from 1967

and "D-I-V-O-R-C-E" from 1968. The same year brought "STAND BY YOUR MAN," perhaps Wynette's most famous recording, and one that continues to inspire controversy due to its message that it's a woman's duty to support her husband, no matter what. More hits came in 1969 with "Singing My Song" and "The Ways to Love a Man."

In 1968 Wynette began a stormy seven-year marriage to hard-drinking country star GEORGE JONES. They often recorded together, including an album of duets in 1972 (a hit in 1973 was "We're Gonna Hold On") and again in 1976. They hit it big with "Golden Ring" and "Near You." Even though they divorced in 1975, they reteamed in 1980, scoring a hit with "Two-Story House." Wynette continued to record through the 1970s, scoring major hits through the middle of the decade, including 1972's "Bedtime Story" and "My Man (Understands)" (which clones the sentiments of "Stand By Your Man"), 1973's "Kids Say the Darndest Things," 1974's "Another Lonely Song," and her last solo number-one country hit, "You and Me" in 1976. Many of these songs were cowritten by Sherrill, and were carefully crafted to fit Wynette's image.

By the early to mid-1980s Wynette's career was in the doldrums. Sherrill's increasingly pop-oriented production was ill suited to her honky-tonk style, and she was reduced to singing warmed-over pop songs like "Sometimes When We Touch" (a duet with Mark Gray). An attempt to remake her for the new country generation in 1987 on her album *Higher Ground,* produced by Steve Buckingham and featuring a duet with RICKY SKAGGS, was a critical, if not financial, success. Wynette even dipped to self-parody, recording with the English-based technorock group KLF, scoring a British hit in 1992 with "Justified and Ancient."

At the end of 1993 Wynette was hospitalized due to a serious infection; she recovered, but was in a weakened condition. In 1994 she reunited with George Jones for an album titled *One* and a follow-up tour, but her physical condition was obviously precarious. Nonetheless, the album was a success, showing the enduring allure of the star-crossed couple. Wynette died of a blood clot on April 6, 1998.

Yearwood, Trisha (b. 1964) *singer*

The daughter of a small-town banker father and schoolteacher mother, Trisha Yearwood was born in Monticello, Georgia, on September 19, 1964. She came to Nashville in 1984 after two years of junior college to pursue a music-business degree at Belmont College. She interned at the publicity department at MTM Records and began doing demo and studio work, where she met another young unknown, GARTH BROOKS. Brooks invited her to back him up on his first albums, as well as to tour as his opening act. She was signed to a solo deal in 1991, producing the megahit "She's in Love with the Boy," an up-tempo ballad. This was followed by the sultry "Wrong Side of Memphis," along with a duet with Brooks on "Like We Never Had a Broken Heart."

Pop-music agent Ken Kragen took Yearwood under his professional wing in 1992. He had helped change KENNY ROGERS's career from pure country into pop superstardom, complete with movie deals, lucrative stays in Las Vegas, and chart-topping pop records. Kragen urged Yearwood to lose some weight, signed her up to a high-visibility contract with Revlon to promote her own perfume, and oversaw the making of her second album. Surprisingly, although the album was well received critically, Yearwood did not achieve the same chart success she had originally and was in danger of becoming a one-hit wonder.

Despite this slight career detour, Yearwood proved her staying power as a country hit maker through the 1990s. Major later career hits include 1994's "XXXs and OOOs (An American Girl)" and 1998's "I'll Still Love You More." In 1997 both she and LEANN RIMES recorded Diane Warren's "How Can I Live Without You"; eventually, Rimes had the bigger hit. Yearwood continued to score hits through the end of the decade; in fall 2001 she released a new album, *Inside Out*. The album's title track and lead single featured her in duet with ex-Eagles member Don Henley (with whom she had previously recorded a light pop duet, "Runaway Joe").

Yoakam, Dwight (b. 1956) *singer and songwriter*

Yoakam was born in Pikeville, Kentucky, on October 23, 1956, where his father was serving in the military; when Dwight was two, the family relocated to Cincinnati, where many other Appalachian families came in the 1950s in search of a better life. The Yoakams continued to visit relatives in Kentucky throughout Dwight's childhood, traveling down Route 23, the link between Cincinnati and the upper South immortalized in Yoakam's song "Readin', Rightin', Rt. 23." After completing high school and spending a couple of years as a philosophy major at Ohio State University, Yoakam moved to Los Angeles. There, he became a fixture in the local punk rock scene; his retro looks and sound seemed to fit in better with a punk sensibility than it did in the day's middle-of-the-road country.

Yoakam's late 1980s and early 1990s hits won him a cult following in rock, pop, and country circles. And, although he has continued to produce minor hits on the country charts, Yoakam stands apart from other new country acts in his slightly ironic take on the country image. His image is both an homage to the urban cowboy and a satire of it, and his music has a disturbing underside that seems to question the country ethos.

The height of Yoakam's chart success in country and pop arenas came in the late 1980s, with songs like "Little Sister" and "Streets of Bakersfield," a duet with BUCK OWENS that brought him his first number-one country tune in 1988. That same year, "I Sang Dixie" followed at the top of the charts. However, his retro hip style started to stale, and his follow-up releases failed to have the same impact. Yoakam's last major country hit came in 1993 with "Ain't That Lonely Yet." Six years later he had a fluke minor pop hit with a cover of Queen's "Crazy Little Thing Called Love," after recording it for a Gap khaki advertisement. He entered the new century with two albums, an all-acoustic career retrospective, and a new country album, featuring another rock cover, this time of Cheap Trick's "I Want You to Want Me."

yodeling

Yodeling, a sudden change from a chest voice to a falsetto head voice, originated centuries ago in the Swiss mountains, and probably entered the repertory of southern country musicians through the traveling tent shows of the 19th century.

Country music scholars commonly believe the first singer to make a record featuring yodeling was Riley Puckett, a popular Georgia country artist. Another early yodeler was the minstrel singer Emmett Miller, who in the late 1920s recorded "Lovesick Blues," later a major hit for HANK WILLIAMS. But it is JIMMIE RODGERS who popularized the yodeling style in his famous recordings of the late 1920s and early 1930s. Scores of yodeling cowboys came along in the wake of Rodgers's popularity, spearheaded by such famous cowboy film stars as GENE AUTRY and ROY ROGERS. During the cowboy craze, a number of cowgirl stars—notably PATSY MONTANA and Carolina Cotton—also were

popular yodelers, incorporating the sound into their major hits. BOB WILLS in his western swing bands used a kind of modified yodel, an expressive "Ah-ha," to express his pleasure at the band's performance, and BILL MONROE introduced the falsetto break into bluegrass music. Even popular R&B vocalist Aaron Neville says he was influenced to create his semi-yodeling vocal technique by listening to Gene Autry when he was a youngster. And GEORGE JONES created a kind of reverse yodel, in which he suddenly drops into the low bass from his normal vocal range as a means of adding emphasis to a song, a trick picked up by RANDY TRAVIS and GARTH BROOKS, among many others.

Actually, traditional southern mountain singing styles have long featured sudden shifts from normal to falsetto voice. For example, North Carolina ballad singer Dillard Chandler often broke into a short falsetto yelp at the end of a stanza, a kind of vocal hiccup that resembles a mini-yodel. Just as yodeling developed as a means of communication in the Alps, "hollerin' " was used among southern mountaineers to communicate across vast distances or to call in the animals. The annual hollerin' contests still held in Spivey Corners, North Carolina, feature much vocalizing that could be called "yodeling."

While the Swiss usually yodel for joy, Jimmie Rodgers introduced the yodel as a lonesome or "blue" expression, coming as it did at the end of a verse in songs like "T.B. Blues." Southern musicians have transformed the yodel into one of the most expressive of all musical techniques.

"You Are My Sunshine" (1940) *hit for Jimmie Davis*

Written by JIMMIE DAVIS with Charles Mitchell, the song was a major hit for Davis. Davis was originally influenced by JIMMIE RODGERS, but he enjoyed a string of pop-style hits in the mid-1930s with his own songs. He used this song's great success to propel him into a career in politics, becoming the governor of his home state of Louisiana. The song, in turn, was adopted as the official state song for

Louisiana. The song has been revived numerous times, notably in the 2001 film, *Oh Brother, Where Art Thou?*.

Young, Faron (1932–1996) *performer and songwriter*

Young was born on February 25, 1932, and raised on a small farm outside of Shreveport, Louisiana. He began playing guitar at an early age, and was already a competent country performer when he entered high school. After a brief stay in college in the early 1950s, Young's musical career interrupted his education. He was signed to the popular *Louisiana Hayride* radio program, where he met another future crooner, WEBB PIERCE, and the duo were soon touring southern honky-tonks and clubs.

In 1951 Young was signed to Capitol, having hits with the barroom tear-jerkers "Tattle Tale Tears" and "Have I Waited Too Long." Young spent two years in the army (1952–54), but in the middle of his army service (he served primarily as an entertainer for the troops) he was invited to join the *Grand Ole Opry*. After his service, he scored his biggest hits, including 1955's country anthem "Live Fast, Love Hard and Die Young." More honky-tonk standards followed, including 1956's "I've Got Five Dollars and It's Saturday Night," 1958's "That's the Way I Feel," and 1959's "Country Girl." In 1956 Young made his big-screen film debut in the horse opera *Hidden Guns*, which launched a brief film career through the early 1960s in similar westerns. *Hidden Guns* also gave him his nickname, "The Young Sheriff," while his band earned the moniker "The Young Deputies." When age caught up with him, Young changed his handle to "The Singing Sheriff."

In 1961 Young helped launch the songwriting career of WILLIE NELSON when he recorded Nelson's "Hello Walls," for a million-selling number-one country hit. However, beginning in the mid-1960s,

Young entered the mainstream Nashville music business with a vengeance. While his recordings continued, they tended to be conventional middle-of-the-road country crooning (1967's "I Guess I Had Too Much to Dream Last Night" being an example of the excesses of this period). He founded an influential music trade paper, *Music City News* and opened his own music publishing company and a racetrack in Nashville.

The 1970s saw Young doing less performing and more business. While he still had hits in the first half of the decade, his music-making gradually dropped off. By the 1980s he was recording only rarely, while continuing to make personal appearances. Through this period Young's personal life and his excessive drinking and womanizing (he once quipped, "I am not an alcoholic, I'm a drunk") often made headlines.

In the 1990s Young's performing career slowed still more, although he did continue to perform in country hot spots like Branson, Missouri, where he cut a live album in 1993. Suffering from emphysema and prostate problems, Young took his own life by a self-inflicted gunshot wound on December 10, 1996.

"Your Cheatin' Heart" (1953) *Hank Williams classic*

Paired with the novelty song "Kaw-Liga," "Your Cheatin' Heart" was the first release following HANK WILLIAMS's tragic death on New Year's Eve 1953. It's a classic weeper, telling the story of a scorned lover who scolds the woman who left him for another. Williams's recent demise and the song's quality made it a classic, and it has been covered numerous times, including pop covers in the 1950s by Frankie Laine and Joni James, as well as many covers by country artists. A 1965 biopic based on Williams's life and career took the song's name as its title; it starred George Hamilton as Williams.

Appendixes

Appendix I

Chronology of Major Events in Country Music

1922

June 22 Fiddlers "Uncle" Eck Robertson and Henry Gilliand record "Sallie Goodin" and "The Arkansas Traveller" for Victor in New York. These are considered to be among the first country recordings.

1923

January 4 Fort Worth radio station WBAP launches its *Barn Dance* program, said to be the first country variety show on radio.

June 14 Ralph Peer records Fiddlin' John Carson's "Little Old Log Cabin in the Lane," considered to be country's earliest hit.

1924

April 19 The *Chicago Barn Dance* debuts on radio station WLS. It is later known as the *National Barn Dance.* It would be broadcast out of Chicago until 1957, and continued to be aired through 1970.

August 14 Vernon Dalhart records "The Prisoner's Song," backed with "The Wreck of the Old 97," the first country record to sell a million copies.

1925

November 28 The *WSM Barn Dance,* later renamed the *Grand Ole Opry,* is first broadcast from Nashville.

1927

June 25 The famous "Bristol Sessions" are held in Bristol, Tennessee/Virginia, by producer Ralph Peer, where both Jimmie Rodgers and the Carter Family make their first records.

1928

September 28 The first recording sessions are held in Nashville when Victor sets up a temporary studio to record early *Grand Ole Opry* stars; this would be the last recording in Nashville until after World War II.

1929

October 9 Gene Autry, who would become America's most popular "Singing Cowboy," makes his first record.

1933

May 24 Jimmie Rodgers concludes his last sessions for Victor in New York City; he dies there two days later.

1935

August 16 Patsy Montana records "I Want to Be a Cowboy's Sweetheart," the earliest country release by a female singer to sell a million copies.

1938

February 19   Roy Acuff joins the *Grand Ole Opry*, marking a transition to a new era of country singers.

1939

October 28   Bill Monroe makes his debut appearance on the *Grand Ole Opry* singing Jimmie Rodgers's "Mule Skinner Blues."

1943

Songwriter Fred Rose and performer Roy Acuff form Acuff-Rose music publishing, which becomes the leading Nashville publisher of country songs.

1945

September 11   Ernest Tubb makes "It Just Don't Matter Now" and "When Love Turns to Hate"; many date the real start of commercial recording in Nashville to this session.

1947

April 21   Hank Williams records his first 78s for MGM.

September 18   Ernest Tubb and Roy Acuff headline New York's Carnegie Hall, the first country music show ever presented there. This was the first of a two-night stand. An overflow crowd came for the shows, and many could not be seated.

1948

January 13   WLW in Cincinnati launches the first country music show on television, *The Midwestern Hayride*.

1949

June 25   Billboard's "Hillbilly Music" chart is renamed the more modern "Country & Western."

1950

March 15   Flatt and Scruggs's classic bluegrass instrumental, "Foggy Mountain Breakdown," is released.

1952

March 15   Hank Thompson has his first number-one hit with the classic honky-tonk ballad "Wild Side of Life." It inspired Kitty Wells's famous answer song, "It Wasn't God Who Made Honky Tonk Angels."

1953

January 1   Hank Williams is discovered dead in the back of his touring car, following a New Year's Eve performance.

January 19   Marty Robbins gives his first performance on the *Grand Ole Opry*.

May 23   Jim Reeves makes his *Grand Ole Opry* debut.

1954

July 21   "I Walk the Line" hits number one for Johnny Cash; it is his first top hit.

1956

January 10   Elvis Presley has his first recording session at RCA's Nashville studios, cutting "Heartbreak Hotel," among other hits.

1957

January 21   Patsy Cline appears for the first time on *Arthur Godfrey's Talent Scouts* on television, launching her popular success.

March 1   Buck Owens signs with Capitol Records.

August 31   Last performance of the *National Barn Dance*, the first country-music radio program, in its Chicago theater.

1958

January 1   Johnny Cash makes his first appearance at California's San Quentin Prison. In the audience, a young inmate, Merle Haggard, hears him perform and is inspired to pursue a career as a country singer and songwriter.

1959

May 4   The first country Grammy Award is announced, for the Kingston Trio's recording of "Tom Dooley."

1960

June 13   "Honky Tonk Girl," Loretta Lynn's first single, released on the tiny Zero label, enters the country charts.

1961

November 3   Fred Rose, Hank Williams, and Jimmie Rodgers are the first inductees into the newly formed Country Music Hall of Fame.

1963

March 5   While touring together, Patsy Cline, Cowboy Copas, and Hawkshaw Hawkins are killed in a plane crash en route to a performance.

1966

May 19   Eddy Arnold makes his first appearance at New York's Carnegie Hall, marking his new style of mainstream pop country.

1967

January 7   Charley Pride makes his first appearance on the *Grand Ole Opry,* the first major African-American performer on the program since harmonica player DeFord Bailey.

April 1   The Country Music Hall of Fame and Museum opens in Nashville.

1969

June 15   Debut showing of *Hee Haw* on CBS TV, beginning a long run for this combination of country music and cornpone humor.

1971

April 27   Opryland USA theme park opens outside Nashville.

August 10   The Nitty Gritty Dirt Band complete their landmark *Will the Circle Be Unbroken* recording sessions, cutting the title song with Roy Acuff, Mother Maybelle Carter, and other country stars.

1973

July 4   Willie Nelson stages his first picnic in Austin, Texas, to feature performances by his "outlaw" friends.

1974

March 9   The *Grand Ole Opry* appears on the stage of the Ryman Auditorium for the last time.

1975

May 13   Bob Wills, legend of western swing, dies in the midst of making his last recordings.

August 8   While climbing Ajax Mountain on the Montana-Idaho border, Hank Williams Jr. suffers a near-fatal fall, leaving him with extensive damage to his face.

1978

June 10   Willie Nelson's *Stardust* album—a collection of pop music standards, unusual for a country artist to release—reaches number one on the country charts and remains on the chart for a record-breaking 551 weeks.

1980

June 5 The film *Urban Cowboy* premieres, launching the countrypolitan music movement.

1982

May 15 Ricky Skaggs joins the *Grand Ole Opry,* one of the first new country stars to be selected for membership.

1983

March 6 The Country Music Television (CMT) cable network goes on the air; the Nashville Network (TNN) will debut two years later (eventually, the two would merge).

1986

July 16 Dolly Parton opens her rural theme park, Dollywood.

1991

April 28 "This Is Garth Brooks" airs on NBC TV; Brooks is the first new country star honored with a network TV concert special.

1992

January 25 Emmylou Harris becomes a member of the *Grand Ole Opry.*

1993

July 3 Alison Krauss joins the *Grand Ole Opry,* the first bluegrass musician to be added to the cast in more than three decades.

1996

January 29 Garth Brooks refuses the "Entertainer of the Year" award at the American Music Awards ceremony, shocking his fans.

1997

April 14 Country.com, a major country music Web site, is launched.

May 3 Ernest Tubb's *Midnight Jamboree* radio program, aired right after the *Grand Ole Opry,* celebrates its 50th anniversary with a street party in downtown Nashville.

Appendix II

Selected Recordings

There are thousands of good country-music records; here's a select list of some recommended CDs by artists highlighted in this volume. In some cases where no current CD was in print, some better out-of-print cassette or album reissues that you might find in a local library have been listed. Remember that recordings are constantly being reissued and repackaged, so what's available today in one form will probably still be available tomorrow—but under a different name with a different catalog number.

Acuff, Roy. *Columbia Historic Edition.* (Columbia 39998. The best overview of Acuff's classic recordings, including four from his first 1936 session.)

Alabama. *Greatest Hits.* (RCA Nashville 61040. Collection of chart-toppers released in 1991.)

Anderson, Bill. *Bright Lights.* (Longhorn 3005. Cassette-only reissue of 1965 album, the only recording currently available from this period.)

Anderson, John. *Greatest Hits.* (Warner Brothers 25619. Chart-toppers from his late 1970s–early 1980s prime recordings.)

Anderson, Lynn. *Greatest Hits.* (Columbia 31641. Cassette-only reissue of her early-to-mid-1970s work.)

Anita Kerr Singers. *Music Is Her Name.* (Sony Music Special Products 48979.)

Arnold, Eddy. *My World.* (DCC 146. CD reissue (released in 1997) of 1965 album featuring "Make the World Go Away.")

Arnold, Eddy. *Pure Gold.* (RCA 58398. One of many budget CDs featuring Arnold's hits from the 1960s.)

Asleep at the Wheel. *Collision Course.* (EMI 53127. Reissue of 1978 Capitol album, the only album from this period currently on CD.)

Asleep at the Wheel. *A Tribute to Bob Wills and The Texas Playboys.* (Liberty/Capitol 81470. 1993 CD featuring new Nashville vocalists, such as Garth Brooks, Dolly Parton, Marty Stuart, and so on, performing Wills's hits backed by the band.)

Atkins, Chet. *Galloping Guitars: The Early Years.* (Bear Family 15174. CD box set of Atkins's classic recordings, before he became the king of the Nashville sound.)

Atkins, Chet. *The RCA Years.* (RCA 61095. A double-CD set.)

Autry, Gene. *Blues Singer.* (Columbia/Legacy 64987. Recordings made 1929–31 while Autry was still emulating the great Jimmie Rodgers.)

Autry, Gene. *The Essential.* (Columbia/Legacy 48957. Fine 1933–46 recordings, featuring swingin' western accompaniments, including previously unissued alternate takes for the collector.)

Bailes Brothers. *Early Radio, Vols. 1–3.* (Old Homestead 103, 104, 109. Radio broadcasts from the 1930s and 1940s reissued on this series of out-of-print LPs.)

Bailey, DeFord. *Harmonica Showcase.* (Matchbox 218. Out-of-print LP reissue of all eleven of Bailey's original recordings, plus five by D. H. "Bert" Bilbro, a white contemporary of his.)

Bailey, DeFord. *The Legendary DeFord Bailey.* (Revenant 208. Recordings from 1974 through 1976 featuring new versions of his legendary harmonica pieces, plus a few pieces played on five-string banjo and guitar.)

Bandy, Moe. *Honky Tonk Amnesia: The Best of Moe Bandy.* (Razor and Tie 2096. Comprehensive career retrospective of the Columbia years, including solo hits and the Moe and Joe tracks.)

Bare, Bobby. *Best Of Bobby Bare.* (Razor and Tie 2043. His 1960s and early 1970s hits collected on CD, including "Detroit City.")

Bare, Bobby. *Bobby Bare Sings Lullabies, Legends and Lies.* (Bear Family 15683. Reissue of 1973 RCA LP consisting entirely of Shel Silverstein compositions.)

Bellamy Brothers. *The Best of the Bellamy Brothers.* (Curb/CEMA 77554. Reissues cuts from the 1980s originally on MCA.)

Bellamy Brothers. *25 Year Collection,* Vols 1–2. (Delta Disc 7002/03. Remastered versions of the big hits of a quarter-century issued on the Bellamy Brothers' own label.)

Black, Clint. *Gospel Classic Series.* (RCA 67624. Budget reissue of 10 of the performer's best-known recordings.)

Black, Clint. *Put Yourself in My Shoes.* (RCA 2372. His best-known recording. Blackwood Quartet.)

Blue Sky Boys. *On Radio, Vols. 1–4.* (Copper Creek 120–21, 146–47. Radio shows 1946–47, including colorful skits and talk as well as songs.)

Bogguss, Suzie. *Country Classics.* (EMI 856038. Budget-priced hits compilation.)

Bond, Johnny. *Ten Little Bottles.* (Richmond 2155. Cassette-only reissue of Starday 333 from 1965 featuring the title hit.)

Bond, Johnny. *That Wild, Wicked but Wonderful West.* (King 147. Reissue of 1961 album of cowpoke songs, his first for Starday and among his best.)

Boone, Debby. *The Best Of Debby Boone.* (Curb/CEMA 77258.)

Boxcar Willie. *King of the Freight Train.* (MCA 20544. 1992. Features guest Willie Nelson on vocals.)

Boyd, Bill. *Bill Boyd and His Cowboy Ramblers.* (RCA/Bluebird 5503. Mid-1970s 2-LP reissue of classic sides, sadly out of print.)

Britt, Elton. *Ridin' with Elton.* (Soundies 4121. CD reissue of late 1930s and early 1940s 78s.)

Brooks, Garth. *No Fences.* (Liberty 93866. Brooks's breakthrough LP.)

Brooks and Dunn. *Greatest Hits.* (Arista 18852. The major hits through the mid-1990s.)

Brown, Junior. *Guit with It.* (Curb 77622. Major-label debut from 1993, with many of his best-known songs.)

Brown, Junior. *Mixed Bag.* (Curb 78719. Release from 2001 offering an eclectic mix of honky-tonk, rock, and country.)

Browns. *The Three Bells.* (Bear Family 15665. Eight CDs of prime Browns recordings, everything they did for RCA from the late 1950s through the late 1960s.)

Burnett and Rutherford. *Complete Record Works, 1926–30.* (Document 8025. CD reissue of all of their 78-rpm recordings, including some that Burnett made on his own or with other partners.)

Byrd, Tracey. *Keepers: Greatest Hits.* (MCA 70048. His 1990s hits.)

Campbell, Glen. *Best of the Early Years.* (Curb 77441. His 1960s Capitol hits.)

Carlisle Brothers. *Busy Body Boogie.* (Bear Family 15172. Band recordings from the 1950s, mostly led by Bill Carlisle.)

Carlisle Brothers. *Cliff Carlisle, Vols. 1 and 2.* (Old Timey 103, 104. Two out-of-print LPs reissuing Cliff's solo recordings and duets with his brother and Wilber Ball.)

Carpenter, Mary Chapin. *Party Doll.* (Columbia 68751. Compilation album from 1999, with live versions of her hits.)

Carson, Fiddlin' John. *Complete Recorded Works, 1926–34.* (Document 8014–8020. Seven CDs of everything Carson recorded, with brief notes.)

Carter Family. *Complete Recordings.* (Rounder 1064–1072. All of the Carter Family's original Victor recordings in chronological order.)

Carter Family. *On Border Radio.* (JEMF 101. Later recordings from their days working in Mexico.)

Carter, Wilf. *Cowboy Songs.* (Bear Family 15939. A second four-CD set.)

Carter, Wilf. *Prairie Legend.* (Bear Family 197542. A massive four-CD set containing everything he recorded between 1944 and 1959.)

Cash, Johnny. *American Recordings I, Unchained, American Recordings III.* (American 45520, 43097, 69691. Sessions from the 1990s produced by Rick Rubin that see Cash tackling everything from traditional ballads (with just his guitar and vocals on volume 1), through more rocking Tom Petty, Beck, and Soundgarden songs with full band accompaniments.)

Cash, Johnny. *Columbia Recordings 1958–1986.* (Columbia 40637. Anthology of Cash's biggest hits recorded during his most popular period as a performer.)

Cash, Johnny. *Complete Live at San Quentin.* (Columbia/Legacy 66017. Landmark live recording made in the late 1960s that helped give Johnny his tough-guy image. Additional tracks on reissue CD.)

Cash, Johnny. *The Sun Years.* (Rhino 70950. Reissue of classic 1950s Sun sessions; a good introduction to his pre-Columbia sound.)

Cash, Roseanne. *Hits 1979–1989.* (Columbia 45054. All the chart-toppers.)

Charles, Ray. *Greatest Country & Western Hits.* (DCC 040. Ray's great 1960s recordings for ABC that launched his country career.)

Chestnutt, Mark. *Top Marks.* (Edsel 646. His first 20 hit songs in one convenient package.)

Chuck Wagon Gang. *Columbia Historic Edition.* (Columbia 40152. Reissues of their finest recordings from 1936 to 1975.)

Clark, Roy. *The Best of Roy Clark.* (Curb 77395. Capitol recordings from the 1960s.)

Clark, Terri. *Fearless.* (Polygram 170157. Album from 2000 that brought her renewed attention.)

Clark, Terri. *Terri Clark.* (Mercury Nashville 526991. Debut album, released in 1995.)

Cline, Patsy. *Birth of a Star.* (Razor and Tie 2108. Radio recordings from the Arthur Godfrey show by a then-unknown Cline.)

Cline, Patsy. *Patsy Cline Story.* (MCA 4038. Originally a 2-LP set released by Decca after Cline's tragic death, this remains a good collection of her best-loved recordings.)

Coe, David Allan. *For the Record: The First Ten Years.* (Columbia 39585. Compilation of his 1970s Columbia recordings that gives a good retrospective of the hits.)

Collie, Mark. *Born and Raised in Black & White.* (MCA 10321. Second album, 1991.)

Collie, Mark. *Hardin County Line.* (MCA 42333. His first album.)

Collins, Tommy. *Leonard.* (Bear Family 15577. Five-CD set of Capitol, Columbia, and Morgan label recordings, with nicely illustrated booklet.)

Conley, Earl Thomas. *Best of Earl Thomas Conley.* (RCA 6700. Big numbers from his years at RCA.)

Cooley, Spade. *Spadella: The Essential.* (Columbia/Legacy 57392. Great, swinging recordings made just after World War II.)

Cowboy Copas. *Tragic Tales of Love and Life.* (King 714. Reissue of a late 1950s album.)

Craddock, Billy "Crash." *Boom, Boom Baby.* (Bear Family 15610. CD reissue of his late 1950s rockabilly recordings for Columbia.)

Craddock, Billy "Crash." *Crashes Smashes.* (Razor & Tie 2095. His 1970s–1980s hits from ABC, Capitol, and other labels.)

Crowell, Rodney. *Collection.* (Warner Brothers 25965. Selected from his first solo recordings.)

Cyrus, Billy Ray. *Some Gave All.* (Mercury 510635. His debut album, a best seller.)

Dalton, Lacy J. *Greatest Hits.* (Columbia 38883. Hits from the early 1980s produced by Billy Sherrill.)

Daniels, Charlie. *A Decade of Hits.* (Epic 38795. A greatest-hits collection with a few surprises.)

Davis, Jimmie. *Nobody's Darling But Mine: 1928–1937.* (Bear Family 15943. Five-CD set reissuing everything Davis recorded during these years, from hokum blues to more mainstream country.)

Davis, Jimmie. *You Are My Sunshine: 1937–1946.* (Bear Family 16216. This five-CD set completes Davis's recordings. These are in a much smoother country style than his earlier, bluesier records.)

Davis, Mac. *Best of Mac Davis.* (Razor & Tie 82216. His late 1960s and early 1970s recordings, when Davis was at his best as a singer and songwriter, if not as successful on the charts.)

Davis, Mac. *Greatest Hits.* (Columbia 36317. The mid-1970s hits.)

Davis, Skeeter. *Essential.* (RCA 66536. Twenty pop and country hits, essentially all of her best-known material from the early to mid-1960s.)

Davis, Skeeter. *Memories.* (Bear Family 15722. Two CDs containing all 60 recordings made by the Davis sisters, along with live cuts, radio appearances, and alternate takes.)

Davis, Skeeter. *She Sings, They Play.* (Rounder 3092. Recorded in 1986 with backup by NRBQ; a rockin' collection of remakes.)

Delmore Brothers. *Freight Train Boogie.* (Ace 455. Their post–World War II King recordings.)

Delmore Brothers. *Sand Mountain Blues.* (Country 110. Uptempo country boogie recordings originally issued by the King label between 1944 and 1949.)

Denver, John. *Rocky Mountain Collection.* (RRAC 66837. Two-CD set offering all the hits and a good career retrospective.)

Diamond Rio. *Super Hits.* (Arista 18884. Skimpy nine-track compilation of their big 1990s hits.)

Dickens, Little Jimmie. *Country Boy.* (Bear Family 15848. Four-CD set collecting all of Dickens's Columbia recordings made between 1949 and 1957, including previously unreleased gems.)

Diffie, Joe. *Greatest Hits.* (Epic 69137. Twelve of his big numbers through 1998.)

Dixie Chicks. *Fly.* (Monument 69678. Their best-selling second album.)

Duncan, Tommy. *Beneath a Neon Star in Honky Tonk.* (Bear Family 159572. Recordings from 1951 through 1953 in a more straight-country vein than his earlier work with Bob Wills.)

Duncan, Tommy. *Texas Moon.* (Bear Family 159072. Capitol and smaller label recordings from 1959, in a latter-day western swing style.)

Earle, Steve. *The Mountain.* (E Squared 51064. Features the Del McCrory band as accompaniment to new songs by Earle that reflect traditional sounds and themes.)

Edwards, Don. *Best of Don Edwards.* (Warner 46892. His best recordings from the mid-1990s for Warner Western.)

Edwards, Don. *Kin to the Wind.* (Shanachie 6051. Album from 2001 in homage to Marty Robbins.)

Edwards, Stoney. *Poor Folks Stick Together: The Best of Stoney Edwards.* (Razor & Tie 82169. Twenty tracks, some previously unissued, featuring most of his 1970s hits.)

Evans, Sara. *Born to Fly.* (RCA 67964. Her 2000 breakthrough album.)

Everly Brothers. *Classic Everly Brothers.* (Bear Family 15168. Includes some early radio shows, all of their early recordings for Columbia, and their four albums for Cadence, beautifully packaged as a four-CD set.)

Everly Brothers. *Songs Our Daddy Taught Us.* (Rhino 70212. Reissue of the classic LP.)

Fargo, Donna. *Best of Donna Fargo.* (Varese 5567. All of her hits.)

Fender, Freddy. *Canciones de Mi Barrio: The Roots of Tejano Rock.* (Arhoolie 366. Ideal label recordings from 1959 to 1964. Sung mostly in Spanish, these songs show a rockabilly/Tex Mex blend.)

Fender, Freddy. *The Freddy Fender Collection.* (Reprise 26638. One of many reissues of Fender's mid-1970s hits.)

Flatt and Scruggs. *Foggy Mountain Banjo.* (County 100. All-instrumental album from 1961 that was highly influential on the budding bluegrass revival.)

Flatt and Scruggs. *The Mercury Sessions, Vols. 1 and 2.* (Mercury 512644. Reissues all of their Mercury recordings made between 1948 and 1950. Also available on two CDs from Rounder with more complete notes.)

Foley, Red. *Complete Recordings, Vol 1: 1937–39.* (Document 6024. Early recordings by Foley with just guitar and vocal.)

Foley, Red. *Country Music Hall of Fame.* (MCA 10084. Selections from his Decca recordings.)

Ford, Tennessee Ernie. *Sixteen Tons of Country Boogie.* (Rhino 70975. Compilation of his better earlier recordings.)

Ford, Tennessee Ernie. *Ultimate Collection, 1949–65.* (Razor & Tie 2134. Two-CD compilation of all his best-known recordings.)

Flying Burrito Brothers. *Hot Burritos.* (A&M 490610. Two-CD set reissuing their first three albums in their entirety, plus other rare tracks.)

Forrester Sisters. *Talkin' about Men.* (Warner Brothers 26500.)

Foster and Lloyd. *Essential.* (BMG 66825. Two-CD compilation of the duo's biggest hits.)

Fricke, Janie. *Anthology.* (Renaissance 206. Twenty-six of her big chart hits from the 1970s and 1980s.)

Frizzell, Lefty. *Look What Thoughts Will Do.* (Columbia/Legacy 64880. Recordings 1950–63 with all the hits and some alternate takes, on a two-CD set.)

Gatlin Brothers. *Best Of the Gatlin Brothers.* (Columbia/Legacy 64760. Eighteen hits recorded from 1975 to 1988.)

Gayle, Crystal. *Certified Hits.* (Capitol 34499. CD reissue from 2001 of her 1970s recordings.)

Gentry, Bobbie. *Greatest Hits.* (Curb 77387. Mid-1960s Capitol recordings.)

Gibson, Don. *All Time Greatest Hits.* (RCA 2295. Similar to the Bear Family set, although less lavishly produced.)

Gibson, Don. *A Legend in My Time.* (Bear Family 15401. Classic RCA recordings originally made between 1957 and 1964, lovingly remastered, with excellent documentation.)

Gill, Vince. *Essential.* (RCA 66535. Collects his early 1980s tracks, before he was a major hit maker.)

Gill, Vince. *Souvenirs.* (MCA 11394. His later 1980s and early 1990s hits.)

Gimble, Johnny. *Texas Fiddle Collection.* (CMH 9027. Mid-1970s recordings with many of the old Texas Playboys on hand.)

Girls of the Golden Southwest. *Songs of the West.* (Old Homestead 143. This out-of-print LP reissues 1930s recordings, plus a 1963 reunion cut with Bradley Kincaid.)

Glaser Brothers. *The Outlaw.* (Bear Family 15606. Combines two LPs made for ABC/Dot in the late 1970s by Tompall Glaser.)

Gosdin, Vern. *The Best of Vern Gosdin.* (Warner Brothers 25775. Late 1970s recordings that were reissued after Gosdin's success in the late 1980s.)

Greene, Jack. *Twenty Greatest Hits.* (Deluxe 7808. Budget cassette-only release.)

Griffin, Rex. *Last Letter.* (Bear Family 159112. Three-CD set collecting all of Griffin's 1935–46 recordings, including radio transcriptions and 16 tunes by his brother, Buddy.)

Haggard, Merle. *Merle Haggard.* (Capitol 93181. Part of the Capitol Collector's Series, this CD gives a good overview of his career from the early 1960s through the 1970s.)

Haggard, Merle. *Merle Haggard's Greatest Hits.* (MCA 5386. Budget-priced compilation of 1980s recordings.)

Haggard, Merle. *More of the Best.* (Rhino 70917. Programmed to complement the Capitol release, this includes rarer tracks from Haggard's oeuvre.)

Haggard, Merle. *Same Train: Different Time.* (Bear Family 15740. Reissues Haggard's wonderful tribute to Jimmie Rodgers, along with some additional tracks not originally included.)

Hall, Tom T. *Greatest Hits, Vol. 1* and *Greatest Hits, Vol. 2.* (Mercury 824143, 824144. Cassette-only two-volume overview of his Mercury years.)

Hamblen, Stuart. *I Gotta Feeling.* (Roots of Country 211011. Gospel recordings of unknown vintage.)

Hamilton, George, IV. *Country Boy.* (BMG 39340. Reissue of budget-priced hits collection from his RCA years.)

Hamilton, George, IV. *1954–65.* (Bear Family 15773. Six-CD set of all of his recordings from this period, for the diehard fan.)

Harris, Emmylou. *Blue Kentucky Girl*. (Warner Brothers 3318. One of her better early albums.)

Harris, Emmylou. *Roses in the Snow*. (Warner Brothers 3422. Her most traditional album, with arrangements by Ricky Skaggs and picking by Skaggs, Jerry Douglas, Tony Rice, and other progressive bluegrass musicians.)

Hart, Freddie. *Best of Freddie Hart*. (CEMA 19030. Budget-priced 10-song collection of his Capitol label hits.)

Hawkins, Hawkshaw. *Hawksaw Hawkins*. (Bear Family 15539. His mid-1950s recordings for RCA, which pale in comparison to his earlier King sides.)

Hawkins, Hawkshaw. *Volume 1*. (King 587. CD reissue of 1958 LP that included recordings made from the late 1940s through the early 1950s, including his hit "Sunny Side of the Mountain.")

Highway 101. *Greatest Hits*. (Warner Brothers 26253. Best of the original band.)

Hill, Faith. *Breathe*. (Warner Brothers 47373. Album from 1999 featuring several massive mainstream hits.)

Hofner, Adolph. *South Texas Swing*. (Arhoolie 7029. Classic recordings from the late 1920s through the 1950s, mostly centering on his swing material.)

Hofner, Adolph. *Texas-Czech, Bohemian & Moravian Bands*. (Arhoolie/Folklyric 7026. Five tracks feature Hofner and group singing in Czech.)

Holly, Buddy. *From the Original Master Tapes*. (MCA 5540. Twenty of his most famous hits.)

Homer and Jethro. *America's Favorite Song Butchers*. (Razor & Tie 2130. Nice compilation of 20 of their best parodies.)

Hoosier Hot Shots. *Rural Rhythm*. (Columbia/Legacy 52735. Twenty-song compilation.)

Horton, Johnny. *American Original*. (Columbia 45071. Favorite hits on one CD.)

Houston, David. *American Originals*. (Columbia/Legacy 45074. 1963–70 recordings, including all the big hits.)

Husky, Ferlin. *Ferlin Husky*. (Capitol 91629. Overview of his country career.)

Jackson, Alan. *Greatest Hits*. (Arista 18801. The hits through the mid-1990s.)

Jennings, Waylon. *Only Daddy That'll Walk the Line*. (RCA 66299. Two-CD set documenting Jennings's recordings from the mid-1960s through the 1990s.)

Jennings, Waylon. *Waylon and Willie*. (RCA 8401. Cassette-only reissue of a classic collaboration.)

Jones, George. *The Best of George Jones*. (Rhino 70531. Recordings 1955–87 in a hard-country vein.)

Jones, George. *Greatest Hits, Vols. 1 and 2*. (Epic 34716, 48839. Jones with Tammy Wynette on their greatest weepers and honky-tonkers.)

Jones, Grandpa. *Grandpa Jones Story*. (CMH 9007. Cassette-only reissue of 1970s recordings, with Jones's wife Ramona on a couple of cuts.)

Judd, Cledus T. *I Stoled This Record*. (Razor & Tie 2825. The album that established Judd as a country comic star.)

Judds. *Collection*. (MCA 11583. Hits from Wynona Judds's first three solo albums from the 1990s.)

Keith, Toby. *Greatest Hits*. (Mercury 558962. The hits through 1998.)

Kershaw, Doug. *Best of Doug & Rusty Kershaw*. (Curb 77466. Twelve cuts made by Doug with his brother Rusty in the early 1960s for Hickory Records.)

Kershaw, Doug. *The Best of Doug Kershaw*. (Warner Brothers 25964. Kershaw's later solo recordings.)

King, Pee Wee. *Rompin', Stompin', Singin', Swingin'*. (Bear Family 15101. Great swinging sides from the mid-1940s through the mid-1950s.)

Krauss, Alison. *Now That I've Found You: A Collection*. (Rounder 285. Her first megaselling album.)

Kristofferson, Kris. *Jesus Was a Capricorn*. (Monument 47064. Another early album that shows Kristofferson at his best.)

Kristofferson, Kris. *Me and Bobby McGee*. (Monument 44351. His breakthrough early 1970s album.)

lang, k. d. *Absolute Torch and Twang*. (Sire 25877. Her breakthrough album.)

Lee, Brenda. *Anthology.* (MCA 10384. Two-CD set and a great booklet that gives a good overview of her career.)

Lee, Johnny. *The Best of Johnny Lee.* (Curb 77322. Later hits.)

Lewis, Jerry Lee. *Killer: The Mercury Years.* (Mercury 935, 938, 941. Three-volume set covering his 1960s country, rock, and gospel recordings for Mercury and its subsidiary, Smash.)

Lewis, Jerry Lee. *Milestones.* (Rhino 71499. Includes his great Sun hits, plus his better later recordings for Mercury.)

Louvin Brothers. *Close Harmony.* (Bear Family 15561. Eight CDs containing 220 songs recorded for Capitol and MGM between 1947 and 1965. Great notes by Charles Wolfe and rare pictures accompany these classic sides.)

Louvin Brothers. *Greatest Hits.* (Capitol 57222. Nine hits from the 1950s and 1960s on this cassette-only release.)

Louvin Brothers. *Radio Favorites, 1951–1957.* (Country Music Foundation 009. Air checks from the 1950s.)

Loveless, Patty. *Classics.* (Epic 69809. Hits of the Epic label years 1993–99.)

Loveless, Patty. *20th Century Masters.* (MCA 112352. Her hits recorded for MCA during the mid-1980s–early 1990s.)

Lovett, Lyle. *And His Large Band.* (MCA 42263. Lovett's third album (1989) with a western swing feel.)

Lovett, Lyle. *Step Inside This House.* (MCA 11831. Release from 1998 featuring songs by his favorite Texas songwriters.)

Lynn, Loretta. *Coal Miner's Daughter.* (MCA 936. Early 1970s collection released to cash in on the movie of the same name; representative of her work when she was at her peak.)

Lynn, Loretta. *Honky Tonk Girl.* (MCA 11070. Three-CD set covering her career from 1960 to 1988; the best introductory collection.)

Macon, Uncle Dave. *Go Long Mule.* (County 3505. Recordings from 1926–34, among Macon's best, with excellent sound quality.)

Macon, Uncle Dave. *Travelin' Down the Road.* (County/BMG 115. Bluebird sessions from 1935.)

Maddox, Rose. *America's Most Colorful Hillbilly Band.* (Arhoolie 391. Reissues of wonderful Maddox Brothers and Rose Maddox recordings cut between 1946 and 1951.)

Mainer, J. E. *J. E. Mainer's Crazy Mountaineers.* (Old Timey 106, 107. Two out-of-print LPs reissuing early recordings by Mainer's band.)

Mandrell, Barbara. *The Best of Barbara Mandrell.* (MCA 31107. Her best mid-1970s recordings.)

Mandrell, Barbara. *Super Hits.* (Sony 68507. Early 1970s recordings.)

Maphis, Joe. *Fire on the Strings.* (Sony 62148. Reissue of 1957 Columbia album.)

Maphis, Joe. *Flying Fingers.* (Bear Family 16103. Columbia recordings from the mid-to-late 1950s.)

Mattea, Kathy. *A Collection of Hits.* (Mercury 84230. The hits up to 1990.)

McBride, Martina. *Greatest Hits.* (RCA 67012. Compilation album from 2001.)

McCall, C. W. *Greatest Hits.* (Polydor 825793. Cassette-only reissue of mid-1970s and early 1980s recordings.)

McCoy, Charlie. *The Fastest Harp in the South.* (Monument 44354. Reissue of 1960s recordings.)

McCoy, Charlie. *Harpin' the Blues.* (Monument 47087. Tribute to Chicago blues harmonica masters.)

McDaniel, Mel. *Greatest Hits.* (Alliance 46867. Reissues 1970s Capitol recordings.)

McDonald, Skeets. *Don't Let the Stars Get in Your Eyes.* (Bear Family 15937. Complete 1950s Capitol recordings in a lavish boxed set.)

McEntire, Reba. *Greatest Hits.* (MCA 5979. The hits through 1987.)

McEntire, Reba. *Greatest Hits, Vol. 2.* (MCA 10906. The hits 1987–93.)

McEntire, Reba. *Greatest Hits, Vol. 3.* (MCA 170202. The hits 1994–2001.)

McGraw, Tim. *Greatest Hits.* (Curb 77978. Fifteen big ones from the 1990s.)

Messina, Jo Dee. *Burn.* (Curb 77977. Her breakthrough third album of 2000.)

Miller, Roger. *The Best of Roger Miller, Vols. 1 and 2.* (Mercury 848977, 512646. His Smash recordings from the 1960s. The first volume focuses more on country styles and the second on his pop hits, including "King of the Road.")

Milsap, Ronnie. *40 Greatest Hits.* (Virgin 48871. Actually has 43 tracks (two newly recorded), drawn from his RCA recordings.)

Monroe, Bill. *Essential Bill Monroe & The Monroe Brothers.* (RCA 67450. 25 RCA/Bluebird recordings from the 1930s-early 1940s featuring the Monroe Brothers and Monroe's early Bluegrass Boys band.)

Monroe, Bill. *Essential, 1945–48.* (Columbia/Legacy 52478. Two-CD set of all the Columbia recordings, although 16 of the 40 tracks are represented by alternate takes rather than the better-known originals. Includes the classic Flatt and Scruggs/Chubby Wise band.)

Montana, Patsy. *Columbia Historic Edition.* (Columbia 38909. Reissues her classic 1930s recordings.)

Montgomery, Melba. *Golden Moments.* (Classic World 2100. Ten-song budget compilation of hits.)

Morgan, George. *Roomful of Roses.* (Razor & Tie 82109. Good introduction to Morgan's hits of the 1940s and 1950s.)

Mullican, Moon. *Moonshine Jamboree.* (Ace 458. King recordings from 1946 to 1954, a great introduction to Mullican's best work.)

Mullican, Moon. *Showboy Special.* (West Side 800. His first recordings for King, cut in 1946, mixing western swing with honky-tonk weepers.)

Mullican, Moon. *Sings His All Time Hits.* (King 555. Various recordings from the King archives.)

Murphey, Michael Martin. *Best of Country.* (Curb 77336. His early to mid-1970s hits.)

Murray, Anne. *The Best . . . So Far.* (Capitol 31158. Twenty-song collection of hits.)

Nelson, Willie. *Early Years.* (Scotti Bros 75437. Demos made in the early 1960s before Nelson had a recording contract.)

Nelson, Willie. *Essential.* (RCA 66590. His RCA label recordings made between 1965 and 1971.)

Nelson, Willie. *Nite Life.* (Rhino 70987. Early, hard-to-find tracks.)

Nelson, Willie. *Red Headed Stranger.* (Columbia Legacy 63589. Reissue of the 1975 concept album.)

Nelson, Willie. *Revolutions of Time.* (Sony 85667. Three-CD compilation of Columbia recordings made between 1975 and 1993, Nelson's most successful years.)

Newman, Jimmy C. *Bop A Hula-Diggy Liggy Lo.* (Bear Family 15469. Two-CD compilation of his Dot recordings made between 1953 and 1958, featuring Cajun-style country and rockabilly.)

Nickel Creek. *Nickel Creek.* (Sugar Hill 3909. Debut album (2000), heavily promoted on country music TV.)

Nitty Gritty Dirt Band. *Twenty Years of Dirt.* (Warner Brothers 25382. Best of collection covering recordings from 1966 to 1986.)

Nitty Gritty Dirt Band. *Will the Circle Be Unbroken.* (EMI 46589. Reissue of the famous three-LP set on two CDs.)

Oslin, K. T. *Greatest Hits: Songs from an Aging Sex Bomb.* (RCA 662277. Compilation of her best-known work from the late 1980s.)

Owens, Buck. *The Buck Owens Collection (1959–1990).* (Rhino 71016. Three CDs covering Owens's entire career; great sound and 76-page illustrated booklet by country authority Rich Hierzle.)

Paisley, Brad. *Part II.* (Arista 67008. His second album, featuring four major hits.)

Parton, Dolly. *The RCA Years, 1957–1986.* (RCA 66127. Two-CD set featuring 30 songs from her early tracks to her countrypolitan heyday.)

Parton, Dolly. *Trio.* (Warner Brothers 25491. With Linda Ronstadt and Emmylou Harris; pleasant, if understated.)

Paycheck, Johnny. *Take This Job and Shove It.* (Richmond 2300. Reissue of his most famous album, with the big hit title cut.)

Perkins, Carl. *Original Sun Greatest Hits.* (Rhino 75890. Sixteen of his classic Sun recordings.)

Perkins, Carl. *Restless.* (Columbia/Legacy 48986. Mostly teen-pop material from Columbia cut in the late 1950s and early 1960s, although it also includes tracks from late 1970s sessions with NRBQ.)

Pierce, Webb. *King of the Honky Tonk.* (Country Music Foundation 19. Compilation of his biggest Decca hits from the 1950s.)

Price, Ray. *The Essential.* (Columbia Legacy 48532. His best recordings cut between 1952 and 1961.)

Pride, Charley. *Super Hits.* (RCA 66947. Budget compilation giving an overview of the hits.)

Rabbitt, Eddie. *All Time Greatest Hits.* (Warners 26467. His biggest 1970s hits.)

Rascal Flatts. *Rascal Flatts.* (Lyric Street/Hollywood 166011. Debut album (2000) that soared up the charts.)

Reed, Jerry. *RCA Country Legends.* (Buddha 99776. Sixteen-track compilation of his late 1960s–early 1970s country recordings for RCA.)

Reeves, Jim. *Singles, 1953–60.* (BMG 57118. Two-CD set including all of his hits from the early period cut for RCA.)

Rich, Charlie. *American Originals.* (Columbia 45073. Drawn from his years with Epic, from the late 1960s through his mid-1970s.)

Riley, Jeannie C. *Harper Valley PTA: The Very Best.* (Collectables 6022. Twenty-four prime 1968–74 recordings including most of the hits.)

Rimes, LeAnn. *Blue.* (Curb 77821. Her 1996 debut disc, and her most country in orientation.)

Ritter, Tex. *Country Music Hall of Fame.* (MCA 10188. Sixteen of his Decca recordings from the mid-1930s; not his best-known work, but of interest to fans and collectors.)

Robbins, Marty. *The Essential Marty Robbins.* (Columbia/Legacy 48537. Two-CD set covering his career from 1951 to 1982.)

Rodgers, Jimmie. *Singing Brakeman.* (Bear Family 15540. Lavishly produced six-CD set with notes by Nolan Porterfield; all of his Victor recordings, 145 songs in all. The same material was issued on six individual CDs by Rounder Records without the booklet.)

Rogers, Kenny. *Through the Years.* (Capitol 33183. Four-CD, 80-song compilation covering Rodgers's complete career.)

Rogers, Roy. *The Best of Roy Rogers.* (Curb 77392. Recordings from the 1950s and 1960s.)

Sawyer Brown. *Greatest Hits.* (Curb 77578. The hits up to 1990.)

Sawyer Brown. *Greatest Hits, 1990–95.* (Curb 77689. Picks up with the rest of the band's chart makers.)

Shenandoah. *15 Favorites.* (Capitol 96392. The group's hits from 1992 to 1996; 12 hits and three bonus tracks.)

Shenandoah. *Greatest Hits.* (Columbia 44885. Their Columbia hits up to 1992.)

Skaggs, Ricky. *Country Gentleman: The Best of Ricky Skaggs.* (Epic/Legacy 64883. Two-CD set of his Epic recordings made between 1981 and 1991.)

Smith, Carl. *The Essential Carl Smith, 1950–1956.* (Columbia/Legacy 47996. His best recordings.)

Smith, Connie. *Super Hits.* (RCA 67491. Anthology of her mid-1960s recordings.)

Snow, Hank. *Essential.* (RCA 66931. Twenty of his better-known recordings.)

Sons of the Pioneers. *Columbia Historic Edition.* (Columbia 37439. Drawn from one very fine 1937 session for the budget ARC label.)

Sons of the Pioneers. *Country Music Hall of Fame.* (MCA 10090. Covers their best recordings from 1934 to 1941.)

Sprague, Carl. *Classic Cowboy Songs.* (Bear Family 15456. Recordings from 1972.)

Stanley Brothers. *Best of the Stanley Brothers.* (Mercury 17022. Great mid-1950s recordings.)

Stanley Brothers. *Classic Bluegrass.* (Rebel 1109. Recordings by Ralph Stanley and the Clinch Mountain Boys from 1971 to 1973.)

Stanley Brothers. *Columbia Sessions.* (Columbia/Legacy 53798. The Stanleys' first major label recordings from the late 1940s through the early 1950s.)

Starr, Kay. *Capitol Collectors Series.* (Capitol 94080. Her original 1950s hit recordings.)

Statler Brothers. *The Best of Statler Brothers, Vols. 1 & 2.* (Mercury 822524, 822525. Their biggest hits from the early to later 1970s.)

Statler Brothers. *Flowers on the Wall: The Essential Statler Brothers.* (Columbia/Legacy 64764. Eighteen tracks from the mid-to-later 1960s, including pop and gospel numbers.)

Stoneman, Ernest. *1928 Edison Recordings.* (County 35102. Twenty-two tracks cut by Stoneman with full string band accompaniment.)

Strait, George. *Greatest Hits Vols. 1 & 2.* (MCA 5567, 42304. The hits through the early 1990s.)

Strait, George. *Latest Greatest Straitest Hits.* (MCA 170100. Hits from the 1990s.)

Street, Mel. *Greatest Hits.* (Deluxe 7824. Cassette-only reissue of hits from unknown sources.)

Stringbean. *A Salute to Uncle Dave Macon.* (Hollywood 309. Reissue of a Starday LP from 1963, a collection of songs associated with the famous country banjoist.)

Stuart, Marty. *Marty Party Hit Pack.* (MCA 11204. Collection released in 1995 of his late 1980s through mid-1990s hits.)

Supernaw, Doug. *Encore Collection.* (BMG 44518. Hits through 1976.)

Thompson, Hank. *Best of Hank Thompson.* (Varese 5747. His later recordings for MCA, Dot, and Warner Brothers made between 1966 and 1979.)

Thompson, Hank. *Vintage.* (Capitol 36901. Twenty of his best sides from 1947 to 1961.)

Tillis, Mel. *Greatest Hits.* (Curb 77482. Recordings from the late 1970s and early 1980s of varying quality.)

Tillis, Pam. *Greatest Hits.* (Arista 18836. Most of her 1990s hits after her Warner Brothers years.)

Tillis, Pam. *Super Hits.* (Warner Brothers 47789. Late 1980s through 1992 hits, including "Maybe It Was Memphis.")

Tippin, Aaron. *Greatest Hits . . . and Then Some.* (RCA 67427. His early 1990s hits.)

Travis, Merle. *Folk Songs of the Hills.* (Bear Family 15636. The great late 1940s folk sessions cut for Capitol and a lesser-known return to the folk style in 1963. The 1947 material is also reissued by Capitol, along with some radio transcriptions.)

Travis, Merle. *The Best of Merle Travis.* (Razor & Tie 82214. Twenty of his best numbers from 1946 to 1953, including instrumentals and songs.)

Travis, Randy. *Storms of Life.* (Warner Brothers 25435. Debut album from 1986, still a classic.)

Tritt, Travis. *Greatest Hits—From the Beginning.* (Warner Brothers 46001. His biggest hits through the mid-1990s.)

Tubb, Ernest. *Country Music Hall of Fame.* (MCA 10086. Great cuts recorded from 1941 to 1965.)

Tucker, Tanya. *Super Hits.* (Sony 69065. Early recordings from Tucker's teenage years.)

Tucker, Tanya. *20 Greatest Hits.* (Capitol 22093. Good career retrospective, although primarily focusing on her hits between 1986 and 1997.)

Twain, Shania. *Shania Twain.* (Mercury 514422. Debut album from 1993.)

Twitty, Conway. *The Best of Conway Twitty.* (Mercury 574. Reissues his 1950s hard rockers.)

Twitty, Conway. *Greatest Hits, Vols. 1 and 2.* (MCA 31239, 31240. His country recordings from the mid-1960s through the mid-1970s.)

Urban, Keith. *Keith Urban.* (Capitol 97591. Debut album (1999) that has produced hits through 2001.)

Van Shelton, Ricky. *Greatest Hits Plus.* (Columbia 52753. The hits to 1992.)

Wagoner, Porter. *The Essential Porter Wagoner.* (RCA 66934. Wagoner's solo hits primarily from the 1960s.)

Wagoner, Porter. *The Essential Porter Wagoner and Dolly Parton.* (RCA 66958. Twenty hits for the harmonious pair.)

Walker, Clay. *Greatest Hits.* (Giant 24700. The best from his first four albums.)

Wariner, Steve. *Greatest Hits, Vols. 1 and 2.* (MCA 42032, 10357. The first collection draws on his recordings from 1985 to 1987, the second takes him up to 1991.)

Wells, Kitty. *Country Music Hall of Fame.* (MCA 10081. Reissues Decca recordings cut between 1952 and 1965, including all of her hits in the heartache genre.)

White, Bryan. *Greatest Hits.* (Elektra 47890. Compilation released in 2000 of his 1990s hits.)

Whitley, Keith. *Essential Keith Whitley.* (RCA 66853. Twenty-song compilation of his major hits.)

Williams, Hank. *40 Greatest Hits.* (Polydor 233. Good overall introduction to his MGM/Sterling label recordings.)

Williams, Hank. *Complete Hank Williams.* (Mercury 536077. 10-CD, 224-track compilation of Williams's studio recordings and demos; doesn't include some live and other material available on other Mercury/Polydor releases. Beautiful packaging with great annotation by Colin Escott.)

Williams, Hank. *Rare Demos: First to Last.* (Country Music Foundation 067. Reissues of Williams performing just with his own guitar accompaniment, with great notes by Bob Pinson; originally on two LPs.)

Williams, Hank, Jr. *Bocephus Box 2000.* (Curb/Carbicorn 77940. His rowdy post-MGM career, covering recordings from 1979 to 1999. Originally issued in 1992, the set has been enlarged to cover the rest of the century, although Williams was just barely active during the later 1990s.)

Williams, Hank, Jr. *Living Proof.* (Mercury 320. Traces his MGM recording career from 1964 to 1975, when finally he began to emerge from out of the shadow of his father and take on his own personality.)

Wills, Bob. *Anthology: 1935–1973.* (Rhino 70744. Two-CD set spanning Wills's entire recording career.)

Wills, Bob. *The Essential Bob Wills.* (Columbia/Legacy 48958. Prewar recordings by Wills and his biggest bands.)

Wills, Bob. *The Longhorn Recordings.* (Bear Family 15689. Twenty-three recordings cut by Wills in 1964, including 12 wonderful solo old-time fiddle tunes.)

Womack, Lee Ann. *I Hope You Dance.* (MCA 170099. Breakthrough album (2002) that launched Womack into stardom.)

Wynette, Tammy. *Tears of Fire: 25th Anniversary Collection.* (Epic 52741. A complete overview of her career from a 1964 demo of "You Can Steal Me" through her early 1990s comeback with technorockers KLF.)

Yearwood, Trisha. *Songbook.* (MCA 70011. The hits through 1997.)

Yoakam, Dwight. *Guitars, Cadillacs, etc.* (Reprise 25372. His debut LP on a major label that first introduced his sound to a wide audience.)

Young, Faron. *The Capitol Years.* (Bear Family 15493. Five CDs featuring 157 songs, with notes by Colin Escott.)

Appendix III

Web Sites

Individual artists have "official" Web sites, and there are also many semiofficial and fan sites on line. These can be found using standard search engines (Google, Yahoo, etc.). Following are some useful sites of general interest.

All Music
http://www.allmusic.com
Massive database of artists in all musical styles searchable by artist, album name, or song.

Alt-Country
http://www.nodepression.com
Web site for magazine devoted to alt-country (contemporary country music).

Country Music Association
http://www.CMAworld.com
Official Web site.

Country Music Foundation (CMF)
http://www.countryhalloffame.com
Official Web site for the CMF, which administers the Country Music Hall of Fame.

Country Music Television (CMT)
http://www.country.com
Features news of the day, artist bios, suggested recordings, photos, and other useful material.

Great American Country (GACTV)
http://www.countrystars.com
Similar in style and content to the CMT site.

Rough Stock
http://www.roughstock.com
Offers overall narrative history of country music by genre; nicely written.

Southern Folklife Collection
http://www.lib.unc.edu/mss/sfc1
Web site for the Southern Folklife Collection at the University of North Carolina; indexes the collection that includes photographs and other materials related to traditional country music.

Appendix IV

DVDs and Videos

Dropcap Here is a selection of country DVDs that are worth viewing. Collections of videos by current stars have been avoided in order to focus instead either on documentaries, historic performances, or concerts.

At Town Hall Party (Bear Family). Various 1958–59 shows on six discs (to date) with a wide variety of Southern California country stars.

Bill Monroe: The Father of Bluegrass Music (Winstar Home Entertainment). Nice 1993 documentary with historic clips, interviews with Monroe and his contemporaries, and performances.

Chet Atkins: Rare Performances 1976–1995 (Vestapol). Later career clips from various sources of the country guitar master.

Country Music Classics (Koch Video). Series of DVDs featuring performances from the early 1950s. The artists are accompanied by their road bands (often their recordings of the time were more heavily produced) so they make for interesting viewing and listening. Releases include Webb Pierce and Chet Atkins, Marty Robbins and Ernest Tubb, and Jim Reeves and Ray Price.

Doc Watson: Rare Performances 1963–1981 (Vestapol). Nice two-disc collection from various sources.

Down from the Mountain (Artisan Entertainment). Live concert featuring the artists who performed on the *O Brother, Where Art Thou?* film soundtrack, including Emmylou Harris, John Hartford, Ralph Stanley, and others.

Halloween at Town Hall Party (Bear Family). 1959 broadcast featuring performances by Joe Maphis, Skeets McDonald, Tex Ritter, the Browns, and others.

High Lonesome: The Story of Bluegrass Music (Shanachie). Documentary film from the late 1990s with historic and recent footage of key figures in bluegrass music.

Honky Tonk Blues (Universal Home Video). Wonderful 90-minute documentary (aired as part of the *American Masters* series on PBS in 2004 in a cut version) produced by Colin Escott on the life and times of the great singer Hank Williams.

Honky Tonk Girl (Kulture). Nice documentary about Loretta Lynn.

Johnny Cash at Town Hall Party (Bear Family). Performances from 1958–59 recorded for the famous Southern California TV program showing Cash at his early prime.

Legends of Country Guitar (Vestapol). Various clips of Chet Atkins, Doc Watson, and Merle Travis.

Legends of Flat Picking Guitar (Vestapol). Features Doc Watson, Tony Rice, Norman Blake, and Dan Crary in recent performances.

Legends of Western Swing Guitar (Vestapol). Footage from the 1940s to today featuring Eldon Shamblin, Jim Boyd, Junior Banard, Muriel "Zeke" Campbell, and others.

Marty Robbins at Town Hall Party (Bear Family). Late 1950s TV performances.

Merle Travis: Rare Performances 1946–81 (Vestapol; two discs). Historic footage from various sources, including solo performances from 1951 TV broadcasts.

On the Mississippi (Red Video). Conway Twitty's 1982 TV special shows him back home on a steamboat, performing with Jerry Lee Lewis and Charley Pride, and singing his current hits.

Remembering Patsy (Kultur Video). Nice 1993 documentary on the life and times of Patsy Cline, with performance clips and interviews with family, fellow musicians, and friends.

Road to Nashville (Rhino Video). Film from 1976 with a loose plot serving as a framework for performances by Marty Robbins, Johnny Cash, Waylon Jennings, and Connie Smith, among others.

Times Ain't Like They Used to Be: Early Rural & Popular American Music (Yazoo Video). Historic film clips featuring Jimmie Rodgers, Bob Wills, and others.

Glossary of Music Terms

a cappella   Literally "in the chapel." Used generally to describe unaccompanied vocal music.

accent   Extra emphasis given to a note in a musical composition.

alto   (1) The lowest female voice, below mezzo-soprano and SOPRANO. (2) In musical instruments, an instrument with a range of either a fourth or fifth below the standard range; the viola is tuned a fifth below the violin, for example. (3) The alto CLEF (also known as the C clef) used for notating music for alto instruments and voices.

arpeggio   A broken CHORD; the notes of the chord played in succession, rather than simultaneously.

ballad   (1) In folk traditions, a multiversed song that tells a narrative story, often based on historic or mythological figures. (2) In popular music, a slow lament, usually on the subject of lost love.

bar   See MEASURE.

baritone   (1) The male voice situated between the BASS (lowest) and TENOR (highest). (2) Baritone is sometimes used to describe musical instruments that play an octave below the ordinary range.

barrelhouse   An aggressive two-handed piano style suitable for a piano player working in a noisy room, a bar, or a brothel. The same word is used to describe such a venue.

bass   (1) The lowest male vocal range. (2) The deepest-sounding musical instrument within a family of instruments, such as the bass violin. (3) The lowest instrumental part.

beat   The basic rhythmic unit of a musical composition. In common time (most frequently used in popular music), there are two basic beats to the measure; the first is given more emphasis, and therefore is called the *strong* beat, the second is less emphasized and thus is called the *weak* beat.

bebop   A form of jazz that developed in the late 1940s and 1950s played by small ensembles or combos, which emphasized rapid playing and unusual rhythmic accents. Many bebop musicians took common CHORD PROGRESSIONS of popular songs and composed new melodies for them, allowing the accompanying instruments (piano-bass-drums) a form that could be easily followed while the melody parts (trumpet, saxophone) improvised.

bending notes   Technique used on stringed instruments where the musician pushes against a string with the left hand, causing the note to rise in pitch. On an electric guitar, which has light gauge strings, the pitch may rise as much as a whole tone (two frets).

big band jazz   A popular jazz style of the 1930s and 1940s featuring larger ensembles divided into parts (brass, reeds, rhythm). Riffs, or short melodic phrases, were traded back and forth between the melody instruments.

"Blue Moon" progression   A sequence of four chords associated with the song "Blue Moon," popularized in 1935 by Benny Goodman and others. The chords are I, VI minor, IV (or II minor), and V. In the key of C, they would be: C, A minor, F (or D minor), and G. Each chord might be held for two, four, or eight beats, but they appear in sequence. The progression is very common in doo-wop music.

blues   An African-American vocal and instrumental style that developed in the late 19th to early 20th centuries. The "blues scale" usually features a flattened third and seventh, giving the music a recognizable sound. The classic 12-bar blues features three repeated lines of four bars each, with the first two lines of lyrics repeated, followed by a contrasting line. The chord progression is also fairly standardized, although many blues musicians have found ways to extend and improvise around these rules.

boogie-woogie   Boogie-woogie is a way of playing BLUES on the piano that was first recorded in the 1920s. Its chief characteristic is the left-hand pattern, known as eight-to-the-bar (a note is played on every one of the eight possible eighth notes in a measure of four beats), which provides a propulsive rhythm that seems to have been influenced by the sound of trains. Boogie-woogie became a fad after the 1938 and 1939 From Spirituals to Swing concerts, and was adapted into big band swing, pop, and country music. From there it became part of ROCK 'N' ROLL. To boogie in general slang (as in "I've got to boogie now") means to leave somewhere in a hurry. In musical slang, to boogie means to maintain a repetitive blues-based rhythmic foundation, particularly one associated with the style of John Lee Hooker, similar to the figure in his song, "Boogie Chillen."

brass   Traditionally, musical instruments whose bodies are made out of brass (although sometimes today they are made out of other metals). Usually used to refer to members of the horn family, including trumpets and trombones.

British invasion   Popular groups of the 1960s that dominated the American pop charts. The Beatles led the charge in 1964, but were quickly followed by many soundalike bands, as well as more distinctive groups like the Rolling Stones, The Who, the Kinks, and many others.

cadence   A melodic or harmonic phrase usually used to indicate the ending of a PHRASE or a complete musical composition.

capo   A metal or elastic clamp placed across all of the strings of a guitar that enables players to change key, while still using the same chord fingerings as they would use without the capo.

CD (compact disc)   A recording medium developed in the mid-1980s that enables music to be encoded as digital information on a small disc, and that is "read" by a laser. Various forms of CDs have been developed since to contain higher sound quality and/or other materials (photographs, moving images, etc.)

chord   The basic building block of HARMONY, chords usually feature three or more notes played simultaneously.

chord progression   A sequence of chords, for example in the key of C: C, F, and G7.

chorus   Most commonly used in popular songs to indicate a repeated STANZA that features the same melody and lyrics that falls between each verse. Perhaps because members of the audience might "sing-along" with this part of the song, it came to be known as the chorus (a chorus literally being more than one voice singing at the same time). See VERSE.

clef   The symbol at the beginning of a notated piece of music indicating the note values assigned to each line of the STAFF. The three most common clefs used in popular music are the G clef (or treble clef), usually used to notate the melody; the F clef (or bass clef), usually used for harmony parts; and the less-frequently seen C clef (or tenor clef), used for notating instruments with special ranges, most usually the viola.

country and western (C&W)   A category developed by the music industry in the late 1940s to distinguish folk, cowboy, and other musical styles aimed at the white, rural, working-class listener (as opposed to R&B, aimed at black audiences, and pop, aimed at urban whites). Later, the *western* was dropped.

cover versions The music business has always been competitive, and even before recordings were possible, many artists would do the same song, as can be seen by the multiple editions of the sheet music for certain hits, each with a different artists' photo on the front. In the 1950s the practice of copying records was rampant, particularly by bigger companies, which had more resources (publicity, distribution, influence) and which used their artists to cover songs from independent labels that had started to show promise in the marketplace. A true cover version is one that attempts to stay close to the song on which it is based. Interpretations of existing songs are often called covers, but when artistry is involved in giving an individual treatment to an existing song, that effort is worthy of being considered more than a cover version.

crescendo A gradual increase in volume indicated in music notation by a triangle placed on its side below the STAFF, like this <.

crossover record A record that starts in one musical category, but has a broader appeal and becomes popular in another category. For example B. B. King's "The Thrill Is Gone" started out as an R&B record, but crossed over to the pop category.

cut a record Recording a record.

decrescendo A gradual decrease in volume indicated in music notation by a triangle placed on its side below the STAFF, as in >.

Delta blues Blues music originating in the Mississippi Delta and typically featuring the use of a slide, intense vocal performances, an aggressive, sometimes strummed guitar style with bass notes "popped" by the thumb for a snapping sound.

diatonic harmony The CHORDs implicit in the major scale. The sequence of triads is I major, II minor, III minor, IV major, V major, VI minor, and VII diminished. Because the diminished chord is unstable, it is virtually never used in this context. Because major chords are more common, many songs use only them: I, IV, and V.

disco A dance form of the 1970s developed in urban dance clubs, consisting of a heavily accented, repeated rhythmic part.

Dixieland jazz Jazz style popularized in New Orleans at the beginning of the 20th century by small combos, usually including three horns: a clarinet, a trumpet, and a trombone. The rhythm section includes a banjo, a tuba, a simple drum set, and a piano, and occasionally a saxophone, string bass, or guitar is added.

DIY (Do-It-Yourself) An emphasis on homemade music and recordings, which began with the PUNK movement but outlived it. The message was that everyone could make their own music, and record and market it on their own, using simple, inexpensive instruments and technology.

DJ (deejay) The person who plays records at a dance club or on a radio station. DJs began to create musical compositions by stringing together long sequences of records, and then further manipulated them using techniques such as backspinning (rapidly spinning a turntable backward while a record is being played) and scratching (moving the turntable back and forth rapidly to emphasize a single note or word).

DVD (digital video disc) A form of optical disc designed to hold video or film, but also sometimes used for higher-quality music reproduction. See CD (COMPACT DISC).

easy listening See MOR (MIDDLE-OF-THE-ROAD).

eighth note See NOTE VALUES.

electronic music Music created using electronic means, including SYNTHESIZERS, SEQUENCERS, tape recorders, and other nontraditional instruments.

falsetto A high register vocal sound producing a light texture. Often used in soul music.

finger-picking A style of guitar playing that keeps a steady bass with the thumb while playing melody on the treble strings.

flat A symbol in music NOTATION indicating that the note should be dropped one-half step in PITCH. Compare SHARP.

flat pick A pick held between the thumb and first finger of the right hand that is very effective for playing rapid single note passages or heavy rhythm guitar.

flip side   The other side of a 45 rpm record, typically the nonhit song.

folk music   Traditional music that is passed down from one person to another within a family or a community. Often the original composer or songwriter is unknown.

45   A record that plays at 45 revolutions per minute (rpm). Developed in the 1950s by RCA, the 45 or "single" was the main way of promoting individual songs on the pop and R&B charts through the CD era.

gospel music   Composed black religious music.

half note   See NOTE VALUES.

harmony   Any musical composition with more than one part played simultaneously. In popular music the harmony is usually the accompanying part, made up of CHORDs, that complement the MELODY.

heavy metal   Rock style of the mid-1970s and later that emphasized a thunderous sound, simplified chord progressions, subject matter aimed to appeal to teenage boys (primarily), and flamboyant stage routines. Other variants (death metal, speed metal) developed over the coming decades.

hip-hop   The music (rap), dance (breakdancing), and visual expression (graffiti art) originating in urban areas in the mid-1970s.

holy blues   Songs that combine religious words with blues melodies and accompaniments.

hook   A recurrent musical or lyric phrase that is designed to "hook" the listener into a particular song or record. It is often also the title of a song.

interval   The space between two PITCHES. The first note of a SCALE is considered the first interval; the next note, the second; and so on. Thus, in a C major scale, an "E" is considered a third, and a G a "fifth." The I-III-V combination makes up a major CHORD.

jukebox   A machine designed to play records. Commonly found in bars (known as "juke joints" in the South), these replaced live music by the mid-1950s, and were a major means of promoting hit records. Customers dropped a "nickel in the jukebox" to hear their favorite song.

key   Indicates the range of notes (or SCALE) on which a composition is based.

key signature   The symbol at the beginning of a piece of notation that indicates the basic KEY of the work.

looping   Repeating a short musical PHRASE or RHYTHM. SEQUENCERS can be programmed to "loop" or repeat these parts indefinitely.

LP   A "long-playing" record, playing at 33 revolutions per minute (rpm). Developed in the late 1940s, the LP enabled record companies to present more or longer compositions on a single disc (the previous time limit of 78s was 3 to 5 minutes, while an LP could hold 20 to 25 minutes per side).

major   One of the two primary SCALEs used in popular music. The relation between the seven notes in the major scale is whole step (WS)-WS-half step (HS)-WS-WS-WS-HS. Each scale step has a related CHORD defining major harmony. Compare MINOR.

measure   A unit of musical time in a composition defined by the time signature. In 4/4 time, for example, each measure consists of four beats (and a quarter note is equal to one beat). The bar line (a vertical line across all five lines of the STAFF) indicates the beginning and end of a measure.

melody   Two or more musical tones played in succession, called the "horizontal" part of a musical composition because the notes move horizontally across the staff (as opposed to the HARMONY which is called the "vertical" part because the harmony notes are stacked vertically on the staff). In popular music the melody of a song is the most memorable part of the composition.

meter   The repeated pattern of strong and weak rhythmic pulses in a piece of music. For example, in a waltz, the oom-pah-pah meter is the defining part of the music's style.

MIDI (Musical Instrument Digital Interface) A common programming language that enables SYNTHESIZERS, computers, and SEQUENCERS to communicate with one another.

minor One of the two primary SCALES used in popular music. The relation between the seven notes in the major scale is whole step (WS)-half step (HS)-WS-HS-WS-WS. (There are two variations of this basic pattern found in scales known as the "harmonic" and "melodic" minor.) Each scale step has a related CHORD defining major harmony. Compare MAJOR.

minstrel Performance of African-American songs and dances by white performers in blackface, burnt cork rubbed on their faces beginning in the mid-19th century. Later, black minstrels appeared. Minstrel shows included songs, dances, and humorous skits. Many of these skits and songs made fun of African Americans.

modes A type of SCALE. The two common scales used today (the MAJOR and MINOR) are two types of mode. In the Middle Ages, a system of eight different modes was developed, each with the same intervals but beginning on a different note. The modes are sometimes still heard in folk music, some forms of jazz, and some forms of contemporary classical music.

MOR (middle-of-the-road) Pop music aimed at a wide audience, designed to be as inoffensive and nondisturbing as possible. This term is often used pejoratively by critics. Also sometimes called "easy listening."

movement A section of a longer musical composition.

notation A system developed over many centuries to write down musical compositions using specific symbols to represent PITCH and RHYTHM.

note values The time values of the notes in a musical composition are relational, usually based on the idea of a quarter note equaling one beat (as in ¼ time). In this time signature, a quarter note fills a quarter of the time in the measure; a half-note equals two beats (is twice as long) and a whole note equals four beats (a full measure). Conversely, shorter time values include an eighth-note (half a single beat), a sixteenth (¼ of a single beat), a thirty-second (⅛ of a single beat), etc.

octave An INTERVAL of eight notes, considered the "perfect" consonance. If a string is divided perfectly in half, each half will sound an octave above the full string, so that the ratio between the two notes is expressed as 1:2.

opus A numbering system used in classical composition to indicate the order in which pieces were composed. Some composers only give opus numbers to works they feel are strong enough to be part of their "official" canon.

percussion Instruments used to play the rhythmic part of a composition, which may be "unpitched" (such as drums or cymbals) or "pitched" (such as bells, chimes, and marimbas).

phonograph A mechanical instrument used to reproduce sound recordings. A phonograph consists of some form of turntable, needle, tone arm, amplifier, and speaker. A record is placed on a turntable, a disc that is set to revolve at specific speeds. The needle "reads" the grooves cut into the record itself. The vibrations then are communicated through the tone arm (in which the needle is mounted) into an amplifier (which increases the volume of the sound). A speaker projects the sound out so that it can be heard.

phrase A subsection of the MELODY that expresses a complete musical thought.

Piedmont blues A form of blues from the Carolinas, Georgia, Florida, and Alabama that uses a restrained style of fingerpicking and soft vocal performances. It also often uses ragtime CHORD PROGRESSIONS.

pitch The note defined by its sound; literally, the number of vibrations per second (of a string, air column, bar, or some other vibrating object) that results in a given tone. Pitch is relative; in most tuning systems, a specific note is chosen as the pitch against which others are tuned. In modern music, this is usually A above middle C, defined as vibrating at 440 vps.

pop music　Any music that appeals to a large audience. Originally, the pop charts featured records aimed at white, urban listeners (as opposed to R&B, aimed at blacks, and C&W or country, aimed at rural, lower-class whites). Today, "pop" is applied to any recording that appeals across a wide range of listeners, so that Michael Jackson or Shania Twain could equally be defined as "pop" stars.

power chords　Played on the low strings of an electric guitar, power chords use only the root and the fifth (and often a repeat of the root an octave higher) of a triad, leaving out the third of the CHORD. With no third, the chord is neither MAJOR or MINOR. With only two notes, it is technically not even a chord, but an interval. The use of power chords was pioneered by Link Wray ("Rumble") and the Kinks ("You Really Got Me"), and used extensively in hard rock (Deep Purple's "Smoke on the Water"), heavy metal (Metallica), and grunge (Nirvana's "Smells Like Teen Spirit").

power trio　Three instruments—guitar, bass, and drums—played at loud volumes.

psychedelic　Popular ROCK style of the late 1960s-early 1970s that featured extended musical forms, "spacey" lyrics, and unusual musical timbres often produced by synthesizers. Psychedelic music was supposed to be the "aural equivalent" of the drug experience. See also SYNTHESIZER; TIMBRE.

punk　A movement that began in England and travelled to the United States in the mid-1970s emphasizing a return to simpler musical forms, in response to the growing commercialization of ROCK. Punk also encompassed fashion (including spiked hair, safety pins used as body ornaments, etc.) and sometimes a violent, antiestablishment message.

quarter note　See NOTE VALUES.

race records　Music industry name for African-American popular music recorded in the 1920s until around 1945.

ragtime　Music dating from around the 1890s and usually composed in three or four different sections. The most famous ragtime pieces were for piano, but the style was also adapted in a simplified form for the banjo and the guitar.

record producer　The person in charge of a recording session.

register　The range in notes of a specific part of a musical composition. Also used to define the range of an individual musical instrument or vocal part.

resonator guitar　Guitars with a metal front and back, often used in playing slide guitar, and prized during the 1930s for their volume.

rhythm　The basic pulse of a musical composition. In 4/4 time, the 4 beats per measure provide the pulse that propels the piece. Compare METER.

rhythm and blues (R&B)　Black popular music that emerged around 1945 and peaked in popularity in the 1960s. It usually included gospel-influenced vocal performances, and a rhythm section of piano, bass, and drums. The lead instruments were often guitar and saxophone.

riff　A short, recognizable melodic phrase used repeatedly in a piece of music. Commonly heard in big band jazz or in electric guitar solos.

rock　An outgrowth of ROCK 'N' ROLL in the 1960s that featured more sophisticated arrangements, lyrics, and subject matter. The BRITISH INVASION groups—notably the Beatles and the Rolling Stones—are sometimes credited with extending the style and subjects treated by rock 'n' roll. Rock itself has developed into many different substyles.

rockabilly　Mid-1950s popular music that combined BLUES and COUNTRY music.

rock 'n' roll　The popular music of the mid-1950s aimed at teenage listeners. Popular rock 'n' roll artists included Elvis Presley, Chuck Berry, Little Richard, and Carl Perkins. Compare ROCK.

royalties　Payments to recording artists based on the sales of their records.

salsa   Literally "spice." A form of Latin dance music popularized in the 1970s and 1980s.

scale   A succession of seven notes. The most common scales are the MAJOR and MINOR.

score   The complete notation of a musical composition.

sequencer   An electronic instrument that can record a series of pitches or rhythms and play them back on command.

78   The first form of recorded disc, that revolved on a turntable at 78 revolutions per minute (rpm). The first 78s were 10 inches in diameter and could play for approximately three minutes per side; later, 12-inch 78s were introduced with slightly longer playing times.

sharp   A symbol in a piece of music indicating that a pitch should be raised one half-step in PITCH. Compare FLAT.

side   One side of a recording disc.

slide guitar   Style of guitar in which the player wears a metal or glass tube on one finger or uses a bottle neck to play notes. It creates a distinctive crying sound. Also called bottleneck guitar.

songster   A turn-of-the-20th-century musician with a varied repertoire that included different styles of music.

soprano   The highest female voice, or the highest pitched instrument in a family of instruments.

soul   A black musical style developed in the 1960s that combined elements of GOSPEL MUSIC with RHYTHM AND BLUES.

spirituals   Traditional religious music found in both white and African-American traditions.

staff   The five parallel lines on which the symbols for notes are placed in a notated piece of music. The CLEF at the beginning of the staff indicates the pitch of each note on the staff.

stanza   In poetry, the basic lyrical unit, often consisting of four or six lines. The lyrics to both the VERSE and CHORUS of a popular song follow the stanza form.

strings   Instruments that produce musical sound through the vibration of strings, made out of animal gut or metal. Violins and guitars are stringed instruments.

suite   In classical music, a group of dances played in succession to form a larger musical composition.

symphony   In classical music, a defined form usually consisting of three parts, played Fast-Slow-Fast.

syncopation   Accenting the unexpected or weaker BEAT. Often used in RAGTIME, jazz, and related styles.

synthesizer   An electronic instrument that is capable of creating different musical pitches and timbres.

tempo   The speed at which a piece of music is performed.

tenor   The highest male voice.

theme   A recognizable MELODY that is often repeated within a musical composition.

thumb picks and finger picks   Guitar picks made of metal or plastic worn on the player's right hand fingers and thumb in order to play louder.

timbre   The quality of a PITCH produced by a musical instrument or voice that makes it distinctive. The timbre of a guitar is quite different from that of a flute, for example.

time signature   In notation, the symbol at the beginning of each STAFF that indicates the basic metric pulse and how many beats are contained in a measure. For example, in 4/4 time, a quarter-note is given one beat, and there are four beats per measure; in 6/8 time, an eighth-note is given one beat, and there are six beats in a measure.

Tin Pan Alley   The center of music publishing on West 28th Street in New York City from the late 19th century through the 1930s (so-called because the clatter from competing pianists working in different buildings sounded to passersby like rattling tin pans). Used generally to describe the popular songs of this period.

tone   See PITCH.

tremolo   The rapid repetition of a single note to give a "quivering" or "shaking" sound. Compare VIBRATO.

turnaround   A musical phrase at the end of a verse that briefly outlines the CHORDs of the song before the start of the next verse.

12-bar blues   A 12-bar BLUES has 12 measures of music, or bars, and is the most common blues format, though eight bars and 16 bars are also used.

vamp   A short segment of music that repeats, usually two or four CHORDs. Two chord vamps are common in GOSPEL and ROCK, especially the I and IV chords (C and F in the key of C).

vanity records   Recordings that are conceived and financed by the artists involved. They are called "vanity records" because the motivation comes from the person or group themselves, not from a record company. The reason is to realize a creative project, to promote a career, or just to boost the ego. Previously, singers and musicians would pay to go into a studio and to cover the costs of backup musicians, mixing, mastering, and manufacturing. This continues, but with the rise of home studios, these steps can be done at home, with computerized recording and CD burning. Vanity records now represent perhaps the majority of recordings being made and are more likely to be called independent productions.

verse   The part of a song that features a changing lyric set to a fixed MELODY. The verse is usually performed in alternation with the CHORUS.

vibrato   A rapid moving up and down slightly in PITCH while performing a single note as an ornament. Compare TREMOLO.

walking bass   A style of bass playing that originated in jazz on the upright bass. The bassist plays a new note on every beat, outlining the CHORDs as they pass by in a CHORD PROGRESSION. Chord notes are primary, but passing notes and other decorations enliven the bass line, as well as brief rhythmic variations enliven the bass line. A rock example is Paul McCartney's bass part in the Beatles' "All My Loving" (1964).

whole note   See NOTE VALUES.

woodwinds   A class of instruments traditionally made of wood, although the term is now used for instruments made of brass or metal as well. Clarinets, flutes, and saxophones are usually classified as woodwinds.

Further Reading

Artis, Bob. *Bluegrass*. New York: Hawthorn Books, 1975.

Bufwack, Mary A., and Robert K. Oermann. *Finding Her Voice: Women in Country Music*. New York: Crown, 1993.

Burton, Thomas, ed. *Tennessee Traditional Singers*. Knoxville: University of Tennessee Press, 1981.

Cantwell, Robert. *Bluegrass Breakdown: The Making of the Old Southern Sound*. Urbana: University of Illinois Press, 1984.

Carawan, Guy, and Candie Carawan. *Voices from the Mountains*. New York: Alfred A. Knopf, 1975.

Carlin, Richard. *Country Music: An Encyclopedia*. New York: Routledge, 2003.

———, and Bob Carlin. *Southern Exposure: The Story of Southern Music in Pictures and Words*. New York: Billboard, 2000.

Cash, Johnny, with Patrick Carr. *Cash: The Autobiography*. New York: Harper, 1998.

Ching, Barbara. *Wrong's What I Do Best: Hard Country Music and Contemporary Culture*. New York: Oxford University Press, 2001.

Country Music Foundation Staff. *Country: The Music and the Musicians*. New York: Abbeville Press, 1988.

———. *Country Music Hall of Fame and Museum Book*. Rev. ed. Nashville, Tenn.: Country Music Foundation, 1987.

Daniel, Wayne. *Pickin' on Peachtree: A History of Country Music in Atlanta, Georgia*. Urbana: University of Illinois, 2000.

Dellar, Fred, and Alan Cackett. *The Harmony Illustrated Encyclopedia of Country Music*. Rev. ed. New York: Harmony Books, 1986.

Delmore, Alton. *Truth Is Stranger Than Publicity*. Nashville, Tenn.: Country Music Foundation, 1987.

Ellison, Curtis. *Country Music Culture: From Hard Times to Heaven*. New York: Oxford University Press, 1995.

Erlewine, Michael, ed. *All Music Guide to Country*. San Francisco: Backbeat Books, 1997.

Escott, Colin. *Tattooed on Their Tongues: Lives in Country Music and Early Rock and Roll*. New York: Schirmer Books, 1995.

———, and Kira Florita. *Hank Williams: Snap Shots from the Lost Highway*. New York: Da Capo, 2001.

———, and Martin Hawkins. *Good Rockin' Tonight: The Sun Records Story*. New York: St. Martin's Press, 1989.

———, with George Merritt and William MacEwen. *Hank Williams: The Biography*. Rev. ed. Boston: Little, Brown, 2004.

Ewing, Tom, ed. *The Bill Monroe Reader*. Urbana: University of Illinois Press, 2000.

Feiler, Bruce S. *Dreamin' Out Loud: Garth Brooks, Wynonna Judd, Wade Hayes, and the Changing Face of Nashville*. New York: Spike, 1999.

Fowler, Gene, and Bill Crawford. *Border Radio*. New York: Limelight Editions, 1990.

Greene, Archie. *Only a Miner*. Urbana: University of Illinois Press, 1972.

Guralnick, Peter. *Lost Highway: Journeys and Arrivals of American Musicians*. Boston: David R. Godine, 1979.

Hagan, Chet. *Country Music Legends in the Hall of Fame.* Nashville, Tenn.: Country Music Foundation, 1982.

———. *The Grand Ole Opry.* New York: Henry Holt, 1989.

Horstman, Dorothy. *Sing Your Heart Out, Country Boy.* 3d ed. Nashville: CMF/Vanderbilt University Press, 1996.

Hume, Margaret. *You're So Cold I'm Turning Blue: Guide to the Greatest in Country Music.* New York: Penguin, 1982.

Jensen, Joli. *Nashville Sound: Authenticity, Commercialization, and Country Music.* Nashville: CMF/Vanderbilt University Press, 1998.

Kingsbury, Paul, ed. *Country on Compact Disc: The Essential Guide to the Music.* New York: Grove Press, 1993.

———. *The Country Reader.* Nashville: CMF/Vanderbilt University Press, 1996.

———. *Encyclopedia of Country Music.* New York: Oxford, 1998.

Lomax, John. *Adventures of a Ballad Hunter.* New York: Macmillan, 1947.

Lornell, Kip. *Virginia's Blues, Gospel and Country Records, 1902–1943.* Lexington: University Press of Kentucky, 1989.

Lynn, Loretta, and George Vesey. *Coal Miner's Daughter.* Chicago: Contemporary Books, 1985.

Malone, Bill C. *Country Music USA.* Rev. ed. Austin: University of Texas Press, 1985.

———. *Don't Get Above Your Raisin': Country Music and the Southern Working Class.* Urbana: University of Illinois Press, 2001.

———, and Judith McCulloh, eds. *Stars of Country Music: Uncle Dave Macon to Johnny Rodriguez.* Urbana: University of Illinois Press, 1975.

Marschall, Rick. *Encyclopedia of Country & Western Music.* New York: Simon and Schuster, 1988.

McCloud, Barry. *Definitive Country: The Ultimate Encyclopedia of Country Music and Its Performers.* New York: A Perigee Book, 1995.

Nash, Alanna. *Behind Closed Doors: Talking with the Legends of Country Music.* New York: Alfred A. Knopf, 1988.

Peterson, Richard A. *Creating Country Music: Fabricating Authenticity.* Chicago: University of Chicago Press, 1999.

Porterfield, Nolan. *Jimmie Rodgers: The Life & Times of America's Blue Yodeler.* Urbana: University of Illinois Press, 1979.

Price, Steven D. *Old as the Hills: The Story of Bluegrass Music.* New York: Viking, 1975.

Rooney, Jim. *Bossmen: Bill Monroe and Muddy Waters.* New York: Da Capo, 1989.

Rosenbaum, Art. *Folk Visions and Voices: Traditional Music and Song in North Georgia.* Athens: University of Georgia Press, 1983.

Rosenberg, Neil V. *Bluegrass: A History.* Urbana: University of Illinois Press, 1985.

Shelton, Robert, and Burt Goldblatt. *The Country Music Story.* New York: Castle Books, 1971.

Smith, Richard D. *Bluegrass: An Informal Guide.* Chicago: A Cappella Books, 1996.

———. *Can't You Hear Me Callin': The Life of Bill Monroe, Father of Bluegrass.* New York: Little, Brown, 1999.

Stambler, Irwin, and Grellun Landon. *Country Music: The Encyclopedia.* New York: St. Martin's Press, 1997.

Tichi, Cecelia. *High Lonesome: The American Culture of Country Music.* Chapel Hill: University of North Carolina Press, 1994.

Tosches, Nick. *Country: The Biggest Music in America,* 3d ed. New York: Da Capo, 1996.

———. *Where Dead Voices Gather.* New York: Little, Brown, 2001.

Townsend, Charles S. *San Antonio Rose: The Life and Music of Bob Wills.* Urbana: University of Illinois Press, 1976.

Vaughan, Andrew. *Who's Who in the New Country Music.* New York: St. Martin's Press, 1990.

Wolfe, Charles K. *Tennessee Strings: The Story of Country Music in Tennessee.* Knoxville: University of Tennessee Press, 1977.

————. *Classic Country.* New York: Routledge, 2000.

————. *The Devil's Box: Masters of Southern Fiddling.* Nashville: CMF/Vanderbilt University Press, 1997.

————. *The Grand Ole Opry: The Early Years.* London: Old Time Music, 1978; enlarged and revised as *A Good Natured Riot: The Birth of the Grand Ole Opry.* Nashville: CMF/Vanderbilt University Press, 1999.

Wolff, Kurt, and Orla Duane, eds. *Rough Guide to Country Music.* London: Rough Guides, 2000.

Editorial Board of Advisers

Richard Carlin, general editor, is the author of several books of music, including *Southern Exposure, The Big Book of Country Music, Classical Music: An Informal Guide,* and the five-volume *Worlds of Music.* He has also written and compiled several books of music instruction and songbooks and served as advisory editor on country music for the American National Biography. Carlin has contributed articles on traditional music to various journals, including the *Journal of Ethnomusicology, Sing Out!, Pickin', Frets,* and *Mugwumps.* He has also produced 10 albums of traditional music for Folkways Records. A longtime editor of books on music, dance, and the arts, Carlin is currently executive editor of music and dance at Routledge Publishers. He previously spent six years as executive editor at Schirmer Books and was the founding editor at A Cappella Books, an imprint of the Chicago Review Press.

Barbara Ching, Ph.D., is an associate professor of English at the University of Memphis. She obtained a graduate certificate in women's studies and her doctorate in literature from Duke University. Dr. Ching has written extensively on country music and rural identity, and she is the author of *Wrong's What I Do Best: Hard Country Music and Contemporary Culture* (Oxford University Press) and *Knowing Your Place: Rural Identity and Cultural Hierarchy* (Routledge). She has also contributed articles and chapters to numerous other works on the subject and has presented papers at meetings of the International Association for the Study of Popular Music.

Ronald D. Cohen, Ph.D., is professor emeritus of history at Indiana University–Northwest (Gary). He obtained a doctorate in history from the University of Minnesota–Minneapolis. Dr. Cohen has written extensively on the folk music revival and is the coproducer, with Jeff Place, of *The Best of Broadside: 1962–1988: Anthems of the American Underground from the Pages of Broadside Magazine* (five-CD boxed set with illustrated book, Smithsonian Folkways Recordings, 2000), which was nominated for a Grammy Award in 2001. He is also the author of *Rainbow Quest: The Folk Music Revival and American Society, 1940–1970* (University of Massachusetts Press) and the editor of *Alan Lomax: Selected Writings, 1934–1997* (Routledge). He is also the editor of the Scarecrow Press book series American Folk Music and Musicians.

William Duckworth is the composer of more than 100 pieces of music and the author of six books and numerous articles, the most recent of which is "Making Music on the Web" (*Leonardo Music Journal,* vol. 9, December 1999). In the mid-1990s he and codirector Nora Farrell began *Cathedral,* a multiyear work of music and art for the Web that went online June 10, 1997. Incorporating acoustic and computer music, live Web casts by its own band, and newly created virtual instruments, *Cathedral* is one of the first interactive works of music and art on the Web. Recently, Duckworth and Farrell created Cathedral 2001, a 48-hour World Wide Web event, with 34 events streamed live from five continents.

Index

Page numbers in **bold** indicate main entries; those in *italics* indicate illustrations. Page numbers followed by the letter *c* indicate chronology entries; those followed by *g* indicate glossary entries.